COOKBOÖK

A COLLECTION
OF RECIPES
FROM BEHIND
THE PASS
OF THE UK'S
BEST CHEFS.

VOL.1

'People who cook food and spend time with food – they know what the good stuff is.'

Anthony Bourdain

BEHIND THE PASS

©2022 Luke & Stacey Sherwood-French
& Meze Publishing Ltd. All rights reserved
First edition printed in 2022 in the UK
ISBN: 978-1-910863-94-7

Published by Meze Publishing Limited
Unit 1b, 2 Kelham Square
Kelham Riverside
Sheffield S3 8SD
Web: www.mezepublishing.co.uk
Telephone: 0114 275 7709
Email: info@mezepublishing.co.uk

No part of this book shall be reproduced or transmitted in any form or by any means, electronic or mechanical, including photocopying, recording, or by any information retrieval system without written permission of the publisher.

Although every precaution has been taken in the preparation of this work, the publisher and author assume no responsibility for errors or omissions. Neither is any liability assumed for damages resulting from the use of this information contained herein.

Foreword
By Luke & Stacey Sherwood-French

"We are always learning. We are always evolving. We are always supporting. This is hospitality 2023."

We've been asked a lot when we are going to publish a cookbook and it's definitely something we had considered previously. Then came the pandemic and everything that followed as a result of our industry being turned on its head. This got us thinking about how great our industry is, that even in the face of it all, how many amazing restaurants there are in the UK that currently make up what we believe to be the best culinary scene the UK has ever had.

Every single restaurateur who diversified their business model to survive during that period invested time, thought and soul into their livelihoods, just as they always had. This was nothing new for most and what stood out was the support network that quickly grew, something that's also increasingly prevalent in modern kitchens across the UK. Sharing knowledge and advice along with support means that as an industry we can continue to grow. Chefs are now sharing recipes, techniques, suppliers and even teams! This in turn builds strength and trust amongst peers, and we genuinely believe that without this, the culinary scene would not be what it has become since 2020.

Hot topics are always surrounding our industry, with working hours, work-life balance and fair pay a constant conversation. We've celebrated those that, like us, are working towards a better hospitality industry: one that inspires young people or those with a passion to re-enter. We want them to know that there can be a good work-life balance and fair working hours, unlike the industry we were trained in. We've been there, we've done that, and we've got the stories.

The number one question we get asked by friends, family, guests and followers is where we recommend eating out. From this, Behind The Pass was born. This book is a celebration of and a guide to the places we would recommend, not only based on the food and experience, but all the attributes mentioned above. It features restaurants across the country so that as many people as possible can find one nearby, or to make a special journey to. Believe us, they are worth it! We've been fortunate enough to work with everyone who features in this book, and each individual has contributed a very special insight into their cooking and life to help us create Behind The Pass. This is a unique collection of recipes, including some never published before, and we are extremely grateful to all our contributors.

We have travelled to each of the restaurants and our chefs have kindly given their time and recipes to support us in promoting hospitality across the UK in 2023. Through personal interviews with ourselves and our chefs, we hope to give you an insight into what we know about each of these talented, hardworking people. Thanks to everyone's determination to build a better hospitality industry, you'll also see how these chefs are working to provide careers and inspire ambition.

That's enough from us; we'll let the chefs themselves tell you the rest. We hope you enjoy this experience.

Photo: Zachary Turner

Contents

Foreword by Luke & Stacey Sherwood-French	6
Kitchen Tools	10
Directory	282
Acknowledgements & Contributions	286

THE CHEFS

Luke French and Stacey Sherwood-French — 12
- Barbecued Wortley Wagyu Sirloin with Panzanella — 14
- Korean Fried Chicken — 16
- Rainbow Trout, Smoked Butter Sauce, Yuzu, Wasabi & Parsley — 20
- Alphonso Mango, Pineapple, Kaffir Lime, Coconut & Sansho Pepper — 22
- Cod Crudo, Chilled Aromatic Dashi with Truffles — 24
- Meat & Potato Pie — 26
- My Dishes — 28
- Chewing The Fat with Luke French — 30

Alex Nietosvuori and Ally Thompson — 34
- Beignet Filled with Doddington Cheese and Glazed in Wildflower Honey — 36
- Confit Duck Leg with Duck Liver — 38
- Hand-Dived Scallops, Smoked Cream, Garden Sorrel & Caviar — 40
- Our Food — 42
- Kitchen Q&A — 44
- Our Ethos — 45

Chris McClurg — 46
- Roast Chicken, Manzanilla Sherry, Morels — 48
- Cornish Orchard 'Apple Pie' and Pevensey Blue — 52
- Hot Smoked Salmon, Tartare Butter, Fromage Blanc — 54
- My Recipes — 56
- Meet The Chef — 58
- Life At No.6 — 60

Gareth Ward — 62
- Chilli Crab with a Sweet Steamed Bun — 64
- Hoisin Duck — 66
- Rump Cap in Black Bean Sauce — 68
- Recipe Insights — 70
- Q&A with Gareth Ward — 72

Joshua Overington — 76
- Woodland Pork Cooked Over Coals, Fig and Radicchio Relish, Sauce Civet — 78
- Garganelli with Lamb Belly Pancetta, Egg Yolk, Yorkshire Pecorino, English Peas and Mint — 80
- Line-Caught Pollock Poached in Aged Beef Fat with Senshyu Onions and Lemon Verbena — 82
- My Recipes — 84
- Q&A with Joshua Overington — 86

Kenny Atkinson — 90
- Smoked Jersey Royal Potatoes, Cured Egg Yolk, Asparagus & Wild Garlic — 92
- Peach Tart with Almonds, Lemon Verbena, White Chocolate & Peach Tea Sorbet — 94
- Roast Monkfish, Mussels, Caviar, Lemon & Sea Herbs — 96
- My Recipes — 98
- Chewing The Fat with Kenny Atkinson — 100

Kirk Haworth — 104
- Lightly Smoked Tomatoes, House Ricotta, Beach Asparagus & Wild Garlic Soup — 106
- Smoked Maitake Mushroom, Artichoke Caramel, Black & White Rice — 108
- Rippled Rhubarb Sponge, Liquorice Custard, Wild Pine Oil — 110
- Recipe Notes — 112
- Q&A with Kirk Haworth — 114

Lee Westcott — 116
- Asparagus, Chamomile, Ricotta and Almond — 118
- Lamb, Yoghurt, Sweet Pea, Girolles and Black Garlic — 120
- Slow-Braised Lamb Shank Cooked in Tomato, Herbs and Spices — 124
- Kitchen Q&A — 126
- Kitchen Confidential — 128

Lisa Goodwin-Allen — 132
- Three Lancashire Cheese Pizza, Smoked Bacon, Alliums — 134
- West Coast Scallop, Curried "Pearls", Pomegranate, Coriander, Toasted Almonds — 136
- Chargrilled Yorkshire Asparagus, Sheep's Curd, Sorrel — 138
- Our Recipes — 140
- The Beauty of Barbecuing — 142

Luke Payne — 146
- Manchester Egg — 148
- Mutton Curry — 150
- Salted Caramel Custard Tart — 152
- My Recipes — 154
- Meet The Chef — 156

Paul Leonard — 158
- Hafod Cheddar Gougère — 160
- Beetroots Cooked All Day in Their Own Juices — 162
- Roasted Monkfish with Whey and Fermented Onion Sauce — 164
- Kitchen Confidential — 166
- Tell Us About Your… — 168

Rafael Cagali — 172
- Herb Bouquet — 176
- Pineapple, Coconut, Spice Biscuit — 178
- Moqueca – Brazilian Fish Stew — 180
- Kitchen Confidential — 182

Roberta Hall-McCarron — 184
- Mackerel, Gooseberry, Sunflower Seed Gazpacho — 186
- Beef Tartare and Oyster — 188
- Duck, Radicchio, Rhubarb and Ginger — 190
- Kitchen Confidential — 192
- Tell Us About Your… — 194

Sam Carter — 196
- Tell Us Something We Might Not Know About… — 198
- Turbot, Morels, Australian Winter Truffle, Sauce Bonne Femme — 200
- Lamb Moussaka — 204
- Tiramisu — 206
- In The Kitchen — 210
- In The Restaurant — 212

Santiago Lastra — 214
- Buñuelos with Brie Ice Cream and Sea Buckthorn — 216
- Crab Empanada — 218
- Pork Cheek Carnitas Tacos — 220
- Recipe Notes — 222
- Q&A with Santiago Lastra — 224

Tom Booton — 228
- Beef Ribeye, Stuffed Potato, Mushrooms, Chive Mayonnaise — 230
- Ham, Egg and Chips with Roasted Pineapple — 232
- Lobster, Carrot Bisque, N25 Caviar — 234
- In The Kitchen — 236
- In The Restaurant — 238

Tom Brown — 240
- Sea Bream Tartare, Egg Yolk, Soy, Seaweed — 244
- Smoked Mackerel Pâté with Treacle Soda Bread — 246
- Squid Cacio e Pepe with 36 Month Aged Parmesan — 248
- Recipe Q&A — 250

Tommy Banks — 254
- Beef Short Rib with Glazed Beetroot and Hazelnut Gremolata — 256
- Sea Buckthorn, Chocolate & Chestnut — 258
- Devilled Crab Toast with Brown Crab Custard and Caviar — 260
- My Recipes — 262
- Our Approach To Food — 264

Will Murray & Jack Croft — 268
- Leek, Hen Of The Woods — 270
- Cod's Head, Sriracha Butter Sauce — 272
- Corn Ribs, Lime — 274
- Kitchen Confidential — 276
- Q&A with Will Murray & Jack Croft — 278

Behind The Pass

Kitchen Tools

These bits of kit are all recommended by our chefs. None are necessities and our chefs have provided conventional alternatives throughout, but if you fancy using the professional equipment, take a look at the list below:

Barbecues
These are used a lot by chefs these days – so it's worth getting your hands on a good one. Japanese Konro and Big Green Egg are two of the brands recommended by the chefs in this book.

Charcoal
Big Green Egg and Whittle & Flame are both lump wood charcoal brands used in a number of the kitchens we recommend.

Cold Smoking
Smoking guns infuse food with a distinctive smoky flavour using very little heat. Bradley Smoker and PolyScience smoking guns are both recommended by chefs in the book.

Gastrovac
A compact appliance for cooking, frying and impregnating flavours into food inside a vacuum.

Hand Blender
Another essential piece of kitchen equipment. Bamix and Robot-Coupe are brands commonly used in professional kitchens.

iSi Espuma Gun
This is essentially a cream whipper but chefs also use them for aerating things such as chocolate, as well as creating foams.

Liquid Nitrogen
This is used by chefs to freeze things very quickly, so isn't something to be used without knowing how to do so safely. Mansfield Cryogenics are a well-known supplier used widely by professional kitchens.

Mandoline
This is a Japanese vegetable slicer and sheeter.

Pacojet
This is a very high-powered blender used for churning ice creams, sorbets and purées.

Pizza Oven
These are becoming increasingly popular in domestic as well as professional kitchens. Gozney is the brand that is used in this book's recipes.

Salt Ageing Fridge
This is a specialist refrigerated cabinet with temperature and humidity controls along with Himalayan salt blocks for drying, ageing and curing food products.

Stand Mixer
A multi-purpose piece of kit used mainly for baking recipes as well as combining and mixing foods. KitchenAid is the brand most commonly used by the chefs in this book.

Steamer
A high-pressured combination steam oven; Rational and MKN are commonly used in this book. A classic Chinese bamboo steamer will also do just fine if you do not have a combi oven.

Thermomix
A high-powered food processor that can cook with heat whilst blending and mixing.

Vacuum Seal Machine and Pouches
These are used for storing, marinating and compressing foods to enhance flavour and texture.

Vitamix Blender
A good quality high-powered blender is an essential piece of kitchen equipment.

JÖRO | House of JÖRO | Konjö, Sheffield

Luke French and Stacey Sherwood-French

JÖRO opened in 2016 and is headed up by chef director Luke French and managing director Stacey Sherwood-French. Everything about the restaurant – from the food and drink to the atmosphere and service – is a unique expression of their personalities, with a tasting menu that draws on Asian and Scandinavian flavours but doesn't tie itself down to any one genre or cuisine. Currently based in the Krynkl development, which is made from upcycled shipping containers and based in Sheffield's former industrial quarter, JÖRO will move into the city centre from early 2023 and Konjö – their sister business, serving East Asian inspired street food in a nearby food hall – will take its place in Krynkl.

"I think Luke's cooking is only restricted by the amount of space we currently have," Stacey explains. "We never envisaged that JÖRO would become what it is today; the restaurant was initially intended to be a casual neighbourhood hangout serving small plates, which suddenly turned into a tasting menu that got booked up three months in advance. We've come a long way in a very short time and stretched ourselves to the absolute maximum here. The new venue is going to lift that restriction because it's custom built to do what we do and the equipment will be state of the art."

Luke and Stacey consider their guests' whole experience to create a journey, from the second the booking is made to arriving home after eating at JÖRO. Expanding on this ethos, the husband and wife team created House of JÖRO to provide those from further afield with a home from home while visiting the restaurant. Comprised of four rooms and a private chef's table, House of JÖRO is about the little details that complete a luxurious stay. Their growing portfolio also includes a retail venture that will give the general public access to a wide range of products curated by Luke and Stacey, from their favourite varieties of coffee to the charcoal used in their restaurants.

Three things you should know about us:

Luke: I like there to be a fire in the kitchen whether I'm cooking on it or not; I just like the feeling of it being there. I love the smell too – I've got a candle at home that smells like burning wood.

Stacey: I grew up on a farm with a big family and cooking as a communal, sociable thing is very nostalgic for me. Getting back to basics, being in nature: it all comes back to the name we chose for our business, JÖRO, which means earth.

Luke and Stacey: What we've created is purely out of self-expression. One of the key aspects of hospitality is inviting people into your home and we've always tried to treat it like that.

JÖRO | House of JÖRO | Konjö, Sheffield

Barbecued Wortley Wagyu Sirloin with Panzanella

Preparation time: 10 minutes | Cooking time: 1 hour | Serves 6-8 as a sharing dish

FOR THE SIRLOIN
1 x 1kg bone-in Wortley wagyu sirloin

1 bottle of Momiki black garlic umami sauce

Sea salt flakes

Black peppercorns

FOR THE PANZANELLA SALAD
500g Westlands San Marzano tomatoes

Don Giovani 15-year aged balsamic vinegar

Finca la Barca smoked olive oil

Stale sourdough or focaccia bread, cut or torn into roughly 1cm pieces

1 small red onion, peeled and sliced

1 small tin of drained and sliced artichoke hearts

1 small tin of drained and sliced roasted red peppers

1 small bunch of fresh Genovese basil, leaves only, torn up

1 small bunch of flat leaf parsley, leaves only, roughly chopped

100g Vacche Rosse 24-month aged parmesan

1 tbsp fresh chive flowers

Bring the sirloin to room temperature for at least 1 hour before cooking.

FOR THE PANZANELLA SALAD
Meanwhile, chop the tomatoes into nice bite-size pieces, place them into a large mixing bowl, then toss generously in sea salt. Add a good couple glugs of balsamic vinegar and toss into the tomatoes, followed by a generous amount of the smoked olive oil. Add the stale bread and sliced red onion, then toss again. Allow the tomatoes and bread to macerate in the salt, vinegar and oil for 1 hour while the sirloin comes up to room temperature.

FOR THE SIRLOIN
Preheat your barbecue until the coals are white hot. Preheat your oven to 100°c. Generously sprinkle sea salt all over the sirloin, then allow it to sit for 5 minutes.

Place the sirloin onto the grill over the white-hot coals of the barbecue and heavily char it on all sides. Continue to cook it on the barbecue, turning every 30 seconds for 5 minutes.

Transfer the sirloin to a wire rack set over an ovenproof tray and place in the preheated oven until the core temperature reaches 46°c.

Remove the tray from the oven and allow the sirloin to rest for as long as it took to cook. While it is resting, brush the black garlic sauce all over the sirloin every few minutes. Make sure you keep all the resting juices.

Now finish the salad and carve the steak. Toss the macerated tomatoes with the artichoke hearts, roasted peppers, basil and parsley, then arrange in a serving dish and sprinkle over the shaved parmesan and chive flowers.

Carefully carve the meat away from the bone and slice into 5mm thick pieces, then glaze again with the resting juices and more black garlic sauce. Arrange on a serving dish and pour over all the resting juices, grind over some black pepper and serve with the panzanella.

JÖRO | House of JÖRO | Konjö, Sheffield

Korean Fried Chicken

Preparation time: 30 minutes active + 24 hours inactive | Cooking time: 30 minutes | Serves 4

2 corn-fed free-range chicken legs, cut into thighs and drumsticks

FOR THE BRINE

50g vegetable oil

50g sake

50g buttermilk

50g light soy sauce

10g golden roasted sesame oil

10g caster sugar

5g MSG

FOR THE DREDGING MIX

200g self-raising flour

200g potato flour

100g cornflour

30g table salt

FOR THE SAUCE

75g light soy sauce

60g hon mirin

50g sour apple juice

50g brown rice sake

10g golden roasted sesame oil

100g dark muscovado sugar

50ml rice wine vinegar

3 cloves of garlic, peeled and chopped

2 spring onions, chopped

1 tbsp freshly chopped coriander

1 tsp fresh root ginger, peeled and diced

1 tsp Chinese chicken granules

50g gochujang paste

50g chilli miso

TO SERVE

Spring onions, coriander and sesame seeds

FOR THE BRINE

Combine all the ingredients and blend together using a hand blender. Pour the brine over the prepared chicken thighs and drumsticks, then chill for 24 hours.

FOR THE DREDGING MIX

Combine all the ingredients in a bowl and whisk together, then reserve in an airtight container.

FOR THE SAUCE

Place the soy sauce, mirin, apple juice, sake and sesame oil in a saucepan. Bring to the boil, then transfer to a high-powered blender and blend in all the remaining ingredients except the gochujang and miso. Once combined, add these last ingredients and blend in, then pass the sauce through a sieve and let it cool.

TO PREPARE AND COOK THE CHICKEN

Heat a deep pan of cooking oil to 160°c. Remove the chicken from the brine and dredge it through the flour mix 2-3 times so it is well coated. Deep fry the coated chicken carefully until the core temperature reaches 75°c. If you do not have a temperature probe, the chicken should feel piping hot in the centre and the juices should run clear.

Heat the sauce up, just to warm it. Allow the chicken to cool down slightly and then toss the chicken in the warm sauce, making sure it is coated all over.

Serve with some freshly chopped spring onion, coriander and sesame seeds sprinkled over it.

JÖRO | House of JÖRO | Konjö, Sheffield

Rainbow Trout, Smoked Butter Sauce, Yuzu, Wasabi & Parsley

Preparation time: 30 minutes active + 1 week inactive | Cooking time: 1 hour 30 minutes | Serves 4 as a starter/tasting menu dish

250g fresh rainbow trout fillet, pin-boned

FOR THE TROUT OIL

1 smoked trout head

200g grapeseed oil

6g garlic, peeled and crushed

6g yuzu zest

FOR THE PARSLEY OIL

100g flat leaf parsley leaves

200g grapeseed oil

FOR THE PICKLED PARSLEY

100g rice wine vinegar

50g caster sugar

25g water

2.5g salt

40g flat leaf parsley stalks

FOR THE SMOKED BUTTER SAUCE

50g banana shallot, peeled and thinly sliced

40g chestnut mushrooms, thinly sliced

25g parsley stalks

0.75g black peppercorns

10g grapeseed oil

250g still mineral water

190g cooking sake

125g aged rice wine vinegar

30g salmon dashi

175g smoked butter

125g crème fraiche

20g blonde miso

6g kudzu

5g salt

Fresh yuzu juice, to taste

TO SERVE

Wasabi oil, caviar, wasabi nori, kinome leaves

In the restaurant, we age our trout as whole fish in a salt chamber or fish-ageing fridge for 1 week. This improves texture and flavour.

FOR THE TROUT OIL

Place all the ingredients in a vacuum pack bag and steam at 70°c for 1 hour. Remove the bag from the steamer and allow to chill in the fridge for 1 week. Remove from the fridge and pass the contents of the bag through an oil filter. Reserve the oil and discard the rest. Keep chilled.

FOR THE PARSLEY OIL

Place the ingredients into a high-powered blender and blend to 80°c. Pass through an oil filter and reserve the oil, discarding the rest. Keep chilled.

FOR THE PICKLED PARSLEY

Combine the vinegar, sugar, water and salt in a saucepan, bring to a boil, then remove from the pan and chill completely. Place the parsley stalks in a vacuum pack bag with the chilled pickling liquid and seal on full pressure. Allow to pickle for a short while. Remove the stalks from the bag and finely chop, then reserve in the liquid. Keep chilled.

FOR THE SMOKED BUTTER SAUCE

Sweat off the shallot, mushroom, parsley stalks and peppercorns in the oil until translucent, without colour. Add the water, sake, vinegar and dashi concentrate and reduce by 50%. Pass through a fine sieve. Use a hand blender to blend in the smoked butter and crème fraiche. Blend in the miso, kudzu and salt until dissolved, then gently simmer while stirring for 5 minutes. Pass through a fine sieve. Reserve in a saucepan and keep warm. Just before serving, add fresh yuzu juice to taste.

TO COOK THE TROUT

Bring the trout to room temperature and then brush with the smoked trout oil. Place skin side up on a non-stick ovenproof tray and bake at 100°c until the core temperature reaches 38°c (this should take approximately 6-8 minutes). Remove from the oven, peel off the skin and brush in trout oil again before serving.

TO SERVE

Place a teaspoon of pickled parsley stalks in the bottom of the bowl, followed by a tablespoon of parsley oil. Place the trout next to the parsley, then drizzle over a little wasabi oil, add a generous dollop of caviar and top with a piece of wasabi nori and some kinome leaves. Finally, spoon the butter sauce over the parsley stalks and oil. Serve immediately.

JÖRO | House of JÖRO | Konjö, Sheffield

Alphonso Mango, Pineapple, Kaffir Lime, Coconut & Sansho Pepper

Preparation time: 24 hours | Cooking time: 20 minutes | Serves 10

FOR THE PARFAIT

330g alphonso mango, de-skinned and seeded

230g coconut water

120g coconut purée

90g caster sugar

90g stabiliser

20g mango sake

2g table salt

1g malic acid

FOR THE SORBET

200g 50/50 sugar syrup

1 sheet bloomed bronze gelatine

400g pineapple purée

3 fresh kaffir lime leaves, finely chopped

3g malic acid

2g table salt

FOR THE CARAMEL

50g 20 year aged mirin

50g liquid glucose

5g kuromitsu

FOR THE GARNISH

50g coconut flakes

1 aged pineapple

1 fresh pink grapefruit

1 fresh kaffir lime

Fresh kinome leaves

Green sansho pepper oil

FOR THE PARFAIT

Blend all of the ingredients together until homogenised, then pass through a fine sieve and freeze in 40g portions until solid.

FOR THE SORBET

Warm the syrup and melt the gelatine in it, then blend with the rest of the ingredients and freeze in a Pacojet canister until frozen solid. Churn through the machine and refreeze. Repeat this process until the sorbet is smooth.

FOR THE CARAMEL

Combine the ingredients in a saucepan and bring to the boil. Simmer for 2 minutes, then cool and reserve until needed.

FOR THE GARNISH

Bake the coconut flakes in a single layer on a tray in an oven at 140°c until golden, then allow to cool and keep in an airtight tub until needed.

Peel the pineapple, cut the flesh into 5mm dice, then compress in a vacuum bag. Peel the pink grapefruit, separate into individual cells and freeze.

To build the dish, place the parfait on a serving dish and allow to soften for 5 minutes. Place a spoonful of compressed pineapple dice in the middle and dress with some sansho oil and mirin caramel. Follow with a spoonful of frozen pink grapefruit cells and a spoon of pineapple and kaffir lime sorbet, then arrange the coconut flakes over the top. Drizzle over some more sansho oil and grate over some kaffir lime zest, add a kinome leaf and serve immediately.

JÖRO | House of JÖRO | Konjö, Sheffield

Cod Crudo, Chilled Aromatic Dashi with Truffles

Preparation time: 24 hours | Cooking time: 20 minutes | Serves 10

FOR THE COD CRUDO
1kg trimmed, deboned, and skinned North Sea cod loin

50g sea salt flakes

1g dried ma-kombu seaweed

FOR THE DASHI

STAGE 1
150g still mineral water

4.5g fresh ginger, peeled and sliced

4.5g katsuo-dashi granules

3g dried cep mushroom

STAGE 2
28g shibanuma raw soy sauce

28g aged rice wine vinegar

4.5g arrowroot powder

STAGE 3
20g cleaned and coarsely grated black winter truffles

3.5g black truffle oil

2g light golden roast sesame oil level 3

STAGE 4
5g 2% green yuzu kosho hot sauce

5g 2% fresh yuzu juice

FOR THE GARNISH
Smoked cod bone oil

Freshly grated wasabi

5 large French breakfast radishes

10 small sheets of sea lettuce

Wasabi oil

10g kuki golden roasted sesame seeds

1g Yawataya isogoro bird eye togarashi

1 fresh unwaxed lime

TO MAKE THE DISH

First, cure the cod. Blend the salt with the kombu and coat the cod loin all over. Place it in a non-reactive tray and leave it in the fridge for 3 hours, turning it every 30 minutes.

After 3 hours, rinse the cod, wrap it tightly in clean cheesecloth and then place it into a dry ageing fridge for 21 hours to mature.

Next, make the dashi. Place the Stage 1 ingredients into a saucepan and bring to the boil. Add the Stage 2 ingredients and whisk in, then simmer until it thickens. Remove from the heat and allow it to cool for 10 minutes. Pass through a fine chinois into a clean container.

Stir the Stage 3 ingredients into the dashi and cover it with a lid. Allow to infuse for 2 hours. After 2 hours, chill the dashi completely.

Weigh the chilled dashi and stir in the Stage 4 ingredients. This is now ready to use. Keep it covered and chilled in the meantime.

Slice the cured cod into 4mm pieces and brush with the smoked cod bone oil. Place into a serving dish, then add a little freshly grated wasabi.

Thinly slice the radishes and place in an ice bath for 5 minutes. Marinate the sea lettuce in a small amount of the dashi for 5 minutes, then cover the cod with the marinated sea lettuce. Spoon over the dashi, then arrange the sliced radishes over the top.

Drizzle the cod oil and wasabi oil over the dish, followed by a sprinkle of sesame seeds and togarashi. Finally, finish with a generous amount of freshly grated lime zest and serve immediately.

JÖRO | House of JÖRO | Konjö, Sheffield

Meat & Potato Pie

Preparation time: 1-2 hours | Cooking time: 4 hours | Serves 8

FOR THE PIE FILLING

STAGE 1
900g Wortley wagyu braising steak, diced

8g table salt

75g plain flour

75g beef dripping

STAGE 2
250g diced white onion

175g peeled and diced carrot

110g diced shiitake mushroom (stalks removed)

20g peeled and diced garlic

STAGE 3
330g IPA

STAGE 4
2g fresh thyme leaves

5g dried ma-kombu seaweed, rinsed under cold water for 30 seconds

200g tinned chopped tomatoes

50g double concentrated tomato purée

450g fresh dark chicken stock

450g fresh beef stock

STAGE 5
150g Henderson's Relish

25g IPA vinegar

20g caster sugar

900g peeled and diced waxy potatoes, cooked until tender when pierced with a knife and cooled

25g chopped flat leaf parsley

FOR THE PASTRY

490g unsalted butter, diced, frozen + 35g beef dripping

230g Wildfarmed all-purpose flour

9g table salt

175g cold water

FOR THE PIE FILLING

Heat a cast iron casserole dish over a medium heat. Toss the beef in the salt and flour. Melt the dripping in the casserole dish and brown the beef all over in 3 batches. Remove the beef from the pan and set aside.

Add the Stage 2 ingredients to the casserole dish and cook out until all the veg is golden and caramelised, stirring regularly. Add the beef back to the pan and stir it in. Add the Stage 3 ingredients and bring to the boil, then stir in the Stage 4 ingredients and bring back to the boil. Remove from the heat and place the casserole dish in an oven preheated to 160°c fan for 1 hour 30 minutes.

Remove from the oven after this time and give the mix a good stir. Increase the oven temperature to 180°c fan, place a lid on the casserole dish and return it to the oven. Cook for a further 40 minutes with the lid on, then remove from the oven and stir in the Henderson's Relish, IPA vinegar, sugar, and potatoes. Allow the filling to cool.

TO MAKE THE PASTRY

Combine half the flour with the butter and dripping using the paddle attachment in a KitchenAid stand mixer or food processor (or rub together by hand) until it becomes like breadcrumbs. Mix in the remaining flour and salt. Add the cold water and mix to form a dough, then remove from the bowl and knead gently for 2 minutes.

Roll the dough into a ball and press it into a flat disc 1 inch thick. Wrap this in cling film and refrigerate it for at least 1 hour before using.

Preheat the oven to 180°c fan and grease two 25cm pie tins with beef dripping, butter, or cooking spray. Divide the pastry into 4 pieces and roll them into 3mm thick rounds using a rolling pin on a cold surface lightly dusted with flour.

Line the greased tins with a round of pastry, pressing it gently into the edges. Fill them with the cooled pie mix. Now place the tops on and crimp the pastry together at the edges using your fingers. Brush the tops with a little egg wash (1 egg yolk + 50g milk, whisked together) and then cut a little steam hole in the middle of each pie. Bake them for 30-45 minutes or until golden brown and piping hot in the centre. Allow to cool slightly before serving.

JÖRO | House of JÖRO | Konjö, Sheffield

My Dishes

BARBECUED WORTLEY WAGYU SIRLOIN WITH PANZANELLA

This dish is something I'd cook pretty much every week in summer: invite some friends round, get a nice piece of beef on the bone, bring some amazing tomatoes home from the restaurant. If you're going to cook, you should do it properly or there's no point.

You can cook the beef in two ways, either reverse searing which means letting it get to about 40°c in the oven and then finishing it over the fire, or the other way round which I've done in this recipe. Both give you pretty much the same result, which is meat that's cooked fairly rare but not too pink to make sure the fat has rendered properly, and the smoky flavour is strong enough throughout the meat, which doesn't happen if you sear it too quickly.

Panzanella is one of my favourite things a) to eat and b) to do with tomatoes, especially alongside a smoky, salty piece of meat. All the ingredients I've used in the recipe are literally the stuff I use at home, like the balsamic vinegar which has a really good balance of sweetness, acidity and bitterness that goes so well with my favourite tomatoes. They're from a grower in Evesham and have a very well-rounded flavour with good texture that makes a great salad. We sometimes get heritage tomatoes at home instead though – Stacey loves the green and yellow varieties – and just add a bit more salt or less vinegar or a pinch of sugar, whatever they need to balance. Whatever tomatoes you buy, don't ever put them in a fridge. Just keep them in a warm room where they'll get a good amount of sunlight, so they're continuously ripening and staying at their best.

KOREAN FRIED CHICKEN

We really love to eat this kind of food and that's the reason we created Konjö, where this is on the menu, because it's a mish mash of different cultures and cuisines to represent everything we love about travelling through Asia in one kitchen.

We tried some authentic recipes for Korean fried chicken and then started to think about using what we had in our larder: ingredients that we were already cooking with for other dishes. Gochujang is typically Korean but pretty much everything else we included is Japanese, like the chilli miso and sake. The sauce we eventually developed is our own version of the original but completely unique to us. It's just nice to have a little bit of a twist and put our stamp on it. The brining isn't part of a typical recipe either, so we added that purely for texture and flavour.

Starting with great produce is crucial to getting the end result we want with this dish. Chicken thighs on the bone have the best flavour and I love using corn-fed chicken because it's fattier so the meat tends to be more juicy and succulent with a better texture. The sesame seeds are a mix of roasted white, roasted black and kimchi-flavoured orange so each bring a slightly different flavour to the garnish. The coriander is grown by a friend in Chesterfield, very local to us, and the chicken is from Yorkshire.

RAINBOW TROUT, SMOKED BUTTER SAUCE, YUZU, WASABI & PARSLEY

Everything's really punchy but super well balanced to make this a very light, delicate dish. We get the trout from a farm in Lincolnshire, less than an hour away from the restaurant so it's very fresh, and buy them whole – including the roe sack at the right time of year – to age for up to a week in our Himalayan salt chamber before prepping and cooking. The carcasses and bones are smoked very slowly, then infused into oil with lemon or yuzu peel and fresh garlic. We cook the oil for an hour and then mature it for a week, and that's brushed onto fish as it cooks which gives it this flavour that's almost like fish pie but liquid so it's more intense.

Each element of this dish complements the fish and is there for a reason. We developed our own caviar with Exmoor Caviar, originally for a dish that included kombu seaweed ice cream. That collaboration allowed us to create a product that's unique to us because we worked on the recipe with them to get the curing and salt content just where we wanted it. You get crunch and acidity from the pickled parsley stalks, alongside a bright, grassy flavour from the oil which mixes with the sauce as you eat, helping to season it. Kinome, a delicate leafy garnish we use alongside wasabi and nori, is the shoots of the sansho pepper plant. It isn't something you can typically find in the UK but there are some suppliers growing it, such as The Wasabi Company – you can buy the plants from them here and grow kinome at home or the restaurant.

ALPHONSO MANGO, PINEAPPLE, KAFFIR LIME, COCONUT & SANSHO PEPPER

Alphonso mangoes are so deliciously sweet and tender with deep yellow flesh. We buy ours from the local vegetable markets, but they are grown in India. The season usually spans April to July, but sometimes a little longer. When they are finished, we move on to Thai honey mangoes. We also buy in the mango sake and green sansho pepper oil used in this recipe, sourced from a wealth of over 200 suppliers that we use. The secret to the dish really is the quality of the ingredients used, and they just go together so well. Perfect harmony.

COD CRUDO, CHILLED AROMATIC DASHI WITH TRUFFLES

The word Crudo comes from Italy and really just means sliced, seasoned, raw seafood served with a sauce or dressing. The depth of flavour and earthiness from the black winter truffles work really well with the other ingredients in the dish – ginger, yuzu, lime, seaweed – and is a combination that works brilliantly with fish. Truffle and yuzu are quite commonly used together in raw seafood dishes. The cod bone oil recipe is the same as the recipe for trout bone oil in my trout recipe on page 20 if you wanted to make your own; just replace the trout bones with grilled and smoked cod bones.

MEAT & POTATO PIE

I spent a lot of time developing this recipe to be cooked at home. Autumn and winter is the time of year for pies in my house! Can't beat a nice hot meat and potato pie in some rich, flaky, buttery pastry on a cold day. A little kombu seaweed is the secret, but great quality meat and stocks are what I believe make this a great pie, along with a killer pastry and Henderson's Relish to finish it of course: what's not to love. Ultimately my belief is always the same when it comes to creating a dish: use the best ingredients you can and you don't have to do too much. Jake Tue is the man behind Wortley Wagyu and has become a good friend of mine. I love his beef, it's the best tasting beef there is around this neck of the woods in my opinion. Wildfarmed flour is mega tasty too; they put a lot of effort into the soil first in their farming process which in turn makes the best tasting flour to use in the pastry.

JÖRO | House of JÖRO | Konjö, Sheffield

Chewing The Fat with Luke French

What do you love about cooking over fire?

I love the flavours you get from different woods and charcoals, as well as how intuitive it is. It's just a really fun way to cook but I also think it's a great skill for my younger chefs to learn because it teaches you to understand heat and how to use fat and smoke as flavour and seasoning. Not everything needs that intensity of flavour though, so how much we cook on the fire depends on the season and ingredients. We've always done it to some extent, from day one as a pop up, so it's in JÖRO's DNA.

How do you like to describe your approach to cooking?

Restriction and conforming is my biggest hate. I don't know what to call us except modern, progressive… we're just cooking what we want to cook. But there is a certain identity to it. You see a dish and you know that it's us from the presentation, the ingredients, the way in which we cook. When we started, I was very inspired by Nordic and Japanese cooking, but I don't look to it as much now. What we're doing is us. Being open about it, I think we got a little bit confused along the way and it took me some time to figure it out. The lockdown helped me reflect on that so what we're doing now is completely us and pretty much self-taught. That's what the restaurant is, an interpretation of us and however we're feeling at that moment in time: everything that we love about eating.

Is there an ingredient you couldn't live without?

It would be salt, because it's so useful for cooking with, enhancing taste, bringing out flavours that you didn't know were there. Salt and acid are great at that. We use a lot of malic acid in the kitchen, even adding a little pinch to ice cream. You won't even know it's there, but it elevates the flavours. Also, I absolutely love cooking seafood. Anything that comes from the ocean is fascinating to me in every way: the appearance, texture, smell, flavour, saltiness, the way that it cooks, especially over fire. There's nothing that I don't really like cooking with but unless I love an ingredient, I'll never put it on the menu, so ultimately, it's a true reflection of what I like to eat. How can you cook something to its full potential if you don't think it's amazing?

What's the most important piece of equipment in your kitchen?

Every single section and most recipes in the kitchen require a Thermomix somehow, because we make a lot of oils that involve blending and heating and infusing at the same time. There's an oil in every single dish because they're such a good vessel for flavour. You can also use ingredients that wouldn't otherwise be on the plate that way. We also use the Pacojet for all of our ice creams and sorbets. In my desserts, you'll always find something frozen because I love really cold sweet things.

Which suppliers do you work most closely with?

Jake Tue is our wagyu farmer in Wortley, a 15-minute drive from the restaurant. As a local supplier and producer, he's absolutely incredible. We've got an amazing relationship and we're working on a lot of stuff together including a charcuterie programme with Mangalitsa pigs and his wagyu. The other one is Stuart Turner, known as Sushi Stu by the rest of the world. He's a good friend of mine and has been very important to my cooking in terms of the ingredients we use. He imports the best of the best from Japan to the UK and 90% of what he supplies, you can't really get anywhere else. He does a tasting with us every few months so we can try new products and plan ahead.

If you could go anywhere today for a meal, where would you go?

There's a chef called Björn Frantzén who's got a restaurant in Stockholm called Frantzén which I'd love to eat at. I find him very inspiring and from my perspective, I think we share an excitement for a lot of the same ingredients. In the UK, it would be Ynyshir. That's a really special place for me and Stacey – we think it's the best restaurant in the UK. Everyone else is amazing at what they do but every time we go it just blows my mind with how incredible it is. We've been a few times and I don't understand how it can be so much better every single time; they just level up constantly and it's so progressive, so interesting. Gareth just does what he wants to do. Besides that, Da Terra. Rafael's cooking is on another level, he's thinking outside the box, and everything is really unique. It's restaurants like that that really excite me. Obviously, all the restaurants in the book are big favourites of mine and Stacey's. The ones I've mentioned above are the places we'd go for a special occasion, but everywhere we've included we would absolutely travel to eat at. Some are quite a journey, but it's worth the trip.

Hjem, Hexham, Northumbria

Alex Nietosvuori and Ally Thompson

Hjem is the dream project of Swedish chef Alex Nietosvuori and his partner, Northumberland-born Ally Thompson. They joined forces to create a destination restaurant which represents the very best of their respective backgrounds after spending 20 years gaining experience across some of the top restaurants in Scandinavia and the UK.

Alex began his culinary career in Sweden, where three years with Daniel Berlin were followed by three years at Bror with Sam Nutter and Victor Wågam (formerly sous chefs at Noma) and a stage with Rodolfo Guzman at Boragó. He then took on a position at three Michelin starred Oslo restaurant Maaemo for ten months, before moving to London to work with Tom Anglesea at The Laughing Heart in Hoxton.

Keen to run a business closer to Ally's family home, Alex and Ally were ready to realise their ambition of opening their own restaurant against a stunning Northumberland backdrop. Hjem (pronounced yem) means 'home' in both Scandinavian and Northumbrian, perfectly encapsulating the partnership behind the restaurant and their approach to elevating local produce with creativity and technical skill.

"I think when you eat here, you should look out and think: I'm eating where I am." - Alex Nietosvuori.

HISTORICAL SITE
On this day,
30th November 1734,
absolutely nothing
happened

Hjem, Hexham, Northumbria

Beignet Filled with Doddington Cheese and Glazed in Wildflower Honey

Preparation time: 1 hour | Cooking time: 45 minutes | Makes 30

FOR THE BEIGNET
240g egg

150g water

290g flour

60g sugar

16g honey

3g baking soda

FOR THE CHEESE CREAM
350g milk

4 egg yolks

15g cornflour

200g grated hard cheese (Doddington if possible)

Black pepper

Maldon sea salt

50g smoky whisky

TO ASSEMBLE
50g dried fennel seeds

Oil of your choice, for frying

Wildflower honey, for glazing

FOR THE BEIGNET
Mix all the ingredients together in a stand mixer. Put the batter into an espuma gun, charge with 2 chargers and leave to set.

FOR THE CHEESE CREAM
Put the milk, egg yolks and cornflour in a pan and bring to the boil while whisking. Take the pan off the heat and add the grated cheese. Ensure the cheese is fully melted into the cream, then season with salt and pepper to taste. Let it cool down before folding the whisky through the cheese cream, then transfer to a pipping bag.

TO ASSEMBLE
Toast the fennel seeds in a dry frying pan until golden brown, then set aside. Heat a pan of oil to 180°c. Preheat a small ladle in the oil, and once it's up to temperature fill the ladle with beignet batter and deep fry until golden brown. Repeat with the remaining batter.

Pipe the cheese cream into the beignets, glaze with the wildflower honey, then sprinkle with the toasted fennel seeds and Maldon sea salt to finish.

You can also do a sweet version of this dish by filling the beignets with salted caramel sauce, chocolate sauce or by making a nice fruity dip to enjoy with your fried beignets.

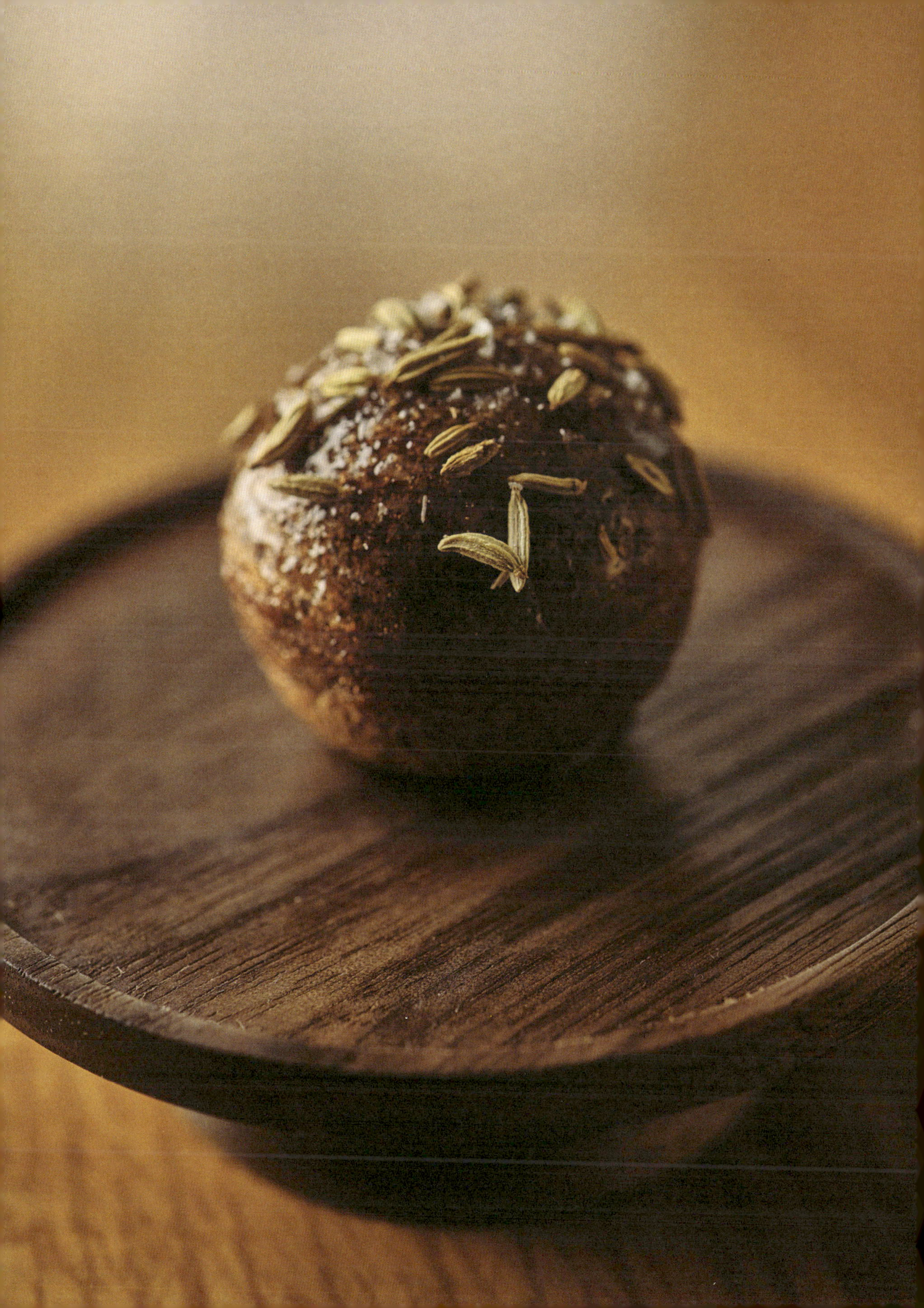

Hjem, Hexham, Northumbria

Confit Duck Leg with Duck Liver

Preparation time: 2 hours, plus 6 hours salting | Cooking time: 4 hours 30 minutes | Serves 2

FOR THE CONFIT DUCK LEG
Salt
2 duck legs (skin on)
500g duck fat
1 bulb of garlic

FOR THE MOREL SAUCE
Olive oil
1 white onion, finely chopped
100g morel mushrooms
100g butter
200g dry white wine
300g chicken stock
300g double cream
100g parsley, finely chopped
50g chives, finely chopped

FOR THE DUCK LIVER
300g duck liver, halved

FOR THE PICKLED ONIONS
10 silverskin onions
600g water
300g sugar
200g vinegar
A few sprigs of thyme (optional)

FOR THE CONFIT DUCK LEG
Salt the duck legs and leave for 6 hours. Heat up the duck fat, add half the garlic bulb and the salted duck legs, then gently simmer for approximately 4 hours. Use a knife to test whether the meat falls away easily from the bone; this means the duck leg is ready. Transfer the duck legs to an ovenproof tray, making sure you keep them as intact as possible.

FOR THE MOREL SAUCE
Heat a large, wide pan on low to ensure even cooking. Put some olive oil into the pan and turn the heat up to medium, then add the chopped white onion and slowly cook out. Do not allow it to colour. When the onion is soft and transparent, add the morels and butter and cook until the morels have a soft texture.

Add the white wine and reduce to an almost dry pan. Add the chicken stock and double cream and reduce until it coats the back of a spoon. Season with salt, then stir the chopped herbs through the sauce.

FOR THE DUCK LIVER
Put a pan on a high heat and when it's smoking, caramelise the duck liver on both sides. Take out of the pan and cool down in the fridge so the pieces keep their shape.

FOR THE PICKLED ONIONS
Peel the silverskin onions, keeping them as whole as possible. Boil the water, sugar and vinegar in a pan, add the onions and let them simmer for approximately 1 minute until soft. Set aside to cool.

TO ASSEMBLE
Preheat the oven to 180°c and put the duck legs in for 20 minutes. After this time, put the duck liver on top of the legs and roast for a further 5 minutes until the liver is warmed through. Meanwhile, heat the morel sauce in a wide pan and season to taste. Add the pickled onions and some more herbs to the sauce if needed or wanted.

Pour the sauce onto a sharing platter and put the duck legs and liver on top. Finish with some more chopped parsley and chives. Serve with potato purée or celeriac gratin.

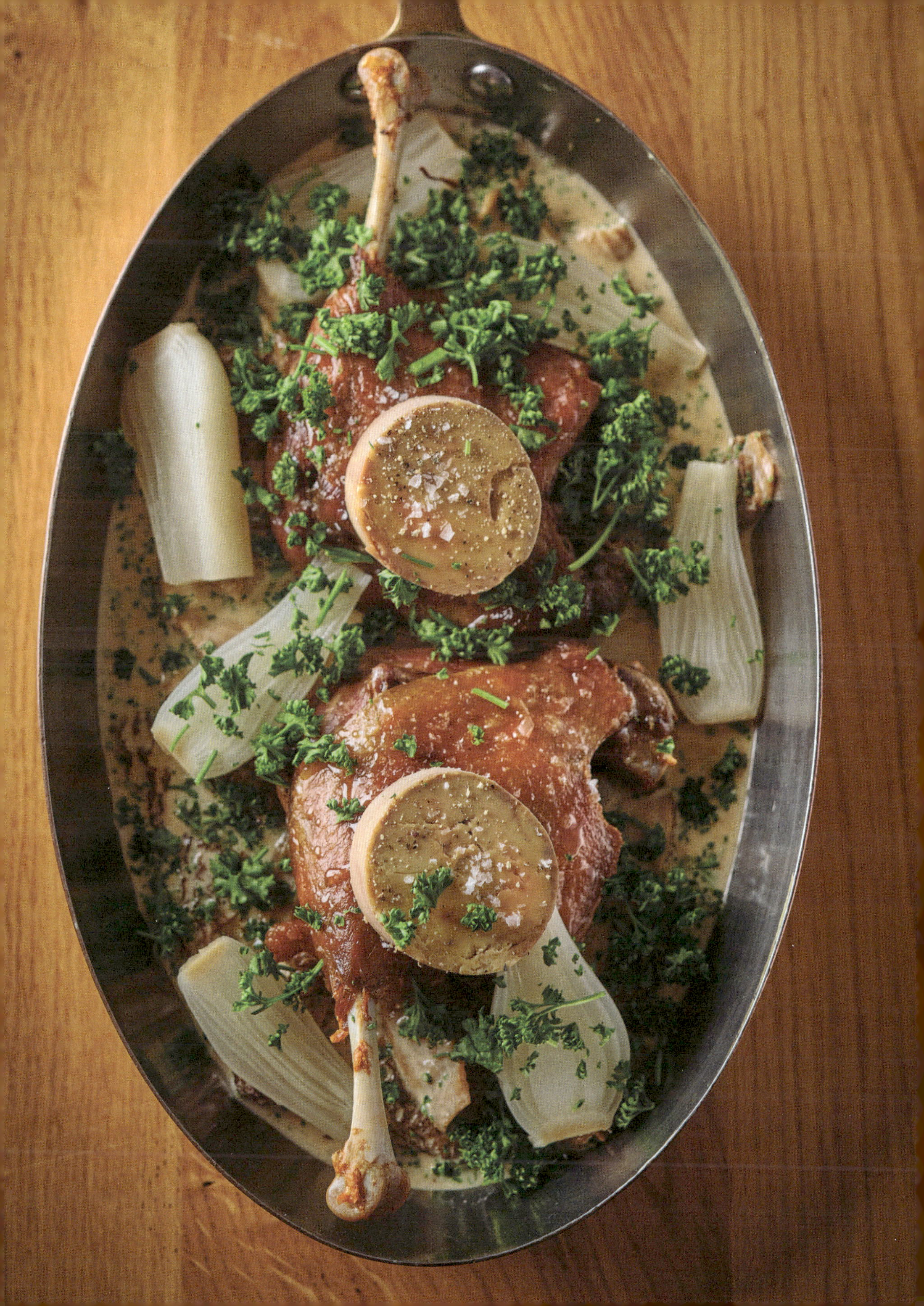

Hjem, Hexham, Northumbria

Hand-Dived Scallops, Smoked Cream, Garden Sorrel & Caviar

Preparation time: 2 hours, plus 24 hours dehydrating | Cooking time: 30 minutes | Serves 8

4 extra-large hand-dived scallops
Garden sorrel
100g crème fraiche
300g double cream
25g rapeseed oil
20-40g caviar (N25 Réserve)

FOR THE SCALLOP
Open your scallops, wash them and put them in a dry container. Keep the scallop roe and cold smoke it for 10 minutes three times before dehydrating in the oven at 70°c until completely dry and you're able to grate it.

FOR THE SORREL
Using a 1.5cm ring cutter, punch out rounds from the sorrel leaves and keep on damp paper, saving all the scraps. Finely chop the sorrel scraps and fold them through the crème fraiche.

FOR THE SMOKED CREAM
Put the double cream in a metal container and cold smoke for 20 minutes. Grate your smoked scallop roe into the cream to taste and then season with salt.

TO FINISH
Cut your scallops into 4 slices of 0.5cm each. Put 2 slices on each plate and season with a little salt, spread the sorrel crème fraiche over each slice and cover with the sorrel rounds. Add the caviar to the plates (if you feel like treating yourself, use a larger amount). Mix the rapeseed oil into the smoked cream, then pour 2 spoonfuls of this sauce between the scallops in the middle of the dish.

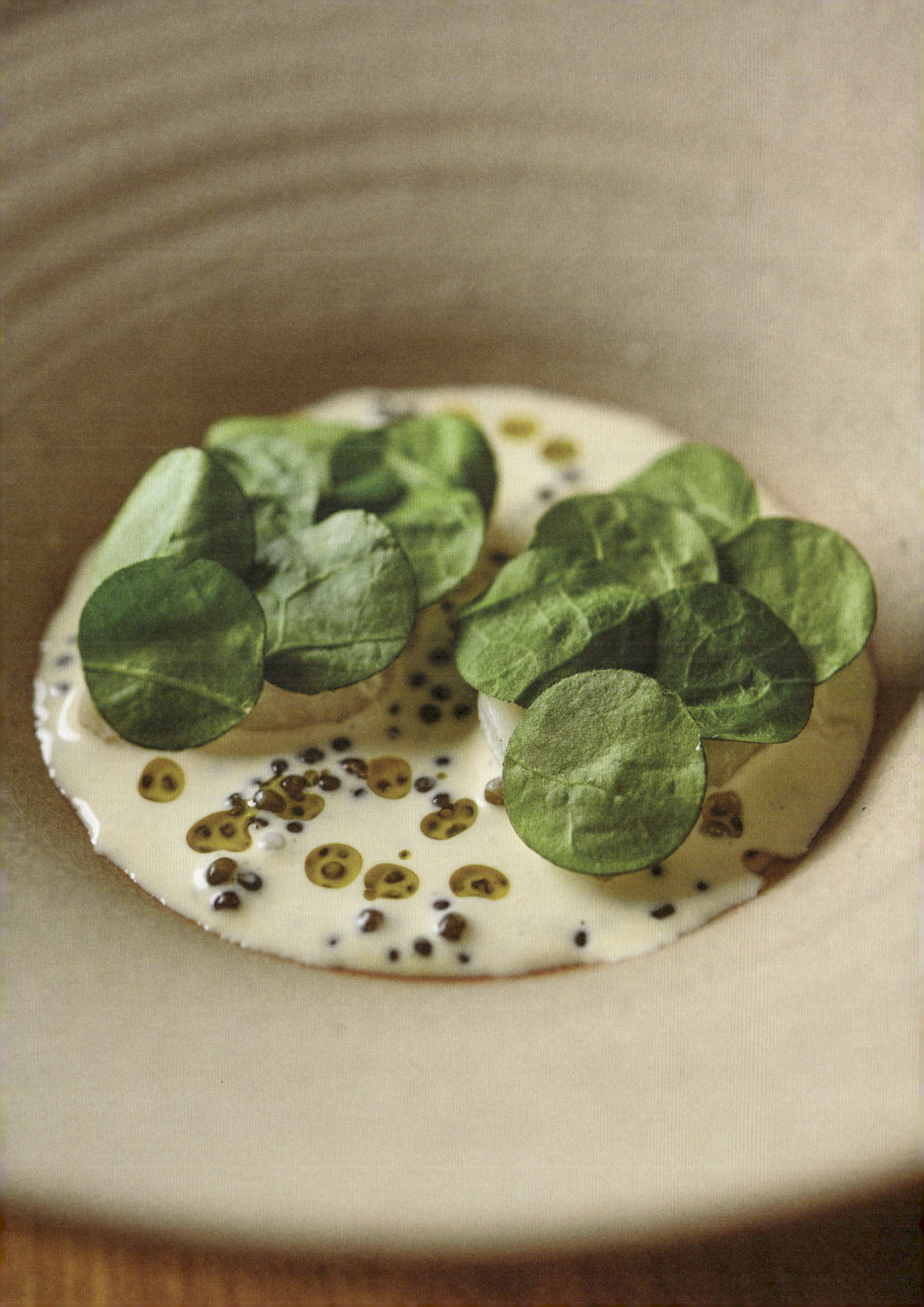

Hjem, Hexham, Northumbria

Our Food

Alex – I'd like to say our cooking style is…interesting. I like to cook things that I like to eat, but every chef says that. We try to take a very simple ingredient and make it as complicated as possible.

Ally – It always looks very simple but it's actually quite technical. The amount of work that goes into making the food look the way it does is quite intense. It's deceptive; you never have more than three or four ingredients on the plate but the processes behind them are often complex. People usually want to say we're Scandinavian in terms of the cooking style, which is inescapable because Alex is Swedish. But we always use what's on our doorstep and work with Northumbrian produce as much as we can – things from the surrounding farms and gardens.

Alex – Though we also have an amazing wild salmon supplier from the only official source in the whole of the UK. They only supply one restaurant aside from us, which is Le Manoir, and Harrods in London.

Ally – You can't guarantee you're going to get any because it just depends on what they catch but what we do get is brilliant.

Alex – We're always changing the menu here anyway…

Ally – Sometimes halfway through service!

Alex – I get a gut feeling. If I don't feel right about a dish, I will change it. It doesn't matter if it's when I'm taking the dish to the guests and then have to do it differently for the next table, I'll change it.

Ally – It's so easy to overthink your food, isn't it? We always say don't compare ourselves to others or try to be something that's not true to us.

Alex – We try not to look at too many other places. I would like to think that we stick to our own thing, but everyone slips up sometimes, you know? There's been millions of times where Ally turns to me and says you need to get back on track. It does help that we don't have too many other people to look at round here, because it's so easy these days with social media – I could probably write 3000 menus just by looking at Instagram. It doesn't make it unique, and it probably doesn't make your food any better. Turn off social media, turn off your phone, create a menu out of your head: that's what makes it better. As a chef I find you always compare yourself to other people, but I think that it can almost become a sickness for you to copy others if you're a creative person.

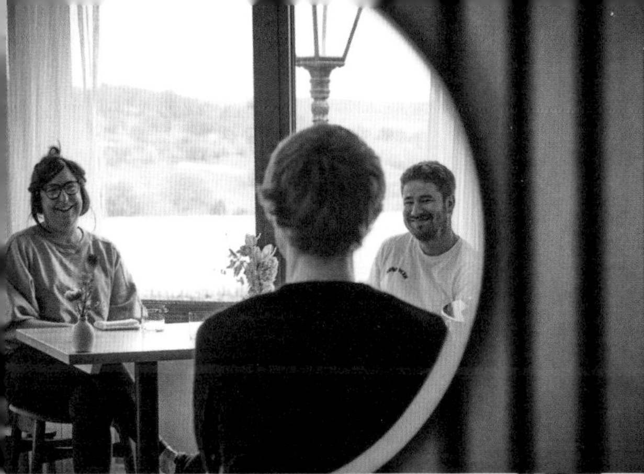
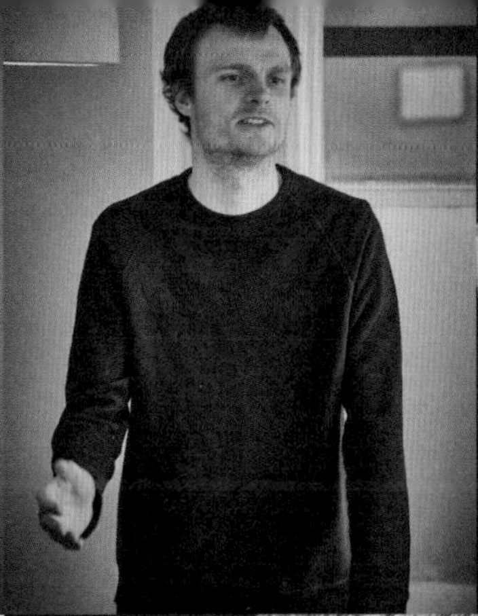
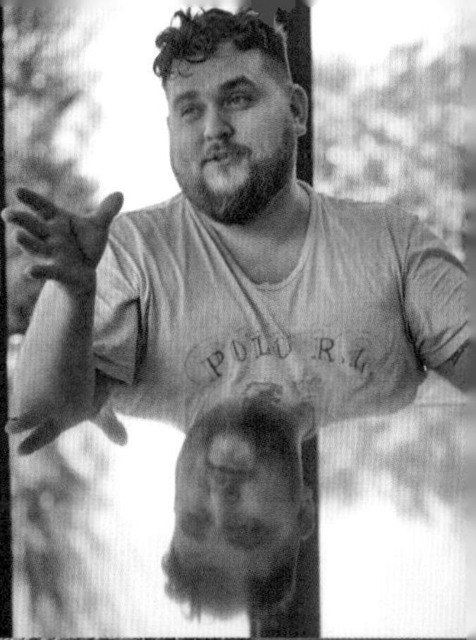
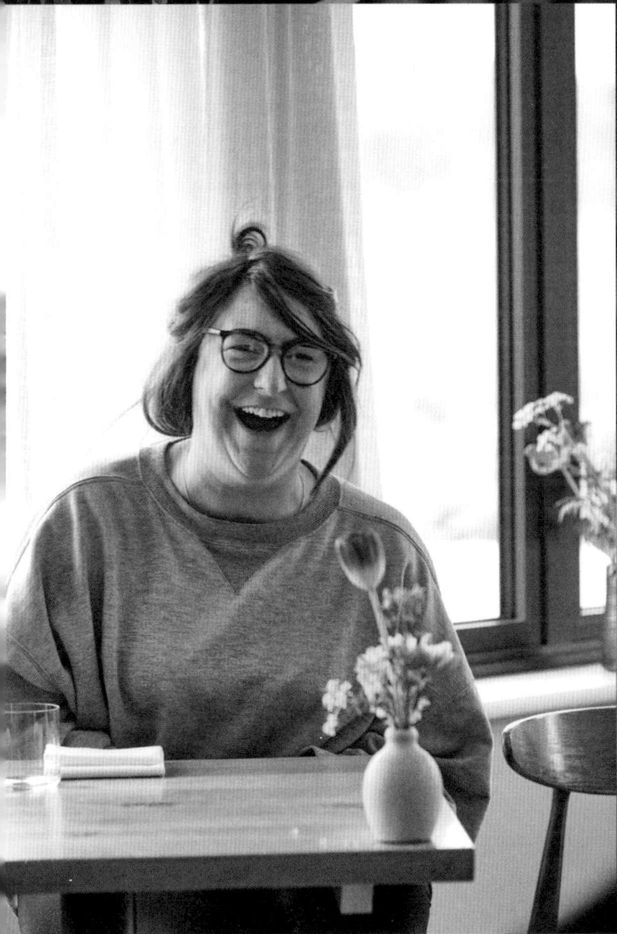
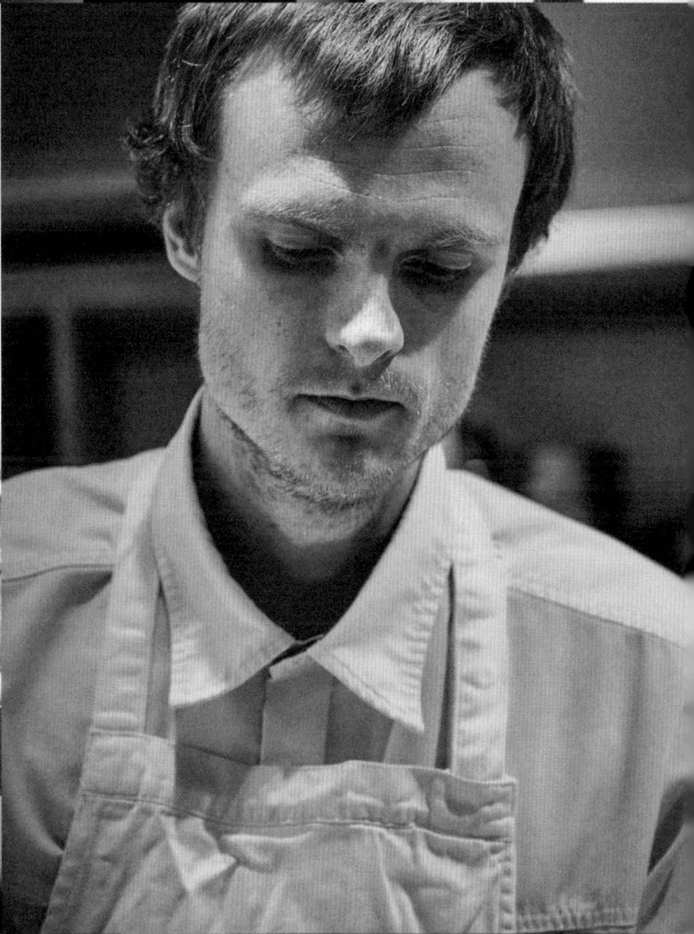
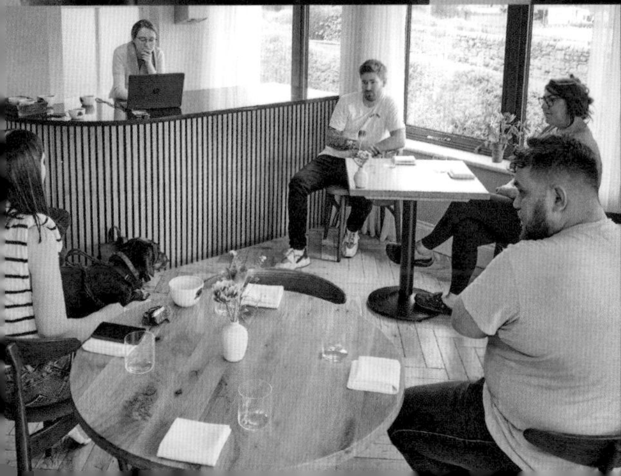
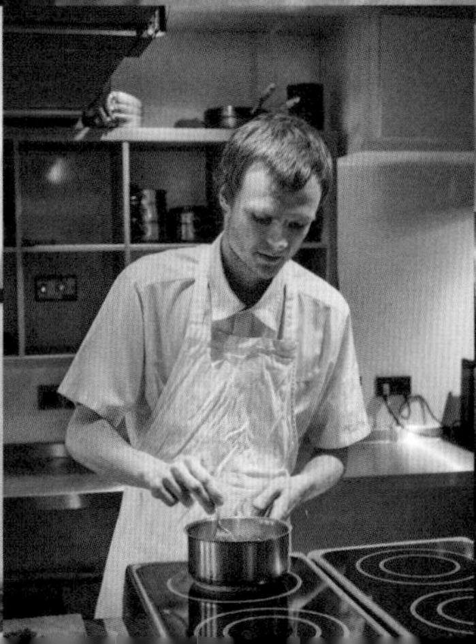
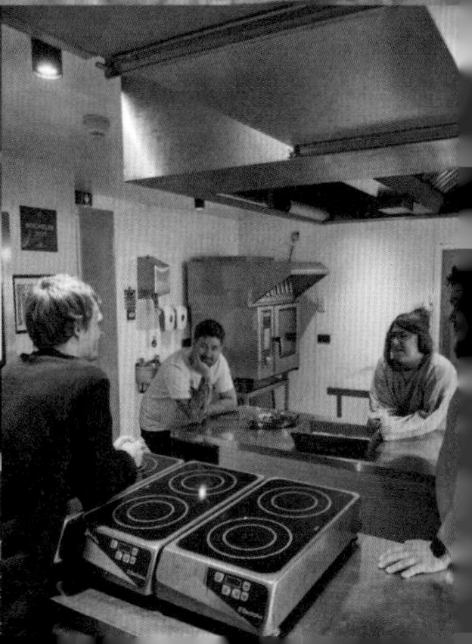

Hjem, Hexham, Northumbria

Kitchen Q&A

What's the secret to a perfect beignet?

You can overwhip the batter, so only shake it once before piping. It should be set – when we're making them for lunch, we make them the night before. At that stage you shake it 24 times in the espuma gun. If overwhipped, they come out flatter but when you get the batter right they're perfectly round, so they can flip themselves over in the oil when deep frying. Get the oil to 160°c and the spoon needs to be hot. Fill the spoon three quarters full, sink it into the oil, wait for the beignet to pop out and then turn itself over. That's it, on to the next one!

Can you talk us through the cold smoking process used in your scallop recipe?

Smoking the cream is straightforward; we just put a lump of hot charcoal wrapped in tinfoil straight into a bowl of cream, then leave it to cool down and infuse. For the roe, first we remove it from the scallops and line it up on a barbecue rack. That's placed within the barbecue on one side of the pit with hay beneath it. This is then lit until it's all burning and the lid is placed on the barbecue, allowing the fire to die and the smoke to spread. We leave that for 10 minutes with the lid on, and then repeat the process three times. The smoked roe is then dehydrated overnight, until it's completely dry and can be grated.

What do you like to cook at home?

We used to cook everything from raw on the barbecue but then we started using the confit process and it works so well. Sear the meat first, then salt the legs, then put the meat into the fat for about 4 hours until it reaches 54 to 56°c in the middle. The confit duck dish in this book would be one I'd cook for a special occasion, served at the table in a big dish for sharing.

How important is the choice of crockery to your dishes?

We've used the same potter since day one at Hjem for our crockery; it was a game changer for us. It's a long wait for the product but you have to respect the craft. Sometimes that can be frustrating because as a chef you like to get everything now, but life doesn't work like that. Ally's dad also made us some beautiful hand-carved wooden bowls and boxes to serve our petit fours in.

What's the best piece of equipment you've invested in for the restaurant?

The dry ageing fridge. I'd like to buy another for fish but at the moment we rotate different meats through it, so lamb for example will age for two weeks, then we take the meat off the bone and poach it in the rendered lamb fat before searing on the barbecue to finish.

We also have a lot of things that people make for us. Not exactly specialist equipment, but custom made, personalised. Ally's dad created a croustade 'machine' from an old chopping board that means we can do four at once – he's very good at turning Alex's briefs into problem-solving gadgets!

Our Ethos

In the beginning with Hjem – maybe because I was very inexperienced with running my own restaurant – I just wanted to cook all the time. But you never think about how the kitchen's going to handle all those new dishes. We'd mess around with some idea for ages and end up running behind every day, whereas now it's very different. I hate kitchens that try to do complicated things just for the sake of it. I've worked in places where you get a lump in your stomach every day because you can't make a particular dish, but the chef keeps it on the menu. I think we're at a stage now where all the guys would tell me: 'Alex, this doesn't work'.

What we want to achieve is a very good menu alongside a better workplace for all our staff. That's the goal. The minute the boys start working 80 to 90 hours a week, that's when you fail. I'm not saying we're always good at that. But if you can achieve that goal, then you have a good balance. If you've got your life, your restaurant, your guests, your team… where do you keep pushing? Working more hours is not always enjoyable or the most productive approach. That's not where you get the Michelin star, either: they don't care how many hours you work. If you can achieve the same thing or greater success with fewer hours but just as much hard work, you can focus on what you're aiming for.

Obviously, as with everything, this is hard to put into practice. It's easy to say, but the reality is a lot more complicated, especially for a small restaurant like ours. I'm not going to say that the guys here only work eight hours a day because they don't. But there's a different ethos. We don't have the stresses and the time pressures that we used to. For example, we used to do massive tastings before service every day, for about an hour and a half, but because of that everyone's in the shit and running late. So Marek and I said let's just stop doing it. The guys can give us some tasters during prep and that's it for the week. That's an hour and a half more time for everybody.

At the end of the day, this project is a joint enterprise. You can't do this without a million people behind you, around you, helping you. We've been quite lucky with our senior team; Marek – our head chef – has been with me for five years and the rest of the chefs have all been here between two to three years. It's the same with front of house. It's a cliché but we are like a family; we work very well together and we look after each other.

No. 6, Padstow, Corwnwall

Chris McClurg

Chris McClurg grew up in County Down and started his career at Shu in Belfast, followed by a stage at Richard Corrigan's Lindsay House, then three years at O'Shea in London and Brussels. He then helped two friends open a cocktail bar back home in Belfast before his return to the kitchen. He joined Paul Ainsworth at his restaurant in Padstow, Cornwall in 2011 as chef de partie and has worked at No. 6 ever since, where Chris is now chef patron. He won the Observer Food Monthly's Young Chef of The Year award in 2018, and has appeared on Great British Menu twice, reaching the finals and winning the dessert course with his Derry Girls inspired trifle in 2022.

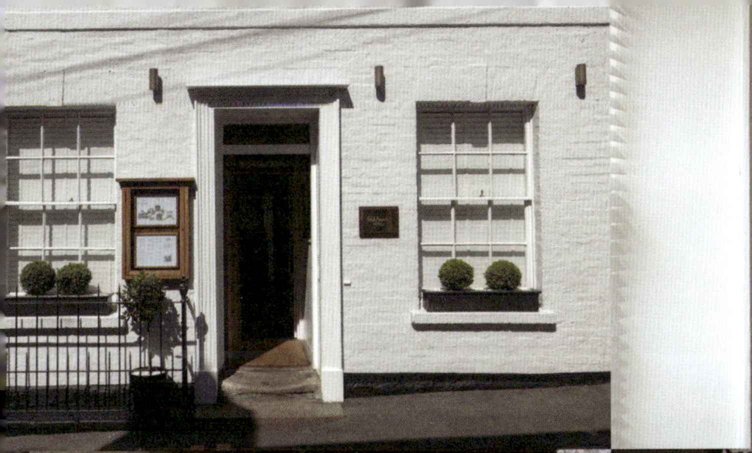
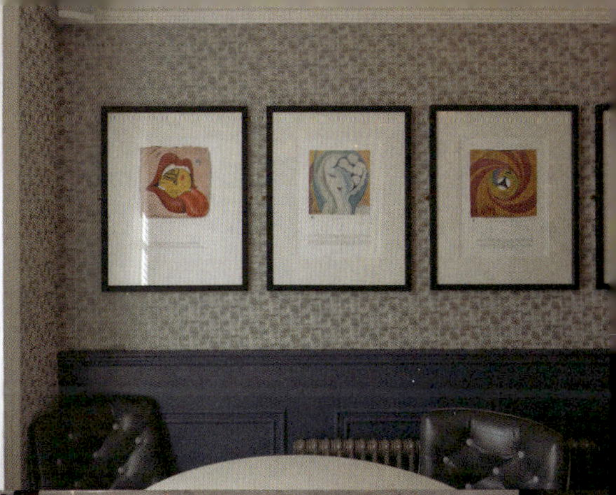
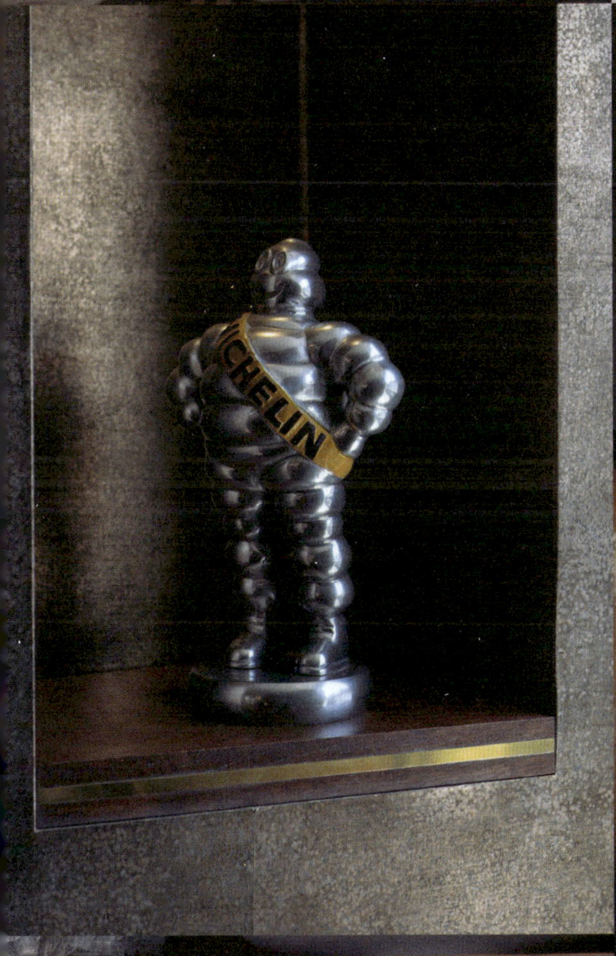
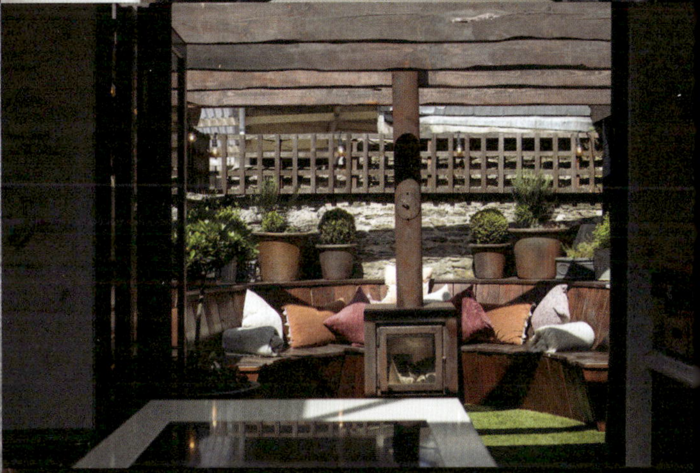
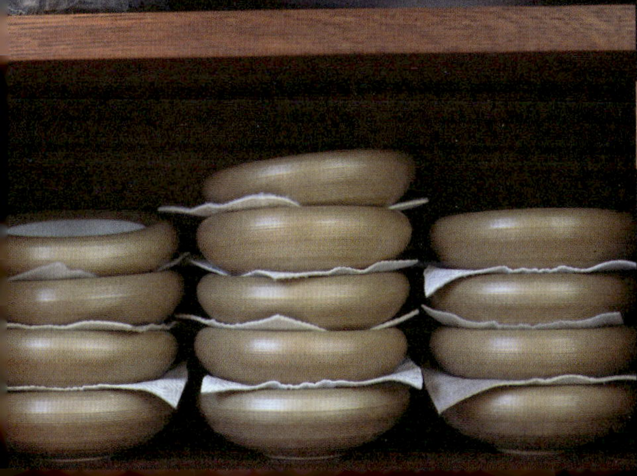
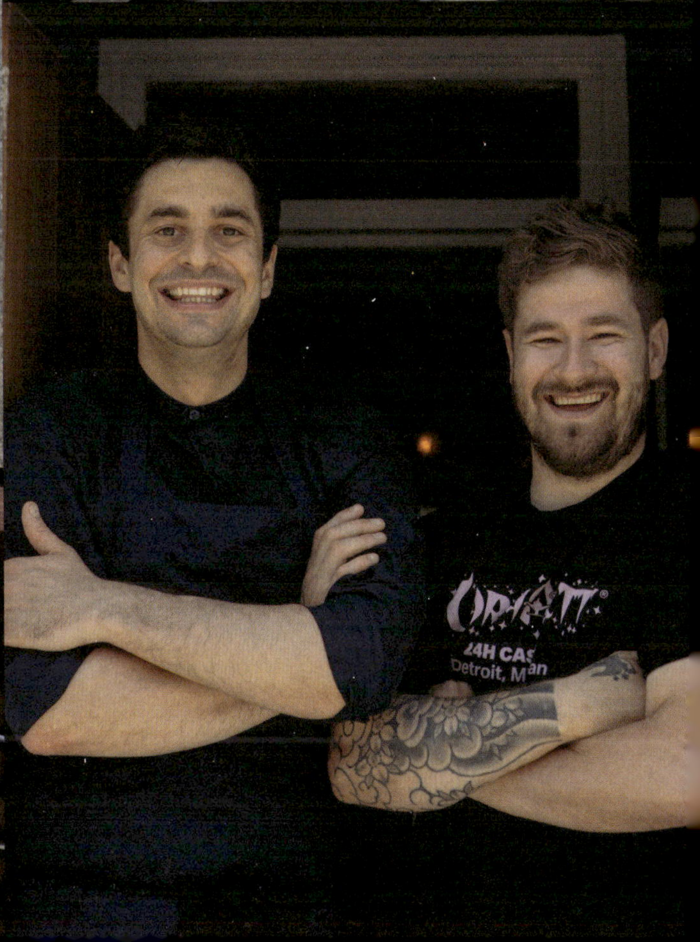

No. 6, Padstow, Corwnwall

Roast Chicken, Manzanilla Sherry, Morels

Preparation time: 1 hour 30 minutes | Cooking time: 3 hours | Serves 6

FOR THE SALSA VERDE

200g flat leaf parsley

200g mint

200g basil

200g chives

2 shallots, sliced

1 clove of garlic

Picked thyme leaves

100ml extra virgin olive oil

5 anchovy fillets

1 tbsp English mustard

1 tbsp capers

Zest of 1 lemon

FOR THE ROAST CHICKEN SAUCE

4kg chopped chicken wings

50g butter

7 large shallots, finely sliced

500g chestnut mushrooms, finely sliced

50g dried ceps

1 garlic bulb

4 star anise

½ bunch of thyme

½ bunch of rosemary

Sherry vinegar, to taste

1 bottle of white wine

½ bottle of Madeira

2 litres reduced beef stock

2 litres reduced chicken stock

50g foie gras

1 tsp soy lecithin

50ml manzanilla sherry

FOR THE SALSA VERDE

First, pick the herbs from the stalks. In a medium saucepan, sweat the shallots for 3-4 minutes in a tablespoon of olive oil with a generous pinch of salt. Add the garlic and thyme, transfer to a small bowl and refrigerate.

In a large pan of rapidly boiling water, blanch the herbs for 1 minute until tender, then immediately chill in a large bowl of heavily iced water, drain and pat dry. Roughly chop the blanched herbs and put them into a blender with all the remaining ingredients, including the chilled shallot mixture.

Blend on full speed until smooth (about 2 minutes) before transferring the salsa to a metal bowl over ice to cool and ensure the colours stay vibrant. We freeze and Pacojet this in the restaurant, but a blender works great at home. Taste the salsa and adjust the seasoning before serving.

FOR THE ROAST CHICKEN SAUCE

Season the chicken wings, then roast at 180°c until deep golden brown, turning every 10 minutes. Meanwhile, heat a little vegetable oil with the butter in a large pan and colour the sliced shallots. Add the chestnut mushrooms, ceps, garlic, star anise, rosemary and thyme, then deglaze with a splash of sherry vinegar. Add the wine and reduce, then add the Madeira and reduce until syrupy.

Add the stocks to the pan, bring to the boil, then turn down to a simmer. Skim the sauce and add the roasted chicken wings. Deglaze the roasting trays with a good glug of water, add this to the pan, then slowly simmer the sauce for 1 hour 30 minutes.

Pass the sauce through a colander followed by a fine strainer. To serve, bring 250ml to a light simmer and emulsify the foie gras with the sauce using a stick blender. Add the soy lecithin and a splash of milk, then adjust the seasoning and balance the flavour with a few drops of sherry vinegar. Finish with the manzanilla sherry and aerate with the stick blender.

No. 6, Padstow, Cornwall

Roast Chicken, Manzanilla Sherry, Morels

Preparation time: 1 hour 30 minutes | Cooking time: 3 hours | Serves 6

FOR THE MOREL FARCE

1 boneless and skinless chicken breast

12 boneless skinless chicken thighs

20g Thai chicken powder (Ros Dee)

200g foie gras

100g veal sweetbread

50g butter

1 large sprig of thyme

1 clove of garlic, cracked

40g double cream

25g Thai oyster sauce

25g confit shallot

25g truffle paste

15 turns of white pepper

3g tarragon

3g chervil

3g chives

FOR THE MARINADE

25g Douglas fir

25g thyme

3 bay leaves

3 cloves of garlic, peeled

100ml extra virgin olive oil

FOR THE MORELS

6-12 large morels (dried are great as you can be selective with size and they picked at their prime and available all year)

FOR THE MOREL FARCE

Dice the chicken breast and thigh into roughly 5cm cubes, season with the chicken powder and freeze on a tray until semi frozen. Dice the foie gras into roughly 5mm cubes and transfer to a flat tray, season with salt, then chill in the fridge to keep firm.

In a medium frying pan, roast the sweetbreads in the butter with the thyme and garlic for 4-5 minutes until crispy and golden, then remove the sweetbreads from the pan and cool on a rack. Chill in the fridge until cold, then dice the same size as the foie gras and reserve in the fridge.

In a food processor, blend the diced chicken until smooth. Transfer to a large metal bowl and combine with all the remaining ingredients. Roll a cocktail sausage amount of this mixture in cling film and simmer in a pan of water for 6 minutes, then remove from the cling film and taste. This is important to check the seasoning of your farce, so adjust the remaining mixture as necessary. When happy, transfer it into piping bags.

FOR THE MARINADE

Chop the fir, thyme and bay, finely slice the garlic, combine them all with the oil and then season with salt and pepper.

FOR THE MORELS

If using dried morels, soak them in fresh water for 30 minutes and then pat dry. If using fresh morels, trim the stalks and wash well. Stuff the morels with the farce from the piping bag, then roll each one in cling film and twist the ends to tighten like a little pert sausage. Steam or poach at 80°c for 8-10 minutes until firm, then remove from the heat and chill rapidly in iced water. Remove the morels from the cling film and pat dry, then add to the marinade and refrigerate.

TO ASSEMBLE THE DISH

Bring the stuffed and marinated morels to room temperature, then gently warm them to 55-60°c over a medium heat barbecue or in a pan of lightly foaming butter. We like to brush them with aged beef fat but melted butter works too. Meanwhile, heat the sauce and froth it up like a cappuccino.

Spoon some of the salsa verde onto a tight centred plate or bowl, place a stuffed morel on top and surround with the sauce. We like to dress the morels with some wild allium flowers and chives when in season. Some little watercress sprigs would work great here too.

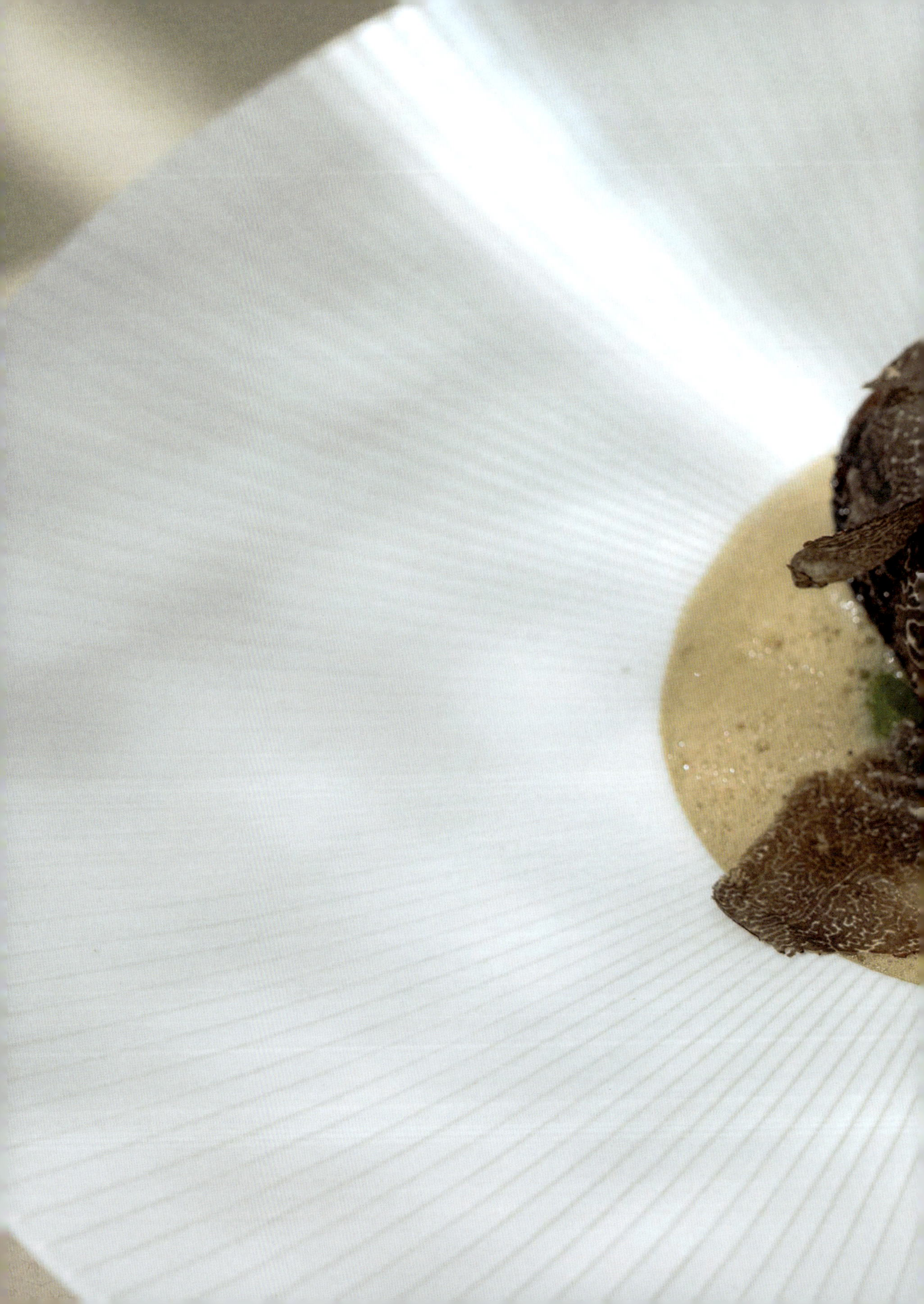

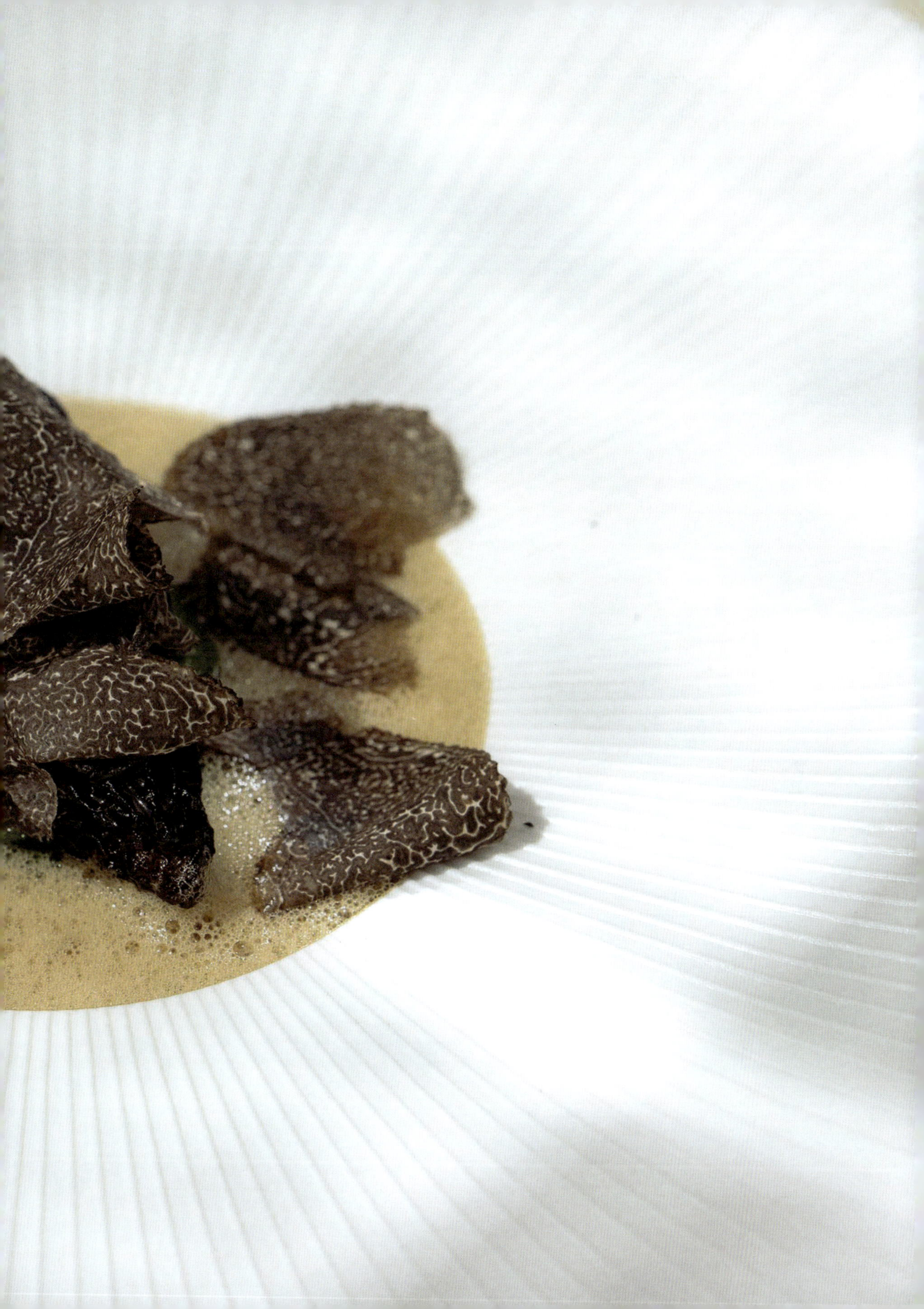

No. 6, Padstow, Corwnwall

Cornish Orchard 'Apple Pie' and Pevensey Blue

Preparation time: 1 hour 30 minutes | Cooking time: 1 hour | Serves 6

FOR THE SEAWEED TART CASE

425g t45 (soft/plain) flour

5g table salt

3g nori sheets, blended to a powder

240g unsalted chilled butter

12.5g dashi granules, mixed into 125g cold water

FOR THE APPLE CARAMEL

1 litre apple juice from concentrate

FOR THE BITTER CARAMEL

500g caster sugar

2 x 184g water

50g unsalted butter

FOR THE CHEESE

250g Pevensey Blue (or a great Stilton works just as well)

FOR THE APPLE TERRINES

8 large Granny Smith apples

A few thyme leaves

FOR THE APPLE BUTTER

Granny Smith apple trim from the terrine (weigh the trim to calculate the quantities)

15% dark soft brown sugar

1% ground cinnamon

TO SERVE

Flaky Cornish sea salt

Picked thyme leaves

FOR THE SEAWEED TART CASE

In a food mixer fitted with a paddle attachment, combine the dry ingredients with the butter until the mixture comes to a fine sandy crumb. Add the dashi water and bring together to form a dough. Transfer to a work surface and roll out between sheets of greaseproof paper until 2mm thick. Chill and rest the dough. Cut the chilled dough with an 80mm ring cutter and place each round between 2 greased 75mm fluted tart cases. Trim and freeze.

Bake the tart cases from frozen at 175°c between 2 heavy baking sheets. After 10 minutes, remove the top tray and trim the edges. Return the tarts to the oven and bake for a further 6 minutes, then check they are cooked before carefully removing the cases. The tarts often take another few minutes in the oven without the cases to finish cooking and achieve an even golden colouring.

FOR THE APPLE CARAMEL

Reduce the juice carefully over a medium heat until syrupy and caramelised (approximately 10% of the original volume). Store at room temperature.

FOR THE BITTER CARAMEL

Combine the caster sugar with 184g of the water in a large stock pot. Start the caramel over a low-medium heat until dissolved, then increase the heat to high and cook to 185-190°c.

Meanwhile, heat the second quantity of water to 50°c. Once the caramel comes to temperature, remove it from the heat and whisk in the warm water. Let the caramel cool before whisking in the butter.

FOR THE CHEESE

With a hot wet knife, remove the rind from the cheese and portion into 28g balls. Press these into a suitable mould lined with cling film to make a uniform shape (individual tart cases work well). Store and serve the cheese balls from chilled.

FOR THE APPLE TERRINE

Sheet the Granny Smith apples on the Japanese vegetable sheeter, then tightly roll into spirals the same diameter as your mould (we use 50mm silicone Yorkshire pudding moulds). Trim the spirals to a depth of 1.5cm (reserving all the excess) and then press into the moulds. Cover each one with 15g of the bitter caramel.

Place the moulds into trays to fit into the vacuum pack machine (ideally, but not necessary at home) and then run the terrine through a cycle on the machine until the caramel is just about to spill over (as above). Bake at 105°c for 40 minutes, then increase the temperature to 150°c and then bake for 8-10 minutes until deep amber. Once tender and caramel in colour, remove and rest the terrine at ambient temperature for 1 hour before serving. Gently warm to remove from the moulds.

FOR THE APPLE BUTTER

Combine all the ingredients, vacuum pack and cook in the water bath at 65°c for a minimum of 4 hours and up to 8. Alternatively, cook in a slow cooker or a bain marie set up in your oven.

Transfer the apple mixture to a clean saucepan and reduce any water until a thick paste is achieved. Blitz in a blender on full power for 2-3 minutes, then pass through a fine meshed sieve and reserve.

TO SERVE

Warm the apple butter just to room temperature. Glaze the terrines with the apple caramel, gently warm in the oven for 3 minutes at 170°c and then glaze with more apple caramel.

Add a teaspoon of apple butter to each seaweed tart case and place a cheese ball on top, followed by the apple terrines. Finish with a few flakes of Cornish sea salt and some picked thyme leaves. Serve with a glass of chilled Cornish orchards heritage cider.

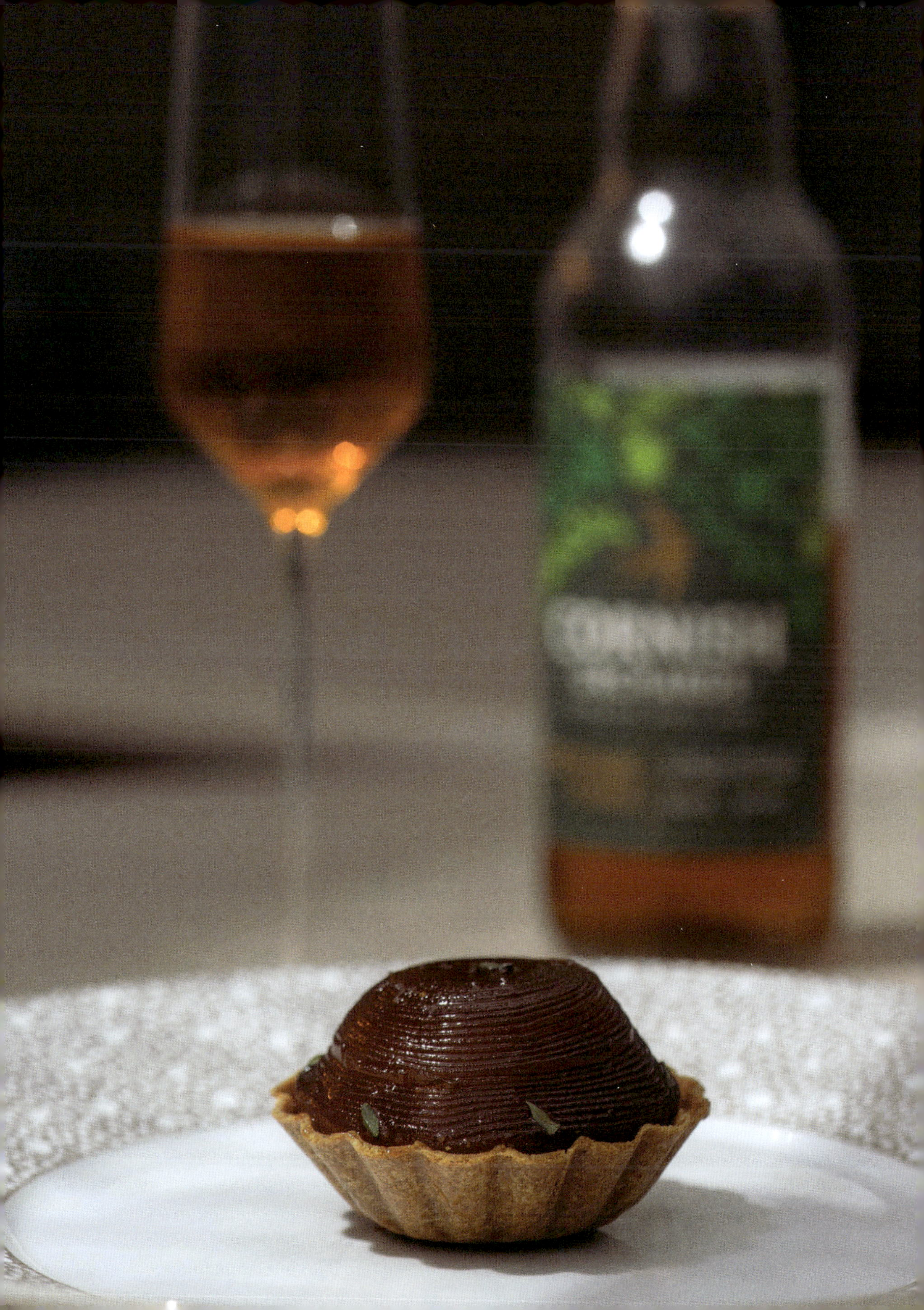

No. 6, Padstow, Corwnwall

Hot Smoked Salmon, Tartare Butter, Fromage Blanc

Preparation time: 30 minutes | Cooking time: 30 minutes | Serves 6

6 best quality free-range eggs

6 best quality English muffins

Caviar (optional)

Chervil

FOR THE TARTARE BUTTER

125g salted butter at room temperature

1 tbsp chopped chives

1 tbsp chopped chervil

1 tbsp chopped parsley

1 tbsp chopped capers

1 tbsp chopped gherkin

1 shallot, finely diced

1 lemon, zested and juiced

1 tsp Dijon mustard

FOR THE SMOKED SALMON

1 'thick end' side of unsliced smoked salmon

500ml pomace olive oil

50g fresh thyme

5 bay leaves

1 garlic bulb

FOR THE FROMAGE BLANC

100g Philadelphia cream cheese

1 tsp chopped dill

1 lemon, zested and juiced

1 pinch of Espelette or cayenne pepper

FOR THE TARTARE BUTTER

In a medium bowl, combine the butter with the herbs, capers, gherkin and shallot. Add the zest followed by the juice of the lemon, then the mustard, and stir to combine. Correct the seasoning and cover but leave at room temperature.

FOR THE SMOKED SALMON

Remove the skin from the salmon. In a pan or tray large enough to hold the salmon, warm the pomace oil with the aromatic herbs and garlic. Heat to around 40-42°c. Slide in the salmon fillet and confit gently for 8-10 minutes, then carefully remove from the oil and place on a wire rack. While still warm, flake the salmon into lovely shells.

FOR THE FROMAGE BLANC

Combine all the ingredients in a medium bowl and refrigerate.

FOR THE POACHED EGGS

Crack 6 of the freshest, largest, richest-yolk eggs you can get your hands on into clean ramekins. Bring a large deep pan of seasoned water to a simmer. Make a little whirlpool in the water and carefully drop in the eggs one by one. Poach until the whites are set but the yolks are still wonderfully gooey. Remove from the pan and chill in iced water to stop them cooking. Trim any messy edges with scissors.

TO FINISH

Cut the English muffins in half, toast well under a hot grill, then butter liberally with the tartare butter. Cover the muffins with the warm smoked salmon shells. Warm the poached eggs and season lightly with salt and pepper, drizzle with good extra virgin olive oil and then pop them on top of the salmon. With a hot wet teaspoon, pull a little rocher (spoonful) of the fromage blanc and pop it beside the egg. Finish with a big dollop of caviar (if using) and a big pellush (fancy chef lingo for small bunch) of chervil. Enjoy this brunch of the gods.

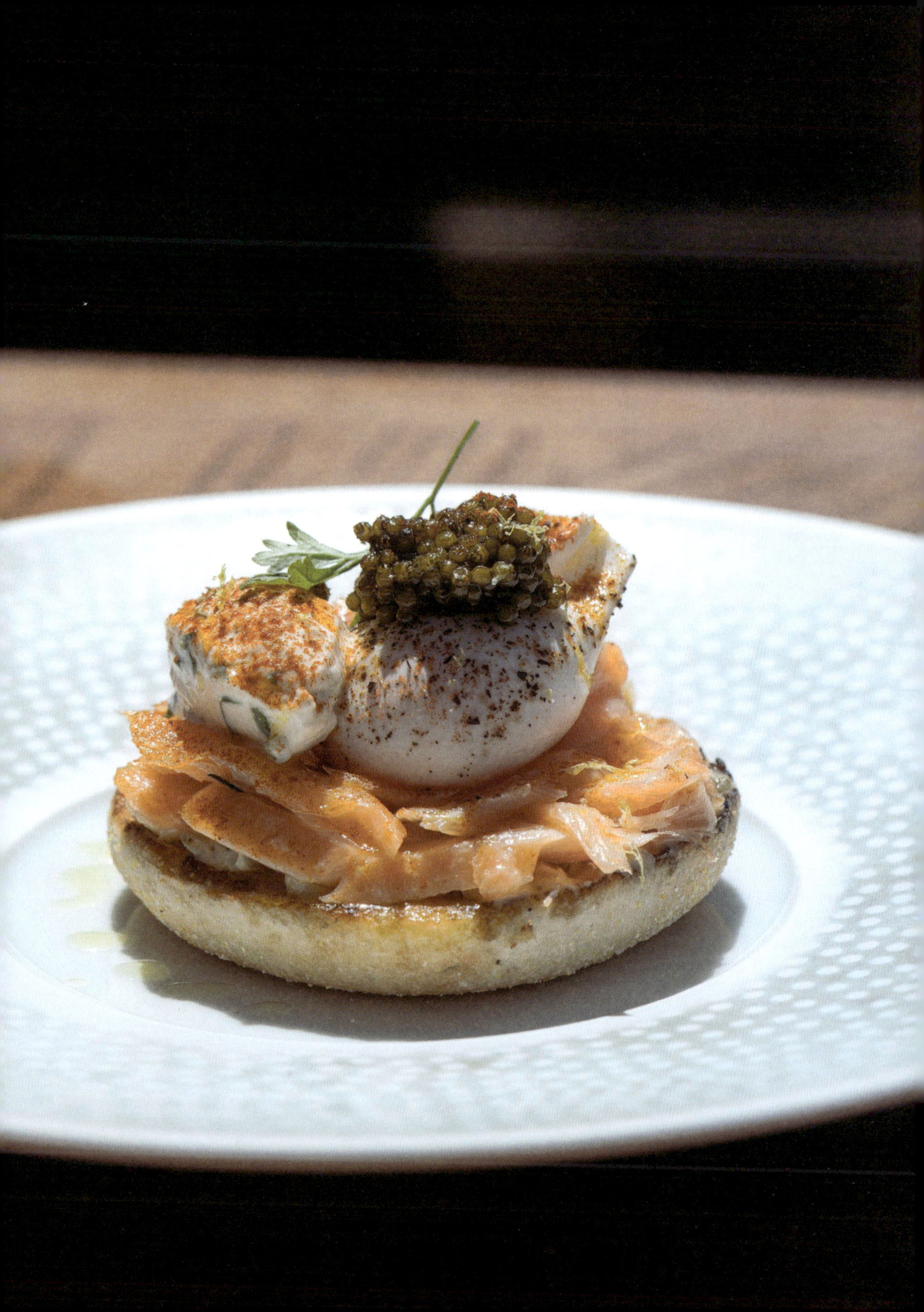

No. 6, Padstow, Cornwall

My Recipes

ROAST CHICKEN, MANZANILLA SHERRY, MORELS

This is an incredible restaurant starter that's simple in its approach and encompasses everything I love about our cuisine right now: great produce cooked with care, respect and knockout flavour at its heart. The recipe makes much more roast chicken sauce and morel farce than you need here but if you go to the effort of making it all, you may as well make plenty. The sauce will be the best chicken gravy for Sunday roasts you will ever have and freezes great. The morel farce can be used to make banging little meatballs, skewers for the barbecue or little chicken sausages.

What's special about manzanilla sherry for you?

It's bone dry. Sherry and mushrooms are really good mates at the best of times – sherry's quite often a secret seasoning in mushroom soups, sauces, purées, that sort of thing – and this dish in its essence is chicken, mushroom and sherry. We make a really intense roast chicken broth from whole roast chickens, loads of button mushrooms, garlic, thyme – classically made, almost like a jus gras, quite high in fat – and then we blend roasted bird's liver into it. When we're finishing that, we blitz it up so it's frothy like a cappuccino, then we finish it with raw manzanilla sherry so it's got that grassy, vegetal, bone dry perfume to it. It's lush.

Where did you first come across the Thai ingredients used here?

We used to do a pinchos style dish at Cici's [the cocktail bar above No. 6] that was basically a chicken wing stuffed with chicken thigh in moo ping dressing, which was based on a very humble, traditional Thai street food dish. Moo ping is always either chicken or pork in Thailand, which is marinated in this dressing and then barbecued, so it gets caramelised and charred. It uses oyster sauce which is super savoury so there's loads of umami flavour. When we made the farce for this dish it was all very classic – chicken mousseline, roasted foie gras, sweetbreads – so we added the moo ping dressing to give it a kick. It's never going to come across as a Thai dish but it's just about accepting influences globally and being open to flavours. If it's delicious and can be part of our narrative then it can be part of our cuisine, it's a simple as that. The origins couldn't be further apart – classic stuffed morels and Thai street food – but it makes the most delicious morel I've ever tasted.

Why are the chicken and foie gras semi frozen for the farce?

We use chicken thighs because texturally they're fantastic and have a lot more flavour than breast, which is traditionally used in a farce, and you freeze them because as you blend, the motion of the blades generates friction which in turn generates heat. If your mix goes anywhere above 2-4°c the heat basically separates the proteins, and as you're aiming for a super smooth finish you want it to stay super chilled, so you start off with very cold apparatus and semi-frozen proteins. The reason we freeze the foie gras is that when you come to combine the ingredients, the end product should have beautifully defined dice throughout when you cut through the morel. Foie gras at room temperature is quite malleable so when you combine the mix you'll end up with a broader distribution, whereas what I want is mousseline, sweetbreads and foie gras as very defined ingredients.

CORNISH ORCHARD 'APPLE PIE' AND PEVENSEY BLUE

This one is a banging cheese course or dessert alternative. The dish is a combination of bittersweet apple, savoury pastry, bittersweet cider, apple butter which is quite sweet, and then this salty but quite mild cheese. In essence it's cheese, chutney and crackers which was inspired by Paul's late father. That's a really important message so the guests who eat this all get a piece of literature that explains the origins. The first version was quite a literal translation of that inspiration – a lump of blue cheese and a tarte tatin – then we reworked it in 2020 and this one is the newest iteration. Like everything we do, it's grown and developed as our cuisine has, but the heritage of the dish is still very personal. Every one we serve is almost like an ode to Paul's father.

What's great about Pevensey Blue?

Pevensey Blue is from East Sussex, and we use that cheese – there are a couple of different ones we use like Barkham Blue and Colston Bassett Stilton – because of the flavour balance we're looking for. It has to be a cheese with really good salinity that's a little bit sharp and a little bit peppery, but quite creamy and not too punchy with a good distribution of veining.

HOT SMOKED SALMON, TARTARE BUTTER, FROMAGE BLANC

This is a banging Sunday brunch dish that I make for myself and my much better half. I'm so well practised at this I could literally do it in my sleep. If you are feeling indulgent or it's a special occasion (XMAS DAY YES PLEASE) then top this bad boy off with a fat spoonful of caviar. For the English muffins, honestly, if you REALLY want to make these yourself then by all means fire away (Richard Bertinet has a great recipe that works every time) but if you are like me and Sunday mornings are valuable chill time, buy some great English muffins or sourdough crumpets from your very best local bakery. We use Saint Ewe eggs which are local, but anything like Burford Browns or whatever you like will work: just keep it local and you want really rich yolks.

Why pomace oil rather than usual olive oil?

A really high quality extra virgin olive oil is cold pressed, so if you then apply 50°c heat to that it's completely counterproductive. You might as well use an ordinary olive oil that has already been extracted at a low heat so the flavour isn't compromised. That's why you don't cook with extra virgin olive oil because the heat will completely change its characteristics. You can cook the salmon in duck fat, caramelised butter, all sorts. It's about using a nice medium that won't impart loads of flavour – I just scent the fat with quite classic aromatics like thyme and garlic – because at the end of the day it's brunch; you don't want to blow your guts on the first meal of the day.

What's your favourite caviar?

We use a company called N25 that a lot of people are using right now, which is fantastic. We've got an exclusive blend at No. 6 and generally speaking the selection will be kaluga or golden osetra, something that's got a really good salinity and loads of umami flavour. Our caviar is four or five month aged which is just mind blowing stuff.

No. 6, Padstow, Cornwnall

Meet the Chef

What ingredient do you most love to cook with?

It changes every week! I adore the British Isles for shellfish. We will always have hand-dived scallops, Cornish lobsters when they come in, langoustines from Orkney… it doesn't have to be within x number of miles because we're just spoilt rotten here and that's really shaped our cuisine.

What's your favourite thing about working in this industry?

I think one of the most exciting things in hospitality right now is how adaptable and industrious we are, even when you throw a pandemic into the mix: everybody pivoted and nobody sat still. I just love our industry for the level of detail and thought that goes into the guest's experience, and I honestly think that people are really starting to get it and understand the value of that experience. There are very few vocations where you get to see the impact you can have on someone's time from start to finish. I eat, sleep and breathe restaurants – I wouldn't change it for the world.

What qualities do you need to work somewhere like No. 6?

You can train people how to cook, how to serve wine – those things are learnable – but I believe being hospitable is an innate attribute. We try to see skills in people that they don't even know they have and that's what ten years being with Paul has really taught me, because that's what he saw in me all those years ago, enough to take the rough with the smooth. None of us are perfect; we've got an incredibly diverse team of individuals at No. 6 from all walks of life but somehow, we all seem to find this common uniting love of what we do and push for the same goals every single day.

What are you inspired by when it comes to food?

Eating out! I really want to go to Jordnær, the new Maaemo and the new Frantzén. I'd love to be in a position one day where I could go to France for a month, not even to eat in restaurants but to visit producers, procurers, growers, farmers, fishermen, foragers and just switch off. It's easy to reel off a load of the best restaurants in cities around the world, but other lifestyles, products, ingredients and cultures are probably more influential now than other restaurants for me.

What advice would you give younger chefs?

I think there's a tendency for young cooks to want a lot very quickly. It's a very attractive industry to come into if you're up for it but what I'm not seeing a lot of, is that desire to show loyalty, to show care for where you are, to be dedicated. So, I would say put yourself somewhere that you really see yourself growing and spending some time. There's nothing worse for me than reading a CV that lists off 16 restaurants in the last few years. Keep your head down, keep your nose clean, listen and learn. I'm quite a traditionalist when it comes to these things.

How do you wind down in your free time?

I like going to the beach for a barbecue with a bottle of wine and losing an afternoon or evening that way, or being up the moor for breakfast at 4 'o clock in the morning when there's no one else there.

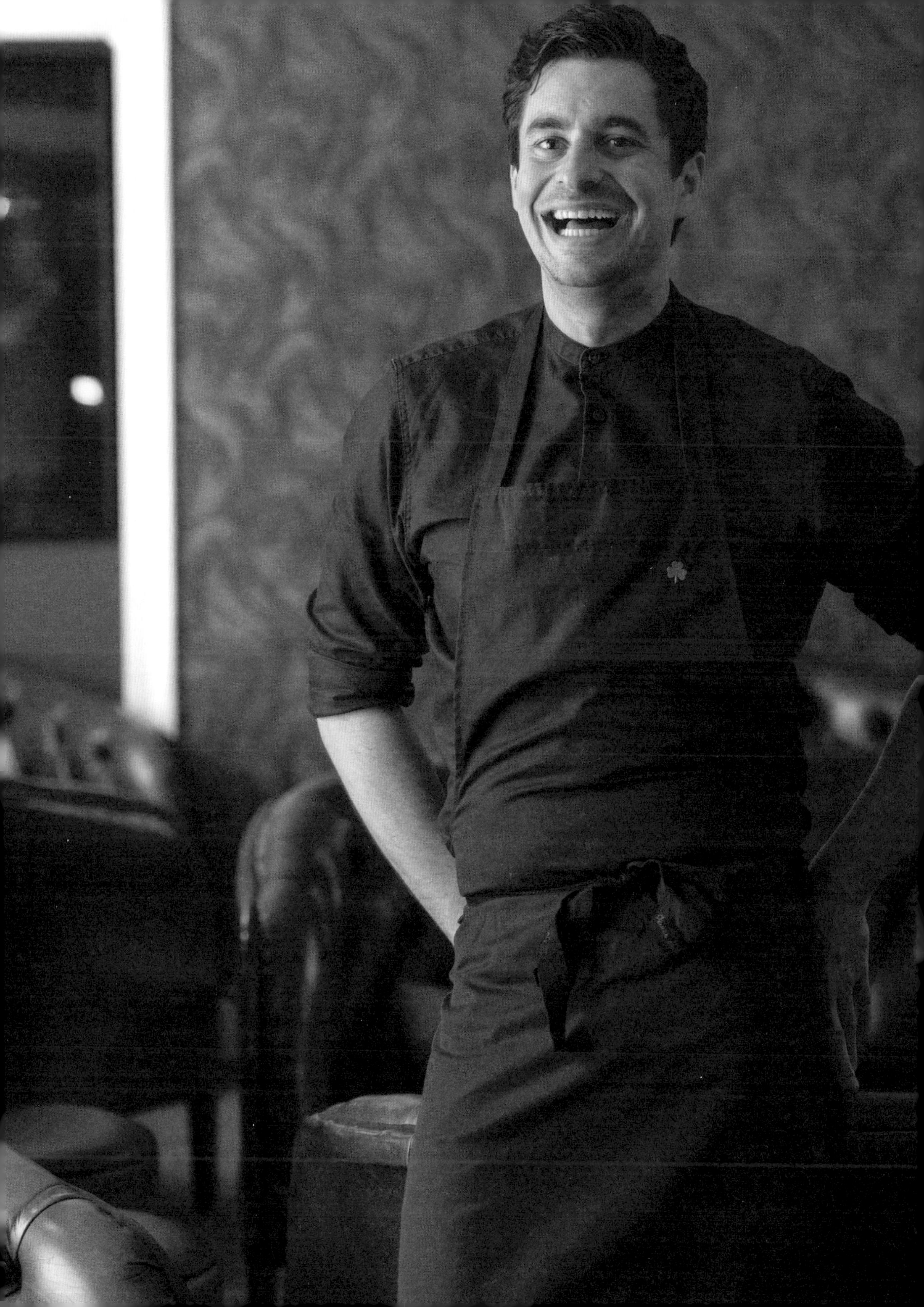

No. 6, Padstow, Cornwall

Life at No.6

As much as we're a one Michelin star restaurant, we're not a restaurant that's happy with one star. We're very quietly but very deliberately pushing as hard as we can to take the restaurant to the next level. Come service time, there can be a vibe in restaurants of a certain level that says to customers 'you should be happy to be here' whereas in all my favourite restaurants it's like 'we're happy to have you here'. It has to be that way round. Yes, you have to cook incredible food and work at a very high level, but ultimately we're cooking food and looking after people. Hospitality is not just a chef's game; people will forget very quickly what they had to eat or drink, but nobody will forget in a million years how you made them feel, and that's our main MO every single day.

I joined No. 6 eleven years ago as chef de partie, wet behind the ears with long curly hair, a Trilby and a bottle of Redbreast 12 in my hand. Paul didn't know whether he was picking up his future head chef or the next frontman for Babyshambles. We all went on this amazing journey together, two years later we won our first star and we've just been chipping away ever since. Paul and Emma had just taken on Caffe Rojano and John Walton was head chef; they were great years, we were under pressure, we had limited equipment but I wouldn't change it for the world. When it came to my time at the helm of No. 6 our focus was the same as it was when Paul first started the restaurant: to cook incredible, delicious food in a relaxed but professional dining room. Paul and I speak every single day and have a lot of creative time together; I look after the day to day operation at the restaurant and although I have an incredible mentor in Paul it's not suffocating, we are growing together. That's a very empowered position to be in. I was made chef patron in 2022. No. 6 is our baby and I love it to bits.

However our journey goes and whatever our next chapter is, it will be with Paul. I've never had anyone else in my life that has got out of me what I've put in – people always tell you that's how it works, but it's never been true with anyone else I've worked for. There was always an element of selfishness for personal and professional gain, which can be short-sighted and short lived: easy come, easy go. Whereas we're slow burning and it honestly feels like every year we're in a new chapter of our careers and our lives. The ceiling within what we do is only as low or as high as you want to make it. In the whole time I've been here, nobody has outgrown the business.

Whenever the curtain comes up for every service, we all turn our focus on creating something that we and our guests think is magical. That's all that matters. The rest of it is immaterial: accolades are great and every once in a while a broader reassurance is nice, but accolades don't pay the bills. There's one that we focus on, that really means the world to us, and that's the Michelin guide. A full restaurant with 10 services a week in a sustainable format is always our goal. We're not the experts in gastronomy or wine or anything like it, we're just experts in what we do. Everything that goes on within these walls, we stick to it and do it with conviction. We don't necessarily get it right all the time but it all comes from a place of love and care.

The thing about No. 6 is that no one's bigger than the team. This thing that we have is way more than the sum of its parts and always has been. That's the real beauty of what we do and everyone gets on board with that. Everyone has a voice. Ciaran, one of my sous chefs, has just been on a three-month paid sabbatical which allowed him to scratch an itch of never having worked elsewhere, while learning at other great restaurants and then coming back into the fold. This is our home – we spend more time here than we do with anyone else.

What I love most day to day is service: cooking for guests and seeing the team doing their thing. Week on week my role is also oriented to front of house, business, future proofing, and succession planning so we're always a few steps ahead of team moves. The fact that I get to cook is great but that's 10% of what we do. I want to be part of a generation that really incites change and doesn't just say that while their team's still working 90 hours a week and being managed in a manner that's not conducive to wellbeing. I can be as impatient and cantankerous as the next person, but I recognise it and I'm very open to change – I want us all to progress.

Mahé

CREATIVITY & DEVELOPMENT

Savoury

Guinea fowl - Albufela Sauce

Ynyshir, Machynlleth, Powys

Gareth Ward

People see some crazy shit that we put on the internet, they see us on TV or read about us in a blog, they follow restaurants and are obsessed with food, or someone tells them about us. That's the beginning of the journey to Ynyshir.

They look on the map and it's further than they think. Then it's further than the SatNav thinks. It's not in the middle of nowhere, it's at the end of nowhere.

They book to eat and to stay over. As soon as they come into Wales, they have to go further and further and further. The further they go, the more incredible the place gets.

Then they see this rusty sign at the side of the road with an arrow pointing this way. They turn onto the track and think that there's nothing there. Then they go over a little bridge with a stream beneath it, and through the gates and you see this huge meadow, full of huge old trees and tipis and a track leading upwards. It's all lit up with rusty orange lights and there's this massive black building set right into concrete pathways. Nestled at the top of the meadow.

They know they're in the right place.

Then they walk inside and see the skull, spray painted in the hallway. They smell the fire from outside. Then they see the most incredible ingredients they'll ever see. Immediately they have a little taste of what is coming later on – the first dish is served straight away, built in front of them by a couple of chefs, before they've even gone to their room.

Welcome to Ynyshir.

By Amelia Eiriksson

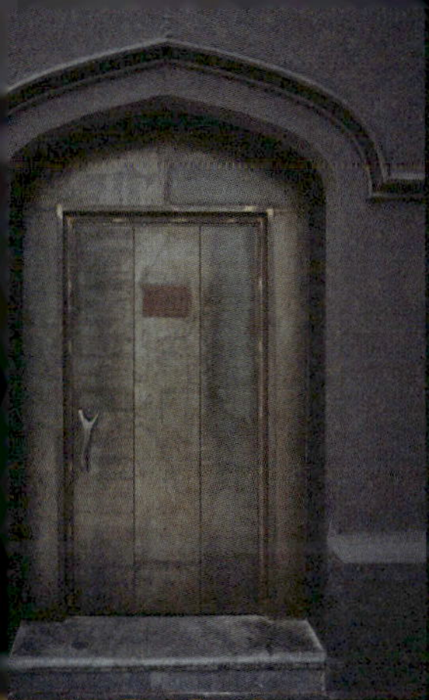
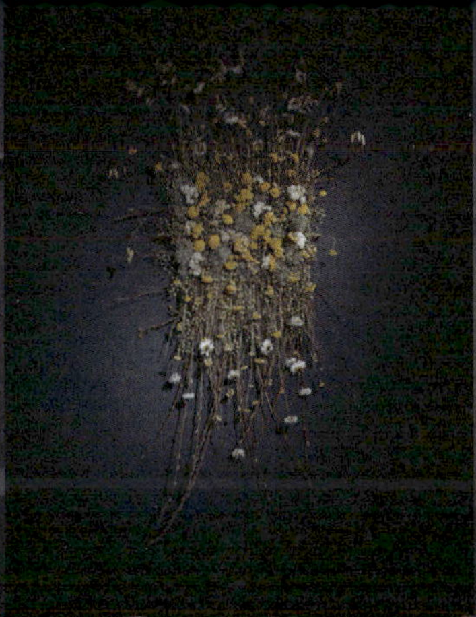
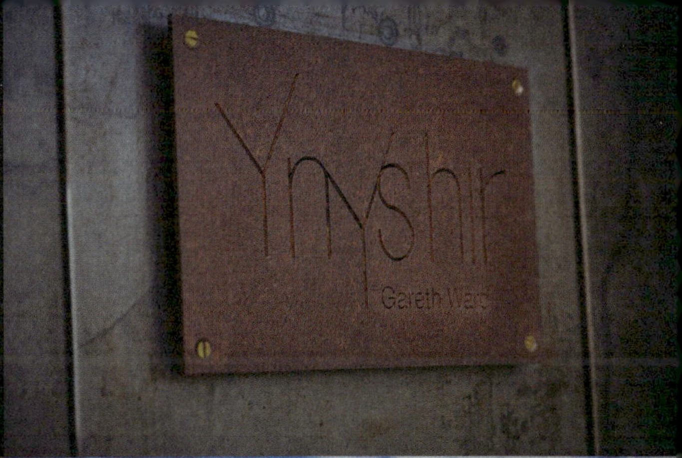
Ynyshir
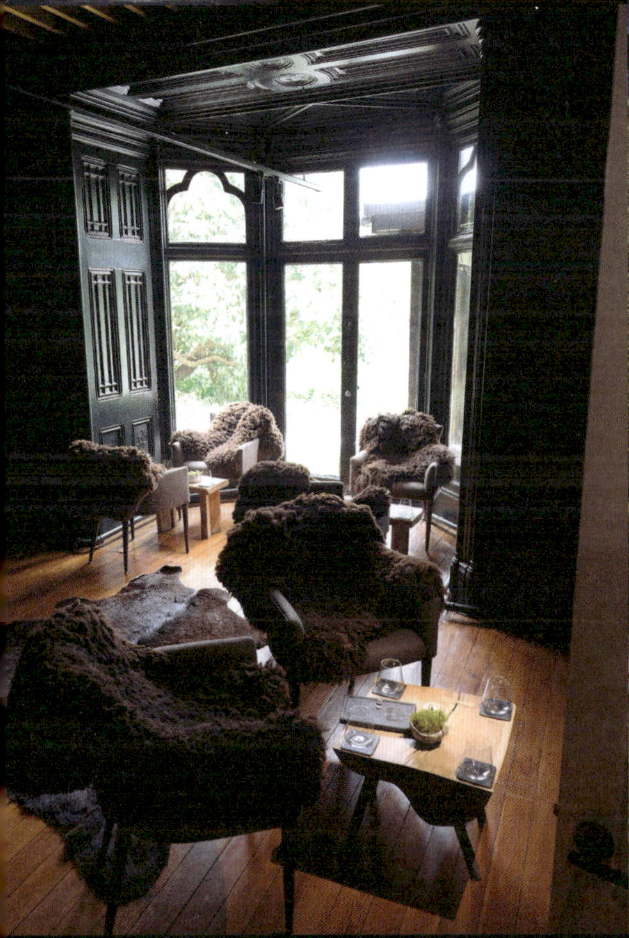
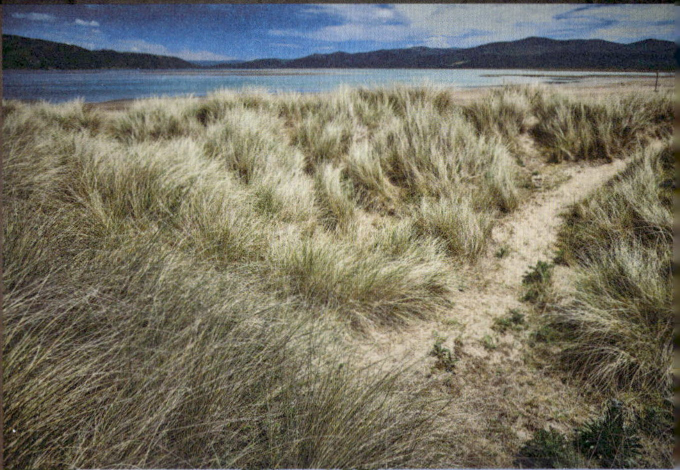
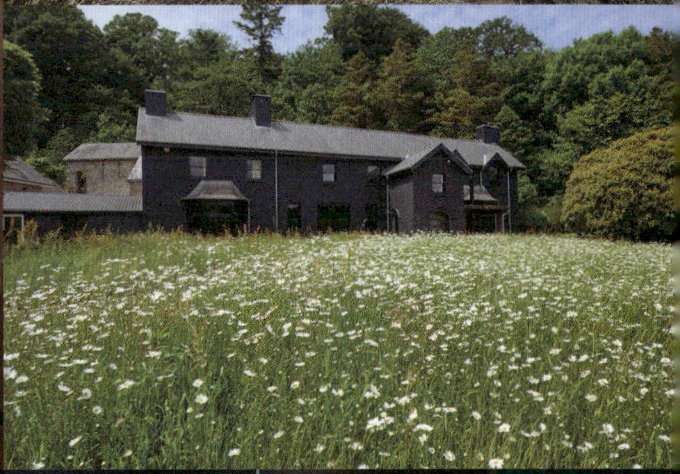
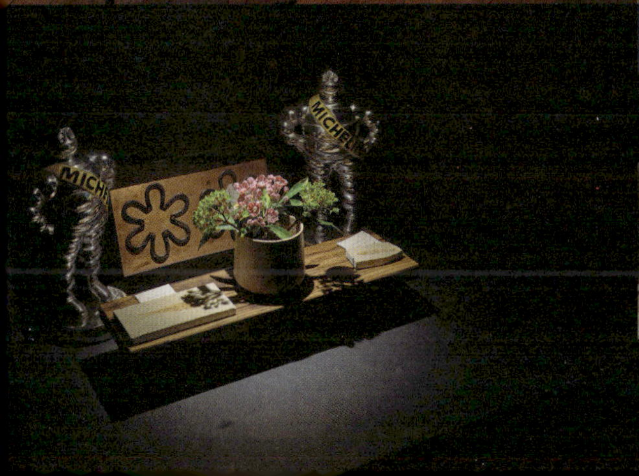
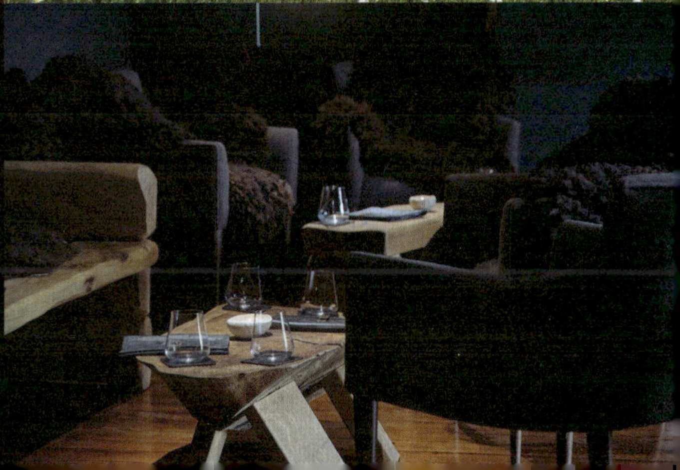

Ynyshir, Machynlleth, Powys

Chilli Crab with a Sweet Steamed Bun

Preparation time: 30 minutes, plus overnight proving | Cooking time: 5 minutes | Serves 4

FOR THE STEAMED BUNS
310g T55OR flour
150g bottled water
50g sugar
25g rapeseed oil
9g fresh yeast
7.5g Maldon salt

FOR THE STOCK
375ml sesame oil
4 large crabs
500g sliced shallots
250g sliced ginger
250g sliced garlic
30g Korean pepper flakes
200g tomato purée
250g honey
1.5 litres dashi

FOR THE SAUCE
15g cornflour
2 egg whites
Fresh coriander, chopped

FOR THE STEAMED BUNS
Beat all the ingredients together in a stand mixer on speed 3 for 8 minutes. Bulk prove the dough overnight. The next morning, bap (portion) the proved dough into 30g rolls. Steam the rolls on the top shelf of the oven at 42°c with full fan and full steam, for 10 minutes until they have doubled in size. Turn the oven off but do not open the door for 6 minutes. Deep fry the steamed buns at 190°c until golden.

FOR THE STOCK
Heat the sesame oil. Fry the bodies, legs and shells of the crabs in the oil until dry, golden and starting to stick to the bottom of the pan. Remove the crab and deglaze the pan with the sliced shallots, ginger and garlic, stirring well but keeping them raw. Add the Korean pepper flakes and tomato purée, stir well, then add the honey, dashi and fried crab shells. Bring to the boil. Pass the stock through a colander, pressing the shells to extract more liquid, then pass it through double muslin. Freeze and then remove the oil on top but keep this for finishing the dish.

FOR THE SAUCE
Defrost the stock and weigh out 500g in a pan. Add the cornflour and bring to the boil, whisking constantly over a gentle heat. You should have a nice, lightly thick crab sauce.

Get the crab claws from the 4 crabs and lightly smash them up with a rolling pin (just crack the shells, don't smash too hard). Heat a frying pan with some sesame oil. Add the claws and cook for a minute or two. Lightly whisk up the egg whites, add to the pan and stir well. Immediately add the thickened crab sauce to the pan, stirring everything together.

Pour the crab sauce and claws straight into a serving bowl. Dress with the reserved frozen stock oil and top with chopped coriander to taste. Get your fingers in there and enjoy!

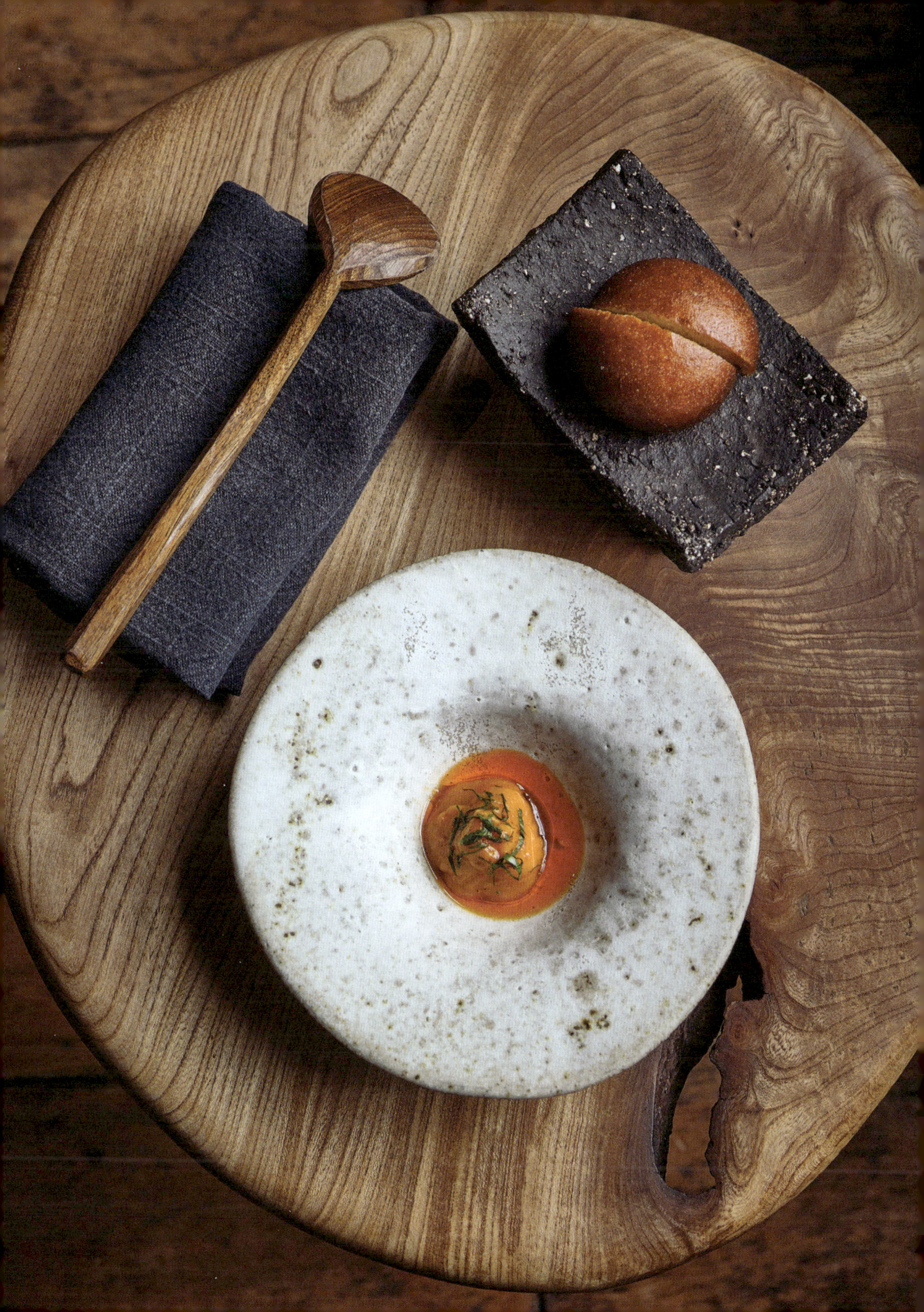

Ynyshir, Machynlleth, Powys

Hoisin Duck

Preparation time: 30 minutes, plus 1 week to dry the duck | Cooking time: 30 minutes | Serves 4

1 duck crown

1.25 litres water

190ml Chinese black vinegar

56g maltose or honey

56ml soy sauce

FOR THE HOISIN

250g Billington's muscovado

87g pickled black bean

63ml box rice vinegar

57ml dashi soy

15g Chinese five spice

10g no.2 sesame oil

9g dashi powder

1 clove of garlic, peeled

FOR THE ONION OIL

300ml sunflower oil

75g chopped chives

75g chopped spring onion tops

FOR THE ROAST GARLIC SALT

Whole garlic bulbs

Splash of dashi

25g Maldon salt

FOR THE PICKLED CUCUMBER

75ml rice vinegar

25g granulated sugar

1 cucumber, peeled and cut into thirds

For the first blanch, bring the water and vinegar to the boil. Hook up the duck crown and dip it in 10 times, waiting for the liquid to come back to the boil each time. Leave the duck to dry overnight, reserving the blanching stock.

For the second blanch, combine the reserved stock with the maltose and soy, bring to the boil and repeat the first blanching process. Dry the duck in a salt chamber for 1 week.

FOR THE HOISIN

Mix the ingredients together and split into two. Blitz each portion in a Vitamix until smooth. Squeeze the sauce through muslin, then blitz again until shiny. Season with mirin until the sauce is light, smooth and just sticky, like the consistency of ketchup.

FOR THE ONION OIL

Blend the oil, chives and spring onion in a Vitamix until it reaches 62°c. Pass through double muslin or a j-cloth. Freeze. Remove the oil and discard the water. Keep the oil frozen.

FOR THE ROAST GARLIC SALT

Slice the root off the whole garlic bulbs so that they're flat on the bottom and the garlic is exposed. Put the bulbs flat side down in a Le Creuset pan. Add a good splash of dashi and cook in the oven at 140°c with a lid on the pan until the garlic is very soft. Pass the roast garlic through a drum sieve and then dehydrate until hard. Blitz 50g of the dried garlic with the Maldon salt, then dehydrate and blitz again to a fine powder.

FOR THE PICKLED CUCUMBER

Mix the rice vinegar and sugar together until the liquid is clear. Put the cucumber into a vacuum pack bag and add lots of the pickling liquid. Vacuum seal the bag 3-4 times and leave to rest for 5 minutes. Thinly slice the pickled cucumber on a mandoline.

TO SERVE

Roast the prepared duck crown in the oven at 100°c until it reaches 65-70°c in the centre, then leave to rest. Turn the temperature up to 220°c. Put the duck back in the oven to crispen up the skin for 5-10 minutes. Leave to rest once again. Remove the breast from the bone, trim and portion it, then season the duck breasts with the garlic salt. Cut the pickled cucumbers to the desired shape and brush with the onion oil. Serve with the duck and hoisin sauce.

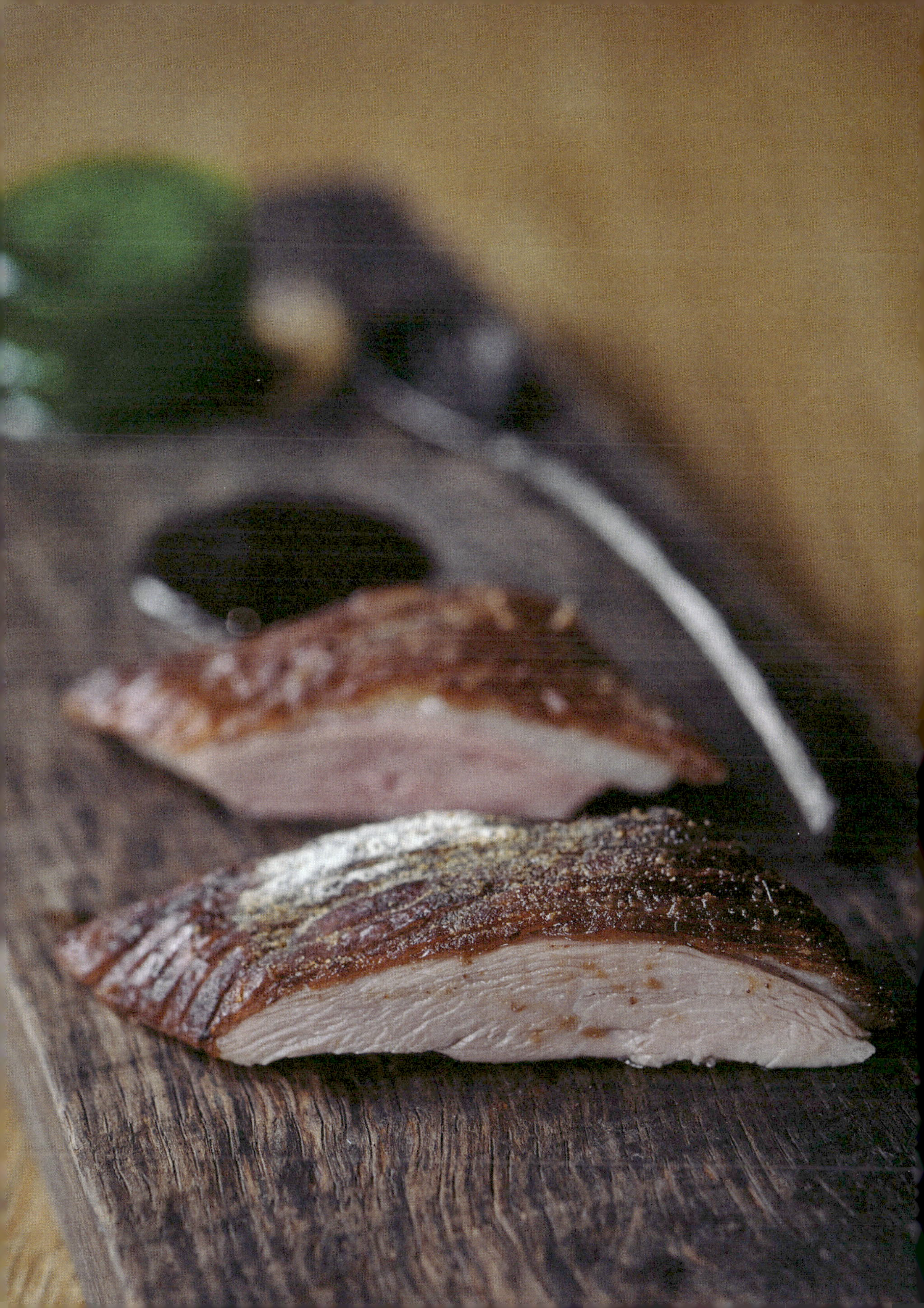

Ynyshir, Machynlleth, Powys

Rump Cap in Black Bean Sauce

Preparation time: 30 minutes, plus 1 month for the pickles | Cooking time: 1 hour | Serves 4

500g beef rump cap (we use A5 Hida)

250g shio koji

25g granulated sugar

12.5g PDS salt

FOR THE PICKLES

75ml rice vinegar

25g granulated sugar

250g fresh jalapeños

No.1 sesame oil

37.5g dried fermented black beans

100g shimeji mushrooms, trimmed

FOR THE BLACK BEAN SAUCE

59g granulated sugar

59ml dashi soy

30ml mirin

29ml dashi

9.5ml no.2 sesame oil

7.5ml rice vinegar

7.5g cornflour

6g minced garlic

6g minced ginger

3g dashi powder

37.5g pickled black beans (washed)

FOR THE PICKLED GARLIC

500ml bottled water

50g granulated sugar

25g PDS salt

250g best quality Isle of White garlic, peeled

500ml Willy's Cider Vinegar

166g granulated sugar

FOR THE ROAST GARLIC SALT

Whole garlic bulbs

Splash of dashi

25g Maldon salt

FOR THE SPRING ONION YOLK SALAD

1 bunch of spring onions

1 egg yolk

Trim the rump cap and spike with a tenderiser on all sides. Blend the shio koji with the sugar and salt to make a brine. Vacuum pack the beef with the brine, chill for 12 hours, then rub off the brine.

FOR THE PICKLES

Mix the rice vinegar and sugar together until the liquid is clear. This is your 3:1 pickle which you will need a batch of for each of the below.

Toss the jalapeños in sesame oil, then cook quickly in small batches on a barbecue. Vacuum pack the jalapeños in the 3:1 pickle and leave for at least 1 month.

Wash the dried fermented black beans under cold water and dry well, then vacuum on full in the 3:1 pickle. Leave for at least 2 weeks.

Vacuum pack the trimmed mushrooms with the 3:1 pickle on full and then leave for 1 week.

FOR THE BLACK BEAN SAUCE

Hand blend everything except the pickled black beans and then leave for 10 minutes. Slowly bring the sauce to the boil, whisking constantly, until thick and shiny. Add the pickled black beans and leave to cook.

FOR THE PICKLED GARLIC

Blitz the water, sugar and salt together. Vacuum pack this liquid with the peeled garlic and leave for 48 hours. Wash the garlic under cold running water for 2-3 hours, then place into a pot and cover with bottled water. Rapidly bring to the boil, then drain and chill the garlic in an ice bath.

Now blitz the cider vinegar and sugar until the sugar has dissolved. Put this into a gastro vac with the garlic and cook at 50°c for 1 hour. Keep releasing the vacuum.

FOR THE ROAST GARLIC SALT

Slice the root off the whole garlic bulbs so that they're flat on the bottom and the garlic is exposed. Put the bulbs flat side down in a Le Creuset pan. Add a good splash of dashi and cook in the oven at 140°c with a lid on the pan until the garlic is very soft. Pass the roast garlic through a drum sieve and then dehydrate until hard. Blitz 50g of the dried garlic with the Maldon salt, then dehydrate and blitz again to a fine powder.

FOR THE SPRING ONION YOLK SALAD

Julienne the inside tender part of the spring onions. Dress them with the raw egg yolk at the last minute.

TO SERVE

Cook the beef at 100°c until it reaches 65-70°c in the centre, then leave to rest. Get your barbecue nice and hot, then very quickly but lightly caramelise the beef on the barbecue. Portion and season the beef with the garlic salt. Serve with the black bean sauce, pickles and spring onion salad.

Ynyshir

Ynyshir, Machynlleth, Powys

Recipe Insights

CHILLI CRAB WITH A SWEET STEAMED BUN

This is a homestyle dish so it's nice to leave some of the meat in the shell and then rip it all apart. We serve it differently in the restaurant but traditionally you would have a whole smashed crab to get stuck into, so we've replicated that here.

What's the secret to great steamed buns?

The strength of flour we use gives the dough a really good texture and nice lightness, then when they're deep fried they go beautifully crispy on the outside.

What would you do with the crab meat that isn't used in the dish?

Anything leftover goes into the stock — nothing gets wasted.

HOISIN DUCK

I love Asian flavours, ingredients and techniques so this dish has developed out of being obsessed with eating that kind of food. Who doesn't love crispy duck with hoisin sauce?!

Where do you like to source duck for the best quality?

We'd been searching for the perfect duck for years when we found Silverhill Duck Farm in Ireland, and theirs are by far the best ducks I've ever tasted in my life. Any Chinese restaurant that's worth its weight uses their produce because their ducks are a proper Peking breed, ideal for cooking. A lot of ducks sold for cooking are ordinary breeds and they're not all great for eating. But these ones are bred for eating so they're absolutely perfect. The fat and the flavour are amazing.

What does the two-stage blanching process do to the texture and/or flavour of the duck?

You're basically creating a skin that gets incredibly crispy when it's cooked. On the first blanch, the skin begins to cook and that layer of fat renders slightly. Then the last blanch in maltose, an inverted sugar, leaves this layer of sugar on the duck which dries so that also makes the skin super crispy.

RUMP CAP IN BLACK BEAN SAUCE

Someone described this as a polished version of Asian street food which was fairly accurate really. We love dishes like Singapore crab, hoisin duck and beef in black bean, but we do them with the best ingredients in the world. That's basically all it is, just using incredible ingredients and having a great time.

What beef do you use in the restaurant?

We use A5 Hida rump cap which refers to the Japanese region it comes from. Beef cattle in Japan are named after the area that they're raised in, so there are over 150 variations that all come from the same breed, a Japanese Black. The finishing process involves the cattle being fed intensively so they put on loads and loads of fat, but the breed of the animal means that instead of just putting fat on their body, it goes into the meat and it marbles. Not every animal does that, although the Dexter does it quite well, but it's also to do with their age because the older the cow, the more easily it puts on fat.

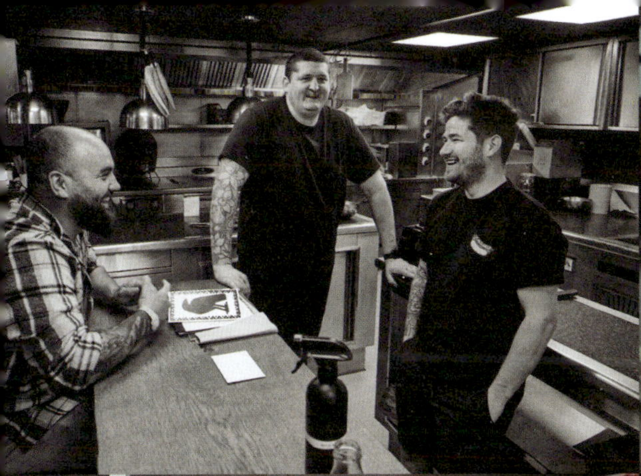
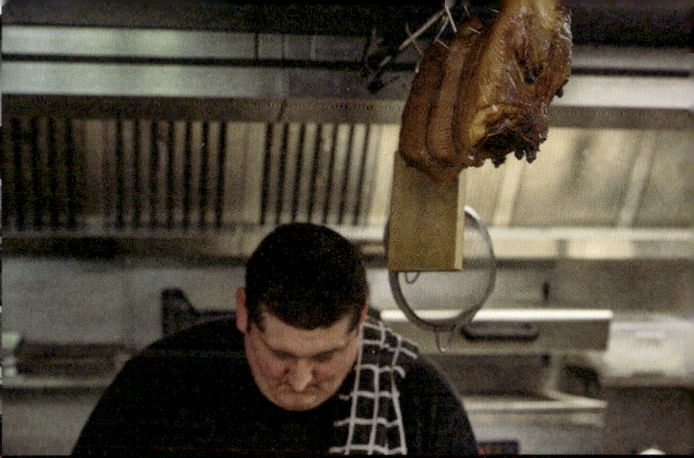
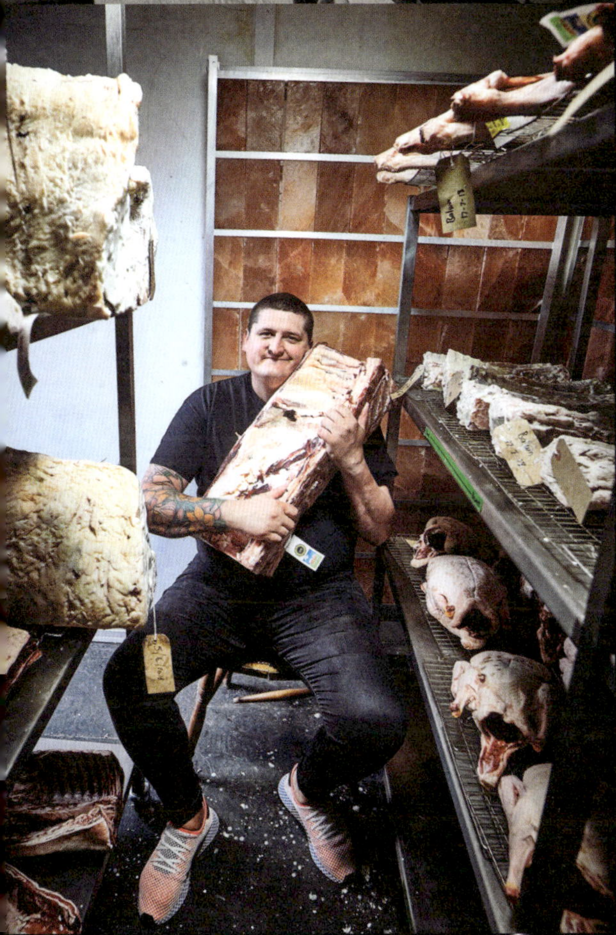
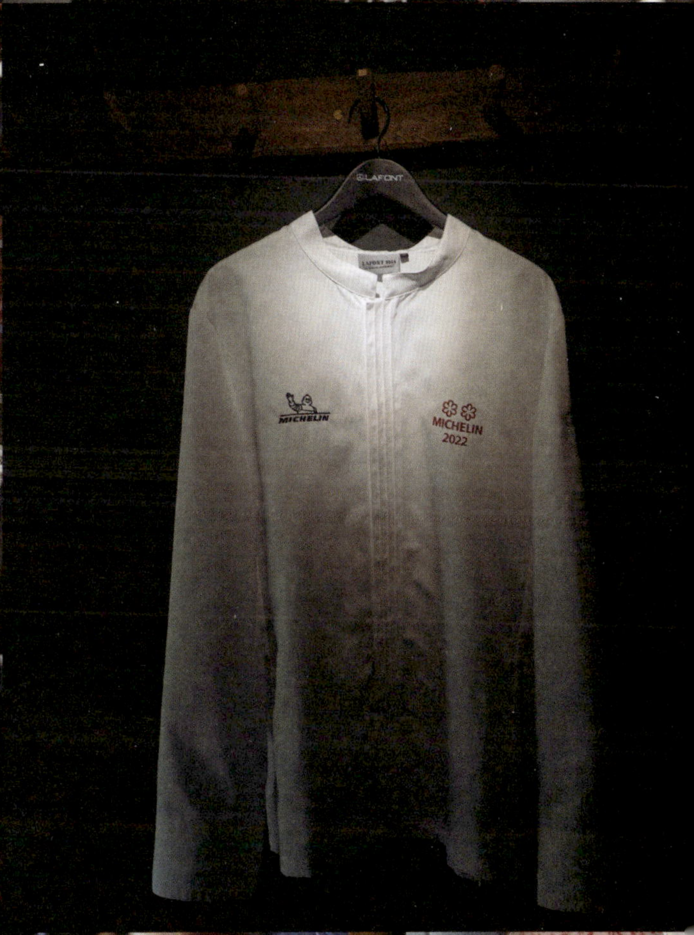
LAFONT
MICHELIN
MICHELIN
2022
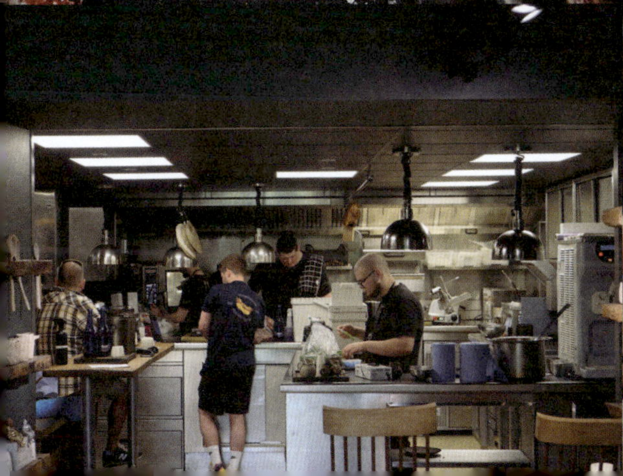
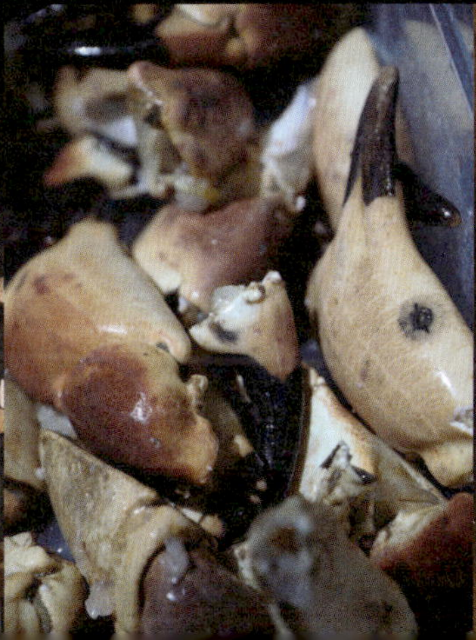
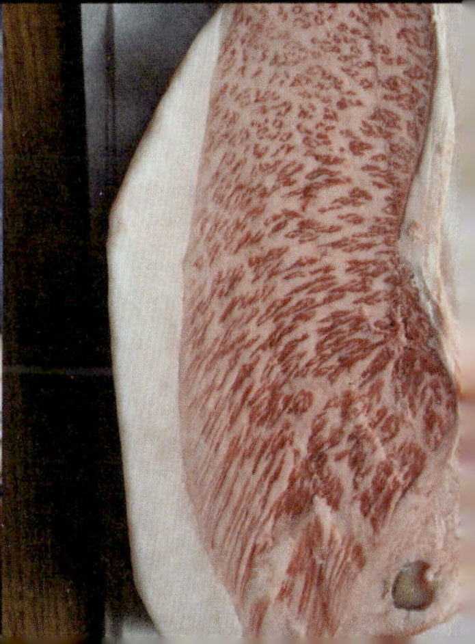

Ynyshir, Machynlleth, Powys

Q&A with Gareth Ward

How would you describe your cooking style and approach to food?
Fun!

What excites you about being a chef and working in this industry?
Actually cooking!

Where did it all begin: what got you interested in food and cooking?
The Seven Stars in Shincliffe.

Has cooking over fire always been part of your cooking DNA?
No, but I love it now.

What piece of kitchen equipment do you use or like working with the most?
The -80°c freezer.

Do you have any absolute favourite ingredients that you love to cook or eat?
Why choose? Variety is the spice of life!

Which cuisines do you lean into for inspiration?
Asian.

What advice would you give to younger people in the industry?
Don't be a dick. Be nice.

Are you happy with where you are now?
Never!

What are your plans and ambitions for the future?
To live in Ibiza.

What do you like to do outside the kitchen in your time off?
See my kids.

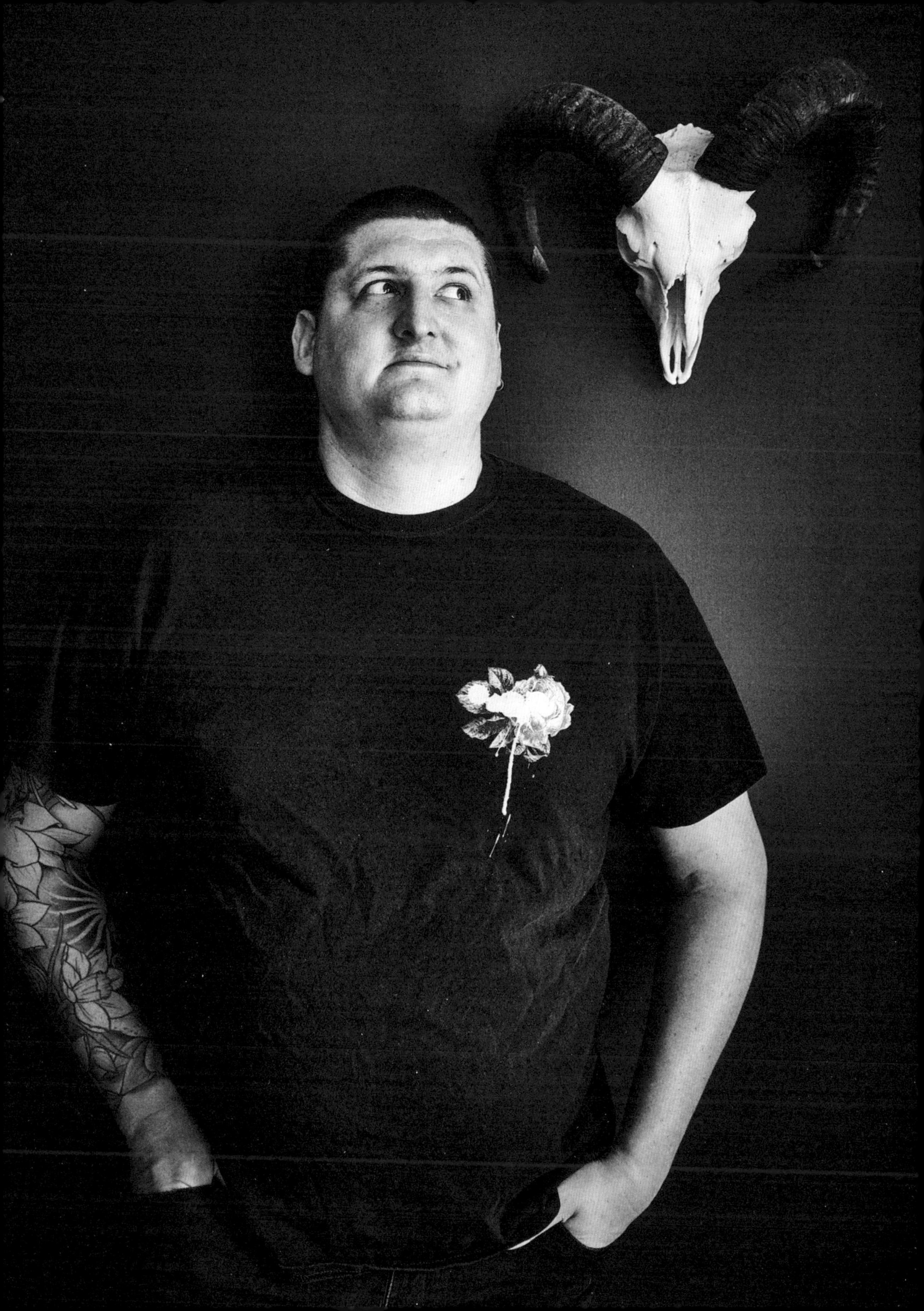

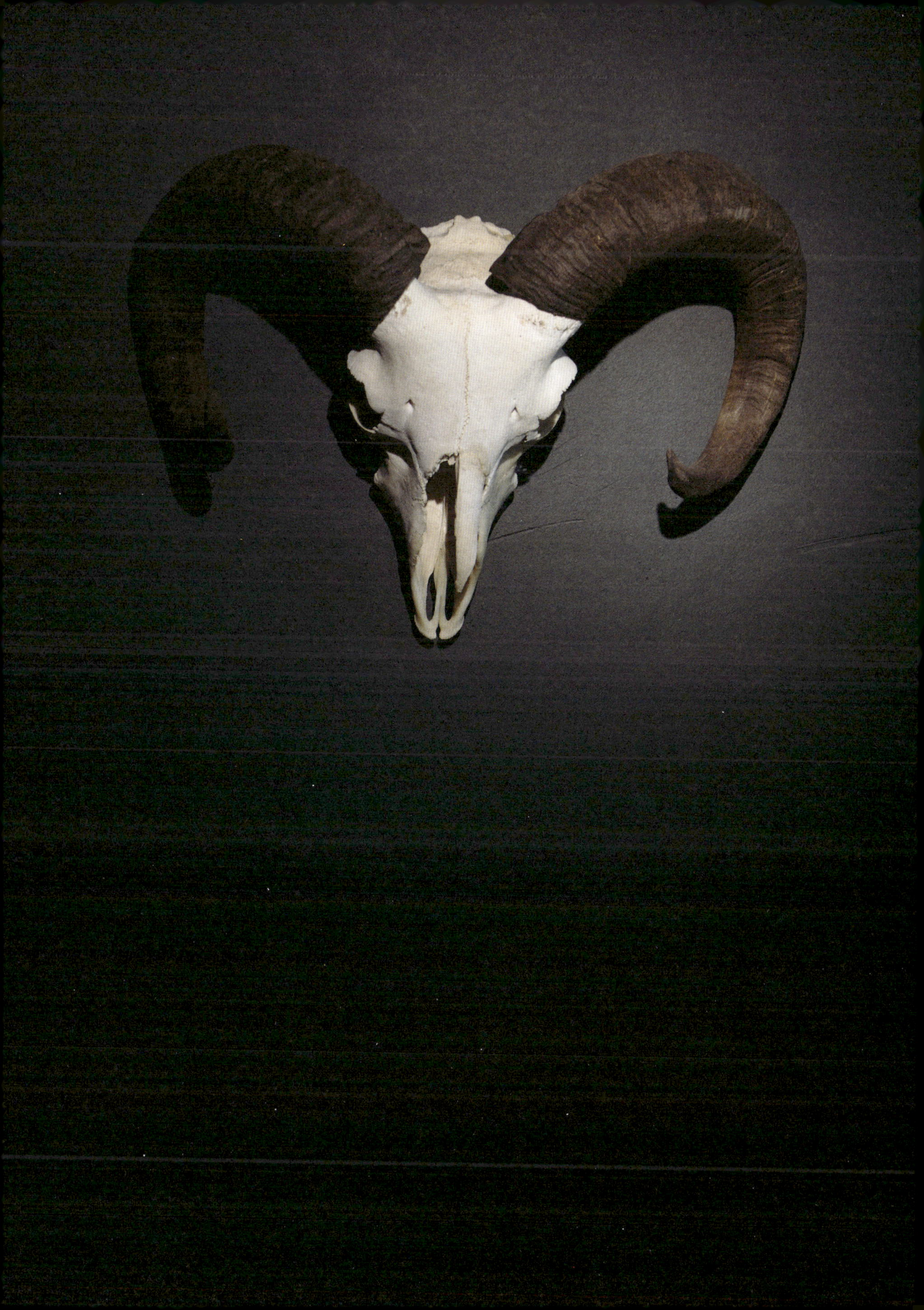

Le Cochon Aveugle | Cave du Cochon, York

Joshua Overington

In partnership with his wife Victoria, the general manager and sommelier for both Le Cochon Aveugle and its sister wine bar and bistro, Cave du Cochon, chef Josh Overington opened his first restaurant in 2014. Having discovered a passion for cooking on his gap year in Australia, Josh went on to train at prestigious restaurants in London and Paris and then enrolled at Le Cordon Bleu, Paris. He was influenced not just by the classical French cooking of world-famous institutions like Pavillon Ledoyen, but by the neo-bistro scene emerging at the time in Paris.

Josh met Victoria while working as a private chef in the Alps, and the pair returned to his hometown of York with the intention of establishing their own neighbourhood restaurant there. Despite being just 26 when Le Cochon Aveugle opened and running the whole place without any other staff or backers, they turned their ambition into great success and Josh quickly gained a reputation as one of the most exciting forerunners of modern French cookery in the UK. They are now ready for the next stage in their journey as restaurateurs which will begin in early 2023.

"The restaurant in its current incarnation will close in November 2022 and we're opening something new in the following year. It's a continuation of ideas that are used within this space but on a slightly bigger scale and with a much more British feel to it. At Le Cochon Aveugle, a lot of the signature dishes have had a French twist to them: a modern take on French classics. The new place is going to be an expression of Yorkshire and the British Isles, moving more towards recipes like those we're showcasing in this book. There will still be flavours from around the world but cooked in our own way, and all the guests will be served at once, dinner party style, with everybody sat round the kitchen looking in. The business is maturing and it's time to take it to the next level. We opened Le Cochon Aveugle at 26 and the restaurant is very urban, incorporating a lot of what we liked at that age. As you get older, your tastes change and so we want to create a new restaurant that reflects who we are now." – Josh and Vicky

A restaurant we love to eat at:

James Knappett's Kitchen Table in London. It's one of our favourites for showcasing exceptional produce. I think it's important for chefs to see what other places are doing better to get you thinking about how to improve.

An ingredient we never cook with:

Josh – I despise Marmite. I'm not a big fan of horseradish either.

Vicky – I love Marmite!

A piece of kitchen equipment we couldn't live without:

It sounds really mad, but I think the Pacojet. We make butters, parfaits, and ice creams in it, so it has become totally integrated into my cooking. That and the konro are our most important pieces of kit.

A meal we enjoy cooking or eating outside the restaurant:

I'll be honest, I don't love cooking at home, but I don't mind doing a barbecue or a roast dinner. On a Sunday though, nothing pleases me more than to go out and eat, even just down at the local pub; it's a release to go out and not have to cook. Everybody's got to switch off sometimes!

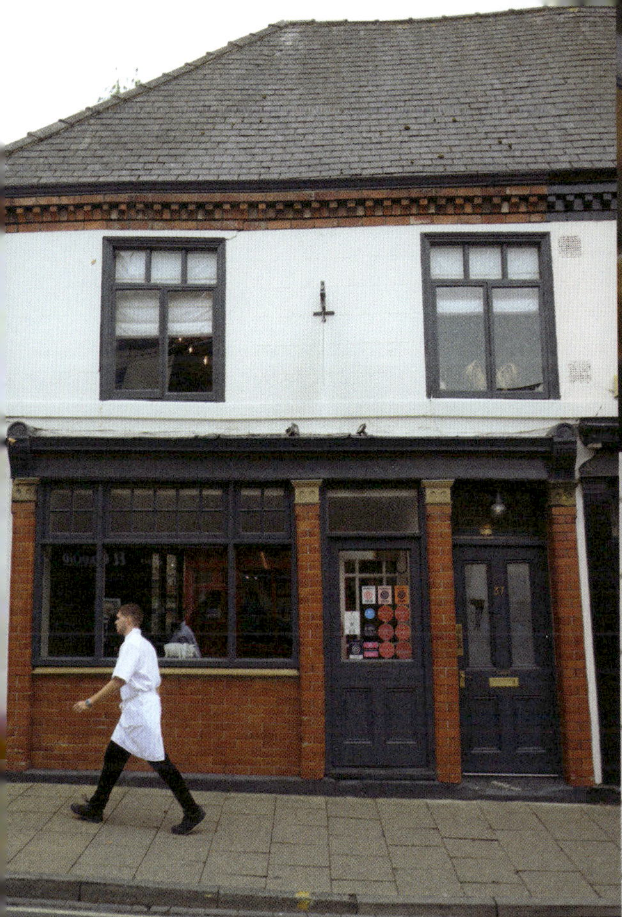
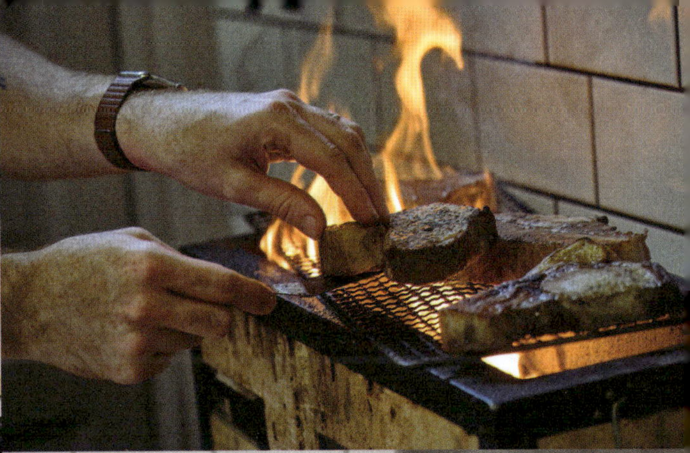
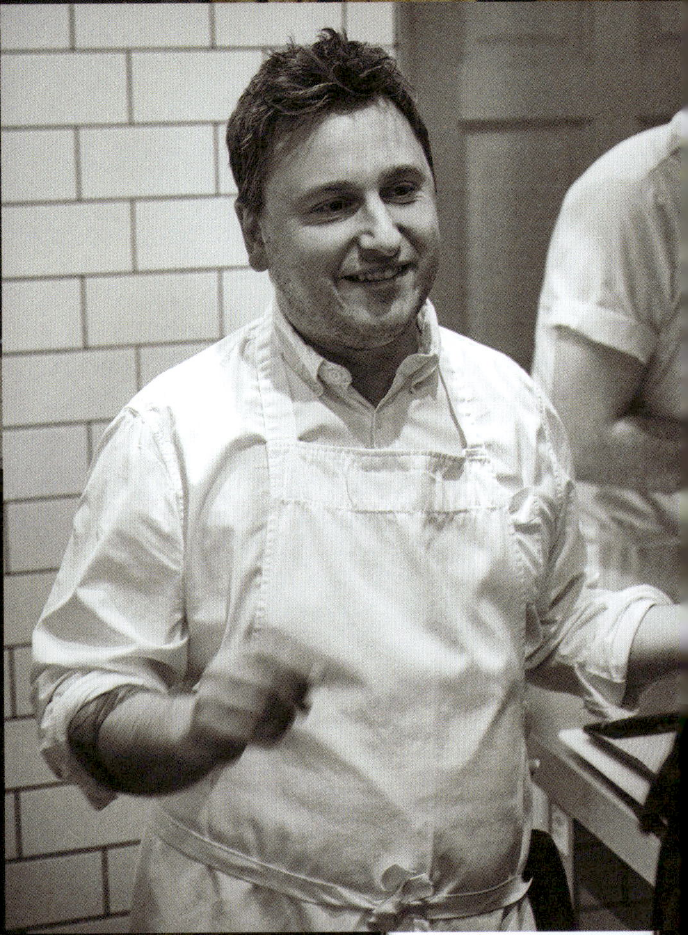
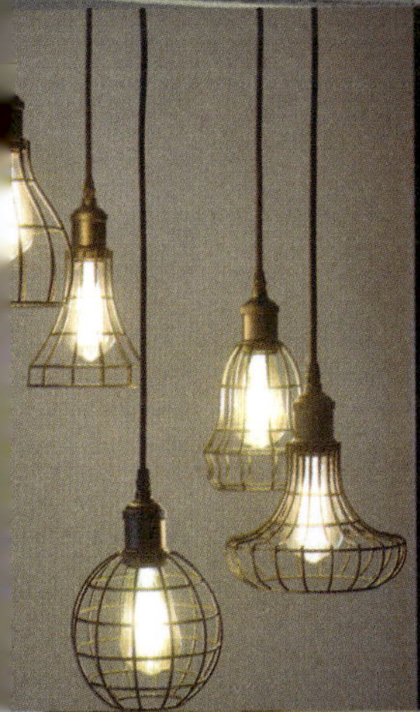
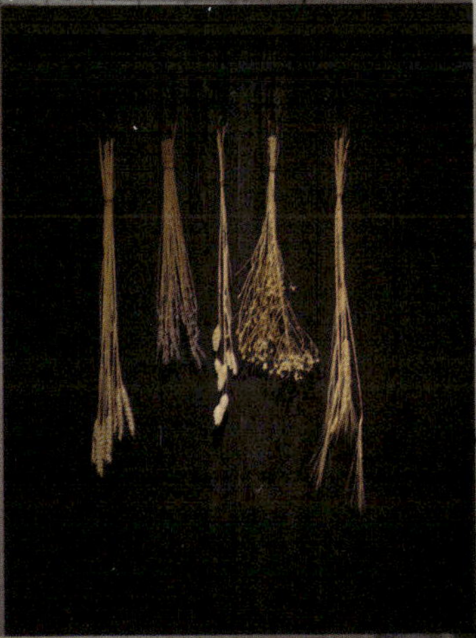
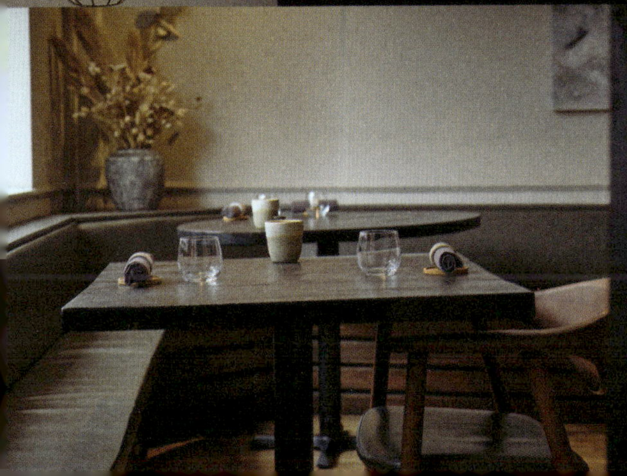
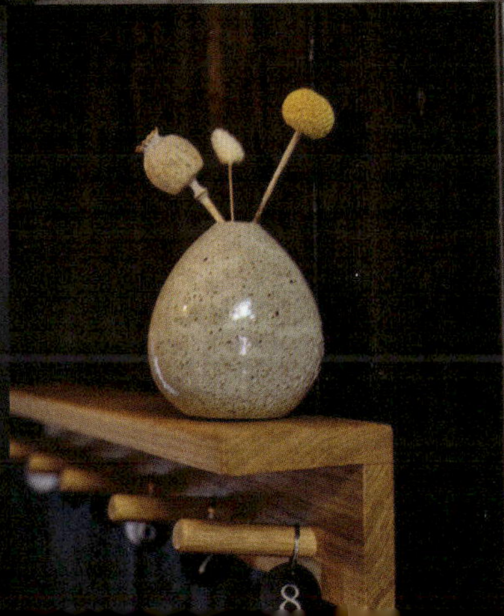
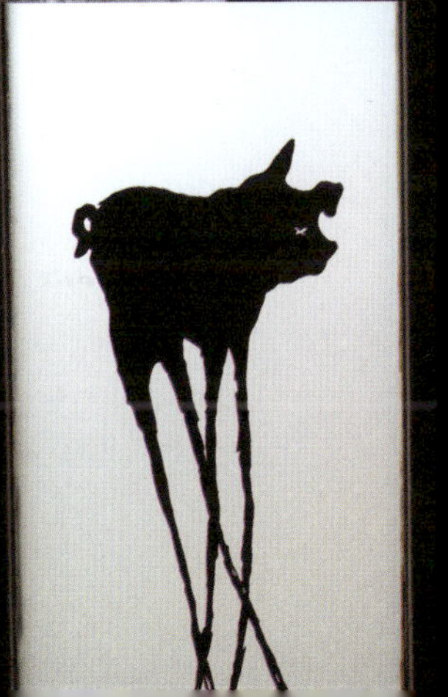

Le Cochon Aveugle | Cave du Cochon, York

Woodland Pork Cooked Over Coals, Fig and Radicchio Relish, Sauce Civet

Preparation time: 2-3 hours | Cooking time: 20 minutes | Serves 2-4

FOR THE RELISH
20ml grapeseed oil

100g dried figs, roughly chopped

200g radicchio, roughly chopped

50g black garlic paste

5g pickled magnolia flowers

5g purple basil leaves

5g salted anchovies

5g capers

1 tbsp sherry vinegar

FOR THE SAUCE CIVET
100g chicken livers, trimmed and sinew removed

1 tbsp grapeseed oil

60g shallot, peeled and sliced

4 cloves of garlic, finely chopped

1 sprig of thyme

4g juniper berries

2g black peppercorns

2g yellow mustard seeds

100ml good quality red wine

1 litre pork stock

25g Dijon mustard

50ml fresh pork blood

4g Maldon sea salt

FOR THE RADICCHIO
500ml apple juice

10g loose leaf Earl Grey tea

3.75g xanthan gum

20g radicchio leaves (I like to use treviso radicchio)

FOR THE PORK
1 Woodland pork chop

50g salted butter, softened

1 clove of garlic, finely grated

3 sprigs of thyme, picked leaves

FOR THE RELISH
This will last for a week, so can be made in advance. Heat the grapeseed oil in a medium pan over a moderate heat. Add all the remaining ingredients except the sherry vinegar to the pan. Cook for 45 minutes, stirring regularly, until cooked down. Season the relish with the vinegar then remove from the heat and place in a blender. Blend to a coarse paste.

FOR THE SAUCE CIVET
In a heavy-based pan over a medium heat, fry the chicken livers in the grapeseed oil until golden. Add the shallot, garlic, thyme and spices to the livers and cook until aromatic. Deglaze with the red wine, bring to the boil and then reduce by half.

Add the pork stock and bring to a simmer, then leave to cook for 30 minutes. Remove from the heat, pass the sauce through a fine sieve into a clean saucepan, then bring it back to a simmer. Add the Dijon mustard, whisking until fully incorporated. Now add the pork blood, whisking constantly. Do not allow it to boil and continue whisking until sauce has thickened enough to coat a spoon. Season with sea salt and set aside.

FOR THE RADICCHIO
In a blender, combine the apple juice and Earl Grey tea on a medium speed. Slowly add the xanthan gum until thickened. In a bowl, generously dress the radicchio leaves with the apple mixture.

FOR THE PORK
Preheat the barbecue until the coals turn white. Allow the pork chop to come to room temperature, then season generously with Maldon sea salt and place on the barbecue. Cook to medium (approximately 4 minutes on each side) and then allow to rest. Meanwhile, mix the butter with the grated garlic and thyme leaves, then use this to liberally baste the chop as it rests.

TO FINISH
Carve 1-2 slices per person from the pork chop and place them on a warmed plate with a quenelle of the fig and radicchio relish. Spoon the warmed sauce civet into the middle and finish with a garnish of the dressed radicchio leaves.

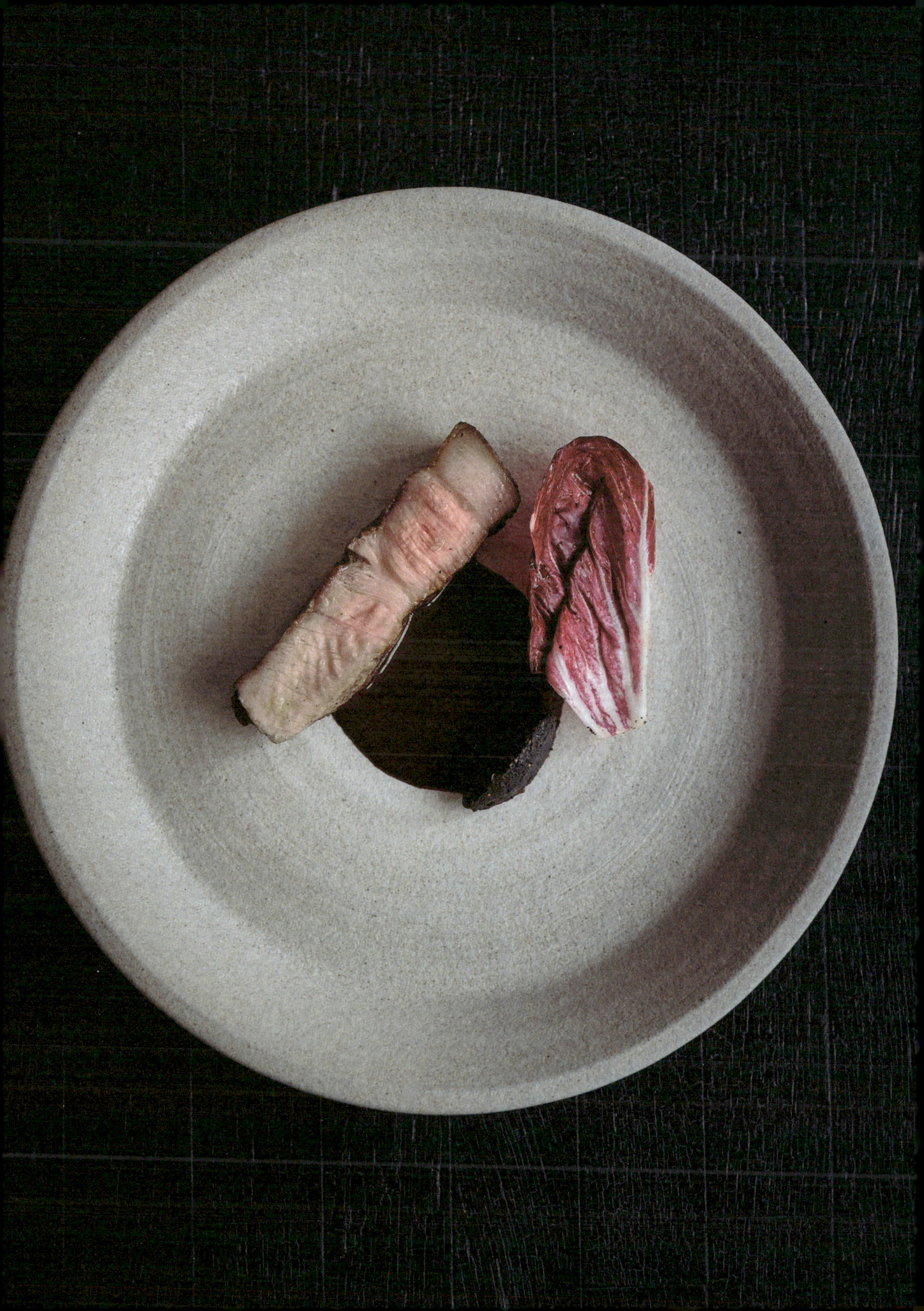

Le Cochon Aveugle | Cave du Cochon, York

Garganelli with Lamb Belly Pancetta, Egg Yolk, Yorkshire Pecorino, English Peas and Mint

Preparation time: 15 minutes | Cooking time: 15 minutes | Serves 2

50ml good quality extra virgin olive oil

100g lamb belly pancetta, cubed

3g cracked black peppercorns

300g dried garganelli pasta (or homemade fresh pasta)

3 free-range medium egg yolks

50g Yorkshire pecorino, grated

50g English peas, shelled

2 sprigs of fresh mint

Maldon sea salt

TO MAKE THE DISH

Bring a large pan of heavily salted (as salty as the sea!) water to boil. Meanwhile, in a frying pan over a low to medium heat, add 40ml of the extra virgin olive oil and then add the lamb pancetta.

Slowly render the pancetta; do not fry this too quickly. After 3-4 minutes, add the black pepper and continue to cook slowly.

Add the pasta to the boiling water and cook until just softer than al dente. Once the pasta is cooked, drain the pasta in a colander, but make sure to reserve some of the pasta water.

Add the pasta to the lamb pancetta along with 2-3 tablespoons of the pasta water. Remove the pan from heat, then add the egg yolks. Use a wooden spoon to stir vigorously and emulsify the water and egg yolk to a thickened sauce.

Add the Yorkshire pecorino, peas and torn mint leaves to the pan and carefully combine. Serve immediately, with a drizzle of the remaining extra virgin olive oil and – if you like! – an extra grating of Yorkshire pecorino on top.

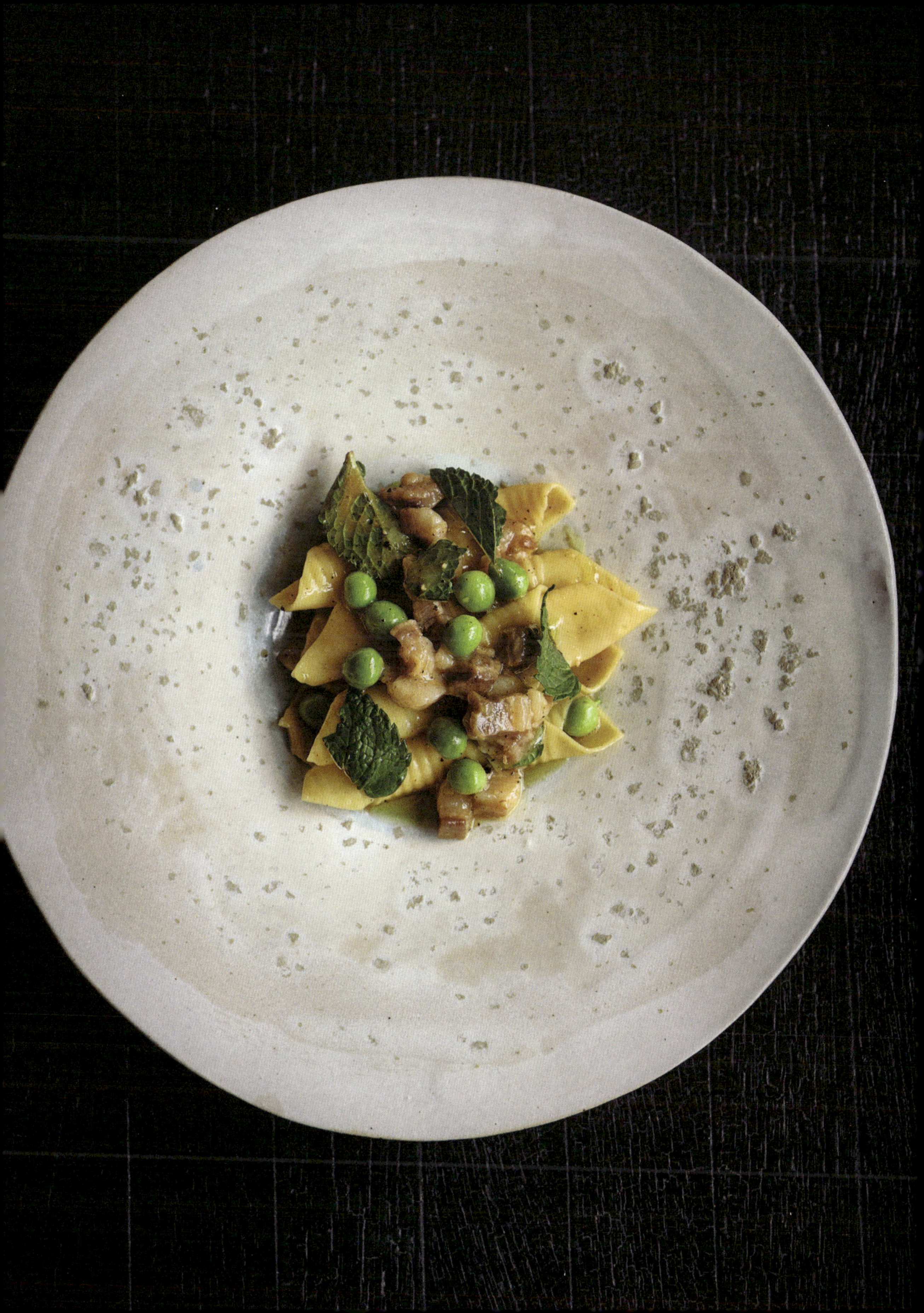

Le Cochon Aveugle | Cave du Cochon, York

Line-Caught Pollock Poached in Aged Beef Fat with Senshyu Onions and Lemon Verbena

Preparation time: 3 days | Cooking time: 30 minutes | Serves 4

FOR THE ONION CONSOMMÉ
2.5kg whole brown onions, peeled
2.5 litres water
1 tsp Maldon sea salt
50ml white soy

FOR THE SENSHYU ONION JAM
3kg senshyu onions, roughly sliced
1 litre dashi
100g aged beef fat, chilled and solid
50ml Banyuls wine vinegar

FOR THE POLLOCK
300g Maldon sea salt
300g dark brown sugar
1 large line-caught pollock fillet
2kg rendered aged beef fat

TO FINISH
50ml lemon verbena oil

FOR THE ONION CONSOMMÉ
Preheat an oven to 90°c fan. Place the peeled whole brown onions, water and salt in a gastro then cover and tightly seal with tin foil. Place in the oven for 3 days and don't be tempted to uncover or stir during this time! After 3 days, remove the tray from the oven and strain the clear liquid into a large bowl. Season with the white soy to taste. Allow to cool, then store in the fridge.

FOR THE SENSHYU ONION JAM
Place the sliced senshyu onions and dashi in a heavy cast iron pan over a low heat and slowly bring to a simmer. Balance a wire cooling rack over the top of the pan and place the aged beef fat on top. The heat from the onions will slowly melt the fat and as it drips down it will slowly incorporate to develop a dark onion jam over approximately 4 hours.

Once all the beef fat has melted, remove the pan from the heat. Place the mixture into a blender and blend until it has a smooth consistency. Once smooth, season with the wine vinegar. This makes more than you need for this dish, but it will keep in the fridge in an airtight container for 2 weeks.

FOR THE POLLOCK
On a large tray or dish, combine the salt and sugar. Roll the fillet gently in this cure, ensuring it is covered all over. Place the fish in the fridge for 45 minutes, then carefully wash off the salt cure in a bowl of cold water. Pat dry with paper towels, then place the fillet on a large sheet of cling film. Tightly wrap the fillet in the cling film and roll into a ballotine shape, securing each end with a knot. Slice the ballotine into four equal portions, each still wrapped in the cling film.

Place the rendered beef fat into a large heavy-based pan, deep enough to cover the pollock. Place over a low heat and slowly warm to 53°c. Place the cured pollock portions in the warm beef fat and poach for 20 minutes. The pollock is cooked when the flesh is pearlescent, and a knife easily glides through without any resistance. Gently remove it from the beef fat and unwrap the cling film.

TO FINISH
While the pollock is poaching, gently reheat 2-3 tablespoons of onion jam and approximately 200ml of the onion consommé in separate saucepans over a low heat until hot.

Place 1 teaspoon of the onion jam in the middle of a warm bowl, then gently place the pollock on top of the jam. Pour the consommé over the fish and finish with a drizzle of lemon verbena oil.

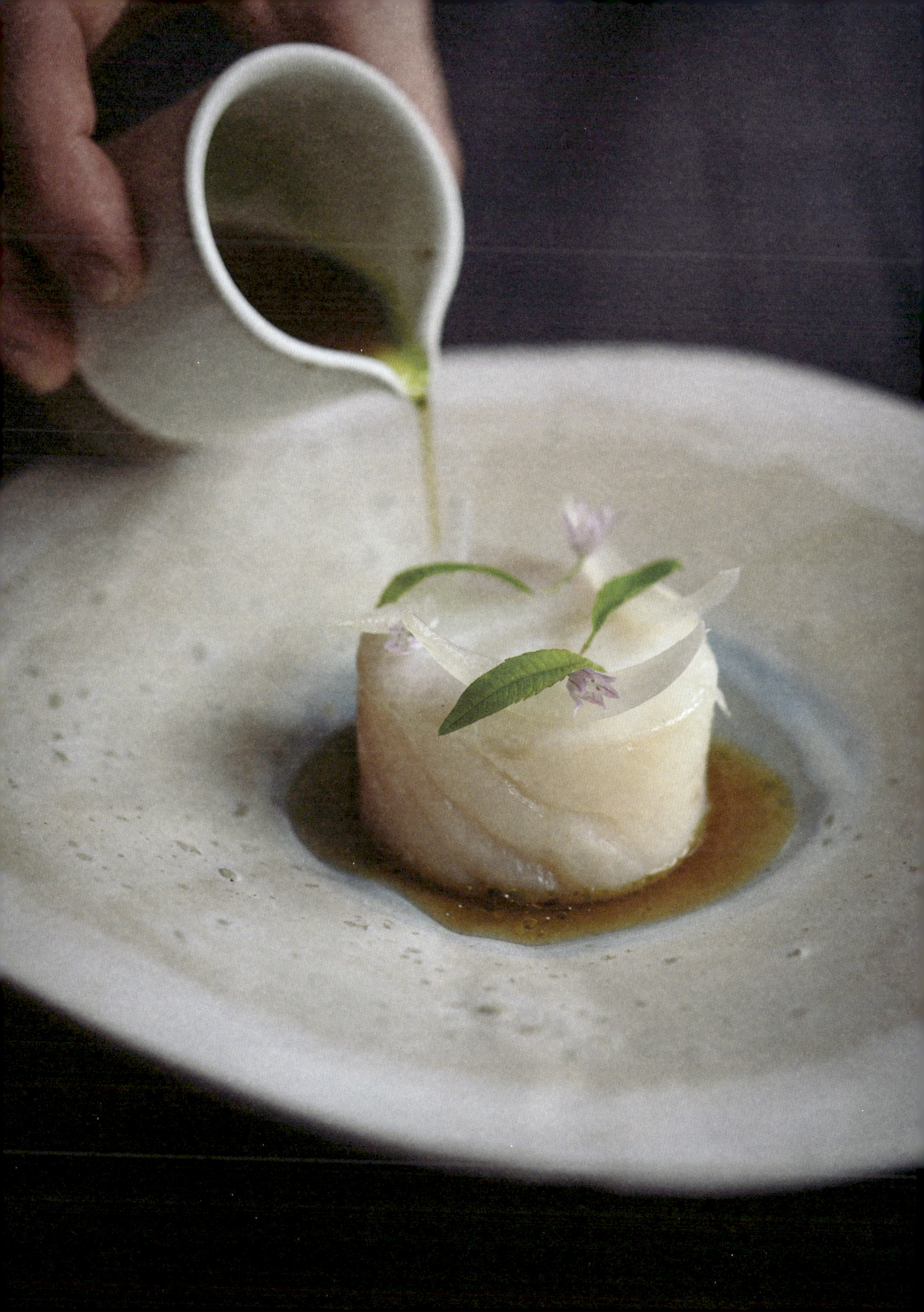

Le Cochon Aveugle | Cave du Cochon, York

My Recipes

WOODLAND PORK COOKED OVER COALS, FIG AND RADICCHIO RELISH, SAUCE CIVET

Why woodland pork – what is special about this produce?

The pigs are reared in the woodlands, just outside York, by a farmer called Fraser Atkins. They're all heritage breeds and the pork has an almost gamey flavour which we really like. It's a high quality and low intensity way of sourcing meat, as Fraser doesn't rear the pigs all year round; he starts around autumn time and goes through the winter and then stops in the spring. It's quite a specific process and product to work with, but we want to use the very best ingredients we possibly can in the restaurant so for us, this is a great choice.

Is cooking over coals your preferred way to work with meat?

Every menu we develop will include something cooked over coals. Our kitchen is very small but we have a large konro barbecue grill which is one of the most important elements of our kitchen. We might use it for fish sometimes, or it might be meat or vegetables, but there's always at least one dish being cooked in that way.

How traditional is the civet sauce in this recipe, or have you put your own twist on it?

I wanted the sauce to essentially taste like black pudding, because I didn't want to do something as obvious as putting a piece of black pudding on the dish. It is based on classical French cookery – you'd normally find it with hare à la Royale, or in English cookery with jugged hare – and we wanted to use that same technique but to create a sauce that was close to hollandaise in consistency. We describe it to customers as a sauce made out of black pudding, which it's not, but saying that has less impact than saying we use pork blood, which is what thickens the sauce and gives it that luscious and glossy texture.

GARGANELLI WITH LAMB BELLY PANCETTA, EGG YOLK, YORKSHIRE PECORINO, ENGLISH PEAS AND MINT

What inspired this English take on a carbonara style pasta dish?

Vicky and I both love carbonara; it's one of our favourite things to eat. It's also one of those dishes that a lot of chefs get wrong or can't cook properly, so I get my team to make carbonara for a lot of the staff meals here and teach them how to do it. Essentially, this version is a carbonara made with excess lamb, because when we have lamb on the menu, we end up with a lot of spare bellies which we then cure and turn into pancetta. That goes on the pizzas at our other restaurant, Cave du Cochon, but usually we'll have some left over, and that's why this dish was created. We use Yorkshire Pecorino because it's made right down the road in Otley, near Leeds, by a guy called Mario Olianas who is originally from the area of central Italy where Pecorino Romano is made and now makes traditional Italian ewe's milk cheeses here. We freshen it all up with mint and peas, then it's finished with lots of pepper, because carbonara should always have a real whack of black pepper.

LINE-CAUGHT POLLOCK POACHED IN AGED BEEF FAT WITH SENSHYU ONIONS AND LEMON VERBENA

What qualities do senshyu onions have that make them work for this dish?

They're a very sweet white onion grown in early spring and summer, with a flavour almost like the bottom of the shallot onions with the green tops you get. We wanted to use senshyu because the dish is quite rich, as the pollock is poached in beef fat, so we needed an onion which would cut through that. All the other elements are there purposefully to cut through the beef fat.

How was the method for making the onion jam developed?

If you just add the beef fat at the end, as if you were using rendered drippings, the mixture won't emulsify properly so what'll happen is once you cool that jam down, it'll just split out again. This technique, where you're very slowly melting the solid fat into the onions drip by drip, is like making a mayonnaise. The concept of adding fat slowly and gradually is the same and that process stabilises the jam because there's nothing else holding the onions and fat together, so you have to get that emulsification right. If you try and cowboy it, it won't happen – trust me, we tried! Originally the method came off Kitchen Table and I think Gareth Ward having a conversation on Twitter or Instagram about cooking their onions like that as a side dish. I thought that would make a really interesting jam, so it was one of those things where you just end up creating your own version. It usually takes about 6 to 8 hours in the restaurant, depending on how much onion we're using and what we're doing with the end product. Since we're so small, we are able to take our time with things like this and that's what makes it special. Our service is always very calm – it's not all "go, go, go" with shouting and screaming – because we've put the time in beforehand. I think that shows in the finished product; you can definitely tell when a dish has had short preparation. All our dishes are purposefully plated to look really simple but actually a lot of work goes into them before that point.

Le Cochon Aveugle | Cave du Cochon, York

Q&A with Joshua Overington

How would you describe your cooking style?

I would say it's 100% product and personality driven. Our dishes will only use produce that is in season and at its very best. I tell our guests that the produce here is some of the best in the UK and that's because we're only serving 14 to 18 people a night. We're literally picking through the crème de la crème and anything that doesn't suit us, we just send back. We have the luxury of being able to pick the very best. I know a lot of restaurants say that but for us it's a huge part of what we do, partly because we can and partly because we have to, to make it worthwhile. This approach is something we've grown into as we've got older, because the simpler and more refined you want a dish to be, the more important the quality of the ingredients becomes.

Would you describe your kitchen as quite technical or more classical in terms of technique?

The food is classically based – although that's not to say the food is classically served, because it certainly isn't. Our food is very modern in the way we plate it, but everything starts with the fundamental question that I think is central to classical cooking: does it taste amazing? If something can be improved with technology then we'll implement that, but we don't do it just for the sake of it, only if it will make the dish better. The two restaurant dishes we've shared in this book – the woodland pork and poached pollock – don't have any technical wizardry behind them: it's just pure cookery, showcasing what we can do pretty much just with heat. When we were buying products that weren't as high quality, we'd need a lot more technique to get them up to standard, whereas we've realised since then that you can just buy absolutely incredible produce that sings for itself with very little intervention. That's the process you learn and develop through as a chef, and the restaurant has matured with us to embrace that more stripped back approach.

Are there any particular cuisines you lean into when you're developing dishes?

That's a really hard question to answer because I want to say everything and everywhere! I think the hardest part is making my food look like it's from York. I don't want it to be Japanese, I don't want it to be Nordic, I don't want it to be French – I want it to be obviously Joshua Overington. Creating your own personal style is challenging so we'll always tweak dishes until they feel like ours. There are elements of Italian, French and English cooking all jumbled together in my food but it's also got to be mine. So everywhere and nowhere has to be the answer!

Is sustainability important in your approach to produce?

It's more about showcasing where the restaurant comes from. For me, sustainability comes into good cookery, in the sense that wasting food makes you a crap chef at the end of the day. If we're throwing out half the products we buy in, that's just nonsense cookery and not something I'm interested in, so I look at sustainability as part of the whole process. At the moment, everything that doesn't get used in our main restaurant is used in the second one, so it's all part of a cycle. Along the same lines, if an ingredient is good locally then we'll use it, but if not we'll go further afield. We've got a lot of produce available to us on our doorstep and we champion that – it's not something that we really have to focus on because it just comes naturally. All our vegetables, for example, are grown on a farm eight miles away. We fully buy into lower food miles and organic produce, but it's not a box-ticking exercise for us, it's just part of the game.

What do you love about being restaurateurs and what keeps you doing it?

Mostly, it's the customer interaction. We have an open kitchen here and I really enjoy chatting when customers come to the pass after their meal – that is still the thrill and the reason why we do it. At the end of the day, as a chef you cook to make people happy and if you're not doing that, what's the point of cooking?

What would you say to someone starting out in the hospitality industry?

I think self-confidence is always a really hard thing. Opening a restaurant when I was 26 meant that I constantly had imposter syndrome, especially when we started getting recognition. You feel like you don't deserve it, but I wish I had the self-belief back then that I do now. I can remember being very nervous when customers ate my food and panicking if anyone important came in, whereas now I know my food is good so I can just get on with it. So, I would tell myself to have less doubt that it's all going to work out. But be prepared for the hard work! It's not an easy route. The change in hospitality is also helping; it's a bit more supportive and inclusive and everyone looks after each other and celebrates each other. When you run a restaurant, you feel like you're in a bubble, especially as a couple because you can bounce off each other. When you make friends in the industry and start sharing experiences though, you realise that others are going through all the same things, so I think the more friends you make in the industry, the easier you'll find it.

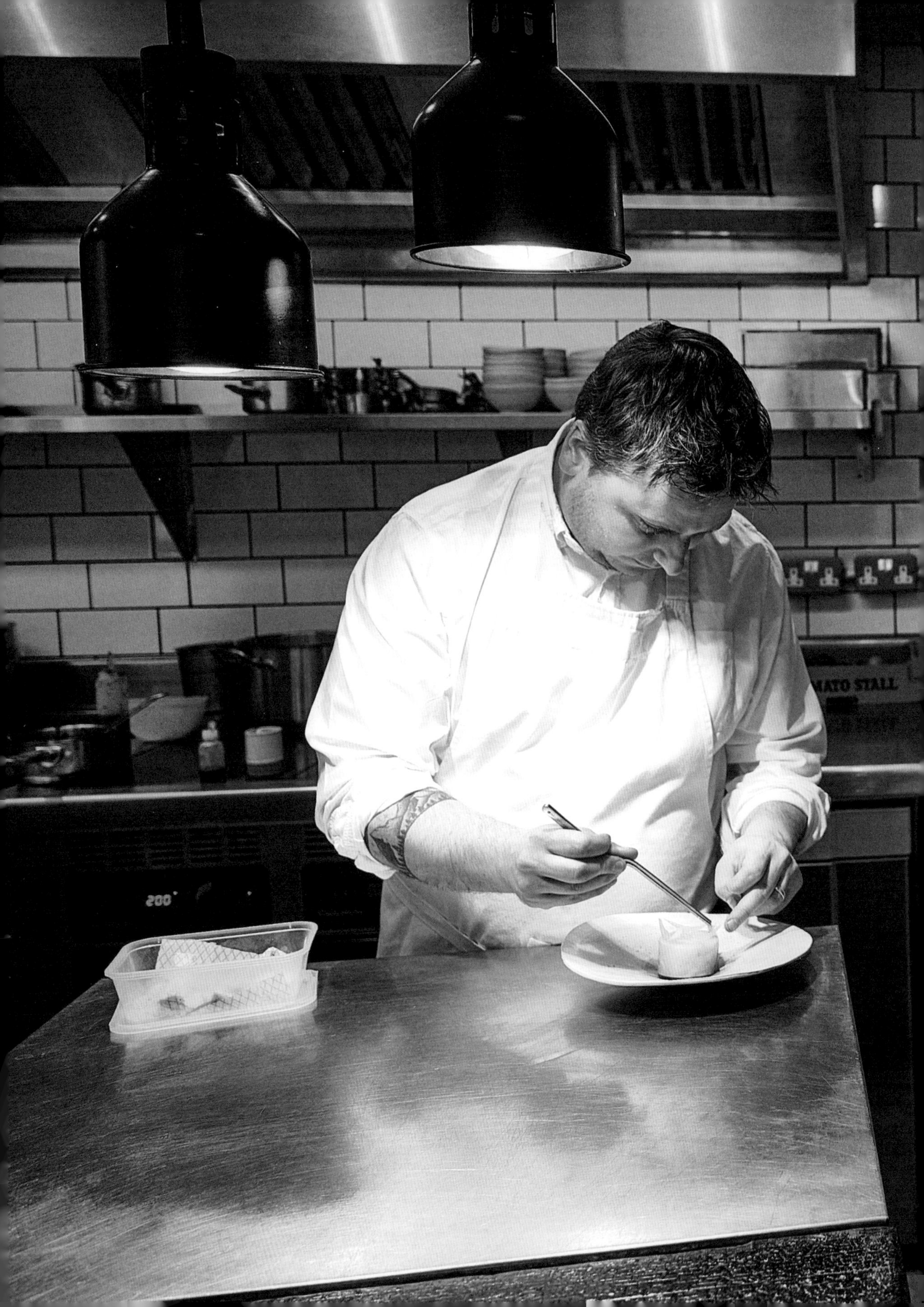

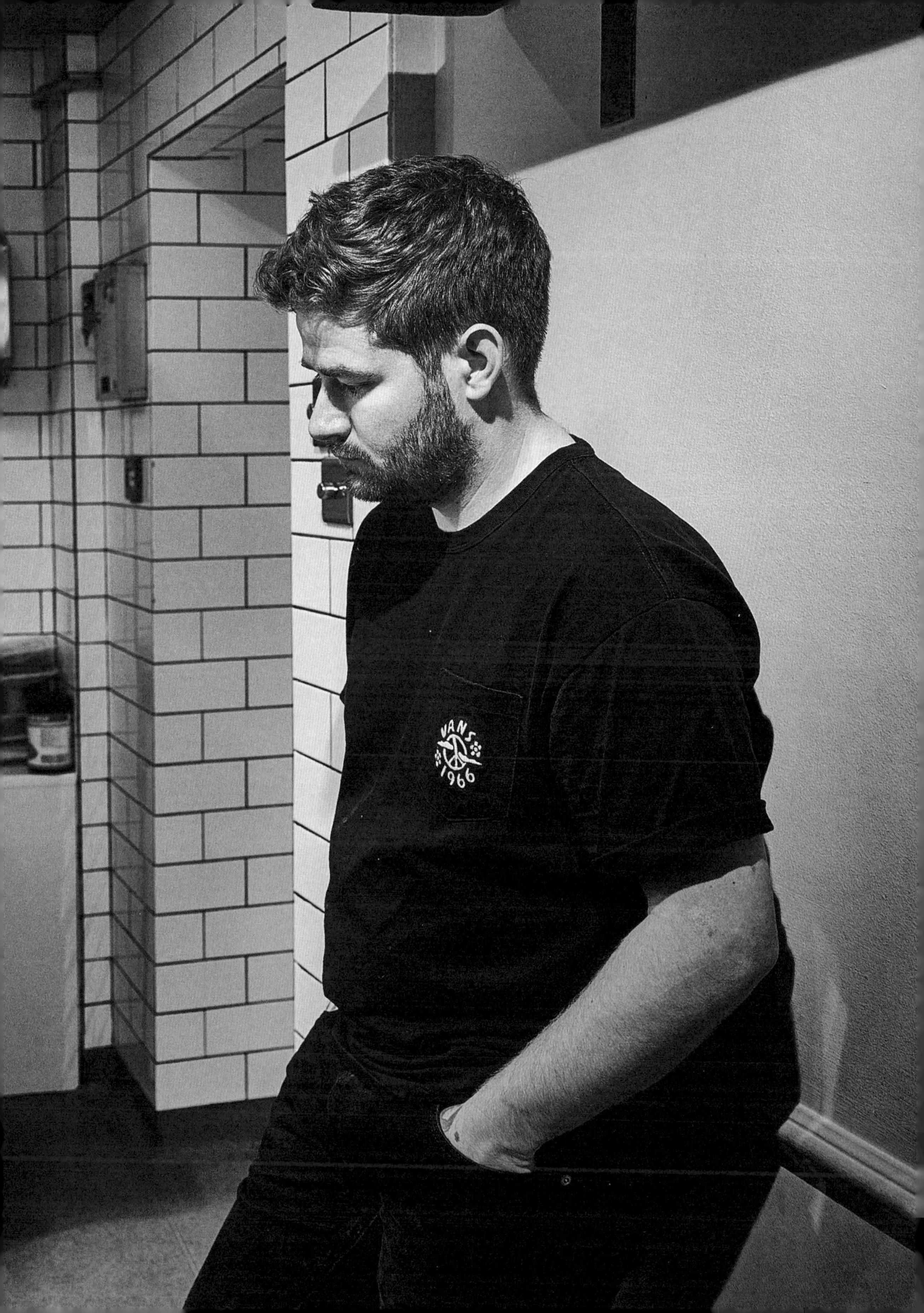
VANS
1966

House of Tides | Solstice, Newcastle Upon Tyne

Kenny Atkinson

Kenny Atkinson was born and bred in Newcastle and spent the first 12 years of his career training at some of the best restaurants in the UK before returning to his roots in the northeast. In 2008, Kenny won his first Michelin star as head chef at St Martins in the Scilly Isles, and his second at the White Room in County Durham. He then became executive chef at Rockliffe Hall near Darlington from 2009 to 2013 and is now chef patron of House of Tides in Newcastle, which he opened in 2014 with his wife Abbie.

Throughout his career, Kenny's bold and ambitious cooking has brought him critical acclaim including a Michelin star and four AA rosettes for House of Tides. He also won The Great British Menu in two consecutive years, 2009 and 2010, and has appeared on various other TV cookery programmes. His first restaurant, set on Newcastle's historic quayside within a Grade 1 listed 16th century former merchant's town house, was joined by a second just around the corner in 2022. Solstice is Kenny and Abbie's new fine dining venture and offers a seasonal tasting menu in the intimate restaurant with an open kitchen.

How I describe my cooking style:

I like doing lots of little courses. House of Tides limits that to some extent because of its size – pastry's on the second floor, restaurant's on the first floor, kitchen's on the ground floor, so the waiters are always running up and down stairs – but I'm trying to be a bit more ambitious at Solstice. I'm getting more into Asian and Middle Eastern ingredients, whereas House of Tides is very classically French. If you don't try new things, it's easy to get stuck in the same style. I've been doing this since I was 18 and over the years you do cook a lot of the same food, so it's nice to try something really different and see where it goes.

Where I want to eat next:

I want to go back to Ramsay's – last time I was there it was my 20th birthday. Last time I was in London I ate at the Ritz and that was stunning. How they haven't got two stars I don't know, everything's impeccable. We also had one of the best meals ever at Alex Dilling's place, The Greenhouse. The Ledbury's open again so that and getting round to friends' places is next for me.

What I eat when I'm not working:

I make quite hearty food at home because I've got three kids, so we'll have a big lasagne or pasta bake, something everyone likes that's easy. Trying to eat out's a nightmare when you have kids!

HOUSE OF TIDES

House of Tides | Solstice, Newcastle Upon Tyne

Smoked Jersey Royal Potatoes, Cured Egg Yolk, Asparagus & Wild Garlic

Preparation time: 1 hour | Cooking time: 1 hour | Serves 4

FOR THE SMOKED POTATOES
300g Jersey Royal potatoes, skin on
1.1 litres (2 pints) smoked oil
5 sprigs of thyme
½ garlic bulb

FOR THE MINT GEL
400g water
250g caster sugar
1 bunch of fresh mint
250g cider vinegar
1g agar agar

FOR THE WILD GARLIC PURÉE
200g wild garlic leaves
150g double cream
400ml water
50g butter
Maldon salt
Ground white pepper
Squeeze of fresh lemon juice

FOR THE ASPARAGUS
8 white asparagus spears
8 green asparagus spears
Fresh thyme
Garlic cloves
Rapeseed oil

FOR THE PICKLED MUSHROOMS
100g Trompette de la Mort mushrooms
1 clove of garlic
2 sprigs of thyme
1 tbsp sherry vinegar
100ml rapeseed oil

FOR THE CURED EGG YOLK
Fine salt
3 egg yolks

TO SERVE
Bitter endive
Micro watercress
Wild garlic flowers

FOR THE SMOKED POTATOES
Slowly simmer the potatoes in a pan of the smoked oil with the thyme and garlic until just cooked, then leave them to cool in the oil. Slice the potatoes into 5 by 2cm discs and reserve until needed.

FOR THE MINT GEL
Bring the water and sugar to the boil, add the mint and leave to infuse overnight. The next day, pass the liquid through a fine sieve. Whisk the vinegar and mint syrup into the agar agar, bring to a simmer, pass through a fine sieve and then leave to set in a tray. Blitz the jelly to a smooth gel and place into a plastic squeezy bottle.

FOR THE WILD GARLIC PURÉE
Blanch the wild garlic in boiling salted water for approximately 1 minute, then refresh in iced water. Remove and squeeze the wild garlic to remove as much liquid as possible. In a pan, bring the cream, water and butter to the boil and then pour this mixture onto the garlic leaves. Blitz to a purée, then season with salt, ground white pepper and lemon juice to taste.

FOR THE ASPARAGUS
Prep and peel all the asparagus spears. Place the white asparagus in a vacuum pack bag with thyme, garlic and rapeseed oil. Cook in the microwave for 30 seconds on full power, then place the sealed bag in iced water to chill. Trim the spears into neat 3cm diamonds and set aside.

Dress the green asparagus in a little rapeseed oil and barbecue on a konro grill or char in a griddle pan for 2 minutes. Season with salt and pepper to finish.

FOR THE PICKLED MUSHROOMS
In a hot pan, sauté the mushrooms for approximately 30 seconds with the garlic and thyme. Add the sherry vinegar to the mushrooms and reduce the liquid until evaporated. Season the mushrooms with salt and add the rapeseed oil.

FOR THE CURED EGG YOLK
Cover the base of a tray with fine salt to a depth of about 1cm. Use the back of a tablespoon to make as many dents in the salt as there are yolks to cure. Separate the yolks thoroughly so there are no whites, then carefully sit them in the dents and completely cover with more salt. Leave in the fridge for 8 hours, or overnight. The next day, remove the yolks and wash them under cold water, then dry them carefully on kitchen paper. Heat your oven to its lowest setting (60°c/40°c fan/Gas Mark ¼ is ideal) and leave the yolks in the oven to dry out on an oiled cooling rack for 3 hours until hard.

TO SERVE
Pipe a nice circle of wild garlic purée into the centre of the plate. Pan fry the sliced potatoes in a little of the smoked oil until golden, then place on a tray and finely grate the cured egg yolk over the potatoes. Neatly arrange 5 of the dressed potato slices around the wild garlic purée.

Dress the white asparagus pieces in a little oil and season with salt, then arrange in between the potatoes. Pipe a few dots of mint gel onto the white asparagus. Neatly arrange the pickled mushrooms and barbecued green asparagus over and around the potatoes. Garnish the dish with bitter endive, micro watercress leaves and wild garlic flowers to finish.

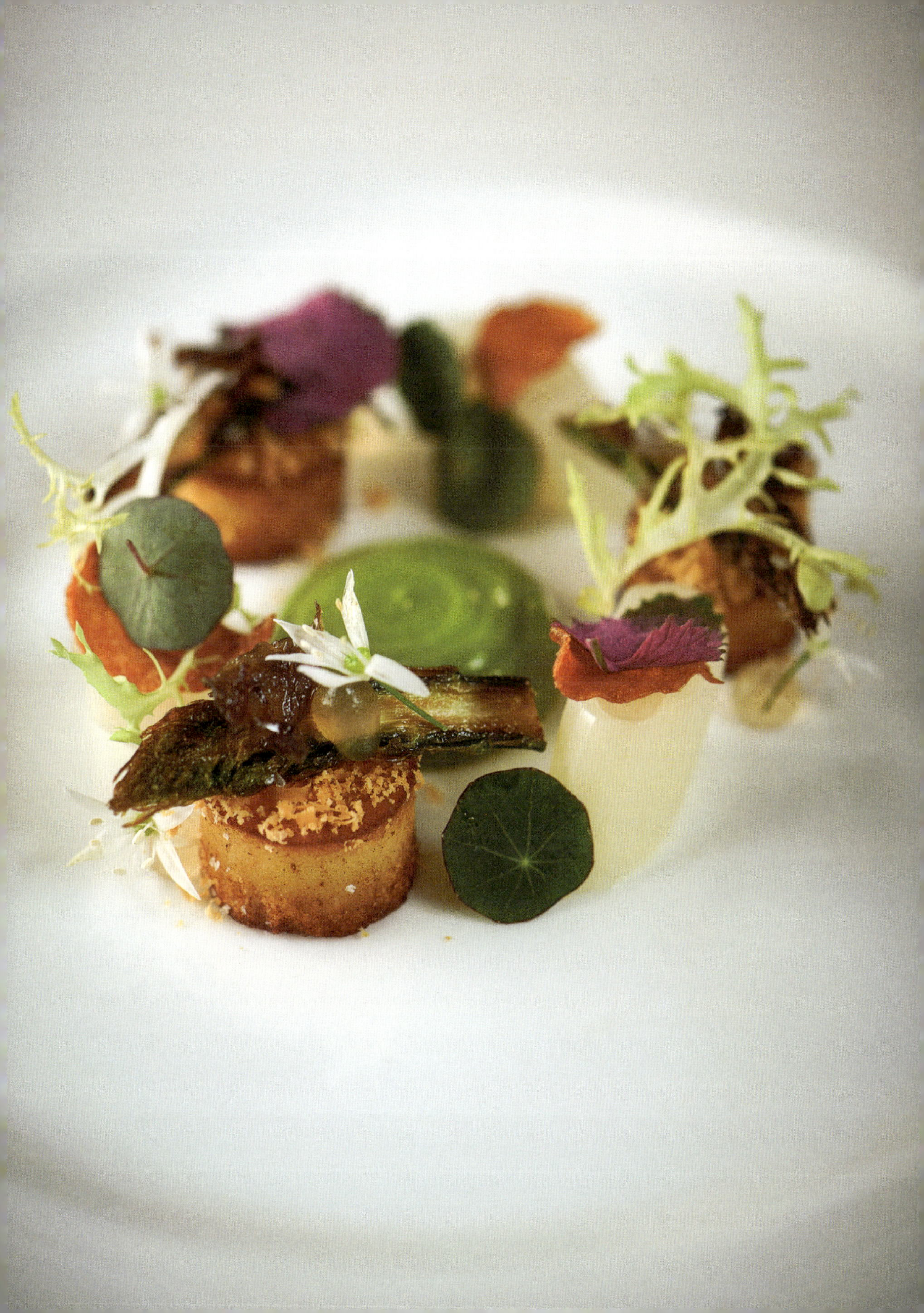

House of Tides | Solstice, Newcastle Upon Tyne

Peach Tart with Almonds, Lemon Verbena, White Chocolate & Peach Tea Sorbet

Preparation time: 2 hours | Cooking time: 1 hour | Serves 4

FOR THE SWEET PASTRY
80g butter

60g icing sugar

1 egg yolk

135g plain flour

10g cornflour

Pinch of salt

FOR THE VERBENA CREAM
50g verbena butter (49g butter blended with 1g lemon verbena)

50g icing sugar

50g pasteurised egg

50g ground almonds

FOR THE PEACH COMPOTE
1.3g ascorbic acid

200g poached peach dice

200g roasted peach purée

20g crème de pêche

FOR THE ALMOND TUILE
25g butter

40g icing sugar

40g ground almonds

14g glucose

5g water

FOR THE WHITE CHOCOLATE MOUSSE
120g white chocolate

200g double cream

1 egg yolk

½ a vanilla pod

FOR THE PEACH TEA SORBET
1.25kg water

75g Earl Grey

20g dried lemon verbena

1kg peach purée

400g stock syrup

35g dextrose

75g sorbet stabiliser

2g gellan gum

FOR THE SWEET PASTRY
Lightly cream the butter and icing sugar together in a stand mixer. Add the egg yolk and mix well. Sieve the flour, cornflour and salt together, then add this to the butter mixture. Mix everything together until fully combined but be careful not to overmix the dough. Wrap in cling film and leave to chill for a couple of hours.

Roll out the pastry on a floured surface to approximately 2cm thick and line 4 x 10cm non-stick tart cases with pastry. Chill for at least 20 minutes. Line the chilled tart cases with baking paper and fill with baking beans or dried peas, then bake at 170°c for 10 minutes until golden. Remove the beans and baking paper, then cook for a further 5 minutes. Leave the tart cases to cool.

FOR THE VERBENA CREAM
Cream the verbena butter and sugar together until light and fluffy, mix in the egg until combined, then add the ground almonds and mix until smooth.

FOR THE PEACH COMPOTE
Combine the ascorbic acid and diced peach in a bowl, fold in the peach purée and then finish with the peach liqueur. Fold in and leave to infuse.

FOR THE ALMOND TUILE
Cream the butter and sugar until light and fluffy. Add the remaining ingredients and mix into the butter and sugar until combined. Roll the mixture out thinly between two sheets of parchment paper. Bake at 160°c for approximately 8 minutes.

FOR THE WHITE CHOCOLATE MOUSSE
Heat the chocolate until half melted over a bain marie while you bring 50g of the double cream and the vanilla pod, split and scraped, to the boil in a separate pan and leave to infuse. Bring the cream back to a simmer, remove the vanilla pod and then pour the hot cream over the chocolate. Whisk in the egg yolk and allow the mixture to cool. Whip the remaining double cream to soft peaks and fold into the chocolate base, then leave the mousse to set.

FOR THE PEACH TEA SORBET
Mix all the ingredients together, bring to a simmer and then leave to infuse. Pass the sorbet mix through a fine sieve. Pour the mix into an ice cream machine and churn until the sorbet is a thick consistency. Store in the freezer until needed.

TO SERVE
Pipe the lemon verbena cream into the tart cases. Spoon a good amount of the peach compote on top of the cream and level flat. Place a disc of the almond tuile on top of the compote. Neatly pipe the white chocolate mousse on one side of the tuile and decorate with picked fresh lemon verbena leaves. Place the tart onto the plate and finish with a rocher of peach tea sorbet to one side.

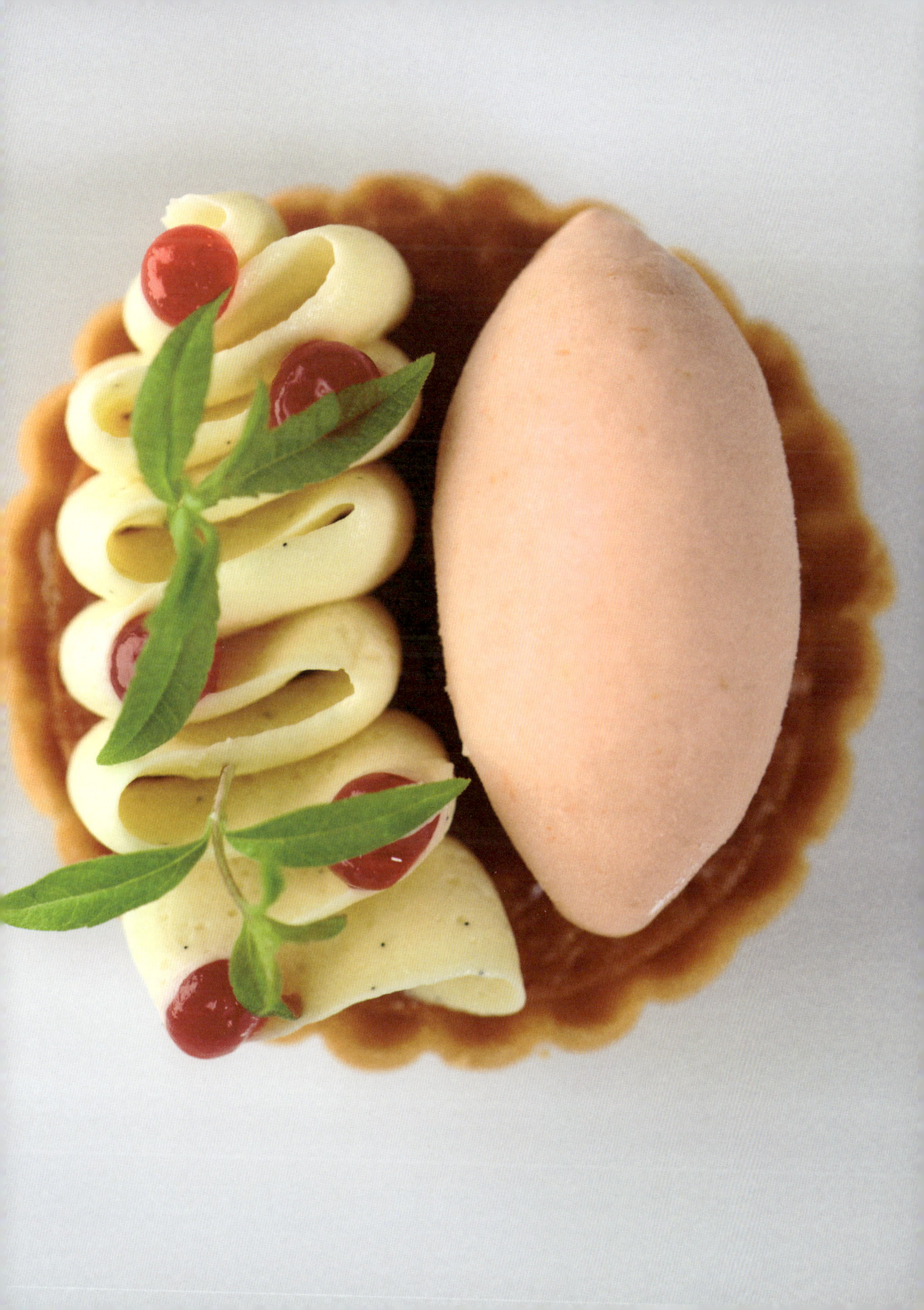

House of Tides | Solstice, Newcastle Upon Tyne

Roast Monkfish, Mussels, Caviar, Lemon & Sea Herbs

Preparation time: 30 minutes | Cooking time: 1 hour | Serves 4

FOR THE ROAST MONKFISH
4 x 100-120g monkfish tail portions
50g butter

FOR THE MUSSELS
200g mussels, cleaned and de-bearded
150g white wine
100ml water

FOR THE MUSSEL SAUCE
1 banana shallot, diced
1 clove of garlic, crushed
25g butter
300ml fish stock
200ml mussel stock
200ml double cream

FOR THE LEMON GEL
300ml water
300g sugar
200ml lemon juice
14g agar agar

TO SERVE
Caviar
Sea herbs such sea fennel, sea purslane or samphire

FOR THE ROAST MONKFISH
Pan fry the monkfish tail in a little oil until golden, then add the butter and cook in the foaming butter for about 6 minutes. Remove the tail and leave to rest in a warm area for 5-6 minutes.

FOR THE MUSSELS
Put the mussels, wine and water into a hot pan, cover with a lid and cook quickly for about 1 minute until the mussel shells have opened. Drain off the mussels in a sieve when cooked, reserving the cooking liquor for the sauce (you will need at least 200ml).

FOR THE MUSSEL SAUCE
In a hot pan, sauté the shallot and garlic in the butter. Add the fish and mussel stocks, then simmer for approximately 20 minutes. Drain and pass the stock into a clean pan, reduce by half, then add the double cream and reduce by half again. Finish the sauce with a touch of seasoning if needed and a little lemon juice.

FOR THE LEMON GEL
Bring the water, sugar and lemon juice to the boil, then whisk in the agar agar and bring back to a simmer. Place into a container and chill until set, then blitz in a blender to a smooth gel. Place into a squeezy bottle and set aside.

TO SERVE
Top and tail the monkfish tail and place into the centre of the bowl. Top with a good dollop of caviar and arrange the mussels around the monkfish. Top the mussels with a little lemon gel, garnish with the sea herbs and finish with the mussel sauce.

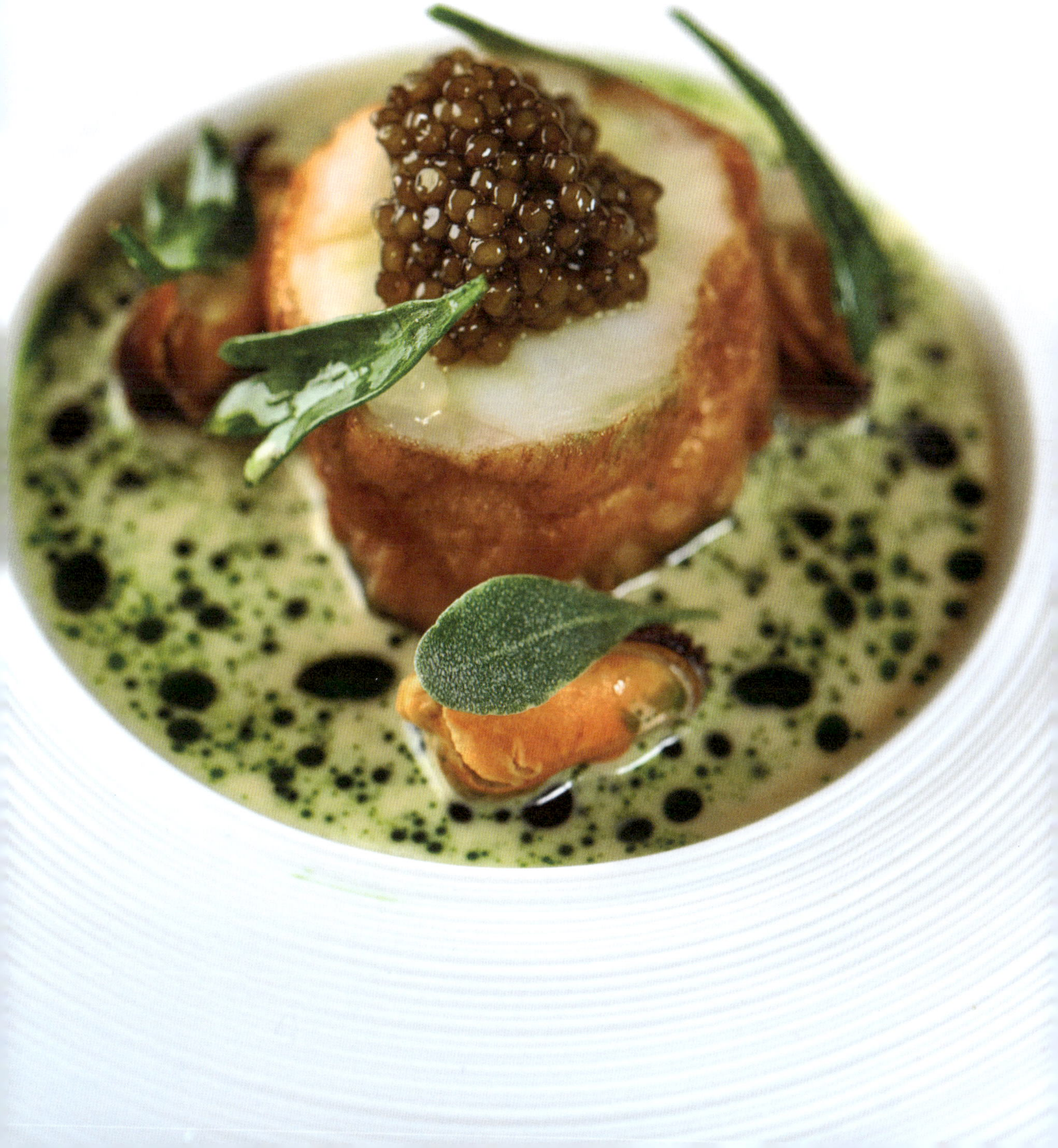

House of Tides | Solstice, Newcastle Upon Tyne

My Recipes

We have a mackerel appetiser, the potato and asparagus starter, then the monkfish, a lamb dish, the peach tart and a chocolate dessert. It's clean, it ticks all the boxes, you're not going to go home disappointed, but it's not going to blow your mind. Most restaurants don't do that and everything's produce-led now anyway. I think there's an element of people watching programmes like Great British Menu and expecting something different because that's all about theatre, but when you come to a restaurant it's got to be consistent. It's about whether the guys in the kitchen can do it to the same standard every time.

SMOKED JERSEY ROYAL POTATOES, CURED EGG YOLK, ASPARAGUS & WILD GARLIC

This is the first course on our menu at House of Tides at the time of writing. It's probably going to change soon as the asparagus season changes. What we'd probably do if we wanted to keep the dish on after that is use salsify instead, and maybe change the garnish a little bit. We cook the Jersey Royals in smoked oil with garlic and thyme, so they're almost confit, then we cut them down and pan roast with a bit more smoked oil. We make our own smoked oil with all the charcoal left over at the end of service; you just get a pan of oil on and drop it all in. We have plenty because everything's barbecued now where it used to be done in water baths. We char things like asparagus on our barbecues and cook our meats on it, just so that not everything's pan fried.

ROAST MONKFISH, MUSSELS, CAVIAR, LEMON & SEA HERBS

We use Petrossian Daurenki caviar on this dish. We went through a phase of using truffle but it's a lot of money for not a lot of flavour, and you'd see some guests not eating any of it…so now on fish dishes we try and keep things nice and clean. The caviar makes it feel more substantial and ties it in to the sea, keeping it nice and fresh.

PEACH TART WITH ALMONDS, LEMON VERBENA, WHITE CHOCOLATE & PEACH TEA SORBET

For this we make a lemon verbena and almond cream that goes on the bottom, then we do roasted peach purée and poached peach, a little almond tuile on top of that, then a nice peach tea sorbet, white chocolate mousse, and blood peach gel. That's the first dessert.

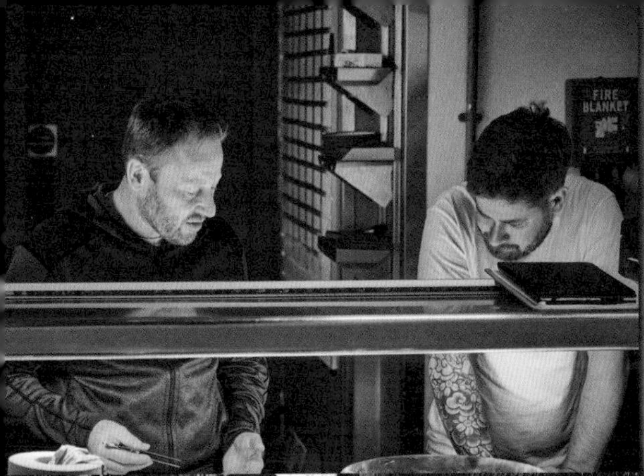
FIRE
BLANKET

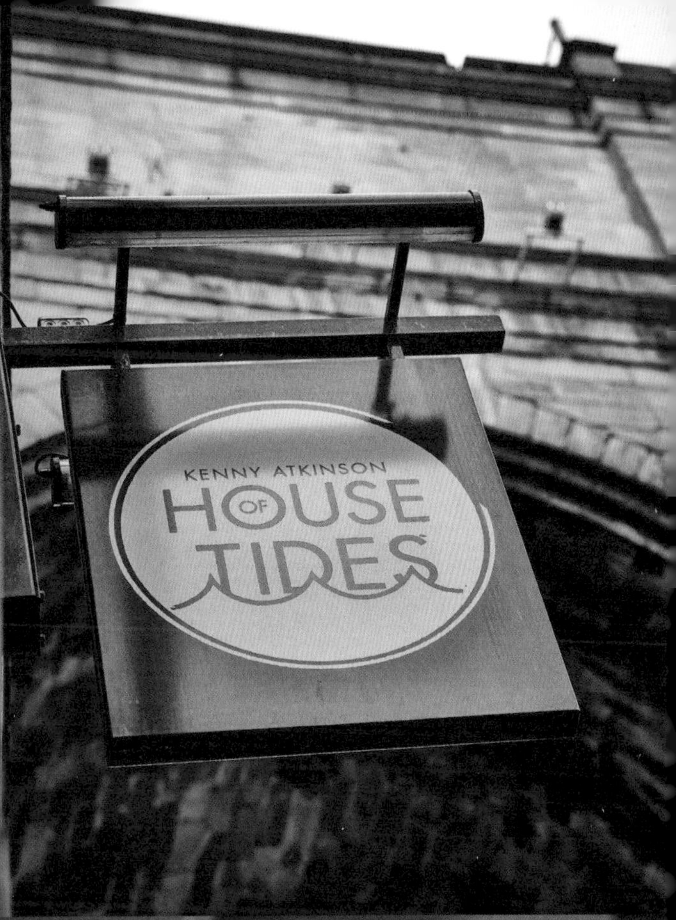
KENNY ATKINSON
HOUSE OF TIDES

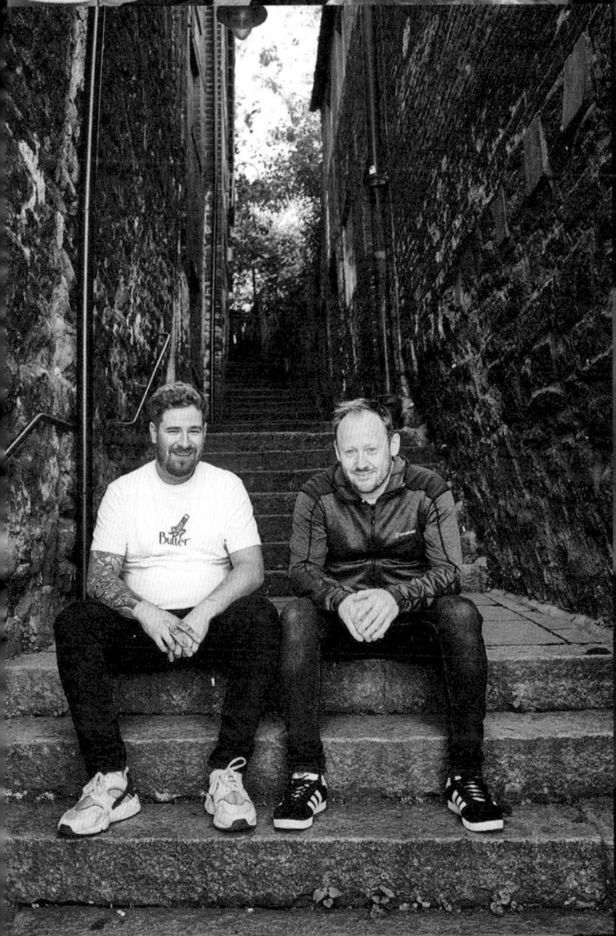
Butter

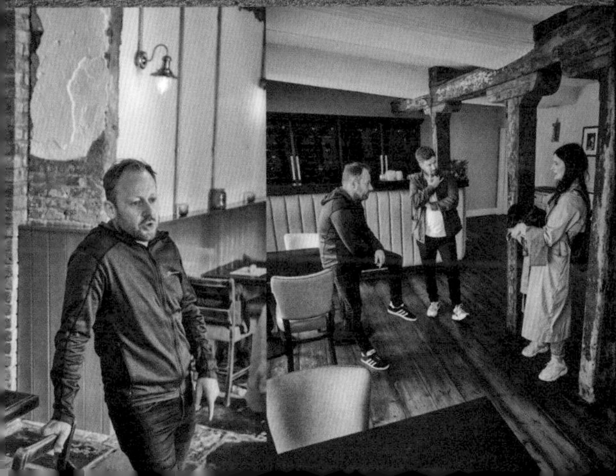

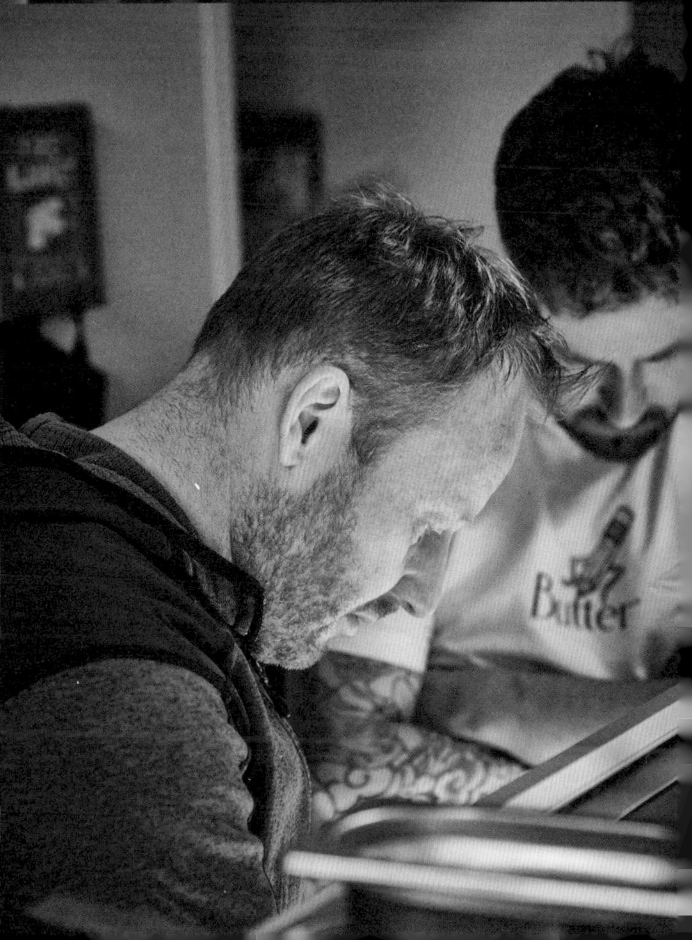
Butter

House of Tides | Solstice, Newcastle Upon Tyne

Chewing The Fat with Kenny Atkinson

How much has the industry changed since you started working in professional kitchens?

I think chefs of my generations have come through the hard way with à la carte menus, being in the shit every day, working all hours, having three or four main courses to get out every service – we've gone through the hard times, and I think that's why the industry has changed. Now we've come up with a system where we're trying to give the guys in the kitchen better working conditions, fewer hours (45-50 a week where I was doing 70-80 at one point) and make the menu more simplistic so there's not too much cooking going on for each dish right before we serve it. In our day there were pomme annas and dauphinois and boulangeres to order, and that was just the potatoes. Now the guys don't break a sweat, service is nice and easy, everything is controlled, and they're home by half ten. They're doing a good job, but I also feel there is a danger of chefs not being chefs anymore. They're almost part of a production line putting the dishes together on the pass. I've got seven chefs in the kitchen at House of Tides, including a couple who are being trained up, and for me it's about getting them to do that classical French cooking with the right skill level.

What have you learnt since becoming a restaurateur?

I think trying to keep our food simple and streamlined so it's achievable is a good thing. We don't know what's going to happen tomorrow; someone could call in sick or not turn up. Since the pandemic we've stripped everything back and reassessed our costs. When you're running a business and looking at your financials, it's easy to wait another month to tighten things up so they keep rolling over, until it all stops. Consistency's the big thing for us now, then you can't go wrong. Personally, I also think the VAT structure for hospitality needs to change massively because it's the only way we can invest more into wages, the business and ultimately the economy. Some restaurants might think that's more for my back pocket but for chefs like ourselves, the first reaction is 'what can I do better?' whether that's better equipment, better produce, an extra chef… Really, I should just open a chicken shop because it would be a lot easier for me to have a restaurant that just makes money, but there's this thing inside, an ego maybe, that gets in the way. I just can't do it.

Has any of that changed you as a chef or decisions you've made about your menu?

Bigger places and chains can offer so many dietary alternatives which is great, and they can absorb that cost because they're getting the volume, but for small businesses the cost and the time just isn't viable. We don't do a vegan menu anymore and won't offer one at Solstice for that reason. Guests would sometimes book as vegan and then get here and say 'oh, go on then, I'll have the full menu' which is difficult because we've already made every alternative purée, sauce and garnish by that point. At Solstice we do cater for vegetarians, but I've reserved the right to make a call about whether it's doable for the team or not. It's a really small kitchen and totally on show, so if the guys are in the shit everyone's going to see it. There are great vegetarian restaurants out there and they specialise in that food, whereas here it might be sub-standard compared to the rest of the menu. I think most chefs want to create their best possible menu and if a guest doesn't like a particular element then we can change that, but I'm not going to say it's always as good as it would have been.

What's your next goal within the industry?

House of Tides has built up a good reputation over the years – it's a good one star restaurant, it doesn't need to be a two star restaurant – but it wasn't cost effective, so we need to get that right and then we can be more creative with Solstice. I've stepped back a lot at House of Tides and given my head chef there a lot more responsibility to strengthen that kitchen as best I can so it runs without me and is self-sufficient. With Solstice, there's a part of me that thinks: can I get two stars with this one? Maybe not, but if I don't try I'll never know. If I get one star, I'll be the first chef with two one star restaurants on the same street and that's an achievement. I want to be able to look back when I'm in my fifties and say I've achieved something – I want to have some sort of legacy. Solstice is more about ambition and development, without being tied to a particular cuisine and with the ability to use luxury produce because it's only small. It's open Tuesday to Friday and closed over the holidays for two reasons: I want a life and I've got three kids who all need my attention, as well as time with my wife. You want to make sure you're there for your guys, for your guests, for your family, but trying to find that balance is hard. When we decided to open Solstice, it was about the business working around our life, not the other way round.

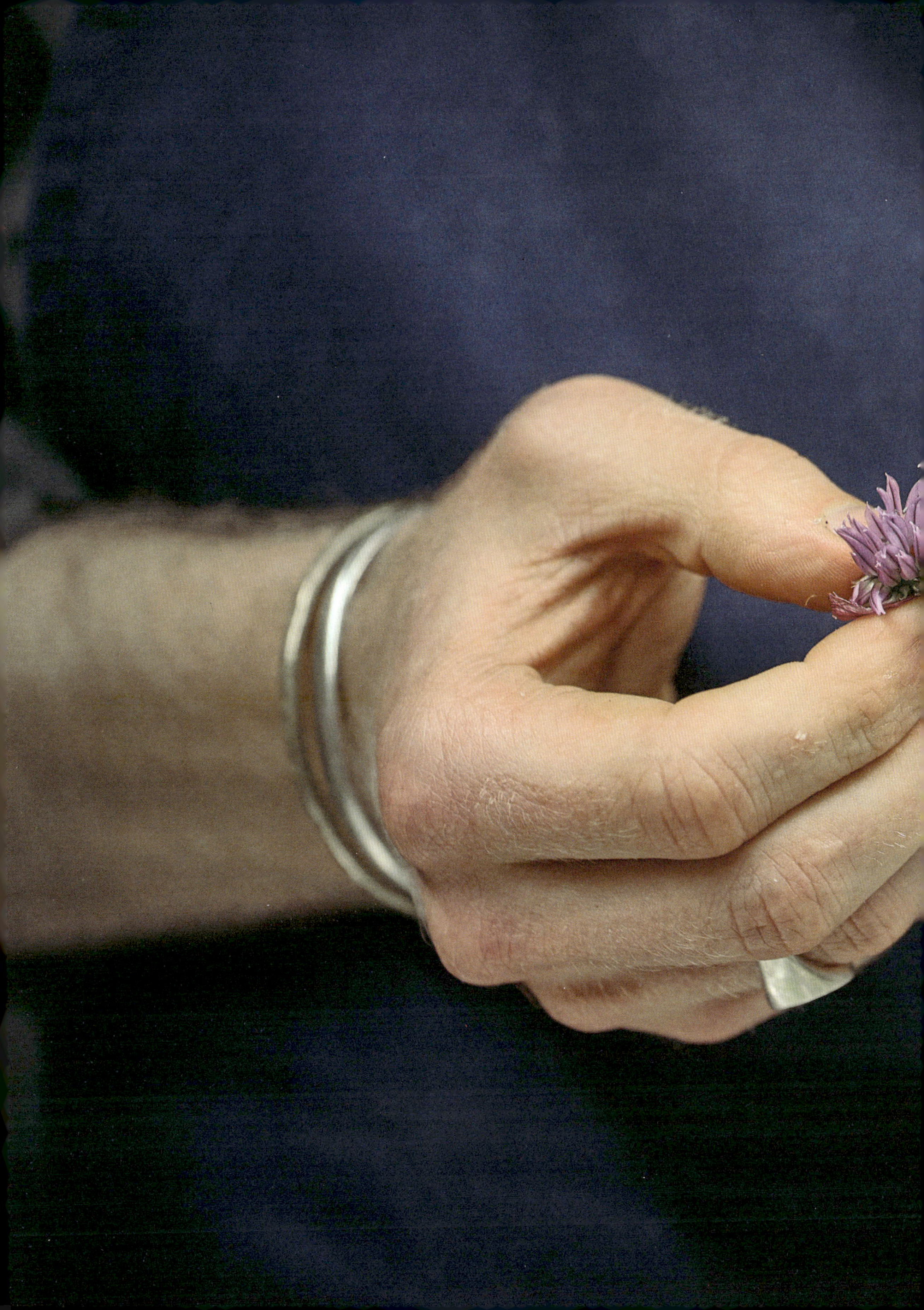

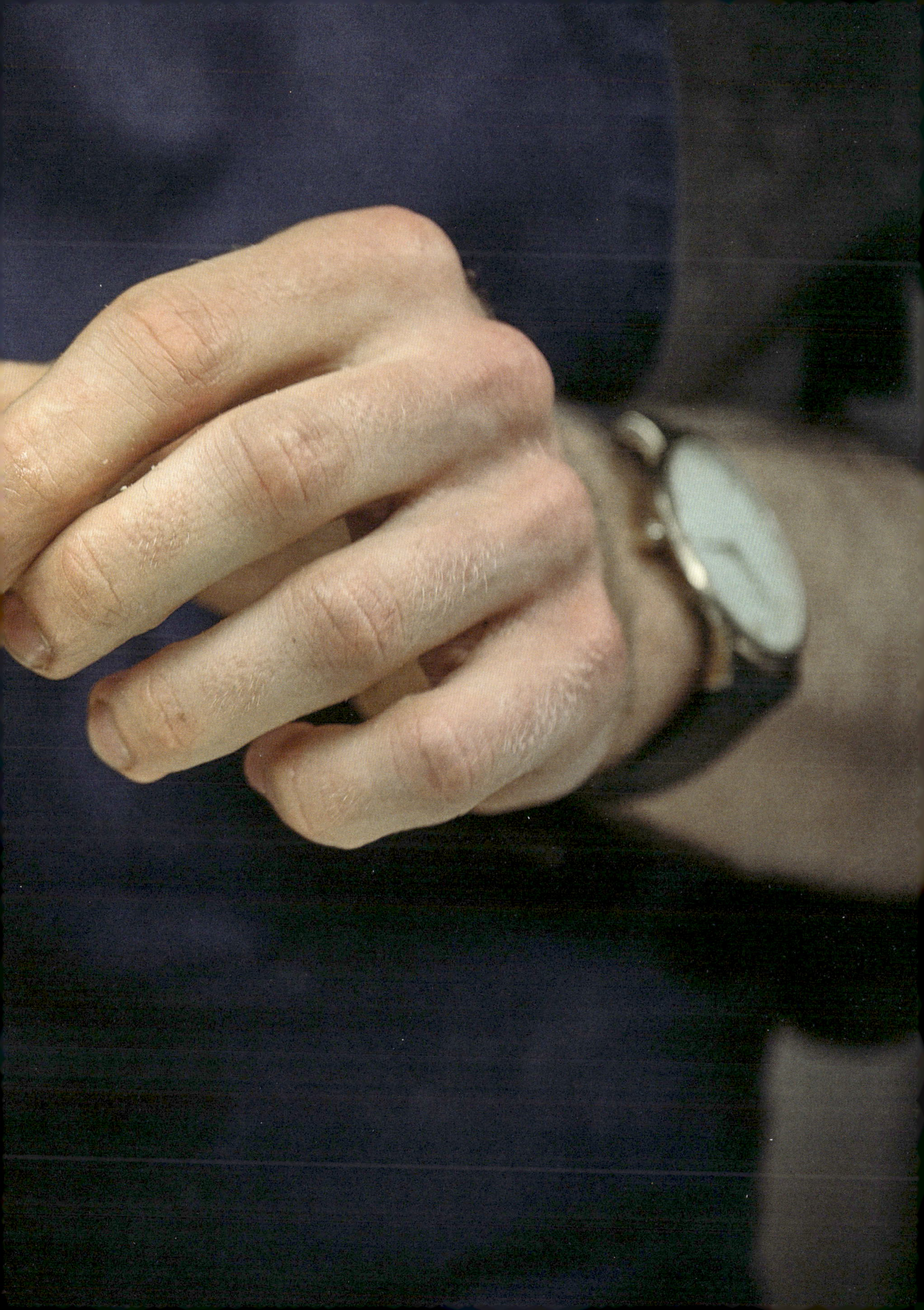

Plates, London

Kirk Haworth

Kirk made a name for himself early in his culinary career by winning the North West Young Chef of the Year award at 17. He went on to work under the world's top chefs at The French Laundry, Restaurant Sat Bains, The Square, The Quay and Northcote. Having spent 16 years perfecting his craft in Michelin-starred restaurants around the world, Kirk and his sister Keeley Haworth co-founded Plates in early 2022.

The restaurant, based on Kingsland Road in London, is entirely plant-based and delivers a modern tasting menu with high-end execution. Plates' ethos was born out of Kirk's own personal journey into eating and cooking differently, which began in 2016 when he was diagnosed with Lyme disease. This led Kirk to overhaul his lifestyle and explore plant-based food in the pursuit of better health, eventually discovering that an anti-inflammatory diet free from meat, gluten, refined sugar and dairy reduced the intensity of his symptoms.

Kirk's unique perspective on food and health nurtures a rare working environment for his team that focuses on balance and wellbeing, without compromising on taste or creativity. With a focus on sustainability for people and the planet, Kirk is becoming a leading figure in British plant-based cookery and is on a mission to improve chefs' wellness in the wider industry.

My cooking style in a few words…

I usually just say 'vegetable cookery' because that's fundamentally what it is. About 90% of what we cook with is organic, because I think you've got to commit everything you believe in and hope it pays off in the future. Who knows what it will be or how I might define it in five years' time though.

An ingredient or food I can't stand…

Gluten-free bread from the supermarket can be pretty awful – so heavy and stodgy – but that's kind of what Plates was inspired by. We want to serve people all the things that I have to eat but make them loads better. Gluten-free food can be great, it's just about finding the ingredients and techniques that work.

Something you probably don't know about me…

I've been doing jujitsu for about six months now, which I find is really good for my mental health. I used to do loads of running but I can't really do the crazy cardio stuff now. But if you do jujitsu, you feel like you can do anything – it's so hard! The discipline and constant failure have taught me a lot.

A bit of life advice…

Enjoy the present moment; you don't know what's around the corner. If you've got good health, that's the most important thing in life, that's all you need. You can't be happy without being healthy.

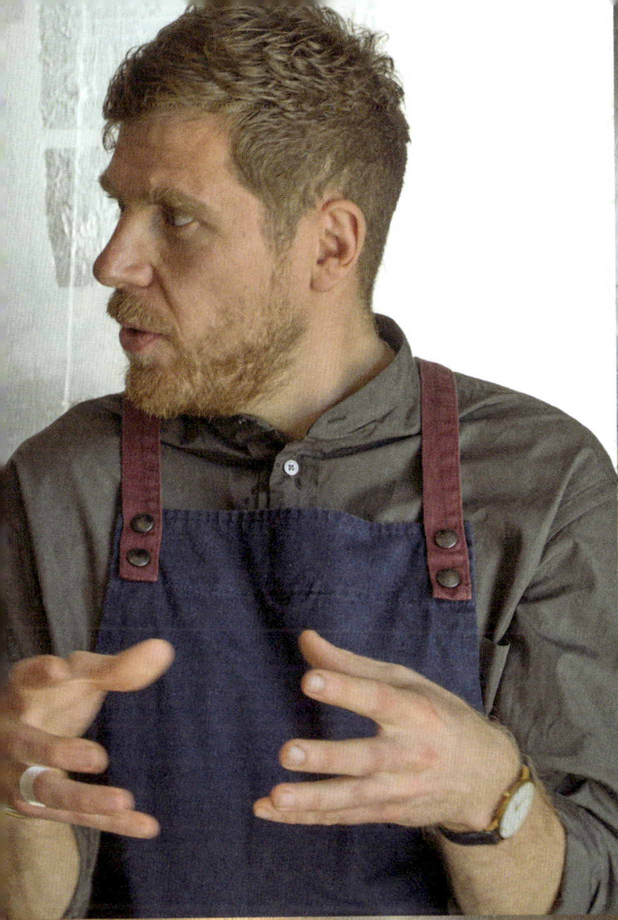
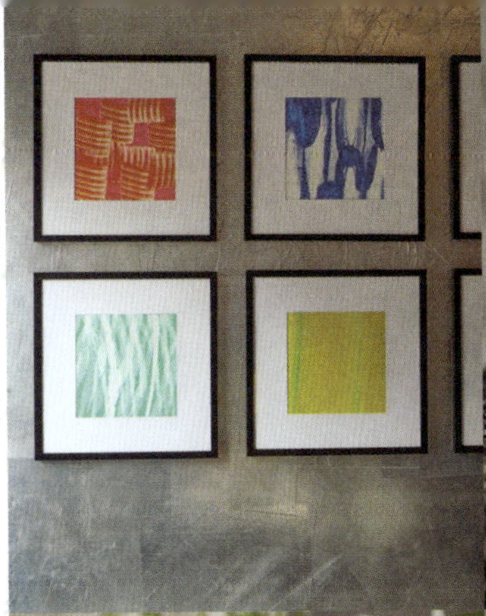
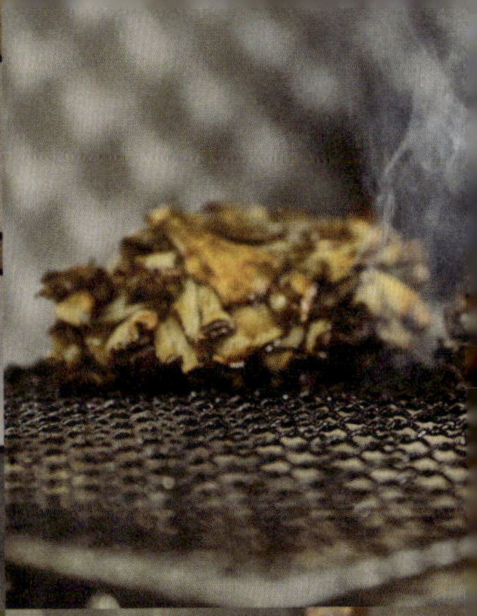
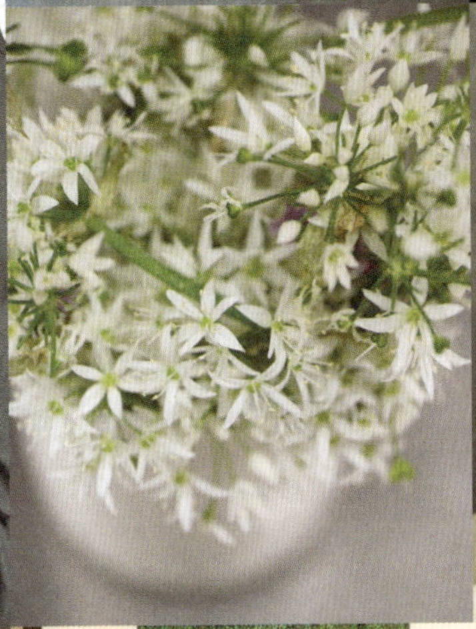
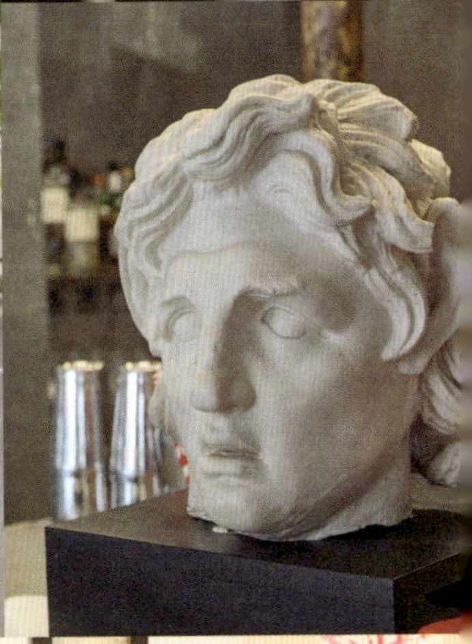
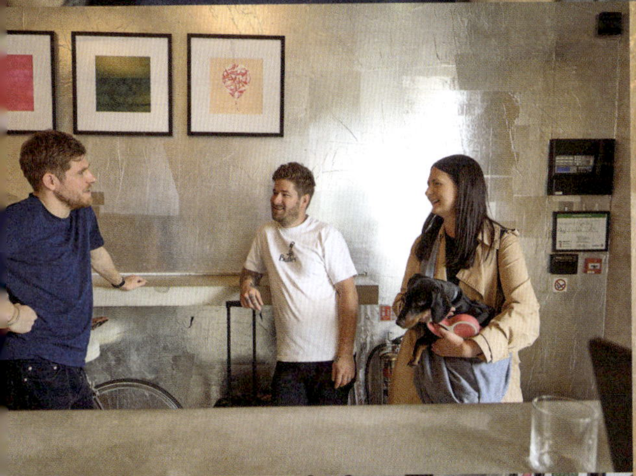
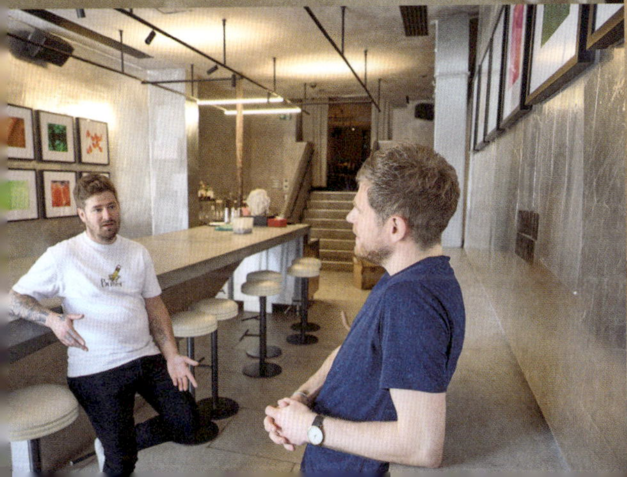
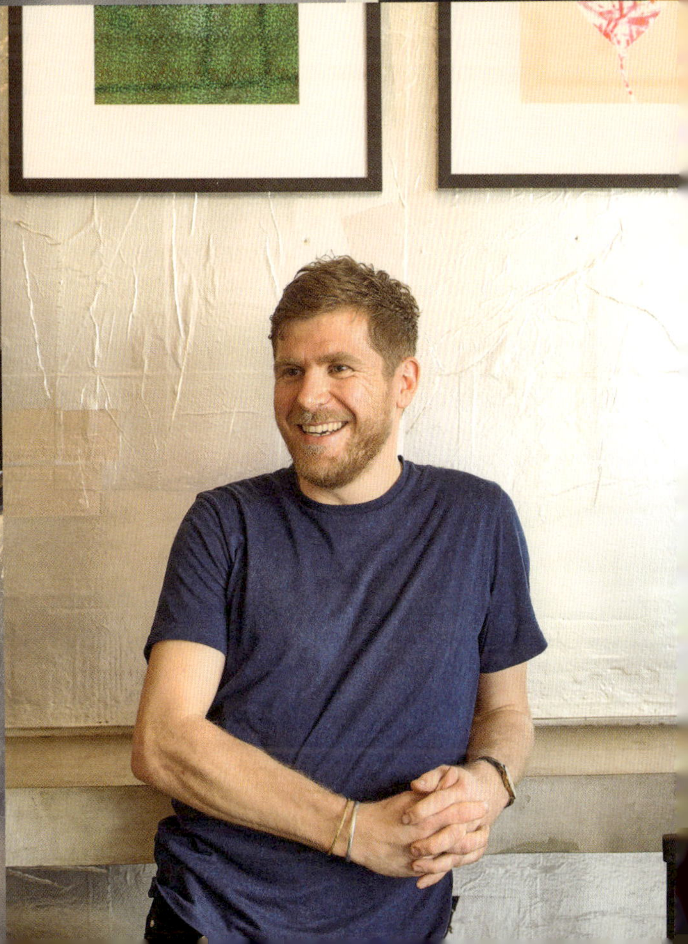

Plates, London

Lightly Smoked Tomatoes, House Ricotta, Beach Asparagus & Wild Garlic Soup

Preparation time: 24 hours | Cooking time: 30 minutes | Serves 2

FOR THE HOUSE RICOTTA
225g raw cashews, soaked overnight

375g water

1 acidophilus capsule or 1g mesophilic culture

10g transglutaminase

FOR THE WILD GARLIC SOUP
2 shallots, finely sliced

50ml olive oil

1 litre filtered water

1 organic vegetable stock cube

100g Maris Piper potatoes

175g wild garlic

FOR THE LIGHTLY SMOKED TOMATOES
Handful of mixed baby organic tomatoes, quartered (2 of each colour)

Handful of good quality meadow hay

Pinch of Maldon salt

10ml olive oil

FOR THE ASPARAGUS
6 spears of beach asparagus

500ml water

1 tsp Himalayan salt

1 tsp olive oil

TO SERVE
Garlic flowers

Chive flowers

Sea purslane

FOR THE HOUSE RICOTTA
Blend the soaked cashews and water together until smooth. Add the culture and blend, then add the transglutaminase and blend again. Pour the 'milk' into a container and cover the surface. Leave for a minimum of 10 hours, then strain through muslin overnight. Place the ricotta into a bowl and season with salt and olive oil to taste. Preserve the whey for other cooking techniques.

FOR THE WILD GARLIC SOUP
Sweat the shallots in the olive oil on a low heat for 20 minutes until tender and translucent. Add the water, stock cube and potatoes, then simmer until the potatoes are cooked through and soft. Put the wild garlic into a blender and pour the hot stock mixture over it, then blitz on high speed for 1 minute until smooth and bright green. Season to taste, then pass onto an ice tray to chill immediately so the soup retains its colour.

FOR THE LIGHTLY SMOKED TOMATOES
Place the tomatoes on a perforated tray with a lid. Put the hay into a large gastro container and set alight, then immediately place the perforated tray on top and leave the tomatoes to smoke for 20 minutes. Once smoked, season with Maldon salt and brush each tomato with good quality olive oil.

FOR THE ASPARAGUS
Bring the water and salt to the boil, add the asparagus and blanch for 15 seconds, then plunge into iced water. Drain and then dress the asparagus with olive oil and a pinch of salt.

TO SERVE
Place a generous spoonful of the house ricotta into a bowl and arrange the smoked tomatoes over and around it, using all the different colours. Lay 3 spears of asparagus around the edge of the bowl, then garnish with the flowers and sea purslane. Serve the wild garlic soup in a small jug on the side to be poured into the dish at the table.

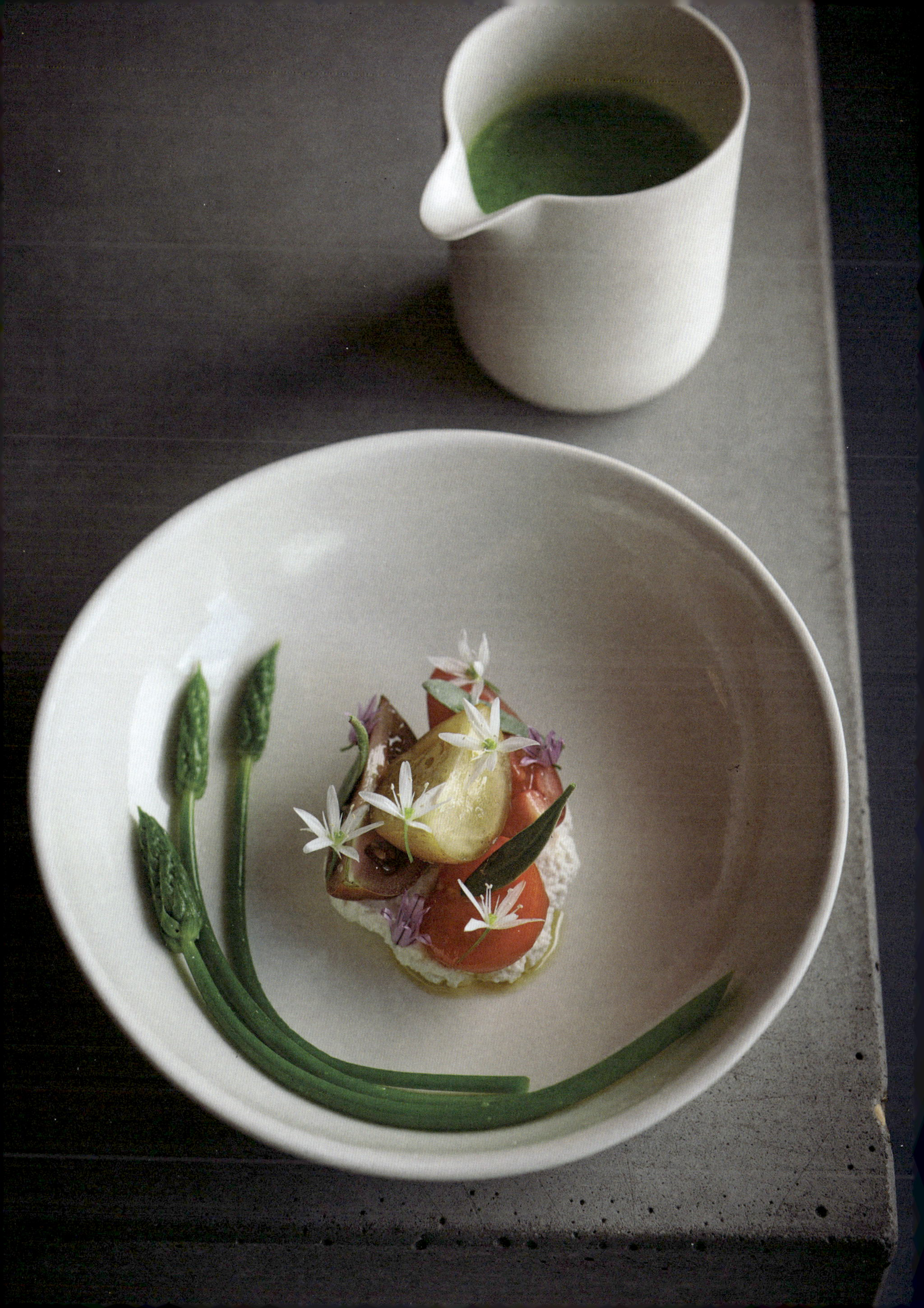

Plates, London

Smoked Maitake Mushroom, Artichoke Caramel, Black & White Rice

Preparation time: 5 days | Cooking time: 5 hours | Serves 2

FOR THE FERMENTED SHIITAKE
250g shiitake mushrooms, sliced
12.5g salt

FOR THE ARTICHOKE CARAMEL
2kg Jerusalem artichokes
10ml apple balsamic vinegar

FOR THE BLACK SILK SAUCE
125g raw black rice
1 tin of organic black beans
175g silken tofu
60g olive oil
50g brown rice miso
30g toasted sesame oil
Fermented shiitake juice, to finish
Pinch of xanthan gum
Salt, to taste

FOR THE PUFFED RICE
500g water
100g sushi rice
250ml sunflower oil

FOR THE STEAMED MAITAKE MUSHROOM
2 maitake mushrooms
25g meadow hay

FOR THE CHICKPEA MAYO (MAKES 6 SERVINGS)
80ml aquafaba (chickpea cooking water)
1 clove of garlic, roasted and puréed
Pinch of xanthan gum
150ml sunflower oil
60ml olive oil
1 tbsp lemon juice
1 tsp apple cider vinegar

FOR THE TOASTED KOMBU POWDER
2 sheets of kombu

FOR THE FERMENTED SHIITAKE
Mix the shiitake mushrooms and salt together in a bowl, vacuum pack and then leave out at room temperature for 5 days. Drain, reserving the fermented mushrooms and the liquid.

FOR THE ARTICHOKE CARAMEL
Wash the artichokes, leave the skin on, cut into quarters and put them through a juicer. Pour the juice into a large saucepan and then weigh the pulp, triple the quantity and weigh out that much water. Add the pulp and water to the pan of juice and bring to the boil. Take it off the heat and leave to infuse for 5 hours. Pass through a fine sieve, then reduce to a syrup consistency. Finish with the apple balsamic vinegar.

FOR THE BLACK SILK SAUCE
Add the rice to a pan with 1 litre of water and cook for around 4 hours on a medium heat until all the water has reduced, and the rice is super overcooked and porridge-like. Allow to cool for 1 hour. Drain the black beans and put them into a Thermomix with the remaining ingredients, including the cooled rice, and blitz on full speed for 10 minutes until super smooth and silky. Pass through a fine sieve and check the seasoning.

FOR THE PUFFED RICE
Bring the water to the boil and add the sushi rice. Cook for around 15 minutes until tender and then drain. Transfer the rice to a dehydrator tray and dehydrate at 60°c for around 2 hours until super dry. Heat the sunflower oil to 210°c in a large pan, add a handful of rice and stir for 2 seconds until the rice puffs up, then drain and place the rice onto a tray. Season with salt.

FOR THE STEAMED MAITAKE MUSHROOM
Steam the maitake mushrooms at 100°c for 6 minutes. Once out of the steamer, lightly season with salt while still warm. Smoke the mushrooms over the hay for 8 minutes and then allow to cool. Place on the barbecue and caramelise while brushing with the artichoke caramel.

FOR THE CHICKPEA MAYO
Place the chickpea water in the bowl of a KitchenAid mixer, add the garlic purée and xanthan gum, then start to whip up using the whisk until the mixture starts to come to a soft peak. Slowly start adding both oils, as you would for a mayonnaise. Once all the oil has been added and the mixture has a mayonnaise-like texture (firm but light), add the lemon juice and apple cider vinegar with a pinch of salt. Taste to check the seasoning, then store the mayo in a squeezy bottle.

FOR THE TOASTED KOMBU POWDER
Place the kombu sheets on a baking tray in the oven at 170°c for 10 minutes until toasted. Allow to cool and then blitz into a powder.

TO SERVE
Reheat the black silk sauce if needed, then spoon into a wide shallow bowl. Pipe the chickpea mayo over the barbecued maitake mushroom, then sprinkle with puffed rice to cover the surface. Place this in the centre of the bowl on top of the sauce and dust with the toasted kombu powder to finish.

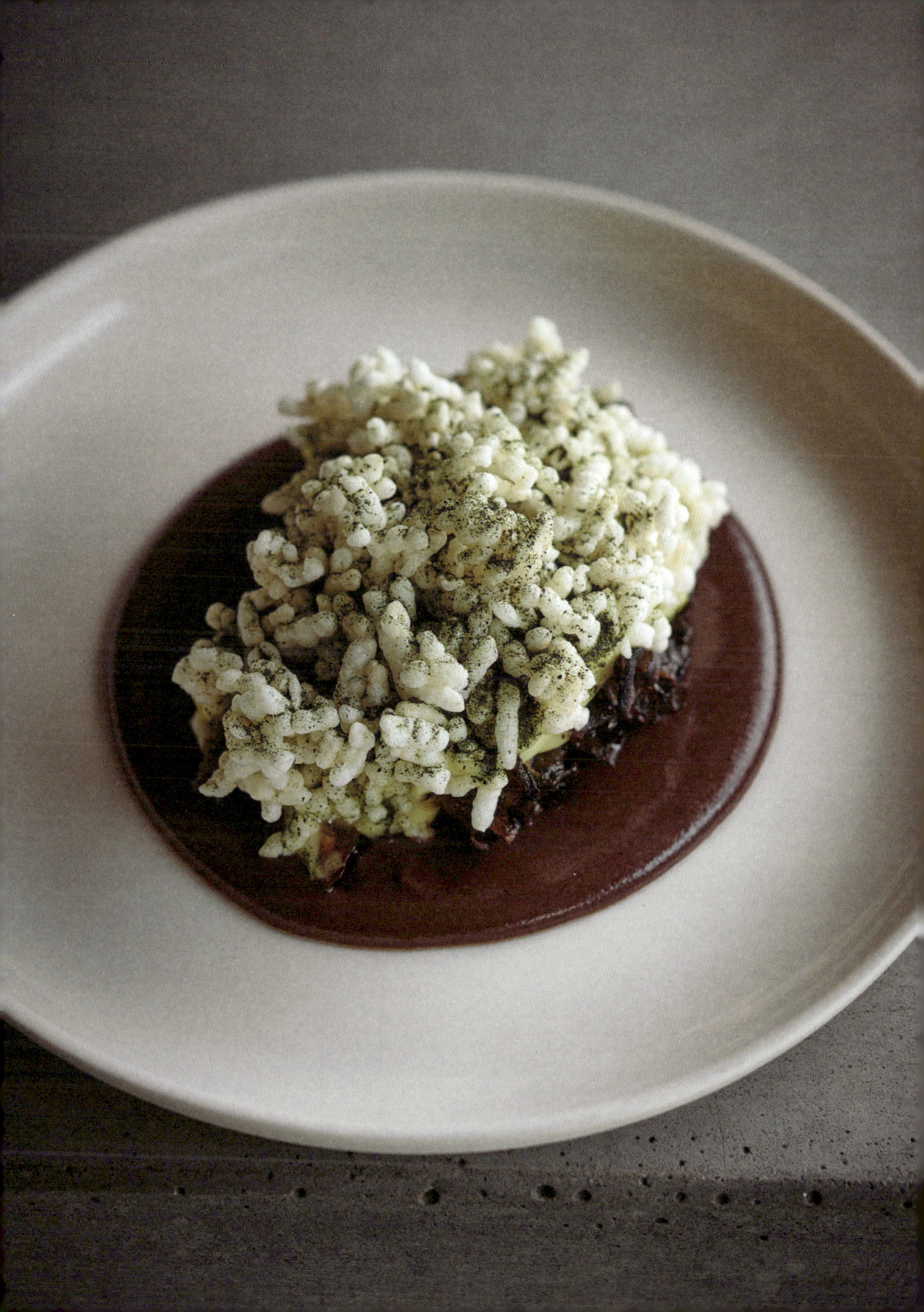

Plates, London

Rippled Rhubarb Sponge, Liquorice Custard, Wild Pine Oil

Preparation time: 1 hour 30 minutes | Cooking time: 1 hour 15 minutes | Serves 4

FOR THE RHUBARB COMPOTE
500g rhubarb

1 litre water

50ml verjus (I use Minus 8)

50g sugar

10g hibiscus

FOR THE RIPPLED SPONGE
120g gluten-free self-raising flour

1 pinch bicarbonate of soda

50g coconut sugar

20g cornflour

3 tbsp olive oil

3 tbsp agave syrup

1 tbsp lemon juice

1 tsp fresh vanilla or essence

220ml coconut milk

FOR THE COCONUT AND LIQUORICE CUSTARD
400ml organic coconut milk

1 tbsp agave syrup

2 sticks of liquorice root, crushed

1 tsp juniper berries, crushed and roasted

2 star anise, crushed

1 tbsp cornflour

1 tbsp water

FOR THE PINE OIL
50g fresh Douglas Fir pine

150ml sunflower oil

150ml olive oil

FOR THE RHUBARB COMPOTE
Cut the rhubarb into 0.5cm pieces. Combine the water, verjus, sugar and hibiscus in a medium pan and bring to a simmer. Leave this to infuse for 10 minutes, then pass the liquid through a fine sieve and add the rhubarb. Gently poach the rhubarb for 15-20 minutes until just tender, then strain. Reduce the rhubarb liquid down to a syrup before adding the cooked rhubarb back in.

FOR THE RIPPLED SPONGE
Mix the dry ingredients together, then add the olive oil, agave syrup, lemon juice and vanilla. Slowly add the coconut milk while mixing with a spatula, then with a whisk until very smooth and shiny. Add one large spoonful of the batter to 4 small individual cake moulds, add a teaspoon of the rhubarb compote, then fill to the top with more batter. Bake in the oven at 160°c for 4 minutes, then turn the tray and bake for another 4 minutes.

FOR THE COCONUT AND LIQUORICE CUSTARD
In a small pan, bring the coconut milk, agave syrup, liquorice, juniper and star anise to a simmer, then take off the heat and leave to infuse for 1 hour. In a small bowl, mix the cornflour and water to form a loose paste. Put the coconut infusion on the heat and slowly whisk in the cornflour paste. Continue whisking over a medium heat for 5 minutes until the custard has slightly thickened.

FOR THE PINE OIL
Add the ingredients to a blender and blitz on high speed for 6-8 minutes until the pine and oil have emulsified. Pass through a fine sieve and place in a squeezy bottle.

TO SERVE
Reheat the custard if needed and spoon some into the centre of a plate or shallow bowl. Place the warm rhubarb sponge on top, then drizzle the pine oil around the sponge over the custard.

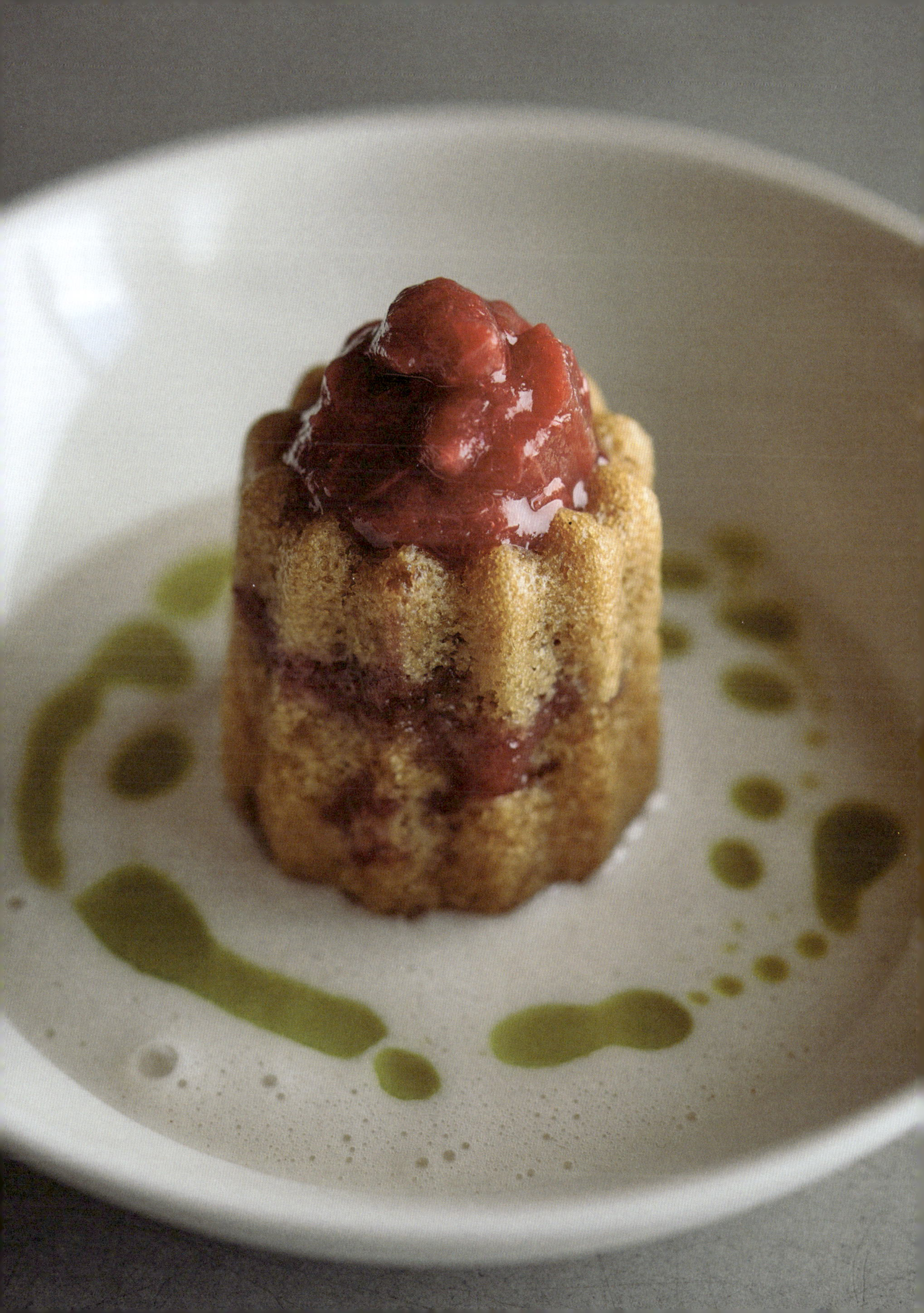

Plates, London

Recipe Notes

LIGHTLY SMOKED TOMATOES, HOUSE RICOTTA, BEACH ASPARAGUS & WILD GARLIC SOUP

I use a mix of seasonal organic tomatoes for this dish, which are cut up and put on a perforated tray with really good meadow hay smoking underneath. Simple but effective.

Our 'house ricotta' is made with cashew milk and what chefs usually call 'meat glue' (transglutaminase) to curdle it. As the name suggests, meat glue would normally be used when butchering a piece of lamb down, for example, so you can take out all the sinew and other bits you don't want, use the glue to stick it back together, then let it set and it's like you never opened the lamb up in the first place.

The leftover 'whey' from the ricotta process is something we're keen to experiment with – the acidic flavour from the culture isn't dissimilar to the whey you get from dairy cheese.

SMOKED MAITAKE MUSHROOM, ARTICHOKE CARAMEL, BLACK & WHITE RICE

Maitake mushrooms are also known as 'hen of the woods' and they have quite a meaty texture and flavour. We brush them with an incredible smoked vinegar while barbecuing.

The black silk sauce for this recipe was developed at an event I went to which was sort of a 'chef raffle' where you get paired up to cook with someone. I was paired with a Korean chef and had to create something inspired by his country's cuisine, so we decided to celebrate rice and developed this sauce which uses rice that's cooked for about 5-6 hours until it's very overdone and soft, which allows it to be blended down to form an incredibly silky sauce.

RIPPLED RHUBARB SPONGE, LIQUORICE CUSTARD, WILD PINE OIL

Did you ever used to have jam sponge at school, a big square of it, with that thick yellow custard? This is a modernised version. It's got to be on the menu, especially in winter. We use an old-school fluted mould shape in miniature for the sponge as a nod to its origins.

The sponge should be warm and the custard should be hot, though occasionally we serve it with ice cream. The poached rhubarb really cuts through the creaminess of either accompaniment.

Sometimes we do a winter version of this dish, with a berry compote instead of the rhubarb. Raspberry essence is the secret weapon in that one: huge flavour in a tiny spoonful.

There's no need to pick the Douglas Fir for the oil – just blend it up, woody bits and all. There's great flavour in the bits we chuck away sometimes.

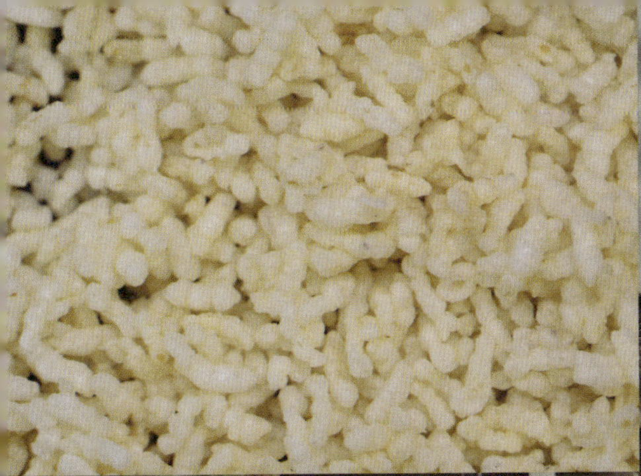
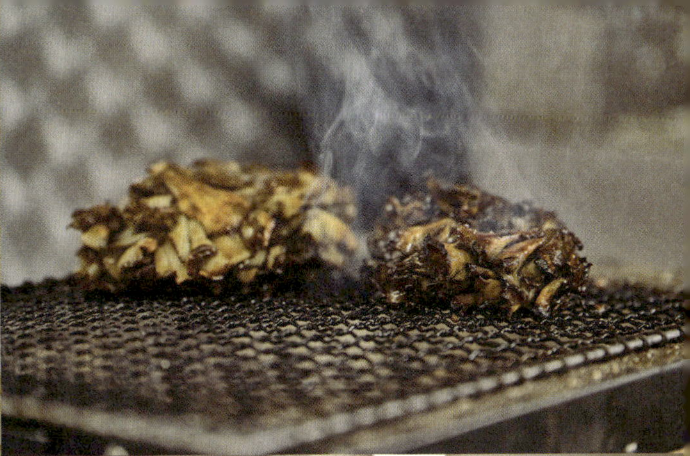
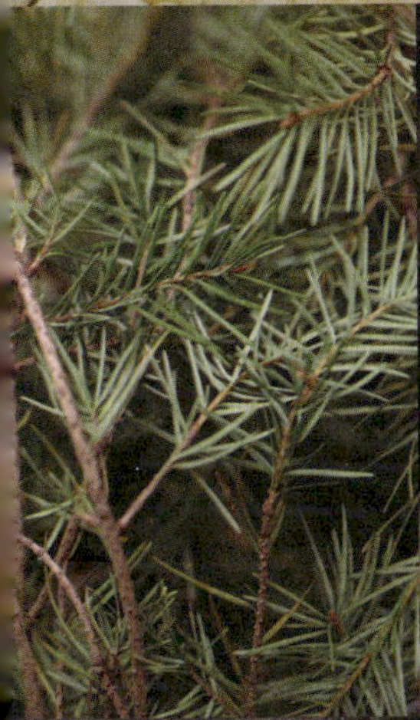
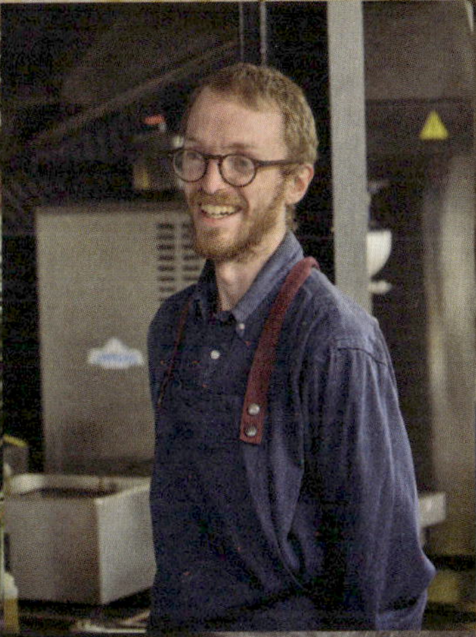
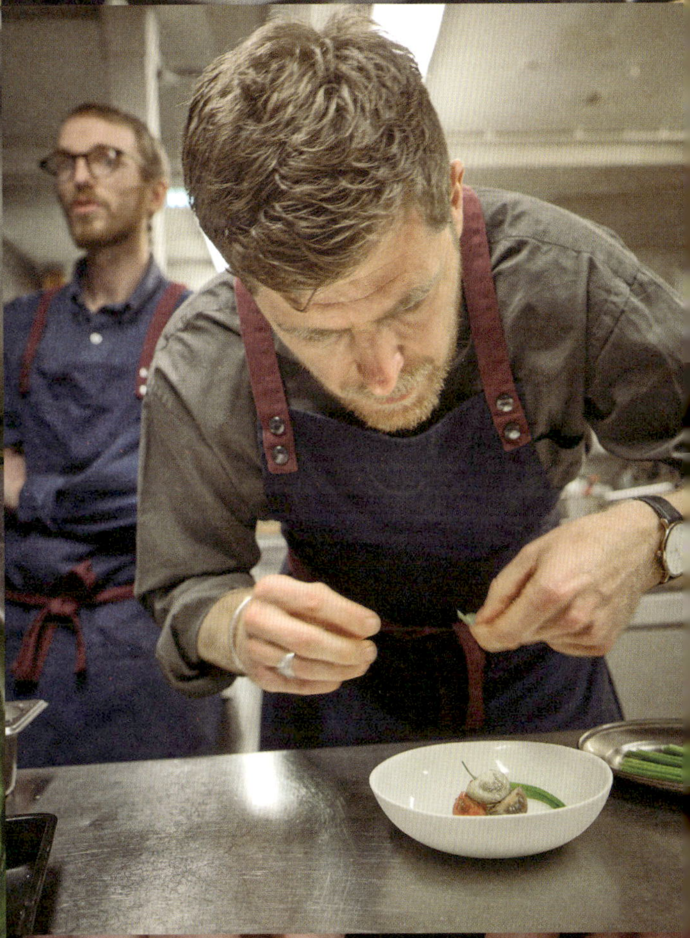
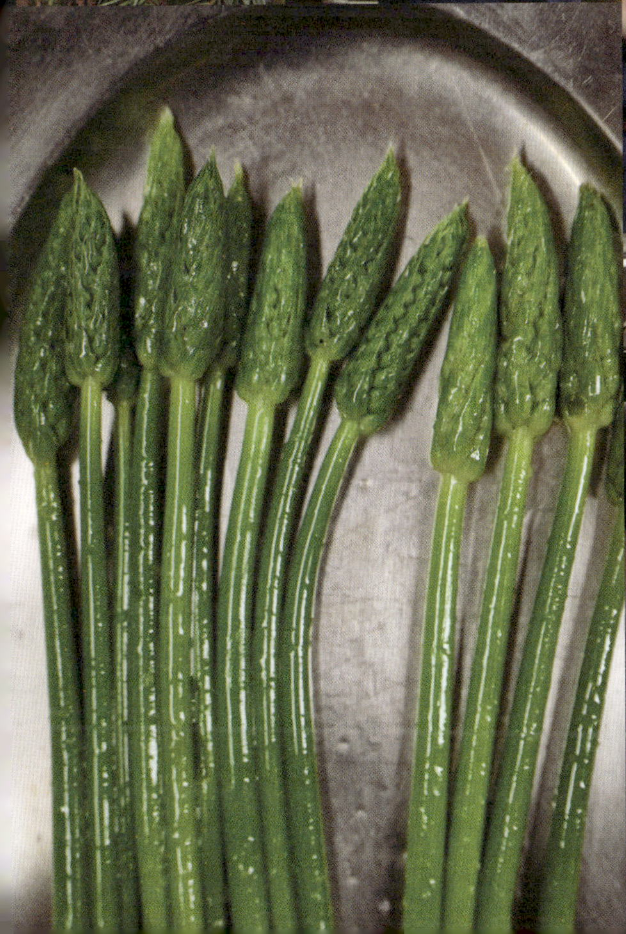
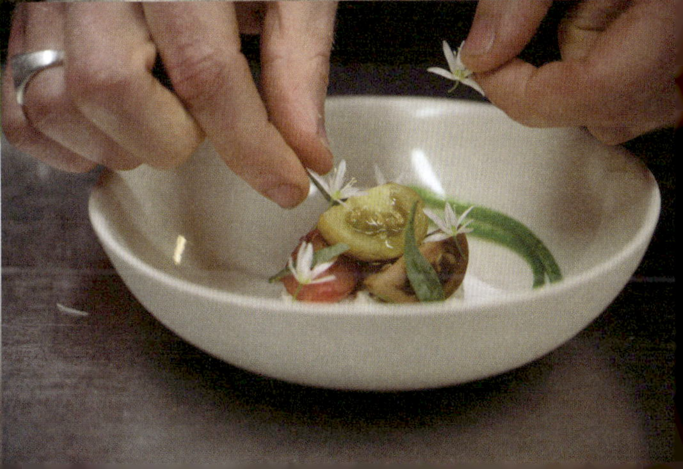

Plates, London

Q&A with Kirk Haworth

Where does your creativity come from as a chef?

In essence the creativity comes from being so restricted in the way I cook, but I'm also a big believer in questioning everything and I spend a lot of time researching plants as I'm fascinated by their medicinal properties. I find that cooking without any dairy or protein – the 'usual' stuff that I used to cook all the time – makes you think so much more. It's a lot more experimental and exciting because I find myself doing stuff that I've never done before. I think if I was doing what I did before I went through my health challenges, I'd probably just be blending in and my food style wouldn't be as unique and personal.

So is Plates a vegan restaurant?

Yes it is, but I don't really describe my cooking as 'vegan' because I'm not really a fan of labels. We should just celebrate everyone for what they're doing. The ethos of what I'm trying to do is to make food that you shouldn't question, so there's no need to say 'where's the meat' or feel like something's missing. 90% of people who eat here at Plates aren't actually vegan and I am trying to create a genre of cooking that's inclusive for everyone.

What surprises or excites you about cooking?

Six years ago when I started on the path of plant-based eating, the first ground-breaking thing for me was cooking without butter and it still tasting delicious! For years I'd been cooking turbot with lots of foaming butter and of course it's delicious – I'd never doubt that – but there's another form of deliciousness over here that also needs to be appreciated. If we look at different oils and cooking techniques, we can create something just as tasty and exciting.

Do you ever feel restricted by only working with plant-based ingredients?

Initially it was so hard to create plant-based dishes and I remember feeling very stuck, but I just kept going and working at it until I got some breakthroughs. Now I feel I've got a certain way I look at ingredients to build an exciting and delicious dish. Occasionally there are things that we can't make a success of, but what it does lead to is all these other ingredients you never knew about – we've got pumpkin seed flour now, for example – and they create a new world of cooking that you never knew existed, because you're forced to look in different places. That's what I find interesting. Sometimes I scour Instagram for small producers and suppliers to see if they can come in with samples. You need that motivation and inspiration because some days your head gets overwhelmed and it can be tiring, but failure and limitation are a driving force in a lot of my most successful ideas.

Do you have any advice for others in the industry?

Food's an opinion and some people aren't going to like everything you do: we have to accept that. In my twenties I used to worry sometimes about what people thought and I'd never say confident things about myself. We should say what we want to be, and what I've realised is that if someone's got a problem with that it's their issue, not yours, so keep believing in your vision and dream. My biggest advice is to focus on yourself and don't be scared to fail because it's all part of the journey. I don't think chefs give themselves enough credit sometimes – you're putting your heart and soul on the line every single time you send out a dish, so be proud. There's so much talent and innovation in our generation, and we're also changing how we look after staff and speak to each other for the better.

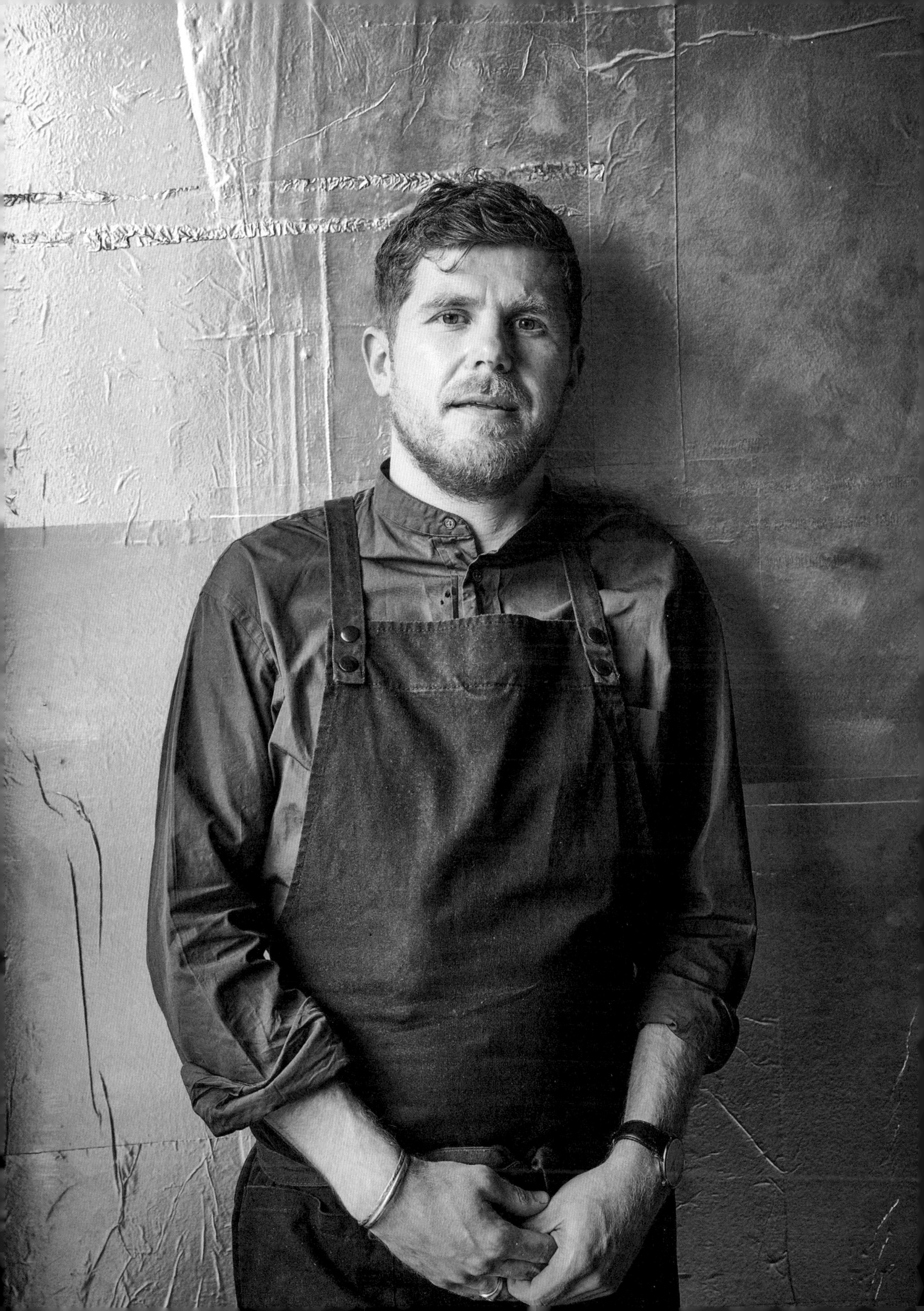

Lee Westcott

Lee Westcott grew up in Hertfordshire and began his career working for the Galvin brothers in London. He then spent four years leading the kitchen as head chef at Restaurant Tom Aikens and also staged at Noma in Denmark and Per Se in New York during that time. Lee was then asked by Jason Atherton to oversee two of his restaurants in Hong Kong, which gave him another platform to develop his own cooking style. On his return to the UK, Lee established the Typing Room Restaurant in London's Town Hall Hotel in Bethnal Green to critical acclaim. The next phase of his culinary career took him to the countryside, where Lee opened Pensons and took full advantage of the local produce as well as the resources to grow some of their own ingredients. Within seven months, the restaurant was awarded a Michelin star among many other accolades. As of 2022, Lee has moved back to the city to focus on his next project.

Tell us about…

Your next steps.

There's nothing concrete yet so I can't say too much, but I have a new concept I've been working on for a while now which will hopefully be opening in the near future – it's just about picking the right time and finding the ideal site.

Your style of food.

I would describe it as British seasonally focused. We are incredibly fortunate to have such amazing produce at our disposal here in the UK and I believe in letting the seasons determine what goes on the plate. We have some of the best ingredients in the world available to us and for me, it's about simply elevating those products by doing as little to them as possible. First and foremost, food must be delicious and to achieve that I really focus on the balance of flavours and textures in each dish. Using foraged ingredients also plays a big part in my cooking approach as I think it adds unique flavour profiles.

The piece of kitchen equipment you couldn't live without.

A spoon. I'm pretty sure I have a spoon in my hand about 90% of the time that I'm in the kitchen. I'm constantly tasting, plating or dressing something. On the other hand, a knife is also a fairly useful tool to have in a kitchen. It's a tough one.

Your signature dish.

It's always evolving but I've had this bread on at both my restaurants and still do it now – it's a sourdough made from IPA and apple juice, served with Marmite butter and roasted yeast. That's become a firm favourite with everybody.

Your influences or inspirations.

The seasons have a big influence on the menu ethos. Seeing what my other chef pals and peers are up to in the industry is also a big influence and an inspiration.

What drives you as a chef.

Putting a smile on a guest's face. Also, teaching and educating the young talent. Cooking is all about bringing people together with great hospitality, having a fun time and feeling fulfilled!

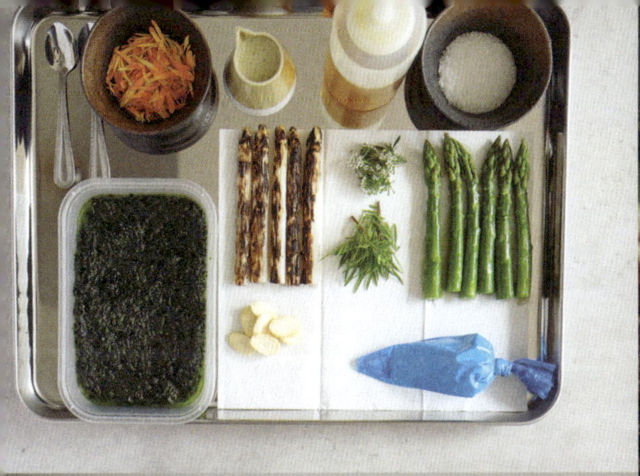
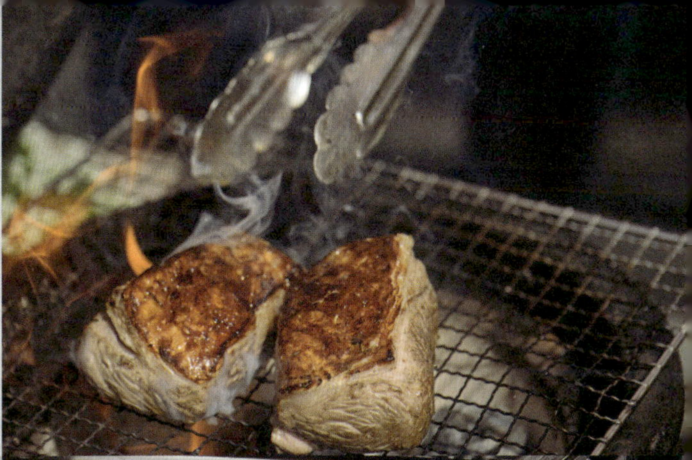
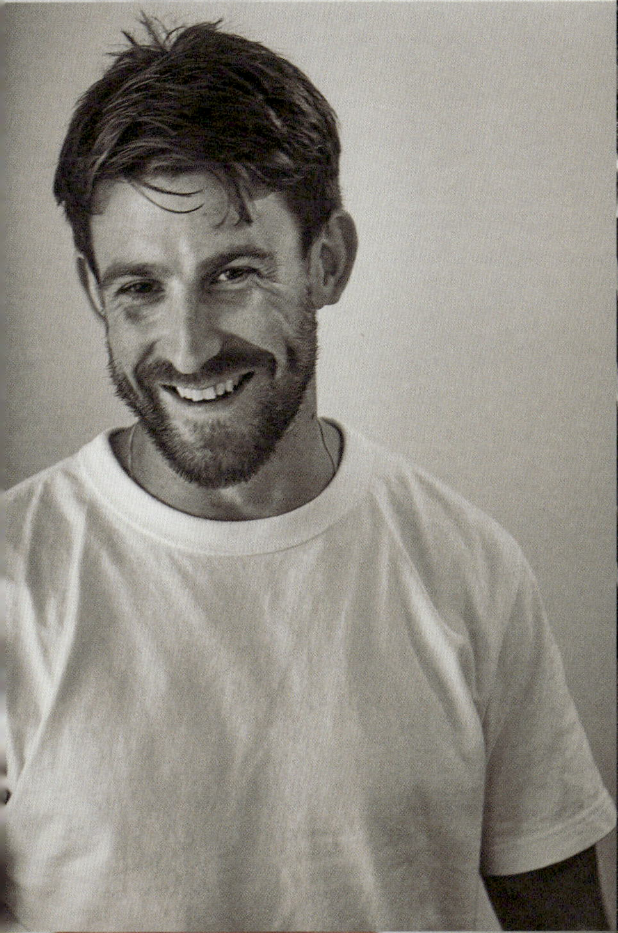
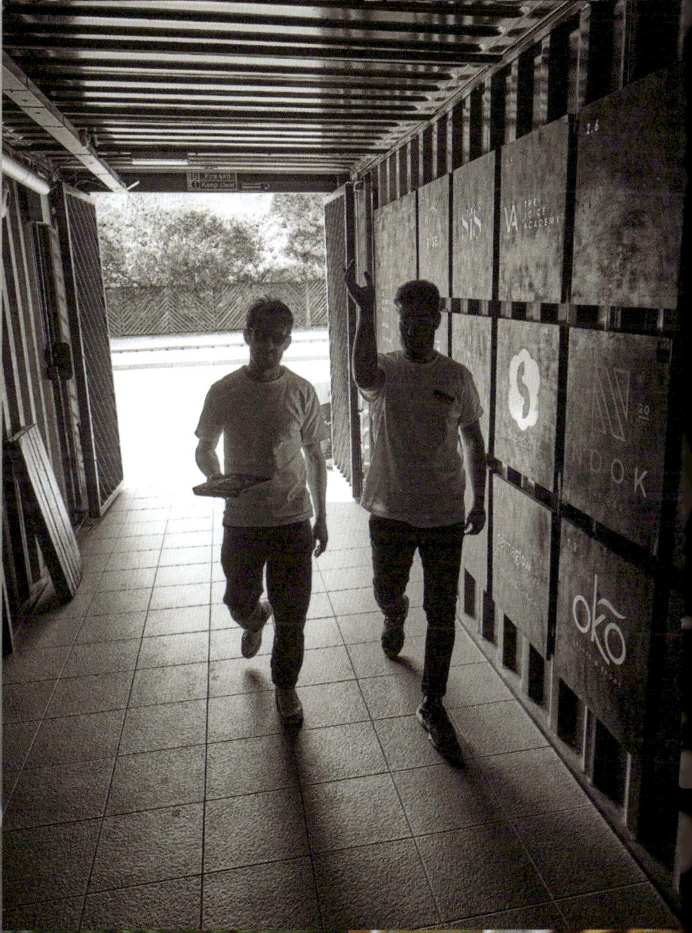
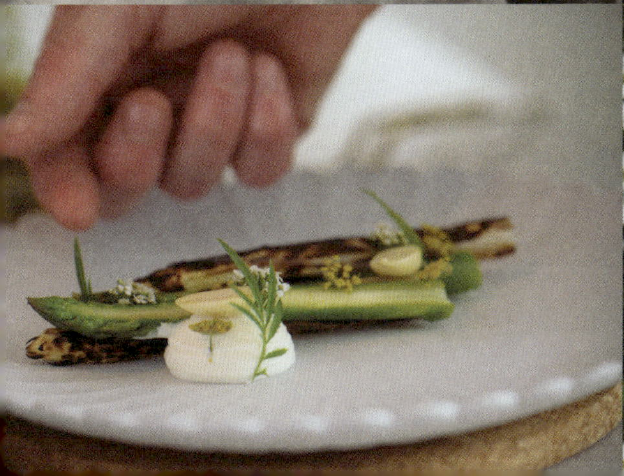
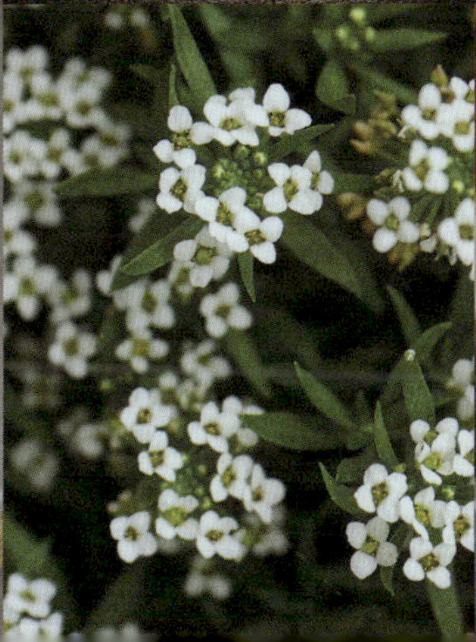
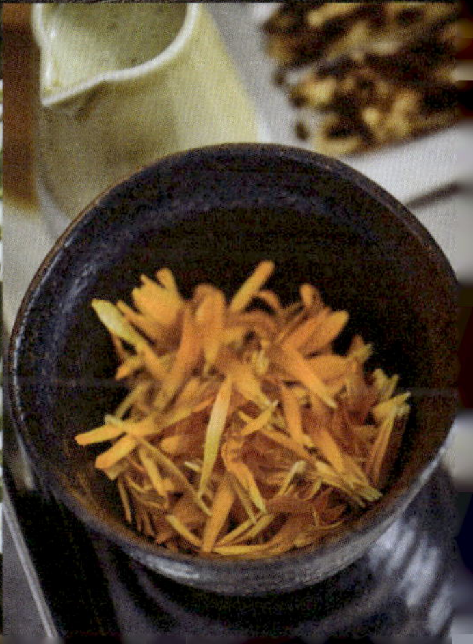

Asparagus, Chamomile, Ricotta and Almond

Preparation time: 8 hours | Cooking time: 30 minutes | Serves 2

FOR THE ASPARAGUS
4 spears of green asparagus, medium thickness, preferably British

4 spears of white asparagus, medium thickness, preferably British

FOR THE CHAMOMILE OIL
100g fresh or dried chamomile buds

300g vegetable oil

FOR THE KALE PESTO
125g curly green kale

¼ bulb of garlic, peeled and micro planed

10g macadamia nut, lightly toasted and micro planed

70ml cold pressed rapeseed oil

FOR THE ALMOND SAUCE
60g flaked almonds

210g natural Greek yoghurt

200g seedless white grapes

120ml almond milk

10g lemon juice

8g picked fresh mint leaves

Pinch of xanthan gum

½ clove of garlic, peeled and finely chopped

Salt and muscatel vinegar, to taste

FOR THE RICOTTA
760g unpasteurised whole milk

12g white wine vinegar

12g lemon juice

2g Maldon salt

1g citric acid

TO SERVE
8 fresh green almonds in the husk or 8 fresh English cobnuts

Marigold shoots, fennel pollen and alyssum flowers

FOR THE ASPARAGUS
Remove an inch from the bottom of each green asparagus spear and discard. Now remove the scaly-looking parts down the length of the asparagus using a small paring knife. Leave the tops intact. Blanch the spears in boiling salted water for 1 minute 30 seconds and then plunge them into iced water. Once cold, drain well and keep in the fridge on kitchen paper until needed.

Remove 1.5 inches from the bottom of each white asparagus spear and discard. Now peel each spear from the tip to the base. A blunt peeler is ideal for this. Now it's time to barbecue the white spears. Drizzle them with a little rapeseed oil and season with fine salt. Place these onto a hot barbecue and grill, turning continually, until they are just cooked and nicely charred all over.

FOR THE CHAMOMILE OIL
Place the chamomile buds and vegetable oil in a vacuum pack bag, seal and then place in a water bath overnight or for 8 hours at 60°c. In the morning, remove the bag and let it cool to room temperature, then place it into the fridge. This is best done well in advance of when you wish to use the oil. Pass the infused oil through muslin when needed.

FOR THE KALE PESTO
Blanch the kale for 3-4 minutes in boiling salted water. Refresh in iced water and squeeze out all the remaining water. Roughly chop through the kale and place it into the blender, then add the garlic and macadamia nut. Blitz this slowly in a blender while adding the oil until it's all bound together nicely. Season to taste with fine salt.

FOR THE ALMOND SAUCE
Toast the flaked almonds in the oven at 150°c for 8 minutes. Blend everything together in the blender until the mixture is very smooth. Do not blend it for too long though as it may go brown. Once smooth, pass the sauce through a chinois over an ice bath. Check the seasoning and adjust if needed with salt and muscatel vinegar.

FOR THE RICOTTA
Bring the milk up to 82°c in a saucepan, ensuring you do not allow it to catch on the bottom. Take the pan off the heat, add the remaining ingredients and quickly stir well. Now leave it undisturbed for 30 minutes, to allow the curds to form at the top.

Carefully pass the solids off through a cheesecloth, reserving the whey. Now allow the curds to continue to drain in the fridge for 1 hour. Blend the ricotta solids until smooth and season to taste with Maldon salt, lemon juice and some of the whey if needed. It should be a thick consistency and be able to hold itself on a plate.

TO PREPARE THE FRESH GREEN ALMONDS OR COBNUTS
Using a hammer, gently but firmly crack the husk and inner shell of the almonds. Using your hands, carefully break apart the husk and shell to reveal the almond inside. Be careful to keep the nut intact and whole. Discard the husk and inner shell. Using a small paring knife, carefully peel the outer skin/membrane off each nut. Now split each nut into two halves. You can do this by gently inserting the tip of a paring knife into the natural groove between the two halves and prising them apart.

TO SERVE
Place a small spoonful of the ricotta at the top of your plate. Using two spoons, place a quenelle of the kale pesto to the right of the ricotta. Dress all the asparagus with chamomile oil and season with Maldon salt. Now arrange your green and white asparagus in between the ricotta and pesto. Place the almonds or cobnuts on and around the asparagus, followed by your foraged marigold, fennel and alyssum. Now pour your almond sauce into a jug and serve.

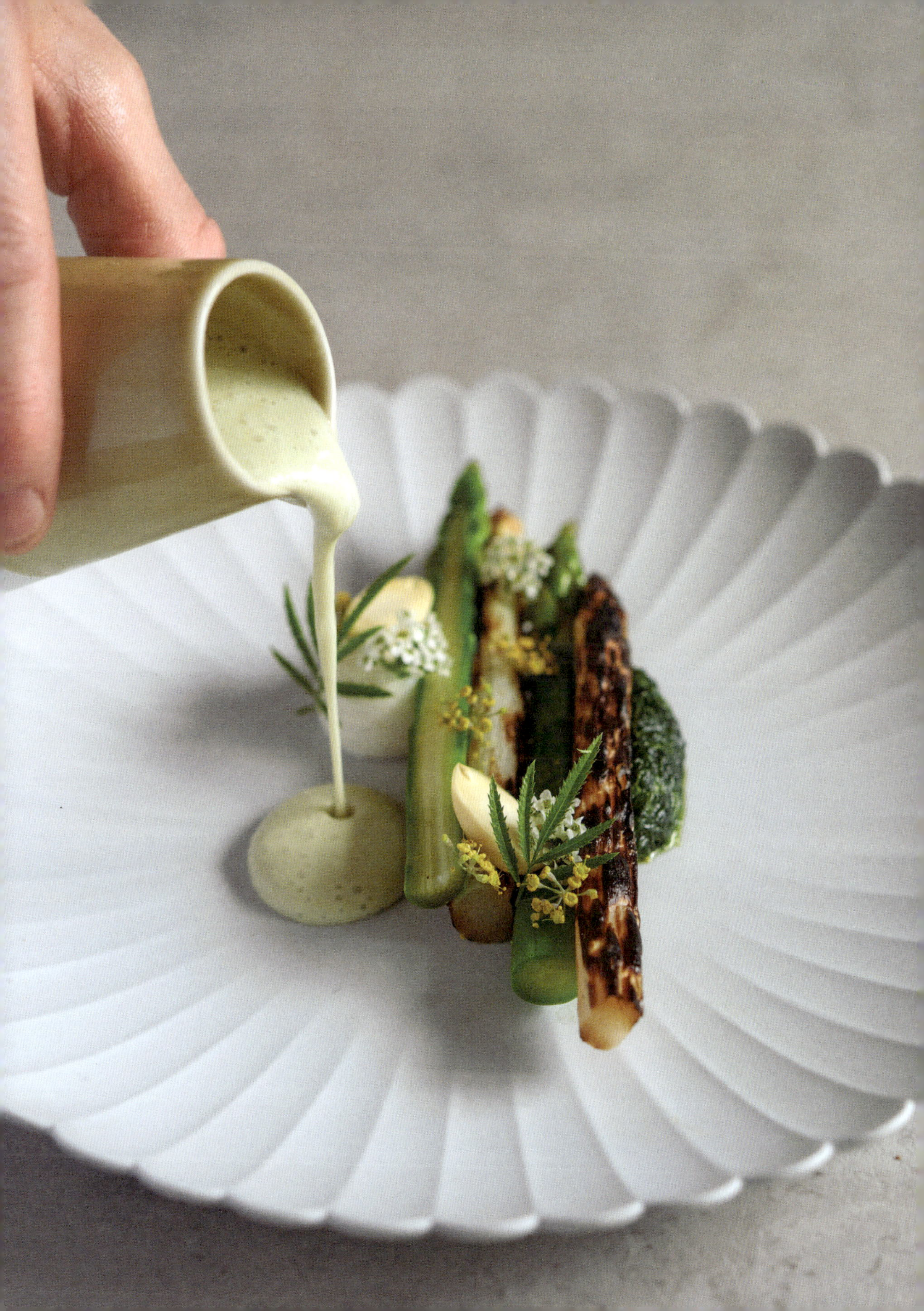

Lamb, Yoghurt, Sweet Pea, Girolles and Black Garlic

Preparation time: 4 days | Cooking time: 1 hour | Serves 2

FOR THE MARINATED LAMB
1 lamb rump, around 250g
400g natural Greek yoghurt
5 cloves of garlic, peeled and sliced
Large handful of chopped fresh thyme
Large handful of chopped fresh rosemary
Pinch of fine salt

FOR THE YOGHURT PURÉE
300g natural Greek yoghurt

FOR THE GIROLLES
80g girolles, trimmed and washed
15g butter, diced
Maldon salt

FOR THE BLACK GARLIC PURÉE
10g agar agar
500ml cold water
75g peeled black garlic
Soy sauce, to taste
Sherry vinegar, to taste
Salt and sugar, to taste

FOR THE GREEN OLIVE SAUCE
100g pitted green olives
50ml white chicken stock
50ml brine
10ml lemon juice
25ml rapeseed oil

FOR THE MARINATED LAMB
Air-dry the lamb rump on a rack in the fridge (without cling film) until the bark is dry. Remove the bark along with any fat if too thick. Combine the yoghurt, garlic, herbs and salt in a large bowl until well mixed, then spread this marinade over the lamb rump until coated. Place into a vacuum pack bag, seal tightly, then leave to marinate for 4 days.

Remove the lamb from the marinade and rub as much yoghurt off as you can using your hands, then a kitchen towel. Vacuum pack the lamb tightly and cook at 56°c for 40 minutes. Once cooked, remove from the water bath and air dry on a resting rack for 10 minutes. Once the course before the lamb dish goes, slowly render the fat of the rump, then quickly sear the meat all over. Add butter, thyme and garlic to baste (fat side down) until cooked pink. Rest the lamb, fat side down, until ready to carve.

FOR THE YOGHURT PURÉE
Hang the Greek yoghurt in muslin overnight with a bowl underneath to catch the liquid. Place the hung yoghurt into a bowl, add a little of the whey back into it and whisk until smooth and the correct consistency is achieved. Season with fine salt to taste.

FOR THE GIROLLES
Pan fry the girolles in the butter and season with salt. Drain on kitchen paper and then cut in half.

FOR THE BLACK GARLIC PURÉE
Whisk the agar agar into the water and cook out on the stove, bringing it to the boil while whisking. Pour this onto a tray and place in the fridge until completely set. Chop the jelly roughly and place half into the Thermomix blender along with the black garlic. Add soy sauce, sherry vinegar, salt and sugar to taste, then blend until smooth. Pass, chill and place into a small squeezy bottle.

FOR THE GREEN OLIVE SAUCE
Blitz together the olives, chicken stock, brine and lemon juice until smooth. Emulsify with the rapeseed oil, then pass through a fine sieve and season with fine salt if needed. Place into a saucepan and heat until warm.

Lamb, Yoghurt, Sweet Pea, Girolles and Black Garlic

Preparation time: 4 days | Cooking time: 1 hour | Serves 2

FOR THE SORREL AND MINT DRESSING
100g large sorrel leaves
20g picked mint leaves
60ml cold-pressed rapeseed oil
20ml white wine vinegar
Fine salt and sugar, to taste

FOR THE CONFIT SHALLOT AND PEAS
2 medium banana shallots, peeled and finely diced
200ml vegetable oil
3 sprigs of thyme
1 clove of garlic
400g fresh young peas in their pods

FOR THE WILD GARLIC OIL
100g wild garlic
150g vegetable oil

TO SERVE
Pea shoots and chickweed

FOR THE SORREL AND MINT DRESSING
Blitz the sorrel, mint, oil and vinegar in a blender until you have a coarse dressing. Season with salt and sugar, then store in the fridge until needed.

FOR THE CONFIT SHALLOT AND PEAS
Place all the ingredients except the peas into a small saucepan and gently cook on the stove for 15 minutes, or until the shallots are nice and tender.

Remove the peas from their pods and when ready to plate, cook in boiling salted water for 30 seconds to 1 minute. Drain well and mix with the confit shallot and some of the sorrel and mint dressing. Season with fine salt.

FOR THE WILD GARLIC OIL
This recipe will make more than you need but the oil is very useful for adding to many other dishes. Place the wild garlic and vegetable oil into the Thermomix and blend on full power for 2 minutes. Turn the heat setting on to 85°c and blend for 8 minutes, then turn the heat setting off and blend for a further 2 minutes on full power. Place the mixture into an ice bath and chill down until very cold. Hang in muslin cloth overnight with a bowl underneath to catch the oil.

TO SERVE
Place a small spoonful of the hung yoghurt onto the plates and make a small hole in the centre. Add some of the black garlic purée into the hole. Garnish with a few pea shoots and chickweed leaves. Carve the lamb into two even slices and place onto the plates, followed by a nice spoonful of the pea, sorrel and shallot mixture. Next, arrange the girolles on your plate and finish with the green olive sauce poured into the centre, followed by a drizzle of the wild garlic oil.

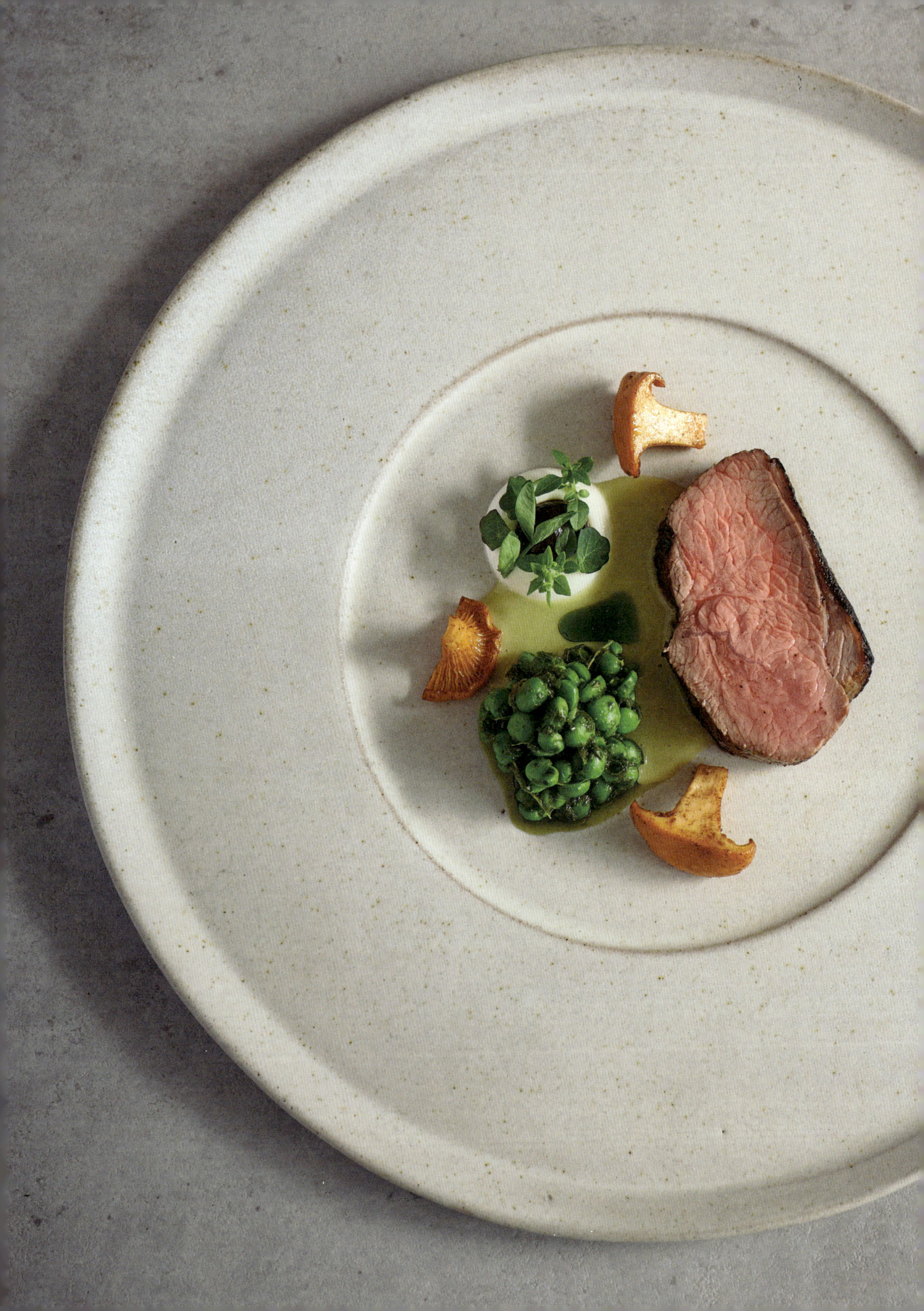

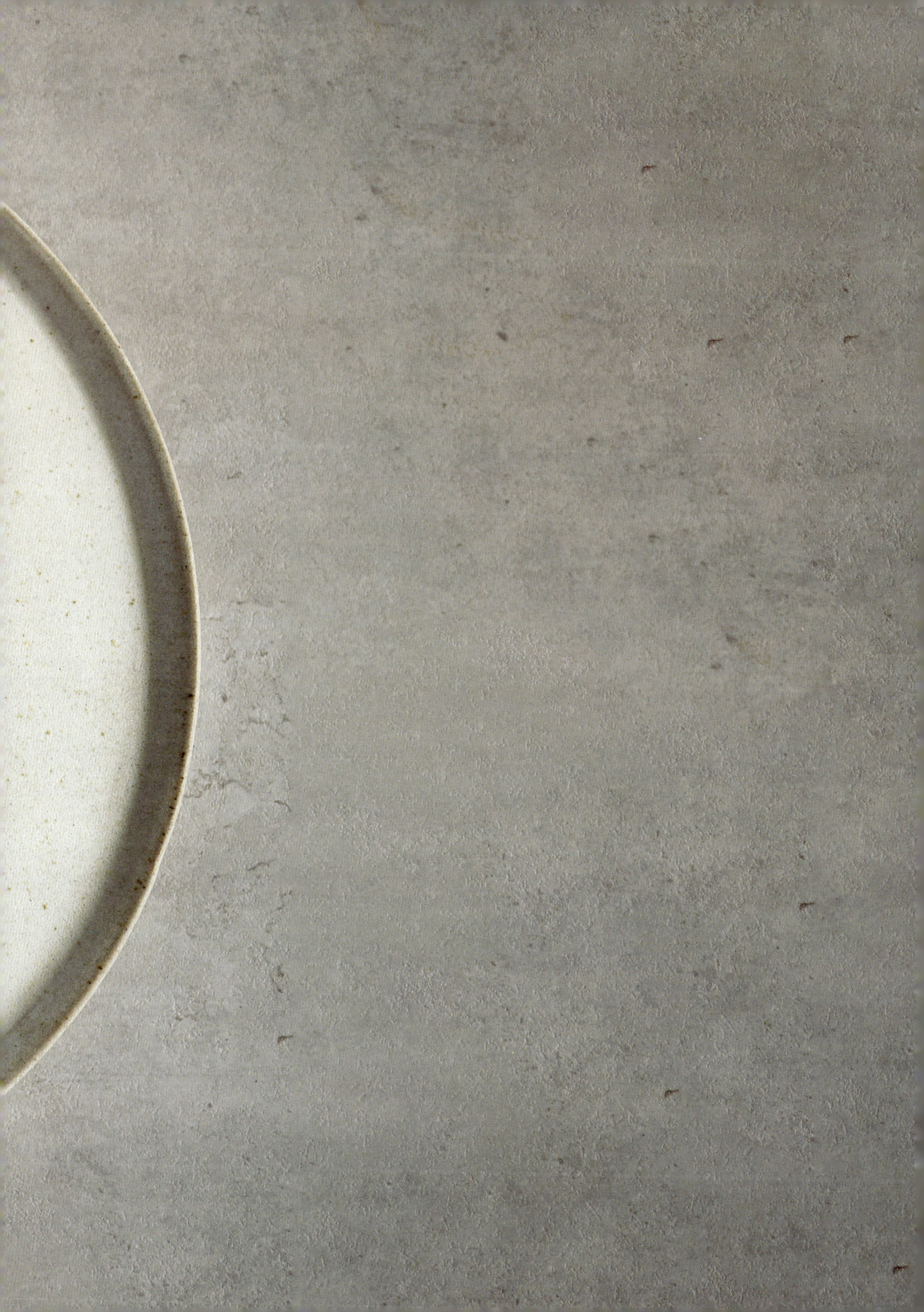

Slow-Braised Lamb Shank Cooked in Tomato, Herbs and Spices

Preparation time: 1 hour | Cooking time: 5 hours | Serves 2

1½ tsp cumin seeds

1½ tsp fennel seeds

1½ tsp coriander seeds

2 lamb shanks, approx. 420g each

300g carrot, peeled and cut into roughly 1cm pieces

300g onion, peeled and cut into roughly 1cm pieces

4 cloves of garlic, peeled and chopped

6 sprigs of thyme, leaves picked (discard the stalks)

2 sprigs of rosemary, leaves picked (discard the stalks)

2 bay leaves

40g tomato purée

2 tbsp plain flour

150ml white wine

150ml red wine

½ tin of chopped tomatoes

500ml white chicken stock

Vegetable oil

Salt and pepper

FOR THE MASH

560g potatoes, peeled, washed and cut into roughly 2cm pieces

120g butter, room temperature

75g semi-skimmed milk, warm

FOR THE LAMB SHANK

Preheat your oven to 180°c. Place the cumin, fennel and coriander seeds into a small piece of muslin cloth and tie them up in a little bundle so they cannot escape, then set aside.

Put a casserole pot on the stove over high heat. This pot needs to be able to go into the oven, have a lid and be big enough to fit the lamb shanks into. Once the pan is slightly smoking, add a drizzle of vegetable oil, then add your lamb shanks and season well with salt and pepper. Colour the lamb shanks well all over, then transfer to a plate and set aside. Do not discard the oil in the pot.

Turn the heat down to medium and add the onions, garlic, thyme, rosemary and bay. Season with a little salt and cook for 4 minutes, stirring occasionally. Add the carrot and cook for another 4 minutes, stirring occasionally. Add the bundle of cumin, fennel and coriander seeds in the cloth.

Add the tomato purée and cook it for 2 minutes, stirring occasionally. Add the plain flour, mix well and cook for 1 minute. Add the white wine and red wine next, letting the liquid reduce by half before adding the chopped tomatoes and chicken stock. Mix well.

Gently place your lamb shanks back into the lovely tomato stock. There should be at least a 1cm gap between the surface of the stock and the top of your casserole pot, to ensure it won't spill over. Place the lid on your casserole pot and carefully place it into the preheated oven. Cook the lamb at 180°c for 30 minutes, then turn the oven down to 160°c and cook for 2 hours 30 minutes. After this time, double-check that it's cooked before turning your oven off. To do this, transfer one of the shanks from the pot onto a plate. Using a fork, make sure the meat moves from the bone with complete ease. If it doesn't, put it back into the stock and cook for a further 30 minutes, or until done. Once cooked, remove from the oven and allow the shanks to rest in the sauce for 20 minutes.

Carefully remove the shanks from the sauce. At this stage, the sauce should be ready to go, but if you want to correct the consistency by either reducing it more or adding a touch of water, you can. Once you're happy, check the seasoning and adjust accordingly. I left everything in the sauce except the cloth bundle with the seeds (I suggest not passing the sauce through a sieve).

FOR THE MASH

Place the potatoes into a saucepan and cover with cold water. Season with fine salt. Bring up to the boil and turn down to a gentle simmer. Simmer the potatoes until they are fully cooked. This means that they break apart easily when you put a fork in them but are not mushy. Drain in a colander and leave to dry out for 2 minutes.

Place the potato back into the pan and gently warm it up, then add the butter. Using a handheld masher, mix and mash the potato for a good 2 minutes. Gradually add the warm milk using a spatula and once all the milk has been added, mix the potato very well, beating it slightly. Season with fine salt. Pass the mash through a fine mesh drum sieve. I used a plastic scraper to do this.

Heat your mashed potato back up. At this stage, I cooked some sliced spring greens in boiling salted water to accompany the dish. Now it's time to plate. First, a nice pile of the silky potato goes on, then place your lamb shank on top, followed by the sauce and greens. Enjoy!

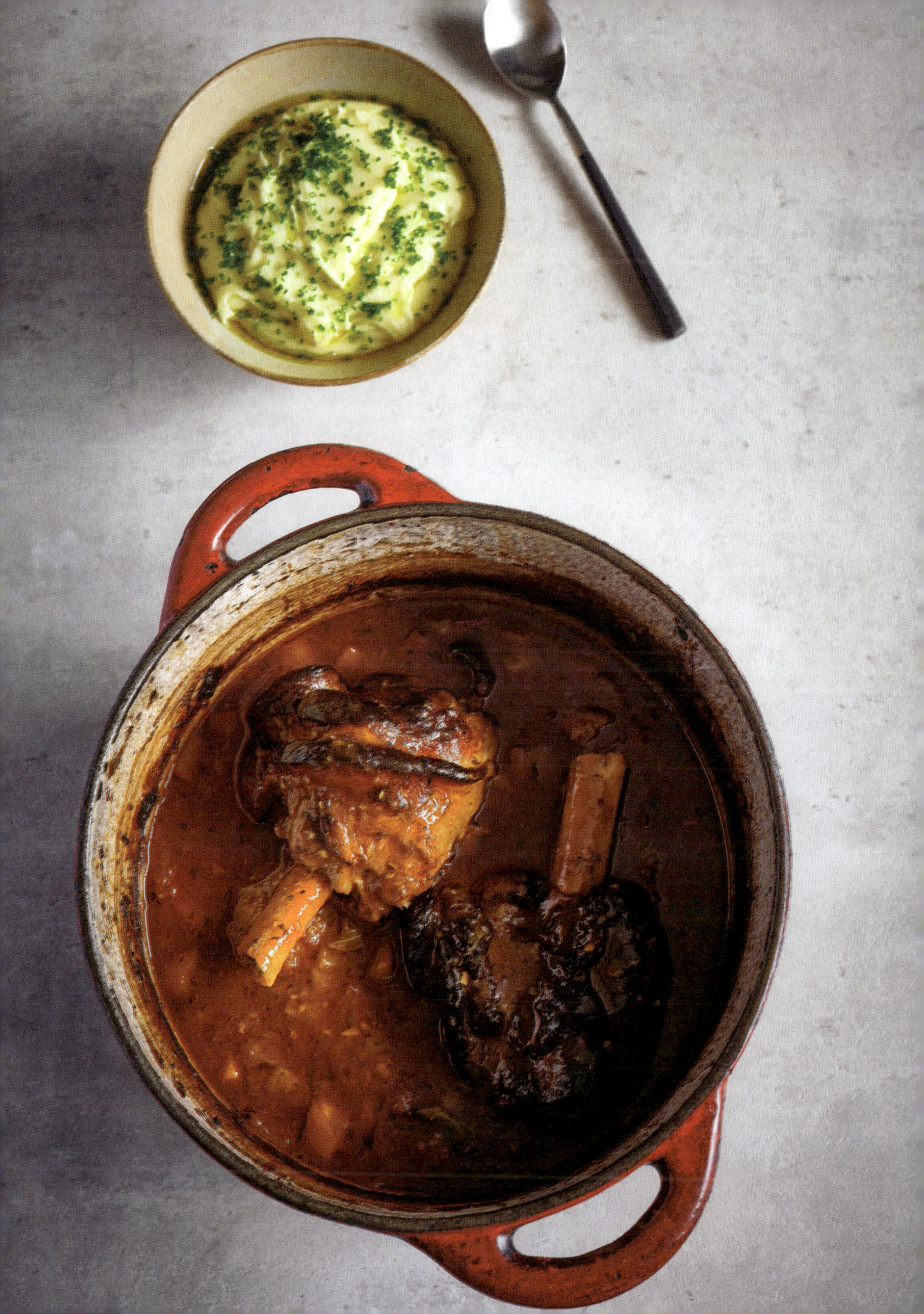

Kitchen Q&A

ASPARAGUS, CHAMOMILE, RICOTTA AND ALMOND

What inspired this combination of flavours?

My cooking approach is based on the British seasons – I really focus on using what's at its absolute peak at that current time. This dish is a true reflection of that and this one is all about spring. Asparagus has quite a short season, so like most other chefs, I take full advantage of it while it's around. Asparagus pairs well with something fresh and creamy and that's where the ricotta comes into its element. I've used both white and green asparagus because I think they both add different contrasts in flavour and texture to the dish. The almond sauce adds a fresh nutty note to the dish, while the chamomile oil brings the dish to another level with a beautiful floral element. Chamomile can be a little hard to forage as it's quite difficult to find, but if you do manage to find some it's definitely worth picking and trying out the oil recipe.

Why make the ricotta yourself rather than source it?

Wherever possible, I prefer to make things myself from scratch. I guess it's the old-school chef mentality kicking in, but I also find a real sense of satisfaction in making ricotta. I think the homemade version tastes fresher, and I also like to use the by-product in other dishes as I have a big no-wastage policy. Turning the whey into an emulsion is a great way of utilising the by-product and creates such a delicious product to cook vegetables in.

What do the green almonds or cobnuts bring to this dish?

On this occasion we decided to use fresh English cobnuts due to the green almonds going out of season a tad earlier this year. Cobnuts are a bit like an English hazelnut. The nut adds freshness and texture to the dish which pairs well with the ricotta and chamomile. You can adjust the recipe and use either the almonds or cobnuts, depending on what you can get hold of or prefer to use.

LAMB, YOGHURT, SWEET PEA, GIROLLES AND BLACK GARLIC

What do all the different processes for the lamb rump do to the end result?

Lamb rumps require a little more work than a prime cut of meat would. Each of the steps in the lamb prep is vital in achieving a tender, flavourful, juicy piece of cooked meat. First, the lamb is marinated in flavourful yoghurt for two to four days. The natural acidity in the yoghurt slightly brines the meat, while the garlic, fresh thyme and rosemary adds a real depth of flavour. Barbecuing the lamb brings a smoky element to the dish, then using a water bath to cook the lamb ensures it stays nice and tender. Finally, by pan frying the lamb in foamy brown butter with garlic and thyme, you get that perfect finish.

Are any of the ingredients in this dish foraged, like the wild garlic?

Yep. I also foraged the fennel pollen in London the day before the shoot. It's in abundance in spring! The wild garlic was foraged and made into the oil a few weeks before. The great thing about wild garlic is when you find a spot where it grows, you will nearly always find lots more in the surrounding area. Grab as much as you can, process and store it for the seasons ahead. It's a great way to add a garlicky element to most savoury dishes throughout the year.

How does seasonality and availability affect this dish?

This dish can be easily modified to suit most seasons. Lamb, yoghurt and black garlic are ingredients that are available all year round, so the base of the dish is there; you would just need to change the peas to an alternative seasonal vegetable. Spring lamb is my preferred choice as it's extremely tender and has a milder flavour than other lamb.

SLOW-BRAISED LAMB SHANK COOKED IN TOMATO, HERBS AND SPICES

Is lamb shank another underused cut and what makes it right for this dish?

Lamb shanks used to be widely used. There was a time when it was on every menu! But not so much these days; it's underused in the restaurant realm. Shanks are perfect for this recipe as you could scale this up quite easily to feed a fair few people. It's also a fair bit cheaper than the prime cuts.

When would you cook this at home?

Most probably on a Sunday. I love a Sunday roast dinner, but they can be a little heavy as late Spring kicks in. This dish is a great one-pot wonder, which requires minimal washing up.

How would you make a white chicken stock at home?

I would take chicken carcasses and place them into a large saucepan, cover them with water and bring to the boil. Skim off any fat that rises to the top, then add lots of chopped vegetables, herbs and spices and gently simmer for 2-3 hours. Pass it through a fine sieve and you're away.

Kitchen Confidential

Where did it all start for you as a chef?

I fell into the trade to begin with. Started washing up while working alongside my brother, then decided that I wanted to pursue cooking as a career and found myself in London doing exactly that. Hospitality is a great community to meet all walks of life and to get out there and see the world. I wanted to be involved in a profession that felt like something that was always growing and evolving.

Which restaurant or stage in your career has been most inspiring?

The stage I did at Noma changed my whole approach to cooking at that time. The restaurant really inspired me to learn so much about the foraging aspect of the dishes there, which allowed me to bring that into my own style. It was a fundamental point of what they were trying to achieve, and I think most chefs who went there learnt a lot from that. Tom Aikens has to get a shout here too as he is one of this country's best talents and cooking alongside him was fundamental to any success I've had in my career.

What cuisines do you like to draw from in your own cooking?

French was the base of my cooking education, so that is still the base of most things I cook. I like that classic element to the dishes. I am really getting into spice recently, so I'm dabbling with that a little more. Nordic cuisine is obviously a firm favourite.

How much does sustainability determine your style of food?

Low wastage is a big priority – you've just got to be a little bit inventive about how you can turn potential waste products into something else. Fermenting, pickling, making oils and vinegars: anything that involves thinking ahead of time so you create products that can be used for the months ahead. Eating and cooking seasonally really does reduce the carbon footprint and lends itself well to utilising the British seasons, which is a big part of my approach.

What do you wish you'd known when you launched your first restaurant?

Probably just how much harder it was going to be than I originally thought – it's always a chef's dream to open a restaurant and you kind of forget how much work it's going to be. You have to become more than just a chef, learning as you go and almost splitting yourself into 20 different people to manage all the different aspects of running a restaurant. My advice to people starting out in the industry is always the same: don't try to progress too quickly and learn all the skills of your trade as there really is nowhere to hide when you're opening a restaurant of your own.

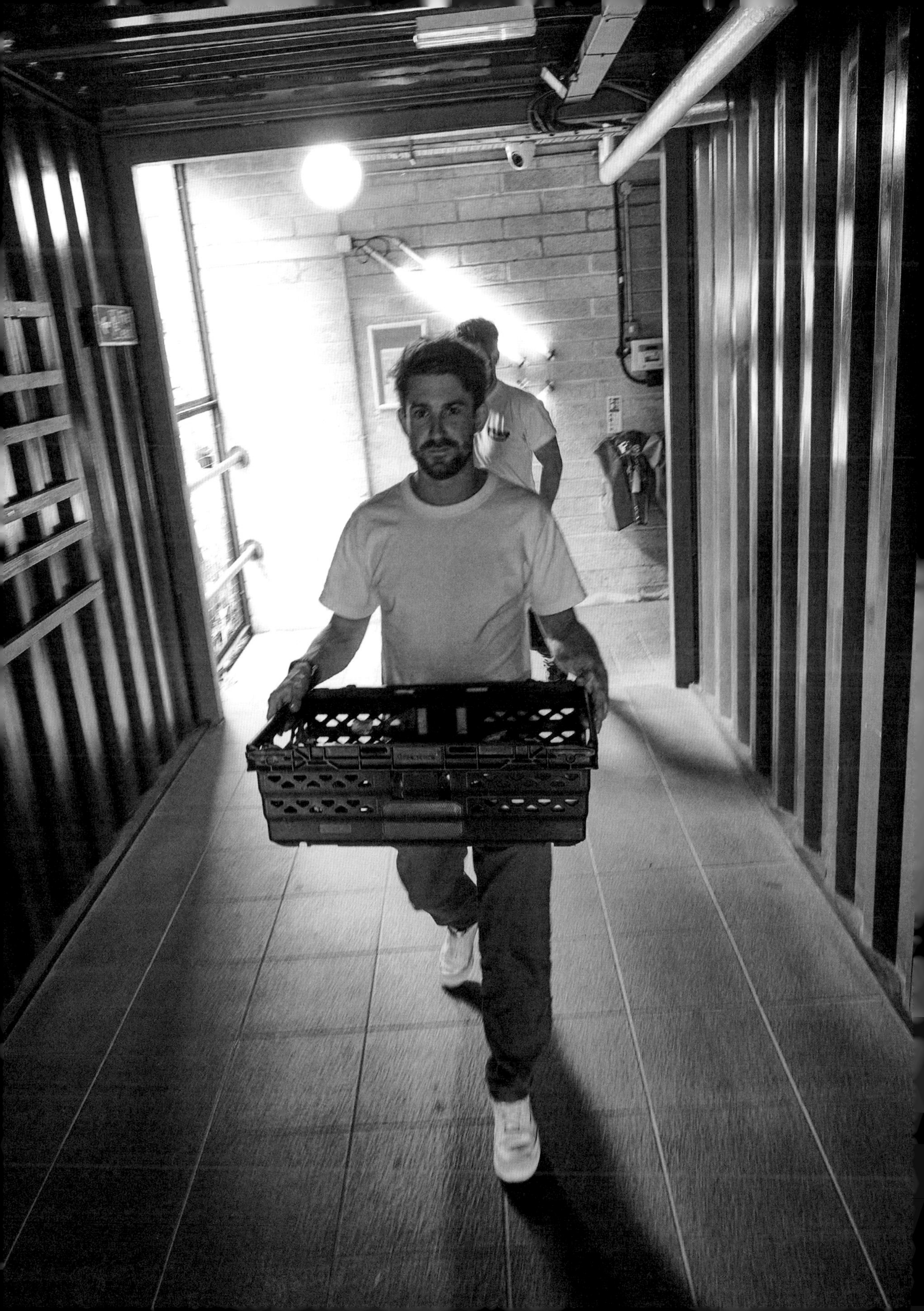

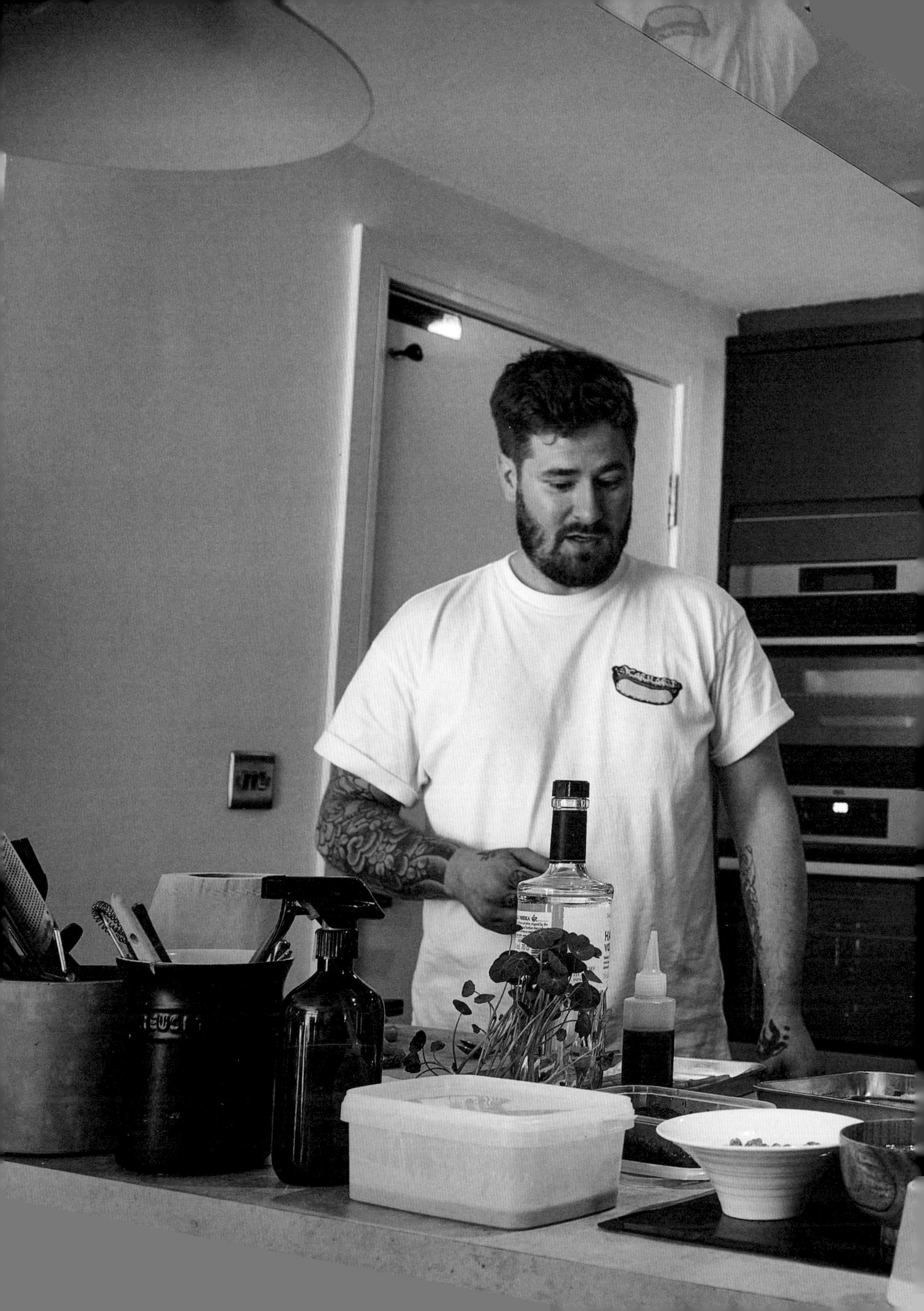

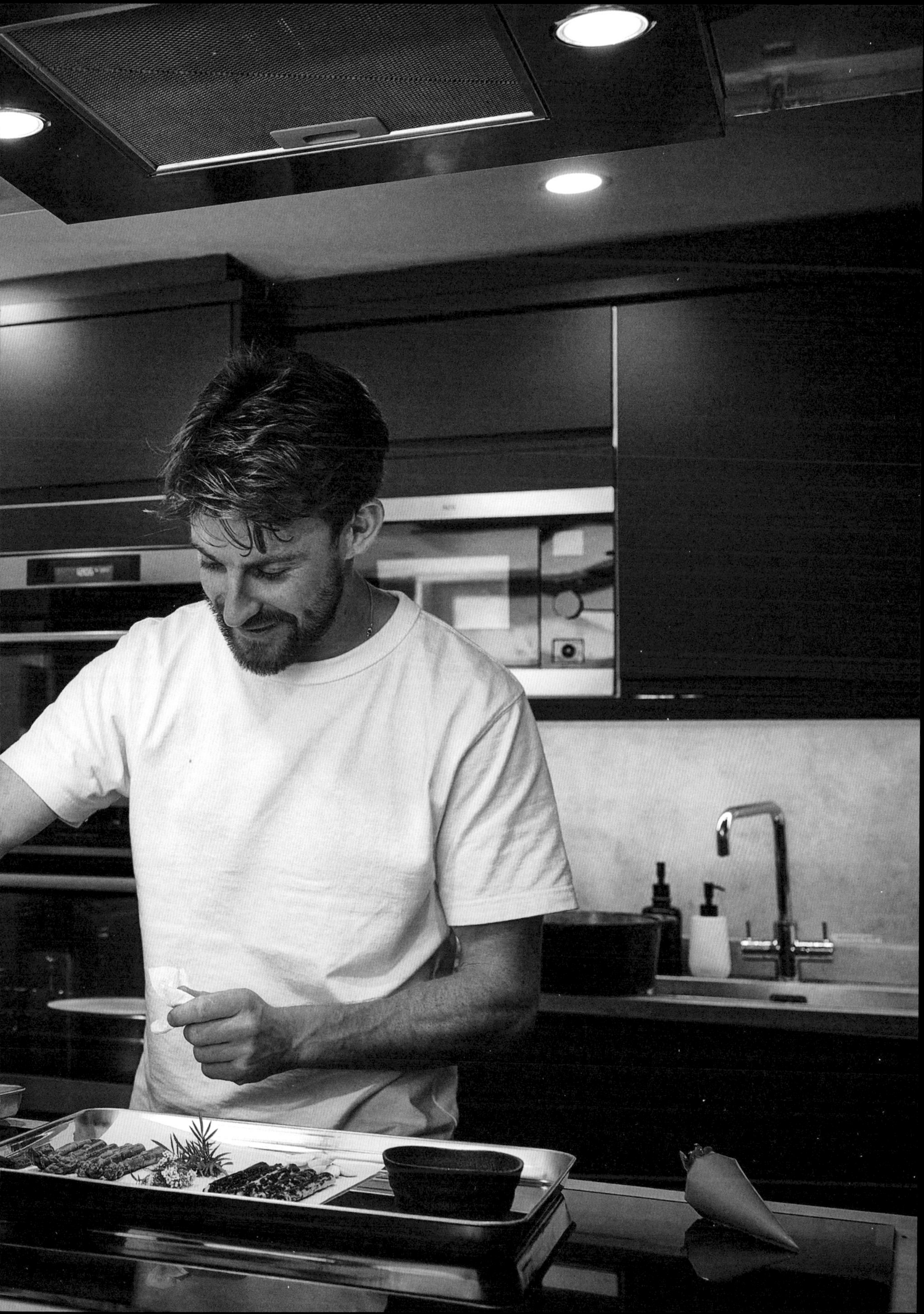

Northcote, Lancashire

Lisa Goodwin-Allen

Having joined Northcote at the age of 20, Lisa became chef de partie after a year, junior sous chef the following year and then was named head chef at 23. She has helped the restaurant maintain its Michelin star which it has held continuously since 1996, and is an instrumental figure in Northcote's gastronomic celebration, Obsession, where she leads the kitchen brigade to cook alongside some of the world's best chefs at the annual event, which was founded in 2001. Lancashire born and bred, Lisa is passionate about championing local producers in line with Northcote's own ethos and also works with a number of charities who support young people in the area. Lisa has won numerous awards within the hospitality industry and will be known to many people from her regular TV appearances.

"Northcote is part of the Stafford Collection which includes The Stafford in London, Norma on Charlotte Street, and a pizza place called Gallo in Canary Wharf. The plan is for them to develop a few more places so there are more opportunities; you can see that they're developing and investing.

People say to me I've been here such a long time and I have – 19 years now – but it's changed so much. Where it was to what it has become are miles apart. It's unbelievable how much we've done with the food as well as the property itself.

I've learnt new things from the process and we've never stagnated. If it didn't move forward, I'd have been gone a long time ago, there's no two ways about it. I'm a very passionate person in what I do and I always want to learn new things.

We get the guys in the kitchen to enter competitions because you need to: if you don't win, that's fine, but you grow your confidence either way. We've got a big 8-seater van so I chuck them in the back and we'll go off to the suppliers, take them on trips so they can see things growing or being produced, chocolate tastings and things like that. That's paramount for the younger people coming through, that we give them as much grounding as possible.

My own position has developed year after year too, which has kept me hungry. When Nigel Haworth left I got the opportunity to stamp my DNA on Northcote, which was something quite special really. I've been executive chef here for about five years now. We're moving along nicely. You've got to – if you stand still, you get forgotten about."

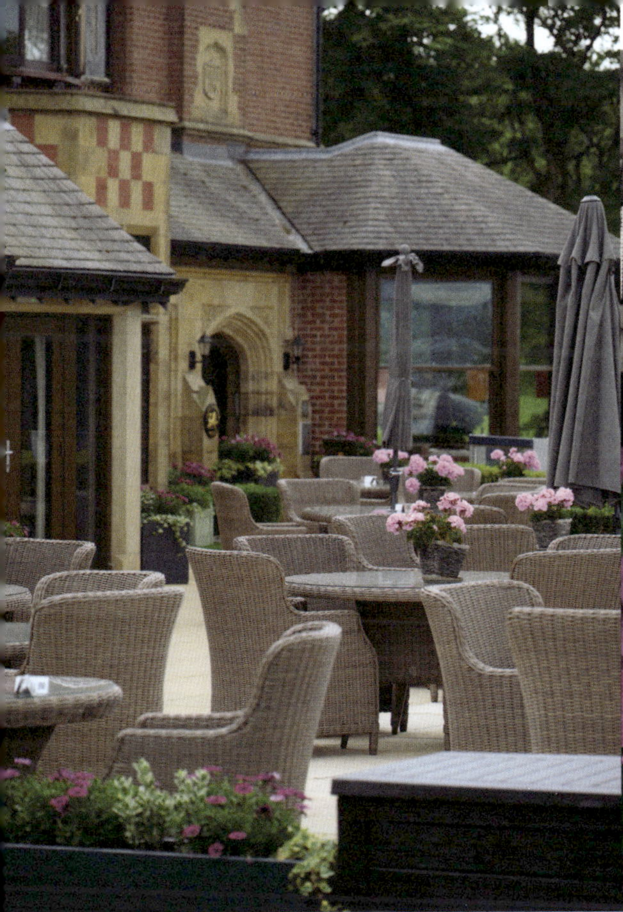

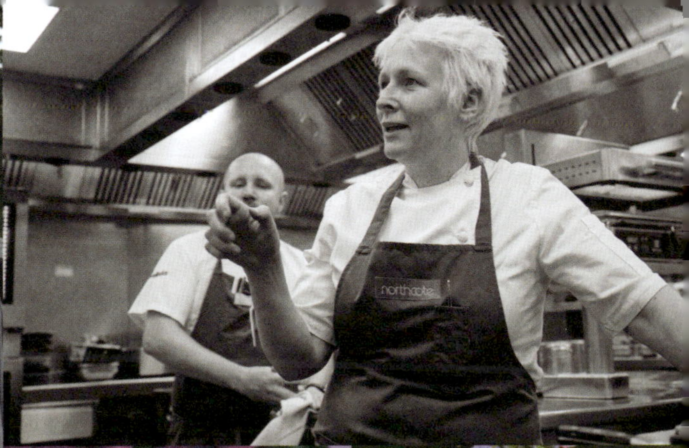
northcote

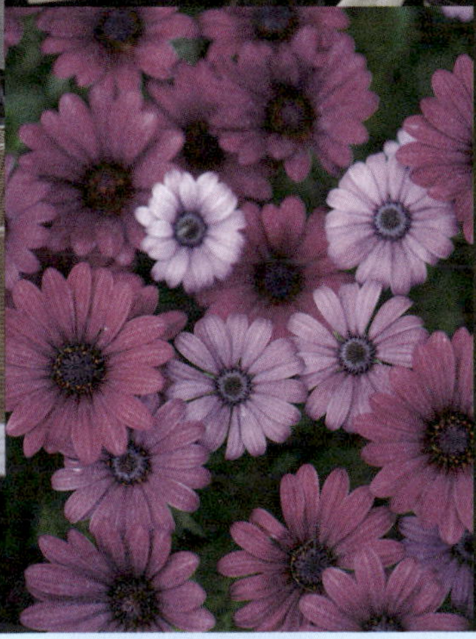

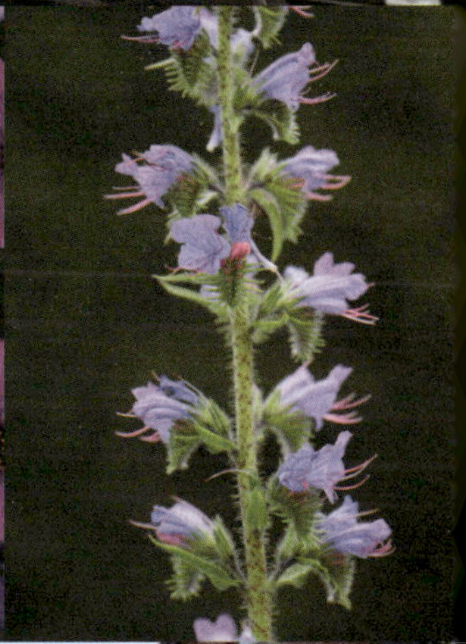

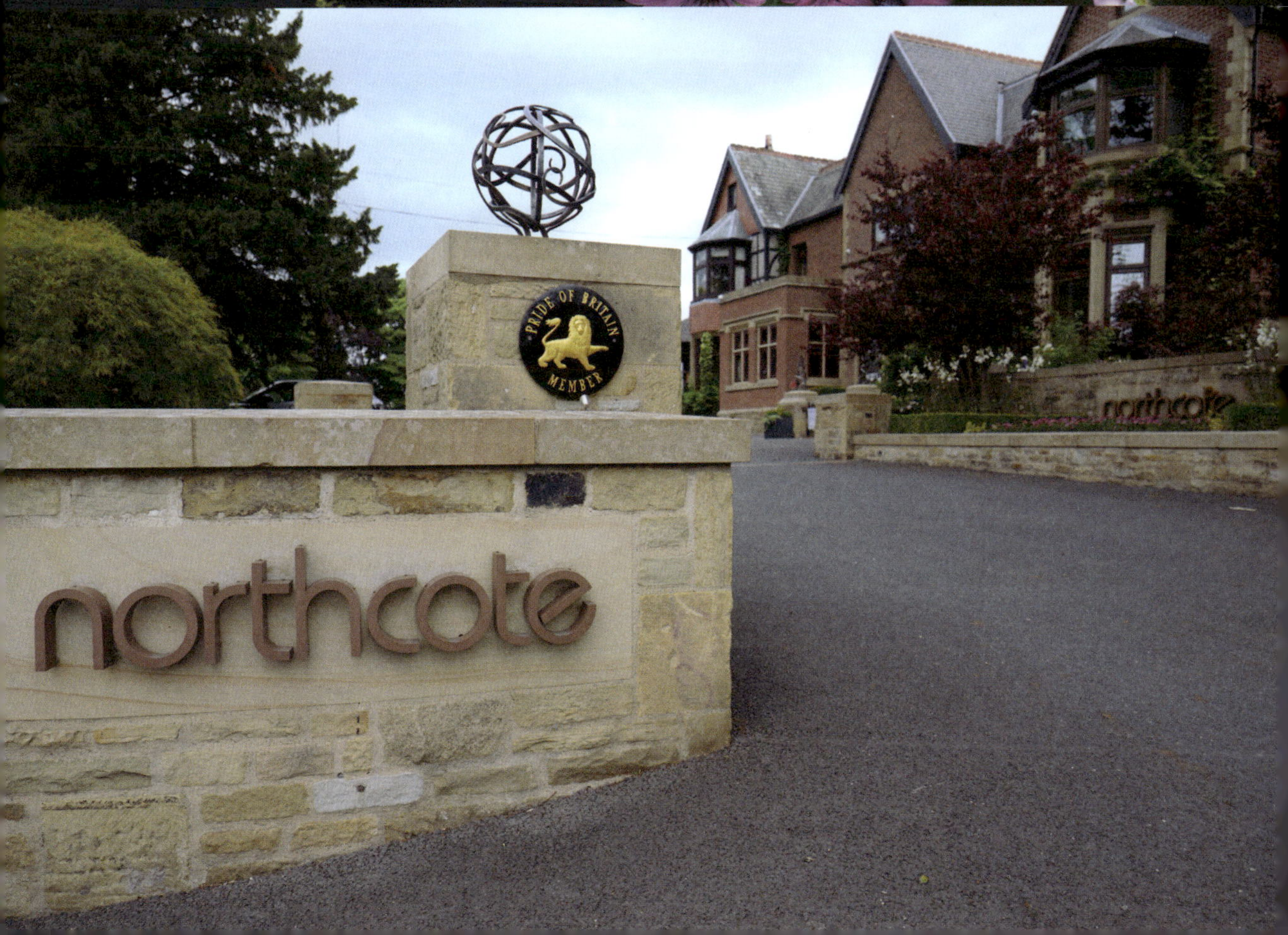
PRIDE OF BRITAIN
MEMBER
northcote
northcote

Northcote, Lancashire

Three Lancashire Cheese Pizza, Smoked Bacon, Alliums

Preparation time: 45 minutes | Cooking time: 1 hour | Serves 1-2

FOR THE SOURDOUGH PIZZA DOUGH
125g strong bread flour

125g '00' flour

1 tsp salt

10g fresh yeast

100ml lukewarm water

Drizzle of extra virgin olive oil

100g sourdough starter

Fine semolina

FOR THE TOMATO SAUCE
Drizzle of olive oil

1 medium-size onion, finely sliced

2 cloves of garlic, crushed

1 red chilli, finely sliced

20g fresh basil

400g good quality plum tomatoes, chopped

200g tinned chopped tomatoes

50g tomato purée

10g roast garlic purée

10g balsamic vinegar

2 tsp sugar

Lime juice and salt, to taste

FOR THE PICKLED ONIONS
200ml white wine vinegar

100ml water

50g sugar

1 juniper berry, crushed

1 star anise, crushed

1 small red onion

FOR THE TOPPINGS
(BASED ON A 9" PIZZA BASE)
20g Shorrocks Lancashire Bomb cheese, grated

20g Mrs. Kirkham's Lancashire cheese, grated

20g Lancashire curd cheese, diced

50g smoked pancetta, diced

2 spring onions, sliced

6-7 basil leaves, roughly torn

FOR THE SOURDOUGH PIZZA DOUGH
Sift the flours and salt together onto the work surface and make a small well in the centre. Use a small whisk to blend the yeast, water and oil together. Pour this liquid into the well along with the sourdough starter and gradually start to incorporate the flour with your fingertips to create a soft dough. Don't worry if some flour remains but remove any excess flour from the work bench before kneading or the dough will become too dry.

Knead the dough for around 10 minutes until it becomes smooth and elastic. Shape the dough into a ball and cover loosely with some lightly oiled cling film. Leave to rest for 30 minutes.

Preheat the oven to 220°c (fan assisted) or use a pizza oven. Knock back the dough and then roll it out around 1cm thick. Sprinkle some fine semolina over a baking tray and lay the pizza dough on top.

FOR THE TOMATO SAUCE
Put the oil into a large pan, heat gently and then add the sliced onion. Cook down slowly to get deep caramelisation. Once caramelised, add the garlic, chilli, basil, tomatoes, purées, balsamic vinegar, sugar, and a good pinch of salt. Mix well and cook for 20-30 minutes until the tomatoes have completely broken down. Season the sauce to taste with salt and lime juice, then pass through a fine sieve. Keep to one side until ready to make the pizza.

FOR THE PICKLED ONIONS
Place the white wine vinegar, water, sugar, juniper and star anise into a pan on a medium heat and heat until the sugar has dissolved. Meanwhile, peel the onion and slice into 1cm rings. Once fully dissolved, allow the pickling liquor to cool slightly before pouring it over the onion. Leave to cool.

TO MAKE THE PIZZA
Spread a good even layer of the tomato sauce over your pizza base, then evenly sprinkle on the three cheeses. Add the pancetta and sliced spring onion, dotting them in and around the cheeses, then season with a couple of turns of black pepper..

Bake in a hot oven until the dough is golden and crispy. Remove from the oven, then add some fresh torn basil leaves, the pickled onion rings and a light drizzle of extra virgin olive oil to serve.

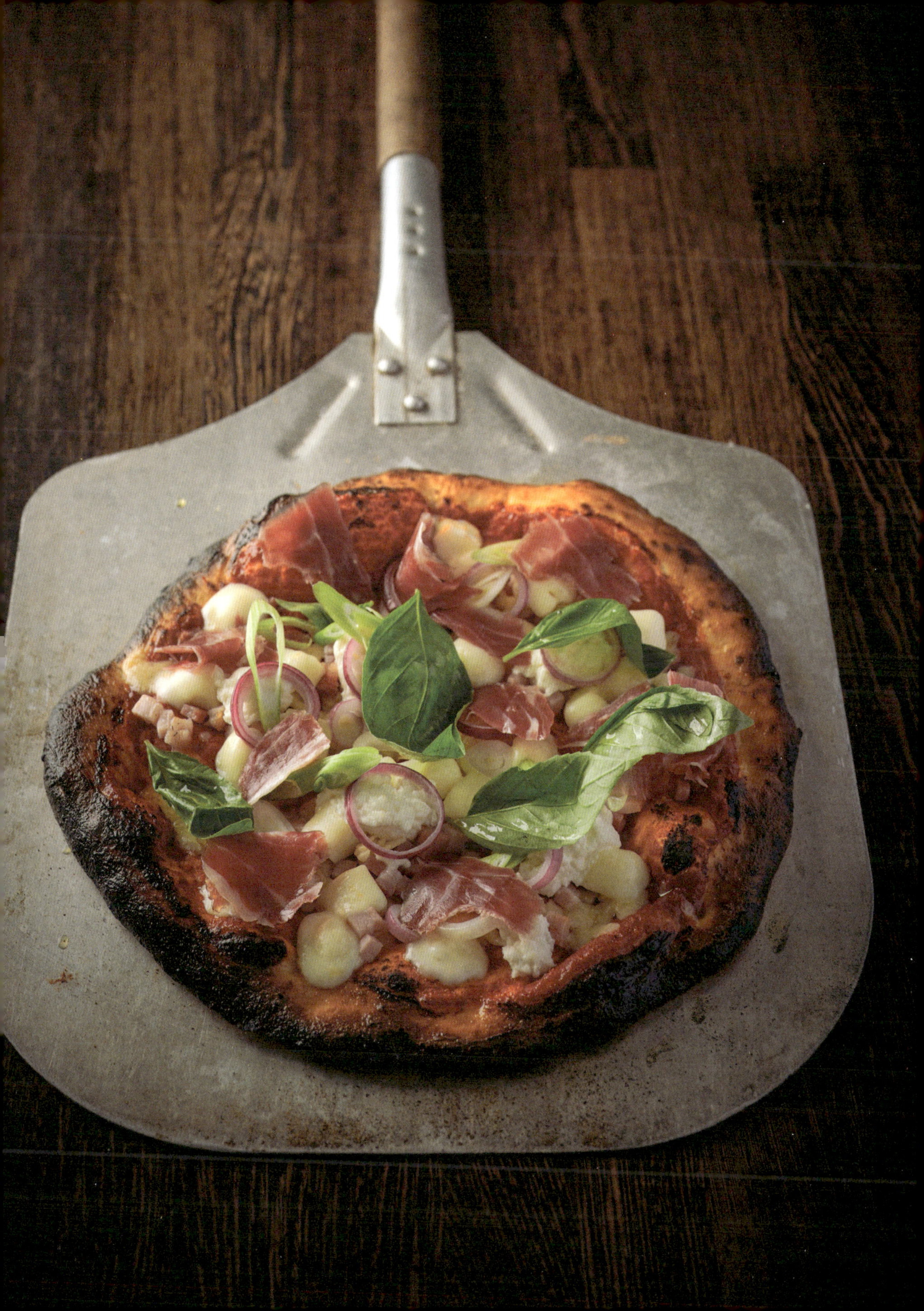

Northcote, Lancashire

West Coast Scallop, Curried "Pearls", Pomegranate, Coriander, Toasted Almonds

Preparation time: 1 hour | Cooking time: 8 hours 30 minutes | Serves 4

FOR THE ONION STOCK
1 large brown onion, skin left on (400g)
500g water

FOR THE CURRY SAUCE
½ tsp ground turmeric
½ tsp cumin seeds
1 tsp coriander seeds
1 tsp chaat masala
2 black cardamom pods, husks removed
100g shallots, finely sliced
15g olive oil
15g lemongrass, crushed
10g root ginger, peeled
1 clove of garlic, peeled
1 kaffir lime leaf, torn
½ red chilli, halved
100g white wine
100g onion stock
100g roast chicken wing stock
100g crème fraiche

FOR THE CORIANDER OIL
50g fresh coriander, picked
150ml sunflower oil
Salt

FOR THE BHAJI CRUMB
50g shallot, finely diced
200g milk
¼ tsp ground turmeric
¼ tsp garlic powder
¼ tsp chaat masala
25g plain flour
3g fresh coriander, picked and shredded

FOR THE COUSCOUS
300g chicken stock
6g curry powder
1g ground turmeric
2g salt
125g giant couscous

FOR THE SCALLOP
4 large West Coast scallops
20g melted butter
Squeeze of lemon juice
100g frozen smoked cod roe
1 whole pomegranate, halved
20g toasted flaked almonds

FOR THE ONION STOCK
Halve the onion, place into a vacuum pack bag with the water and seal tightly. Steam at 85°c for 8 hours. Once ready, leave to cool and then pass off the onion liquor, reserving it for the sauce.

FOR THE CURRY SAUCE
Crush all the dry spices together in a pestle and mortar. In a pan on a medium heat, cook down the shallots and olive oil under cling film until softened with no colour. Add the lemongrass, root ginger, garlic, lime leaves, chilli, and the crushed spice mix. Cook for 1-2 minutes to release all the flavours, then add the white wine and reduce by three quarters until the liquid starts to coat the ingredients. Add both the stocks and bring back to the boil. Boil for 3-4 minutes, then pass through a fine sieve. Place the liquid into a blender with the crème fraiche and blitz until smooth. Pass again and check the seasoning, then leave to one side.

FOR THE CORIANDER OIL
Blanch the coriander in salted boiling water for 30 seconds, then plunge straight into iced water to stop the cooking process and maintain the bright green colour. Wrap the coriander in a cloth and squeeze out all the moisture, then roughly chop and place in a Thermomix with the oil at speed 10 for 6 minutes. Pass the oil through a J-cloth and season with salt to taste.

FOR THE BHAJI CRUMB
Place the diced shallot and milk into a container and leave to soak for 15 minutes. Mix the turmeric, garlic powder, chaat masala, plain flour and a pinch of salt together. Drain the soaked shallots and add them to the spiced flour, making sure they are well coated but only lightly. Sieve or shake off any excess flour. Place the floured shallots into the fryer at 180°c until golden and crisp, then transfer to a tray lined with a J-cloth. While the shallots are still warm, place into a bowl and toss with the shredded coriander, then season with a little salt.

FOR THE COUSCOUS
Put the stock, spices and salt into a pan and bring to the boil. Add the couscous and then take the pan off the heat once it reaches boiling point again. Cling film the pan until ready to use.

FOR THE SCALLOP
Season the scallops with fine sea salt and cook in a hot pan until golden. Turn the scallops over, brush with a little melted butter and a squeeze of lemon juice, cook for a further minute, then remove from the pan and leave to rest. Sprinkle a small amount of bhaji crumb and grate the frozen cod roe over each scallop before serving.

TO SERVE
Add the couscous to your hot curry sauce in a pan and stir gently, then divide equally between 4 bowls. Bash the pomegranate halves with a spoon to remove the seeds, then gently scatter them over the couscous. Drizzle on the coriander oil and add the flaked almonds. Finish with the cooked scallops.

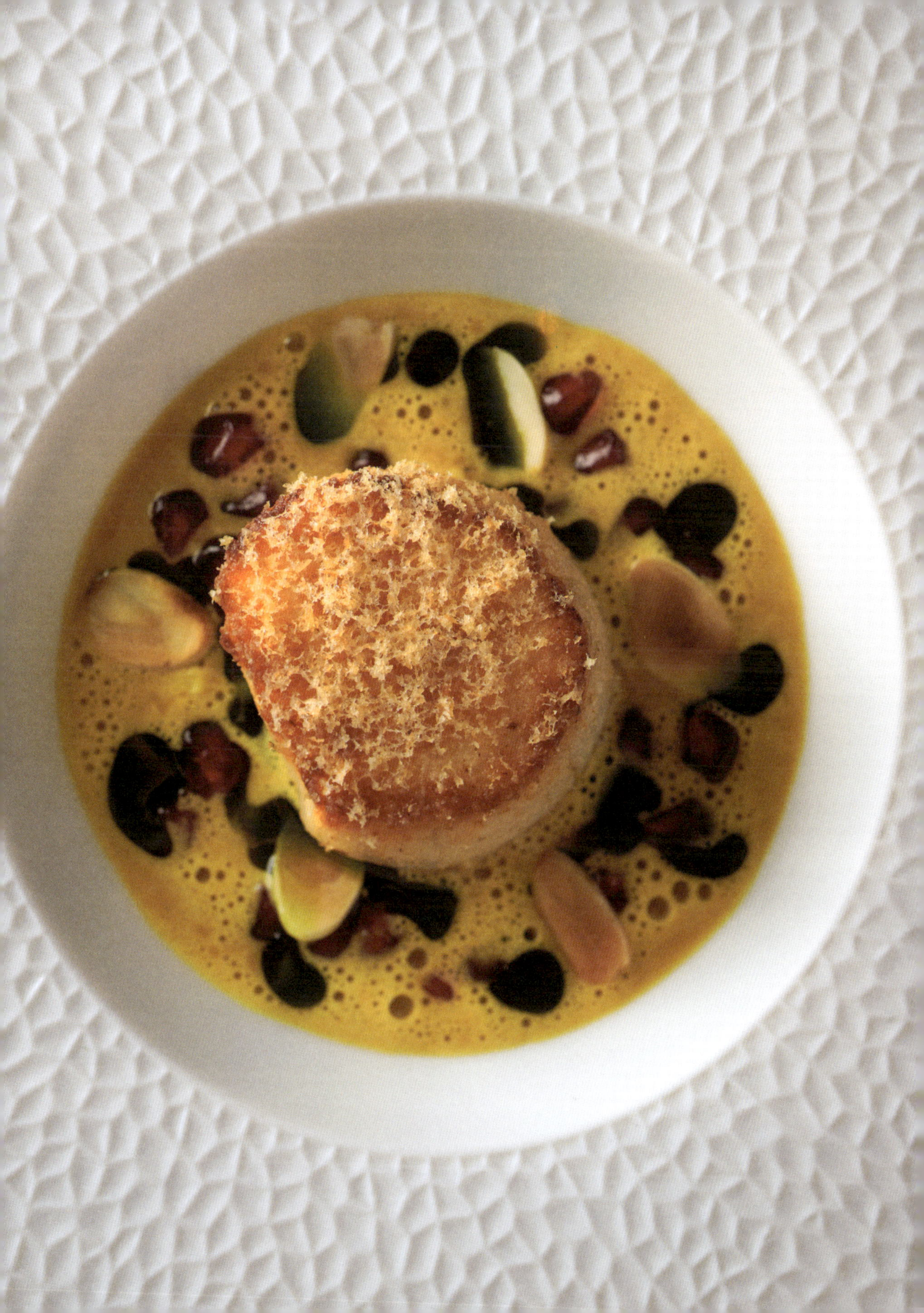

Northcote, Lancashire

Chargrilled Yorkshire Asparagus, Sheep's Curd, Sorrel

Preparation time: 30 minutes | Cooking time: 30 minutes | Serves 4

FOR THE CHARGRILLED ASPARAGUS

12 asparagus spears

500ml water

25g sugar

15g salt

FOR THE SORREL OIL

100g picked spinach

200g sorrel

200g grapeseed oil

FOR THE SHEEP'S CURD DRESSING

100g sheep's curd

50g crème fraiche

25g buttermilk

10g roast garlic

5g lemon juice

FOR THE SOURDOUGH CRUMB

250g butter

50g sourdough starter

8g yeast powder

FOR THE SORREL ICE

150g water

20g sugar

50g lemon juice

25g sorrel

20g spinach

300ml liquid nitrogen

FOR THE GARNISH

16 butterfly sorrel leaves

8 sorrel flowers

FOR THE CHARGRILLED ASPARAGUS

Gently peel the asparagus and remove the woody part of the stalk, either by cutting or snapping at its natural breaking point. Bring the water, sugar and salt to the boil in a pan, then add the asparagus and cook for 40 seconds. Remove from the pan and place straight into the blast chiller to cool.

When the dish is ready to serve, heat a griddle pan. Once hot, lightly oil 8 of the asparagus spears and place them into the griddle pan to get a nice char. Thinly slice the remaining 4 spears into 3 thin slices each. Remove the charred asparagus from the griddle pan and season with a little salt.

FOR THE SORREL OIL

Blitz the spinach, sorrel and oil together in a Thermomix for 2 minutes. Turn the temperature up to 100°c and continue to blend for about 5 minutes until the oil comes to temperature. Pass the oil through a muslin cloth into a bowl over iced water and keep cold at all times.

FOR THE SHEEP'S CURD DRESSING

Place the sheep's curd, crème fraiche, buttermilk, roast garlic and lemon juice into a blender and blitz until smooth. Pass the dressing through a fine sieve and season with a little salt.

FOR THE SOURDOUGH CRUMB

In a large, heavy-bottomed pan, heat the butter to 190°c. Pour the sourdough starter into the butter and whisk vigorously to break up the starter into small grains. Continue to whisk until the grains have become crisp and golden. Strain off the butter and place the crumb onto a cloth. Season with the yeast powder and a little salt, then store in an airtight container until needed.

FOR THE SORREL ICE

In a small pan, gently heat the water and sugar until the sugar has dissolved. Add the lemon juice and allow to cool. Once cool, blitz the sorrel and spinach into the lemon-sugar water until fully incorporated. Transfer to a bowl and chill. Skim off any excess froth, then pass the liquid through a double layer of muslin cloth. Season with salt. Very carefully pour the sorrel liquid into a container of liquid nitrogen while whisking continuously to create a fine frozen crumb.

TO SERVE

Place a spoonful of sheep's curd dressing just off centre on the plate and carefully drag with a small spatula. Put one spear of asparagus next to it, roll another spear in the sourdough crumb, then place it next the other one but slightly further down. Cut a third spear of asparagus into 3 thin slices, slightly curl them and place at the bottom of the whole spears. To the right, make a small pool of sheep's curd and create a well with the back of a teaspoon, then fill this with the sorrel oil. Finish with the butterfly sorrel leaves, sorrel flowers and the sorrel ice.

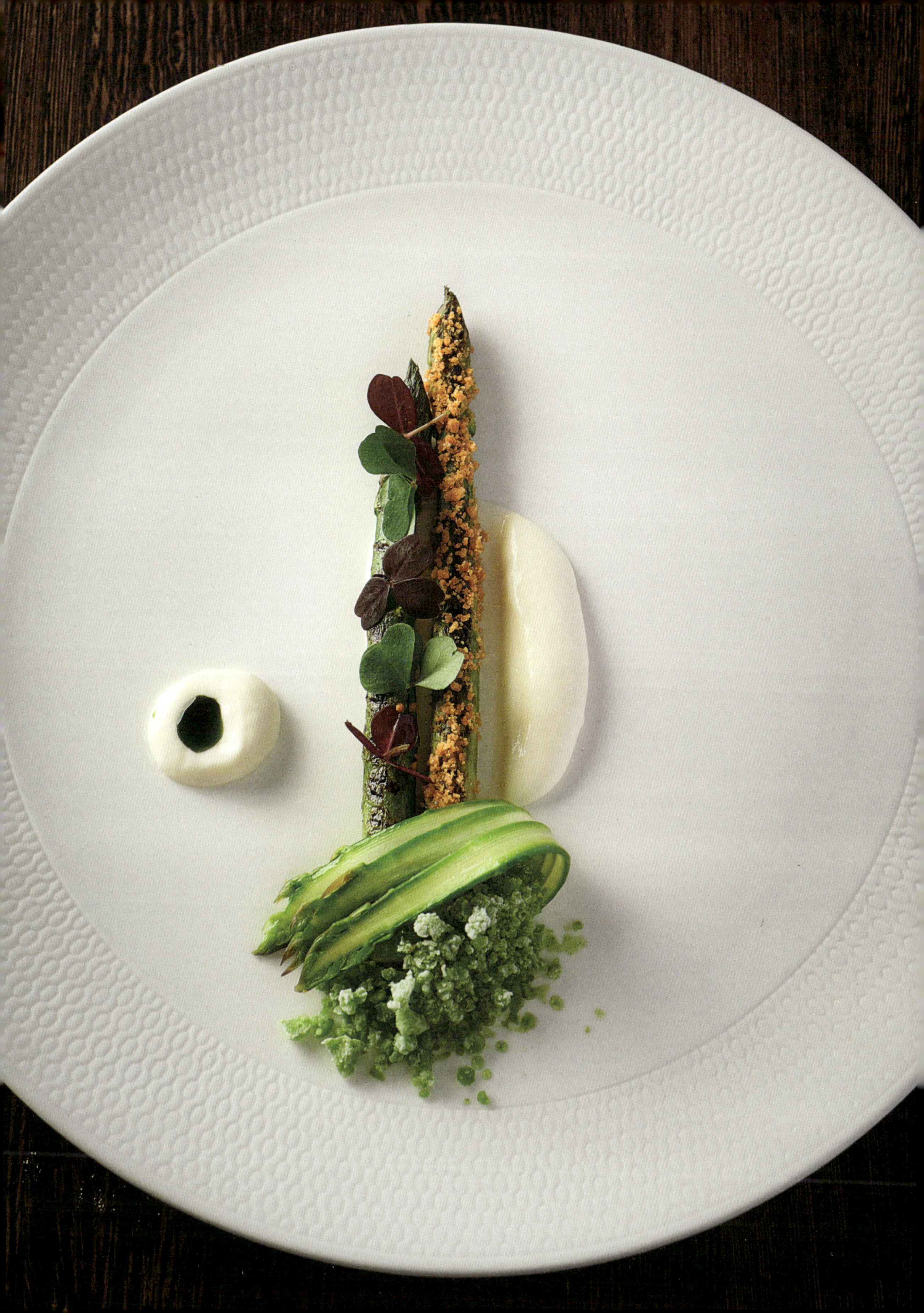

Northcote, Lancashire

Our Recipes

THREE LANCASHIRE CHEESE PIZZA, SMOKED BACON, ALLIUMS

Friday nights are pizza nights. My son's a stickler for that now because he knows it's the only time we get pizza! This one is his favourite, and the three cheeses work really well together as they suit such a quick cook and have different melting qualities. We're very lucky round here to have some amazing cheeses but they all act in a different way, so when we're developing a recipe, we test all the time to see what works with what cheese. In our cheese bread, for example, we use grated Tasty Lancashire because it's so tangy and the fat content isn't as high, so it's more acidic. When it goes into a loaf of bread, it cooks well, whereas if you use a different cheese the flavour won't come through at all. It depends what you're doing with it and whether the cheese will cause interference with the dough. For pizza, the curd is an amazing cheese and the little Lancashire Bomb is quite acidic so that provides a nice contrast. You've got to think about what elements of flavour you're adding, because most people would put sauces on a pizza – like a garlic mayonnaise – so when you take that bite it's got the right balance of acidity, sweetness and tartness. This combination balances smoky bacon, creamy and acidic cheeses, sharp pickled onion and spring onions, then there's the freshness of the basil, which I love. For me, I'd just have a really good tomato base and loads of basil on top. Sometimes the simplest things, when they're done right, are the most delicious.

This dough is the recipe we use for the pizza cookery class at Northcote. The chefs are playing around with it at the moment, so they've done one at 50% hydration and 65-70% hydration. Basically, the higher the hydration, the more bubbles you get which creates a crispier base, but it's harder to handle the dough. With a normal sourdough loaf the hydration can be very high (85-90%) and it's the same with things like baguettes, but it's a very wet dough obviously so that's trickier to make a pizza base with. Then we whack it into our wood-fired pizza oven in the courtyard just out the back, which reaches temperatures of anywhere between 600 and 750°c to cook it to perfection.

WEST COAST SCALLOP, CURRIED 'PEARLS', POMEGRANATE, CORIANDER, TOASTED ALMONDS

It was winter when we developed this dish – we're very seasonal here, so we change the menu four times a year – and I think a curry is that kind of warming, humbling thing that people can really relate to. We took the flavours of a curry sauce and made it very light and aromatic by using chicken wing stock and lots of spices. Then the pomegranate was quite traditional for that time of year. Flavour, for me, is when you close your eyes and taste everything that the menu says is on the dish.

The scallop roe is frozen just so it's easier to grate. We have used cod roe before but started using our own scallop roe, so we cure them in salt and smoke, freeze them and then grate them over the top. It's a good way of getting more of that shellfish flavour into the dish, and also you're using by-products that would otherwise be chucked in the bin. When we're making herb oils in the restaurant, like the coriander oil in this dish, we'll often use the stalks by cooking them in oil at 60°c for about 8 hours. That flavour infuses the oil and you can do this with any soft herbs for all sorts of uses; we might use the oil to make mayonnaise that tastes like chervil, for example.

CHARGRILLED YORKSHIRE ASPARAGUS, SHEEP'S CURD, SORREL

The sheep's curd in this dish is from a local farm where they make it from the leftovers of other cheesemaking processes. It's really soft and made fresh every day, then we enhance that flavour by making it into a purée. The sourdough crumb is mainly there for texture so the key flavours are the sheep's curd, sorrel and asparagus. The granita is there for temperature contrast as well as the flavour of sorrel, which is quite lemony and zingy, so you're adding acid to cut through the creaminess of the curd. That way the dish is doing something that people wouldn't necessarily expect; they're surprised when it comes to the table because the contrast of a cold element with the just charred asparagus is quite a nice thing. We shock the asparagus in salt and sugar water to get the flavour into it, for about 40 seconds, then it goes in the blast chiller – we never cool the spears in iced water because that just washes the flavour away – before being charred on the Japanese barbecue.

Northcote, Lancashire

The Beauty of Barbecuing

We've started to do a lot more barbecue style cooking over the last few years, and we look at that as an application in the restaurant because we're always experimenting with cheaper cuts like brisket. It's a bit of a revelation; you can do paella on the barbecue, we've tried a souffle…we're still working on that one to get the temperature consistent. You can give anything a go, even on an ordinary barbecue at home: we're trying the soufflé in a Weber.

We've got a pretty good set up at home too – my husband's South African so he loves barbecuing. I'm the cook in the house though! Cooking at home's different from cooking at work – you can have a glass of wine, you can experiment, and you just enjoy it. There's no intense pressure when you're creating something and that's when you start experimenting. Northcote did a partnership with Monolith and we did a cook demo for all their clients, so they gave me one. It's a big barrel shape so you can hang chickens and stuff like that; it's great for experimenting. When I was a child, my dad was the owner of an autowreckers and our family barbecue was a five gallon drum, cut in half and welded onto little pegs. People would want to use it for the local cricket club and all sorts. The one we've got now is definitely an upgrade! It's got bars in so you can hang things directly in the barbecue over the heat. The exciting thing about that is the potential for experimenting; we discovered that sausages are great cooked that way, just hung in a string over the coals.

The massive revolution now that people are starting to cotton on to is cooking with direct and indirect heat. We're still learning ourselves at the same time as learning for the cookery school. I teach probably about four times a year and we get different chefs for the range of courses which includes barbecuing – we do that in our courtyard where there are a dozen or so different barbecues just outside the kitchen. The cookery school is a great way of reminding us as chefs that you've got to feel enthused, no matter how long you're working in one place or what you're doing: keep it moving, learning new things, finding new suppliers, coming up with new techniques. Keep yourself energised.

northcote
A STAFFORD COLLECTION HOTEL
STAFFORDCOLLECTION.COM

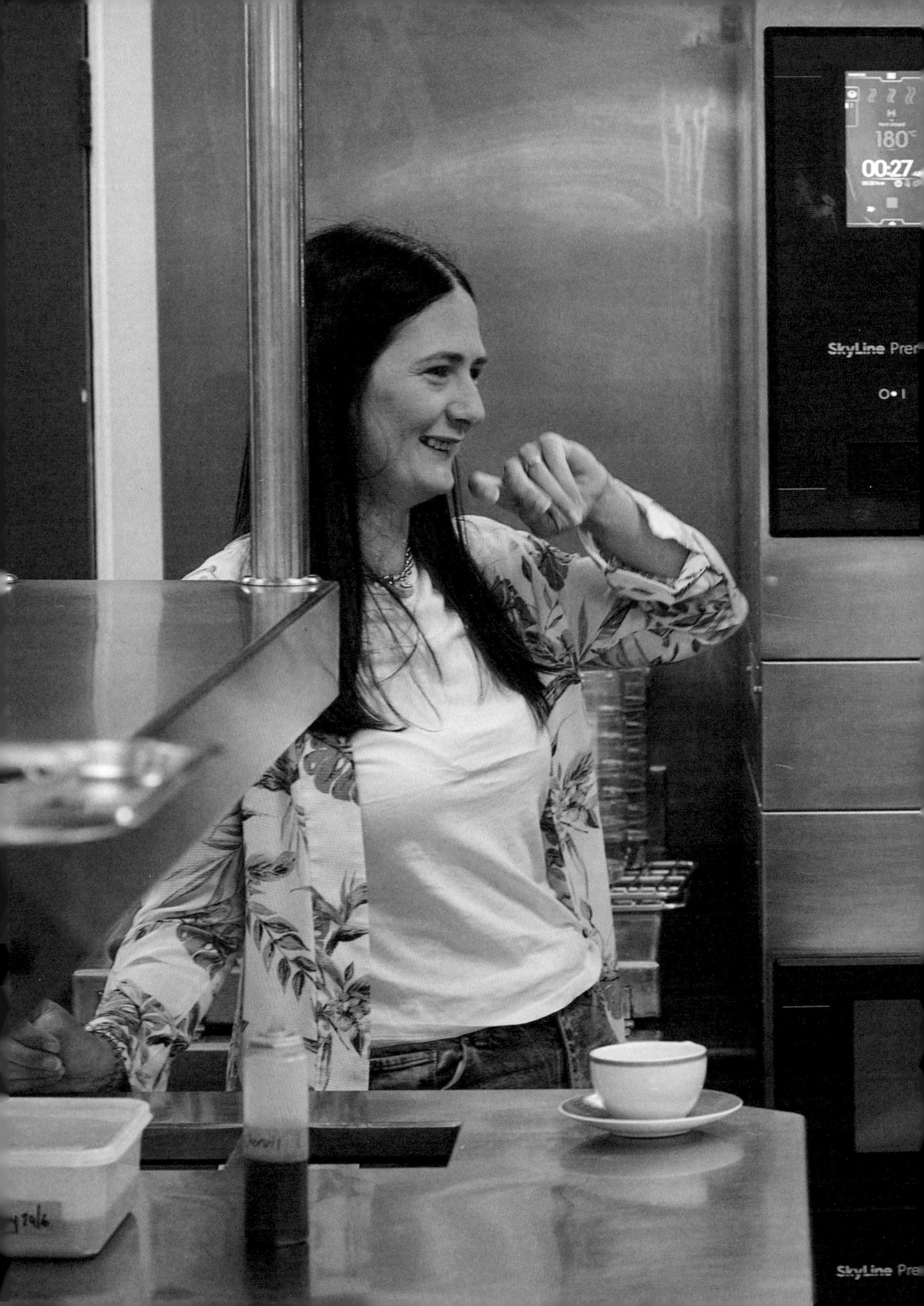
180°C
00:27
SkyLine
SkyLine

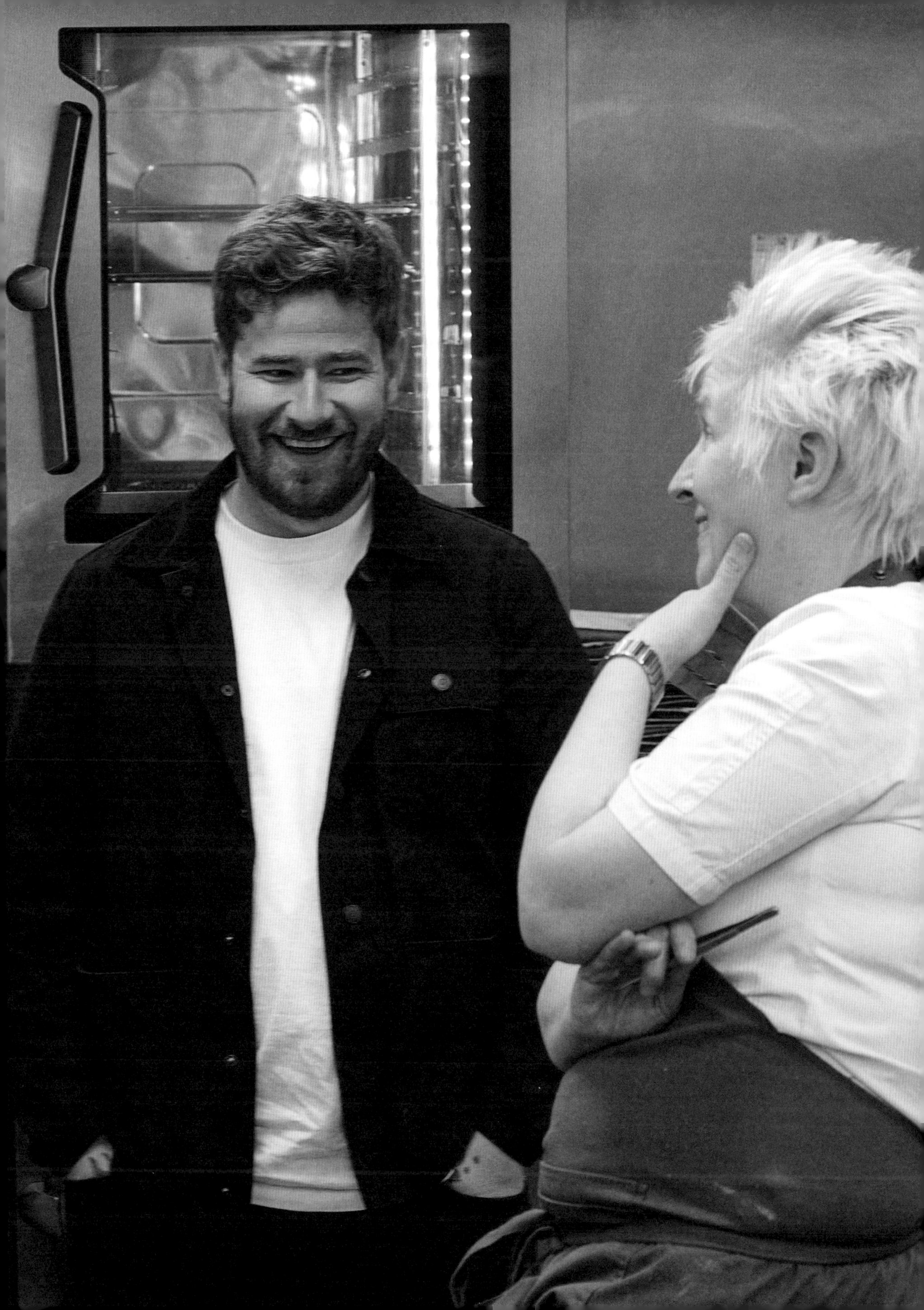

The Pack Horse, Peak District

Luke Payne

Luke Payne is a self-taught chef who worked his way through the ranks in pub chains until he and his partner Emma, who was running managed houses, discovered The Pack Horse and decided to take it on. Under their ownership since 2016, the pub has been recommended in the Michelin Guide and earned a spot in the UK's Top 50 Gastropubs as well as winning the hearts and minds of Peak District locals. Welcoming walkers alongside bookings for their à la carte, bar snacks and Sunday roast menus, The Pack Horse at Hayfield is a rare combination of high-end seasonal cooking within a traditional village pub. Informed by the landscape, local produce and his own passion for great food and great pubs, Luke has created a destination unique to its surroundings.

"The soul of the British dining pub has been lost somewhere and we're trying to get it back. If you think back to when this pub was a rest spot along the Edale to Holmfirth pack horse route, travellers would walk in and probably have had some slow cooked mutton and a barley broth. It would've been hearty, wholesome, a place to recharge after a long day or an indulgent treat for the locals. And it would've utilised local, seasonal produce. I don't know where burgers, fish & chips and pizza in a pub have come from: to me they have nothing to do with proper pub food. It infuriates me that so many people expect all pubs to do the same thing. It's frustrating when our nation's pubs are all so very different from each other and have their own stories, their own mini terroirs. We had to take those safe options away when we started out, because people wouldn't order anything else!

Our bar menu is a great example of us trying to replicate the days of old. There are no sandwiches; instead it focuses on hearty and delicious snacks which are relevant to the surrounding area. The Manchester Egg is our signature bar snack, the original recipe for which was first drawn up in our nearest city. We've got locally made cured meats and bread baked in house with butter from Holmfirth: this is not a venue for an olive oil and balsamic dip. We get a lot of people walking through Hayfield so it's important for us to have a bar menu that has great choice, but also really shouts about how diverse our pubs could and should be, focusing on our unique setting. Our full à la carte menu features none of the pub classics. Once again, we've focused on the great produce surrounding us to lead the way, and we make the most of the best seasonal British produce throughout the year to complement it. The Peak District is poised for a thriving food scene and we are so proud to be at the forefront of that push.

It's also been critical for us to maintain the feeling that this pub is open to everyone, no matter what people may think of the food. The atmosphere is relaxed and unpretentious, and we allow guests to sit at the bar and have tables unreserved for drinkers. There's such a big pub community round here and they've been so nice to us – we never wanted to take the pub away from them by doing something crazy with it. This pub has been part of this community longer than we've been here, it's important we respect that."

Coming soon...
Summer
Tasting menu!
More details to come

Number 32
the UK's Top 50
Gastro Pubs

Welcome to The Pack Horse in Hayfield. Our food changes with the seasons, offering a unique snapshot of the British food calendar using the best local suppliers where possible. We hope you enjoy your visit.

Luke and Emma

WINE OF THE WEEK
Nyetimber, English Sparkling Wine

We are proud to be Hayfield's first entry into the Michelin Guide

The Pack Horse
Hayfield

The Pack Horse, Peak District

Manchester Egg

Preparation time: 4 days | Cooking time: 12 minutes | Makes 8

8 medium free-range eggs
400g black pudding
400g minced pork
8g chopped sage
½ tsp ground mace
½ tsp cayenne pepper
50g fine breadcrumbs
50g cubed lardo
100g plain flour
100ml egg yolk
200g panko breadcrumbs
Oil for frying

FOR THE PICKLE
1 litre white wine
1 litre white wine vinegar
500g caster sugar
½ tsp coriander seeds
¼ tsp fennel seeds
¼ tsp chilli flakes
2 juniper berries
1 allspice berry
1 clove

FOR THE MANCHESTER EGG

Bring a large pan of water to a rolling boil. Fill a 4-litre ice cream tub with iced water. Drop all the eggs simultaneously into the boiling water and boil for 6 minutes, then immediately plunge into the iced water. Once cool throughout, carefully peel off the shell and place the eggs into your pickle. Cover with a baking parchment cartouche and leave in the fridge for 3 days.

Place the black pudding, minced pork, sage, mace, cayenne pepper and breadcrumbs into a food processor and blitz to form a smooth paste. Tip into a mixing bowl and add the lardo cubes, folding through evenly.

Remove the eggs from the pickle and pat dry. Take 100g of the black pudding mix, lightly flour and roll out to 5mm thickness. Place the mix in your hand with the pickled egg on top, then carefully encase the egg tightly in the black pudding mix, making sure all air is removed. Repeat to make 8.

Preheat a deep fryer to 180°c. Roll the encased eggs through the plain flour, egg yolk and then panko breadcrumbs in that order. Deep fry the coated eggs for 7 minutes. Drain off any excess oil and slice in half to serve.

FOR THE PICKLE

Place all the ingredients for the pickle into a large saucepan, bring to the boil then reduce to a simmer for 15 minutes. Set aside and leave to cool to room temperature, then pass through a sieve and place the remaining liquid in the fridge.

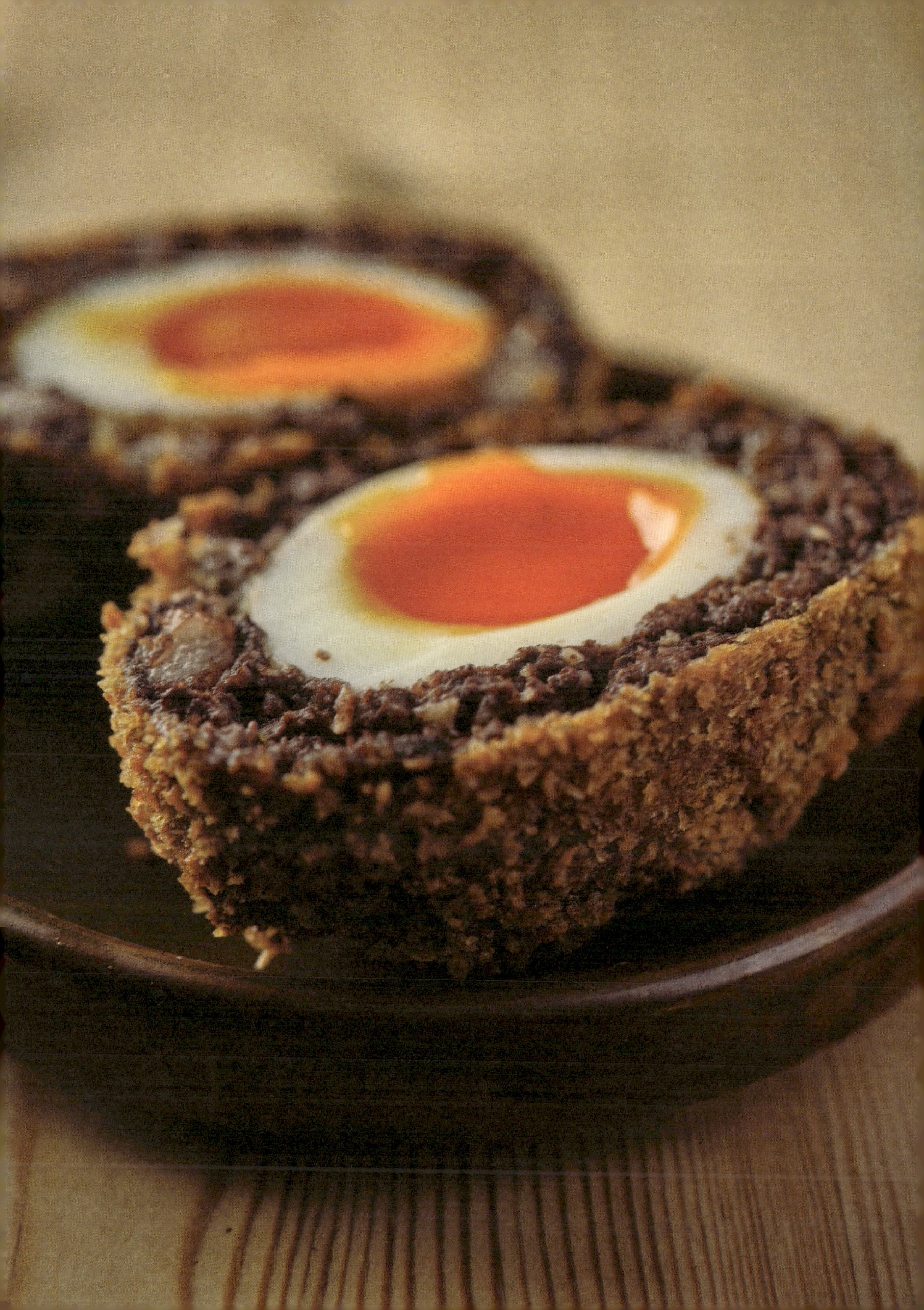

The Pack Horse, Peak District

Mutton Curry

Preparation time: 40 minutes, plus marinating | Cooking time: 4 hours | Serves 6

3 cardamom pods

2 star anise

2 cloves

1 cinnamon stick

1 tbsp cumin seeds

1 tbsp coriander seeds

1kg diced mutton

250ml plain yoghurt

1 tbsp paprika

1 tsp cayenne pepper

2 tsp curry powder

2 red onions, roughly chopped

2 tsp garlic paste

1 tsp ginger paste

Stalks from 15g fresh coriander, chopped

2 tsp sea salt

½ tsp garam masala

50g unsalted butter

400g tinned plum tomatoes

FOR THE MUTTON CURRY

Lightly toast the whole spices (cardamom, star anise, cloves, cinnamon, cumin and coriander) in a hot dry frying pan and then leave to cool.

Mix the diced mutton with the yoghurt, paprika, cayenne pepper, half the curry powder and all the toasted whole spices. Leave to marinate for at least 2 hours, but preferably overnight.

Heat some oil in a pan and add the onion, garlic paste, ginger paste and chopped coriander stalks. Cook slowly until soft, then add the remaining curry powder, salt and garam masala to cook for a further 10 minutes. Blitz to a rough paste and turn the heat right down, adding the butter.

Add the mutton along with all the marinade, turning it through the blitzed paste and butter in the pan, then add the tin of plum tomatoes. Rinse the tin with a splash of water and add it to the pan.

Cook the curry on a very low heat for 3 hours until the meat is soft and yielding, stirring occasionally to ensure even cooking and stop anything burning on the bottom.

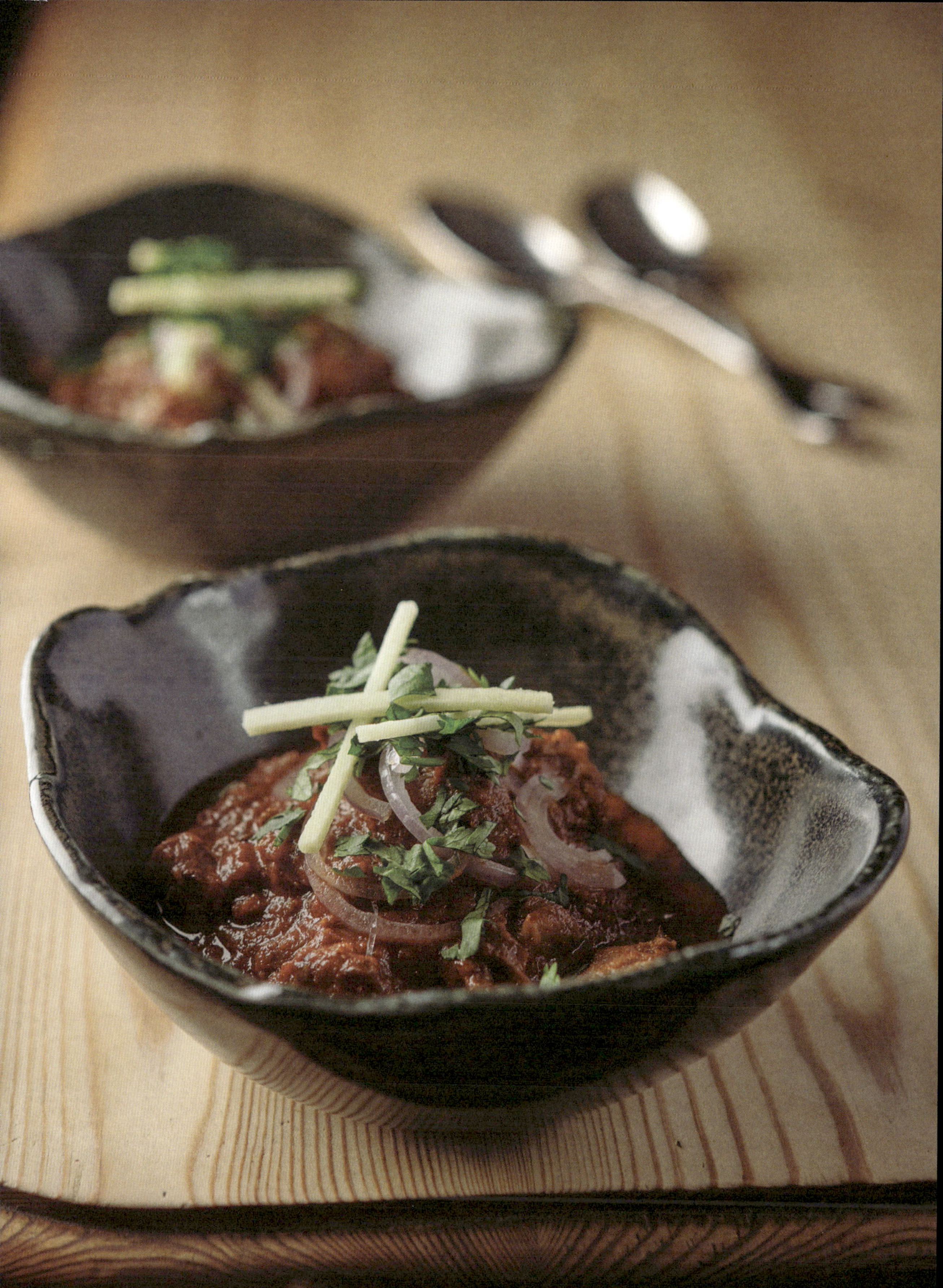

The Pack Horse, Peak District

Salted Caramel Custard Tart

Preparation time: 3 hours | Cooking time: 1 hour 10 minutes | Serves 12

FOR THE PASTRY

350g plain flour

90g icing sugar

175g butter, cubed and chilled

1 egg

30ml water

FOR THE CUSTARD

200ml egg yolk

120g caster sugar

14g Maldon sea salt

850ml double cream

FOR THE CARAMEL

150g caster sugar

40ml water

FOR THE PASTRY

Combine the plain flour and icing sugar in a mixing bowl suitable for use in a planetary mixer. Mix in the butter until the mixture resembles fine breadcrumbs. Add the egg and water and mix until combined. Turn off the mixer and tip the dough out onto a lightly floured work surface. Bring together so it has a smooth texture, then wrap in cling film and set in the fridge for 2 hours.

Preheat a combi oven to 170°c on fan speed 4. Remove the pastry from the fridge and let it soften slightly. On a lightly floured surface, roll out the pastry to 3mm thickness. Lightly grease a 20cm tart tin and gently line it with the pastry, leaving 2cm hanging over the edge all the way round. Wrap a small spherical piece of dough in cling film and use it to press the pastry right into the edges of the tart tin. Gently top with greaseproof paper, fill with baking beans and leave to firm up in the fridge for 20 minutes.

Bake the pastry in the preheated combi oven for 20 minutes. Remove the baking beans and greaseproof paper, then shave the overhanging edges away with a veg peeler. Turn the fan speed down to 2 and bake for a further 10 minutes, then set aside.

FOR THE CUSTARD

Beat the egg yolk and caster sugar together in a mixing bowl. Add the salt and mix thoroughly. Pour the cream into a saucepan and bring to the boil. Once boiling, pour the cream over the egg and sugar mix and whisk as you go, ensuring the mixture is thoroughly combined, then set aside.

FOR THE CARAMEL

Heat the sugar and water in a saucepan. Do not disturb the mix as it cooks, taking the temperature to 155°c. Once reached, carefully pour the caramel into the custard, whisking as you go until smooth. Skim the foam off the top of the mix and pass through a fine sieve into a jug.

Set your combi oven to 130°c on fan speed 2, place the tart base into the oven and pour in the salted caramel custard. Bake for 40 minutes, then leave the tart on the side to cool to room temperature before cutting into 12 slices.

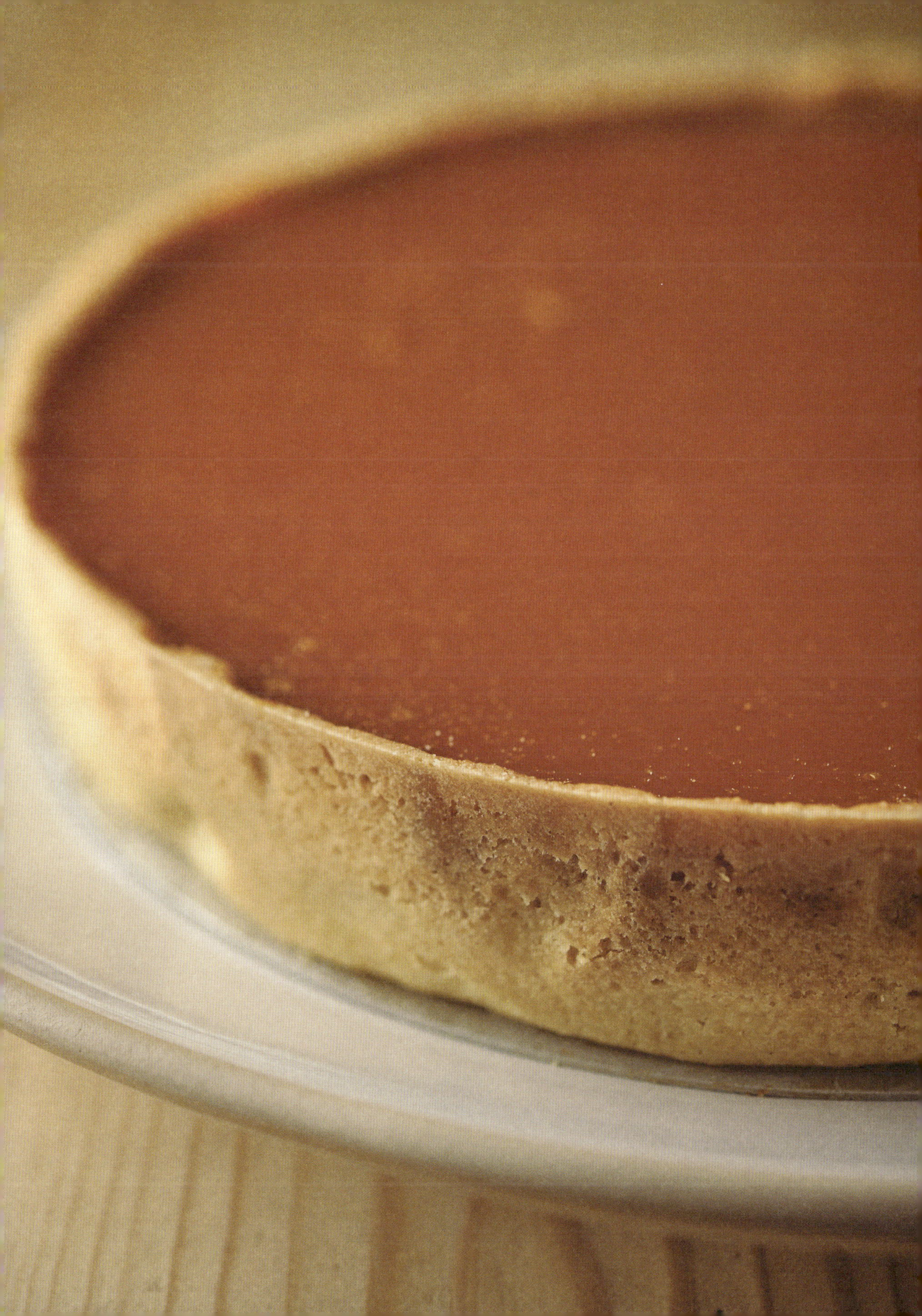

The Pack Horse, Peak District

My Recipes

MANCHESTER EGG

Being so close to Manchester, it was really important to me to have a bar snack that truly represents our location. Unlike a scotch egg, the egg inside a Manchester egg is pickled, and then wrapped in black pudding mix. We soft-boil our eggs before pickling for extra decadence. It's a proper pub snack that's been so popular here, and has become completely synonymous with the pub.

The traditional recipe is 50/50 black pudding and sausage meat, whereas we use minced pork and our own blend of seasoning to ensure total control over the flavour. We use Arlington White eggs from the Cotswolds which have this incredible deep coloured rich yolk; visually it's so striking. Sourcing the right black pudding was key – I needed a black pudding that was soft and creamy enough for us to shape and protect the egg, but still packed with flavour. We settled on Doreen's famous black pudding from Haigh's, quite possibly the best black pudding I've ever eaten, and it's perfect for our Manchester eggs. Just don't tell the Mancunians that it's from Yorkshire!

MUTTON CURRY

I feel like mutton is due a renaissance. It has so much flavour, and it is perfect for a curry because the meat is so robust and has such a strong intensity that can handle the punchy spices. Mettrick's, our butchers, have locally sourced mutton readily available and I always check in to see if they've got any in the dry-ager. We are incredibly lucky here in the Peak District to be surrounded by the most beautiful rolling hills and grazing pasture for livestock. John and Steven Mettrick work tirelessly to source the best high-welfare cattle, pigs, and sheep from within the Peak District wherever possible, and they also have their own co-located abattoir. We can see the fields of sheep from our window, and it's a real pleasure to be able to say the lamb on our menu has had a 10 mile round trip from field to butcher and back to us. It's something to really celebrate, and it's always on the menu, making use of hogget and mutton when the seasons dictate.

I absolutely love curry, and this is one of my favourite recipes to do on a day off upstairs, chilling out in the flat. It takes a little forward planning and some time to cook, but it is so worth it. And the washing up is minimal which is always a bonus!

SALTED CARAMEL CUSTARD TART

We have this on the menu all year round – without doubt it's our signature dessert. We have Adam Byatt to thank for this one; I ate the OG salted caramel custard tart at his restaurant, Trinity in London, six years ago and I've been trying to replicate it ever since. He actually came visit to us and ate our version of the tart a few months ago and he absolutely loved it, which is just incredible and very humbling. We make a fresh tart for every service, so for lunch we've got 12 and if we've got any left over for dinner, that's it. If you do have it at lunch, it's usually still warm which is a real treat.

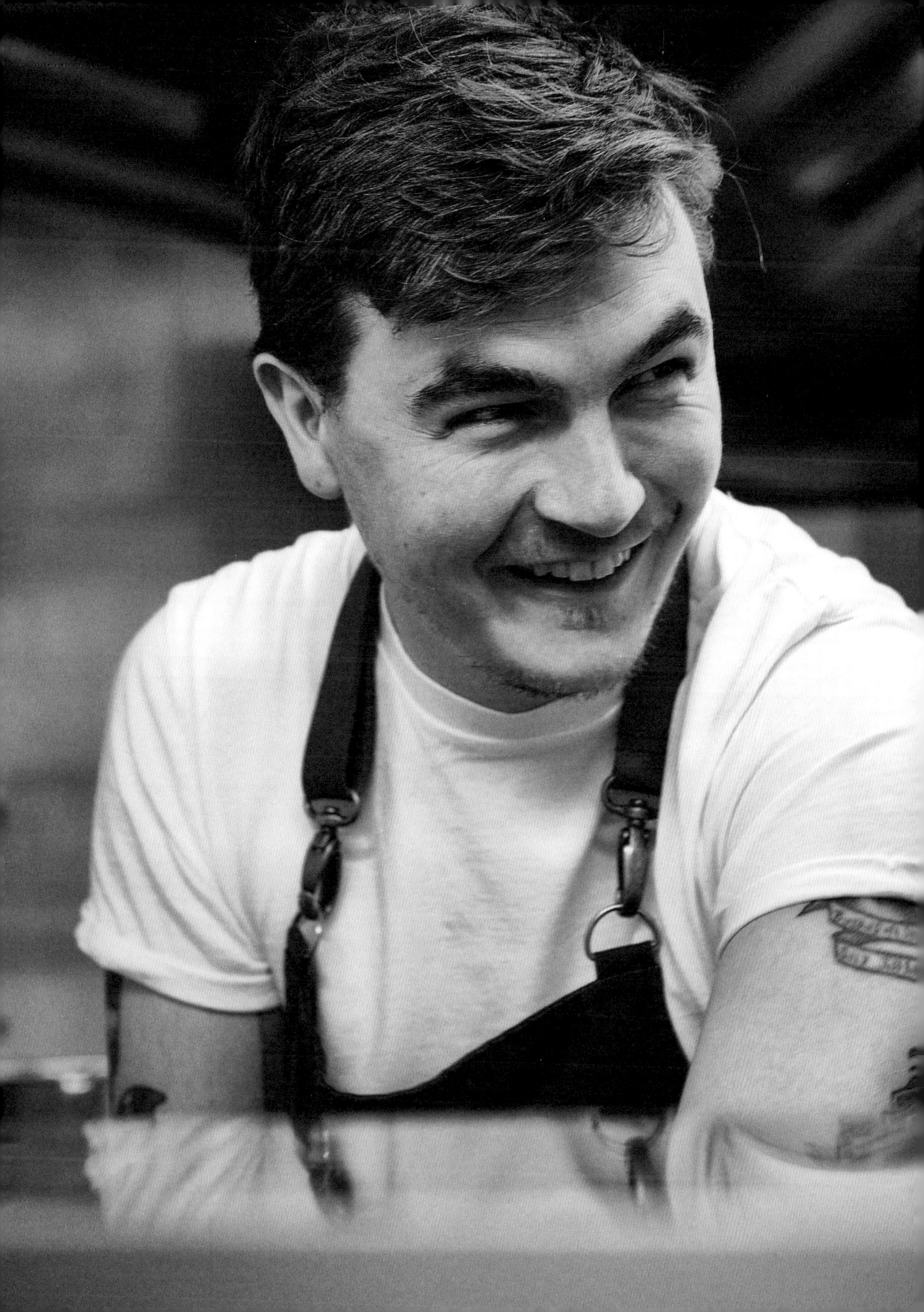

The Pack Horse, Peak District

Meet the Chef

My Background

I studied drama at university in London and fell in love with cooking as a student. I remember my first trip to a restaurant in Soho called Polpo – it was so cool, so different. You couldn't book, there were no wine glasses, the playlist was amazing, and the food was Venetian small plates. It was unlike anything else I'd experienced in a restaurant, and I wanted it. As soon as I graduated, I got a job washing dishes for a pub chain and eventually worked my way up to head chef. By this point my passion for the job was wavering: it was high volume, pre-made, frozen food. It taught me a lot about the logistics of running a team but nothing about cooking and the passion was being sucked out of me, so much so that I planned to walk away from the industry and had an interview lined up for something else. Three days before that interview, I went for a drive and drove straight past The Pack Horse. Something just felt right about it. That evening my partner Emma and I returned to Hayfield, and eight weeks later we had the keys to the pub. Some things are meant to be.

Our first menu was pretty much all pub classics. I knew that was never the end goal though; I needed a creative outlet and began experimenting with new ideas, so one by one the classic dishes fell off the menu. They were outselling everything three to one, so it was a huge risk, but it paid off. We found people were reading the whole menu and getting interested by it, and we've not looked back. Every menu change became a step forward with my learning. Back when I didn't have the understanding I do now of putting a dish together, I'd read other menus and essentially copy them, and in tasting those dishes my repertoire built up from that process of development. With no mentor or guidance, I've had to find my own way with it. Initially I felt like a fraud because I was trusting my intuition alone a lot of the way and it made me feel like an imposter when we started getting great reviews from within the industry. It's taken a while for me believe in myself a bit.

My Influences

Hugh Fearnley-Whittingstall at River Cottage is a key early influence. He made me think about food in a really different way. There was a series of River Cottage on TV while I was at university where Hugh went vegetarian for a few weeks and I did it along with the show, experimenting with new ingredients and recipes and rewarding myself with a meaty meal at the end. That was a lightbulb moment. Hugh gave me the foundation of cooking with great produce, following the seasons, sourcing ingredients properly. I feel like I owe him, but obviously he's got no idea who I am! I bought River Cottage Meat – in my opinion one of the best cookbooks ever written, and I've amassed over 150 in my quest for knowledge – which is always in the pub kitchen for reference, along with The Book of St. John by Fergus Henderson, The Sportsman by Stephen Harris, a signed copy of Adam Byatt's book, and the eponymous book from Nathan Outlaw.

I must mention Luke at JÖRO, because thanks to his social media I began to experiment with all the different types of soy sauce, seaweed dashi and vinegars: all kinds of things I'd never have gone near before without Luke thinking outside the box and shouting about these amazing ingredients. He's always got time to help and support as well.

My Food

Keeping The Pack Horse accessible has been the key to balancing great food with being a country pub. We try to do food that makes people smile, and we cook with the seasons. The menu always follows the rhythm of nature and it changes weekly depending on what's available and at its best. I particularly love doing autumn menus as that time of year lends itself so well to my style, because it's all about robust root vegetables, hearty flavour, loads of butter and cream, red wine sauces… autumnal produce is the best, especially as most of it is British grown as well. There's so much to choose from, and the first delivery of mixed squashes is a delight. I love autumnal fruit too, and I grew up next to an orchard, so it always reminds me of home.

My Future

We've committed to another five years here and don't see ourselves leaving any time soon. Emma and I have a family and a home here, we're part of the village and we're running a sustainable business, so why would we? We've also got some exciting plans for an open kitchen coming soon, which is a big step! I think I would like to open somewhere else eventually, not necessarily another pub. I'd love to open a restaurant that really plays to our strengths: good drinks, good food, accessible and unfussy. I've got so many ideas but it's time and money, as well as building a strong team around us who share our passion. It'll happen one day. We love what we do, I'm obsessed with this industry. The workload is immense, but every single element of it excites me.

Forest Side, Lake District

Paul Leonard

Following a fascination with food and hospitality training in his hometown, Paul moved to London at the age of 21 to work at Pétrus by Gordon Ramsay. He built up a wealth of experience in various restaurants around the north of England before taking up a role with Andrew Fairlie at his restaurant in Gleneagles. Paul moved on to managing his own kitchen at the Isle of Eriska on Scotland's West Coast, retaining the establishment's Michelin star, before becoming head chef at the Devonshire Arms in Bolton Abbey which won four AA Rosettes within a year.

Paul jumped at the offer to join Forest Side and was appointed head chef in 2019. The restaurant has since achieved four AA Rosettes, holds a Michelin star and is known for its celebration of local produce, including many ingredients from the hotel's extensive kitchen garden and grounds. Paul's own ethos developed around a love of cooking with great ingredients, and his thoughtful yet deceptively simple approach marries perfectly with the culinary experience at Forest Side, which is designed to reflect the Lake District landscape in which it sits.

"I've loved this place since it opened; we came here for my wife Robyn's birthday and both fell in love with it. You come up the drive and see it's quite grand, but then you walk in and it's so open and light. I love the dining room and I thought our food would fit in here. So when the opportunity came up, it was a no brainer. I was a bit nervous, because obviously Kevin Tickle [Forest Side's previous head chef] built it up from nothing and spent a long time making sure it had a really good name, but it seemed to be the right place for us – it's our little journey. I just want to enjoy it and build on the great base we've got here. Having confidence in yourself, a bit more maturity, building the team – I think all that reflects on the plate. So that's what we're excited for in the future."

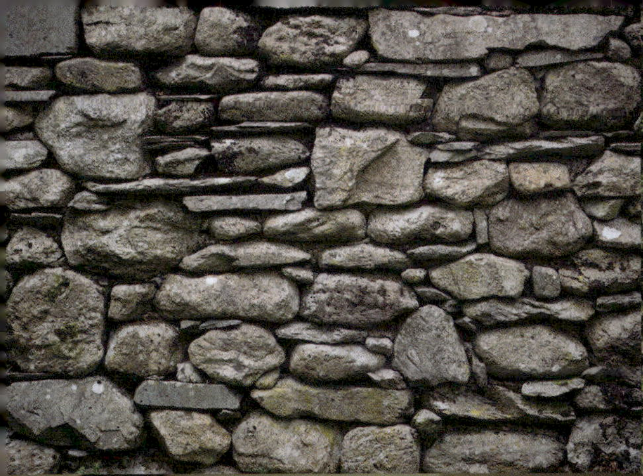
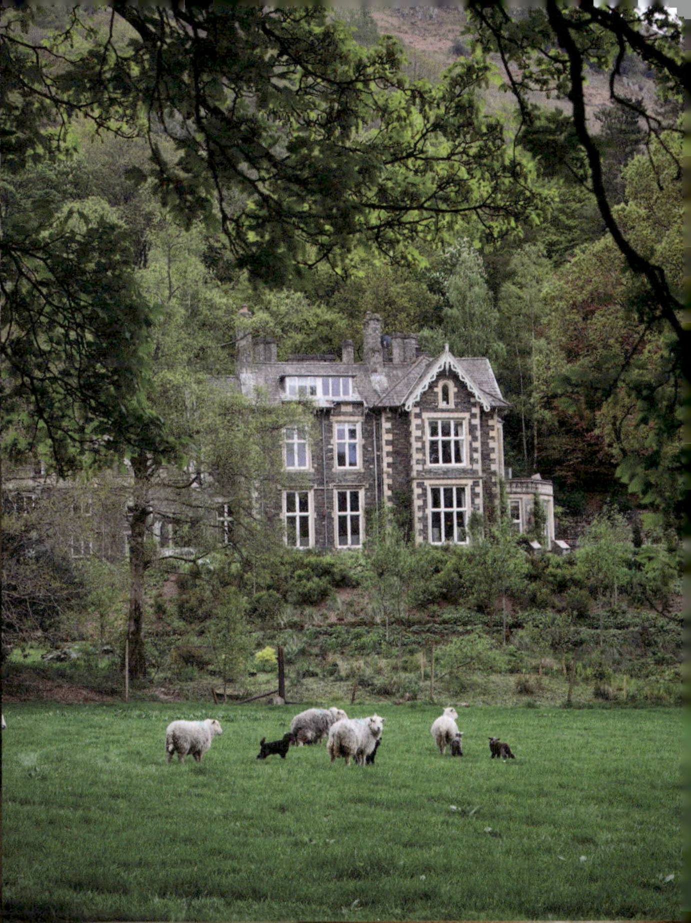
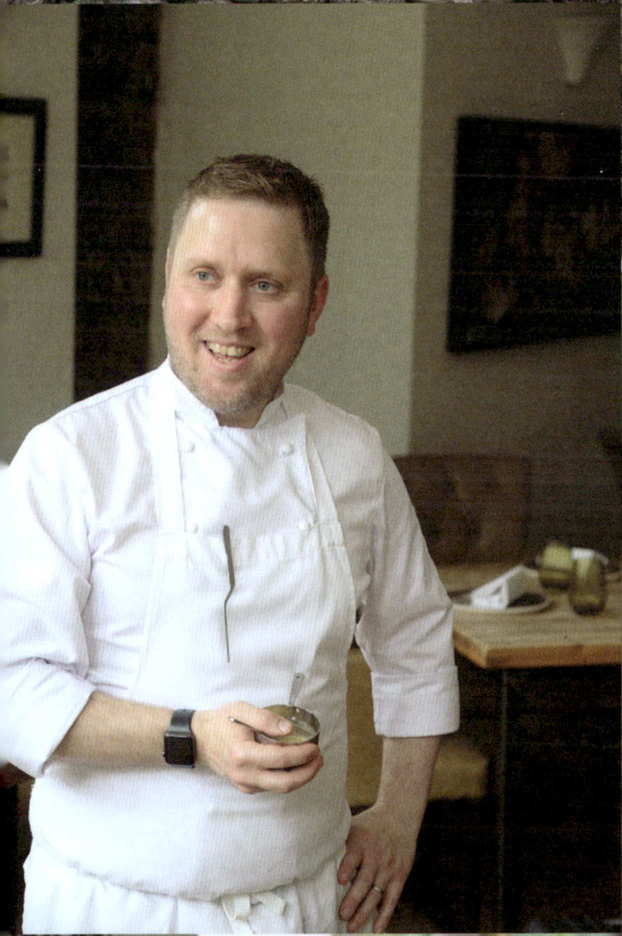
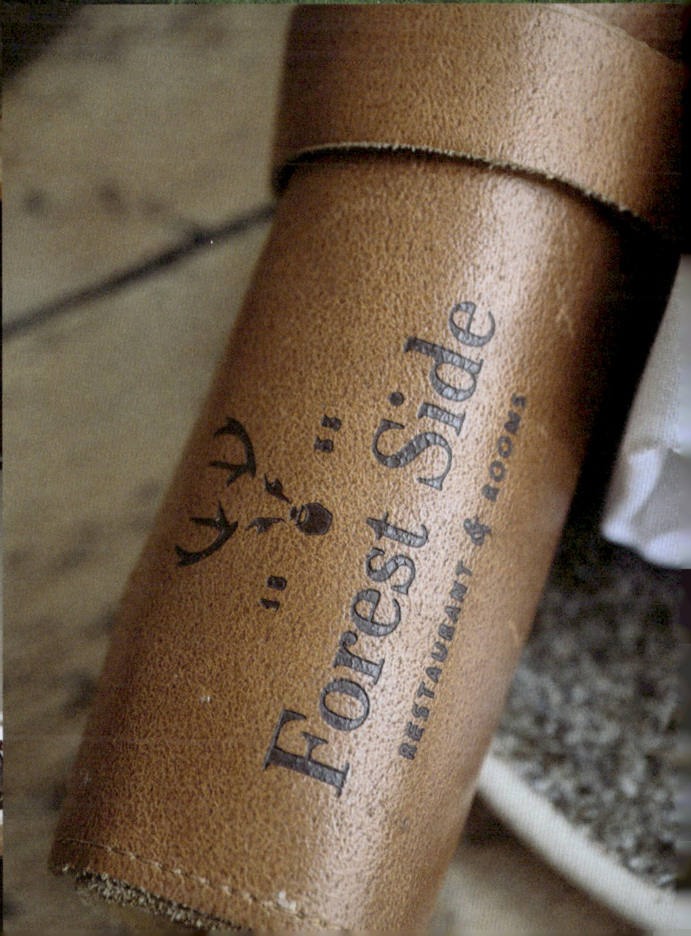
Forest Side
RESTAURANT & ROOMS
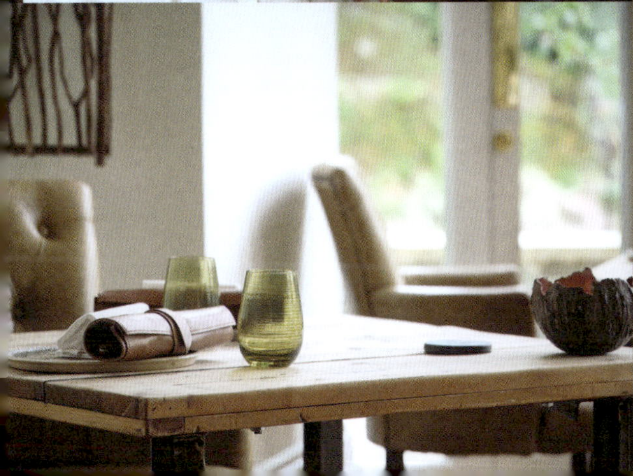

Forest Side, Lake District

Hafod Cheddar Gougère

Preparation time: 2 hours | Cooking time: 2 hours 30 minutes | Makes 50

FOR THE CHOUX
375ml water
125ml white wine
225g cultured butter
300g flour
10g salt
100g Hafod cheddar, finely grated
475g whole free-range eggs

FOR THE FONDUE
350ml raw milk
350ml double cream
280g free-range egg yolks
300g Hafod cheddar, grated

TO ASSEMBLE
200g cheap mild cheddar

FOR THE CHOUX
Weigh everything out. In a saucepan on a medium heat, warm the water, wine and butter until the butter has melted. Do not let the liquid boil.

Sift the flour and salt into the butter mix, stirring to make a smooth dough-like roux. Keep cooking this on a medium heat for around 4 minutes until it is not sticking to the sides of the pan.

Transfer the dough into a stand mixer with a paddle attachment. Start mixing on a medium speed, adding the finely grated cheese first. Whisk the eggs, pass and start adding slowly into the mixer. Once all the eggs are added, set a timer for 16 minutes and keep mixing until you have a cold dough with a smooth ribbon-like consistency.

Pipe the dough into 1cm spherical moulds and freeze overnight.

FOR THE FONDUE
Mix the milk, cream and egg yolks together, then pass into a large bowl. Cook this mixture over a bain marie for around 2 hours, mixing with a whisk every now and again. The mixture will resemble a dry scrambled egg.

Transfer the egg mixture into a Thermomix along with the grated Hafod cheddar. Blitz at 70°c on speed 5 for 12 minutes, then pass and cool.

TO ASSEMBLE
When you are ready to cook, pop your gougères out of their moulds and place on Silpats. Slice your cheap mild cheddar to around 0.5cm thick and cut into 3cm rounds with a cutter.

Once the gougères are defrosted, place a cheddar cheese round on each one and then cook in a preheated oven at 190°c with 0% humidity for 9 minutes. After this time, turn the oven down to 160°c and cook for a further 10 minutes. Once out of the oven, place on a cooling rack.

Pierce the bottom of each gougère and pipe in the cheese fondue until completely full. Reheat in the oven at 160°c for 2 minutes prior to serving.

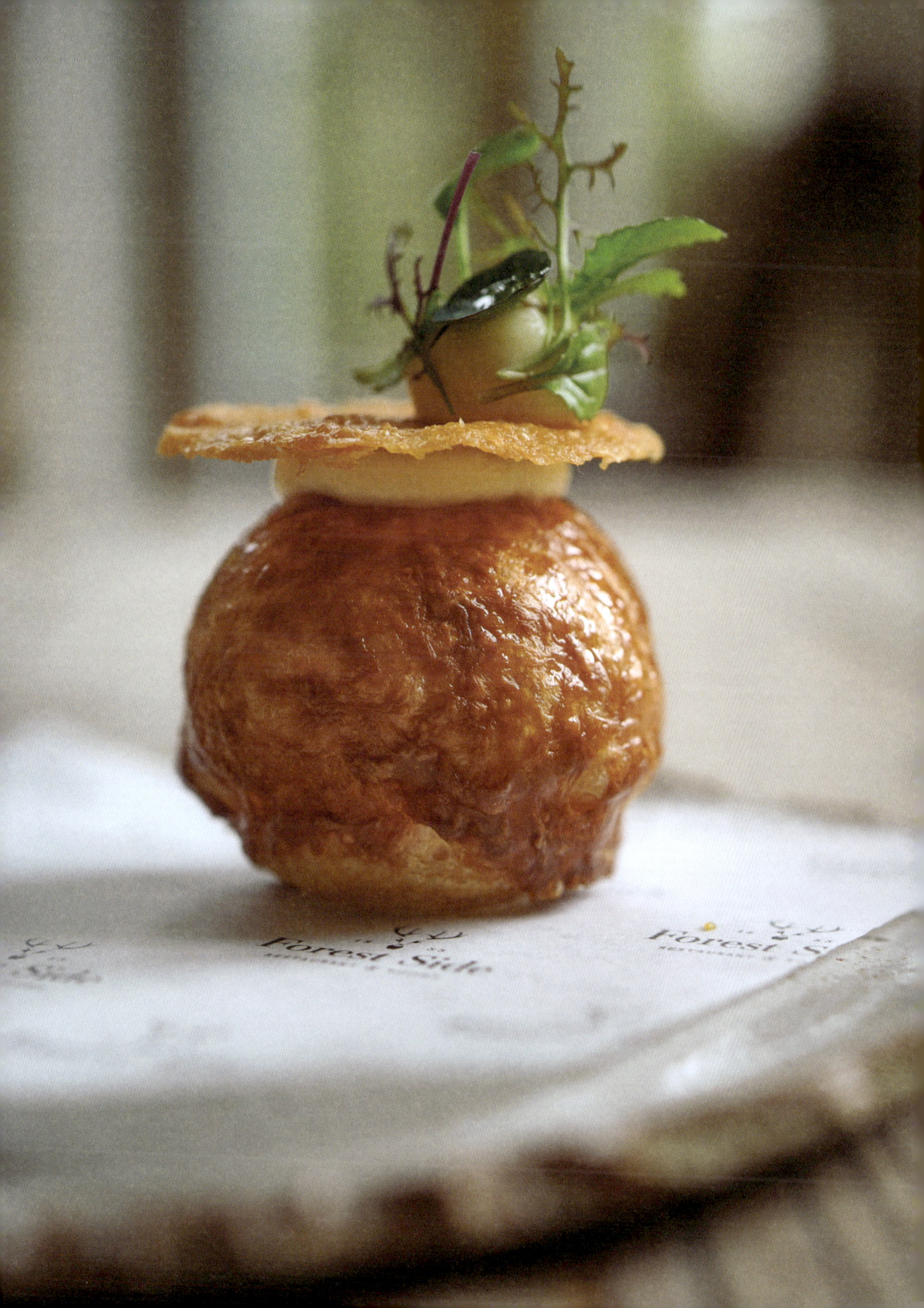

Forest Side, Lake District

Beetroots Cooked All Day in Their Own Juices

Preparation time: 48 hours | Cooking time: 9 hours | Serves 8

FOR THE COOKED BEETROOTS
1kg crapaudine beetroots
2 litres beetroot juice
300ml cabernet sauvignon vinegar
200g caster sugar

FOR THE PICKLED BEETROOTS
4 extra-large red beetroots
300ml blackberry vinegar
150ml water
50g caster sugar

FOR THE SMOKED COD'S ROE
80g smoked cod's roe
50g cold water
6g Dijon mustard
200ml grapeseed oil
Lemon juice, to taste

FOR THE SHEEP'S YOGHURT
200ml sheep's yoghurt

FOR THE CIDER VINEGAR GEL
250ml apple cider vinegar from Minus 8
50ml water
3.6g agar agar

FOR THE BEETROOT DRESSING
1 egg yolk
10g Dijon mustard
10g cider vinegar
100ml grapeseed oil
250ml beetroot juice
20ml cabernet sauvignon vinegar

FOR THE JUNIPER OIL
100g green juniper berries
200ml grapeseed oil

TO SERVE
1 Granny Smith apple

FOR THE COOKED BEETROOT
Wash the crapaudine beetroots, making sure any soil is removed. Place the vinegar, beetroot juice and sugar in a pan. Warm until the sugar has dissolved, then add the beetroots and cover with a cartouche. Cook on a medium heat for around 9 hours. The temperature of the cooking liquor should be around 85°c. Top up with water as necessary.

Once cooked, remove the beets from the liquor and set aside to cool. Pass the liquor through a fine chinois and reduce by half, then season with fine sea salt to taste. Set this aside for the next day.

Peel and halve the cooked beetroots, then place in the dehydrator at 63°c for 12 hours. Place the dehydrated beetroots and some of the reduced cooking liquor into a vacuum pouch and vacuum at full power. Leave to rehydrate for 36 hours before using.

FOR THE PICKLED BEETROOTS
Peel the red beetroots and spin on a Japanese mandoline. Cut the sheets into 10cm lengths, then into ribbons around 1cm wide. This should resemble tagliatelle. Mix the blackberry vinegar, water and sugar over a super low heat just until the sugar is dissolved. Once cool, pour the pickling liquor over the beetroot ribbons and vacuum pack until required.

FOR THE SMOKED COD'S ROE
Using a Vita-Prep, blitz the cod's roe, water and Dijon until smooth. Slowly start adding the grapeseed oil, emulsifying as though you are making a mayonnaise. Once thick and creamy, pass through a fine drum sieve and season with fine sea salt and lemon juice. Place in a piping bag.

FOR THE SHEEP'S YOGHURT
Hang the sheep's yoghurt in muslin cloth overnight to remove any excess whey. The next morning, season with some fine sea salt then place in a piping bag.

FOR THE CIDER VINEGAR GEL
Warm the cider vinegar and water in a pan, then add the agar agar and whisk well. Boil for 1 minute, then place in a container to set in the fridge. Once cool and set, blitz in a Nutribullet until smooth, pass and place into a piping bag.

FOR THE BEETROOT DRESSING
First, we have to make a mayonnaise, so whisk the egg yolk, Dijon mustard and cider vinegar together. Slowly emulsify in your grapeseed oil until thick and creamy. Using a hand blender, mix the beetroot juice and vinegar together, then add 2 tablespoons of the mayonnaise. Season the dressing with fine sea salt to taste.

FOR THE JUNIPER OIL
Vacuum pack the green juniper berries with the grapeseed oil and infuse for 12 hours at 70°c. Pass off and place in a nice squeezy bottle.

TO SERVE
We serve this dish at room temperature. Weigh out 24g of the cooked beetroot and 6 ribbons of pickled beetroot per portion. Pipe a good amount of the sheep's yoghurt onto a nice plate, then add the cooked beetroot, seasoned with a touch more fine sea salt.

Pipe two small dots of the vinegar gel and 3 larger dots of the cod's roe emulsion onto the beetroot. Dice the Granny Smith apple into 0.5cm cubes and place 4 of these onto the dish.

Cover all of this with the pickled beetroot ribbons, then finish with some oxalis cress and fennel. Drop a few drops of the juniper oil over the ribbons and serve the beetroot dressing at the table.

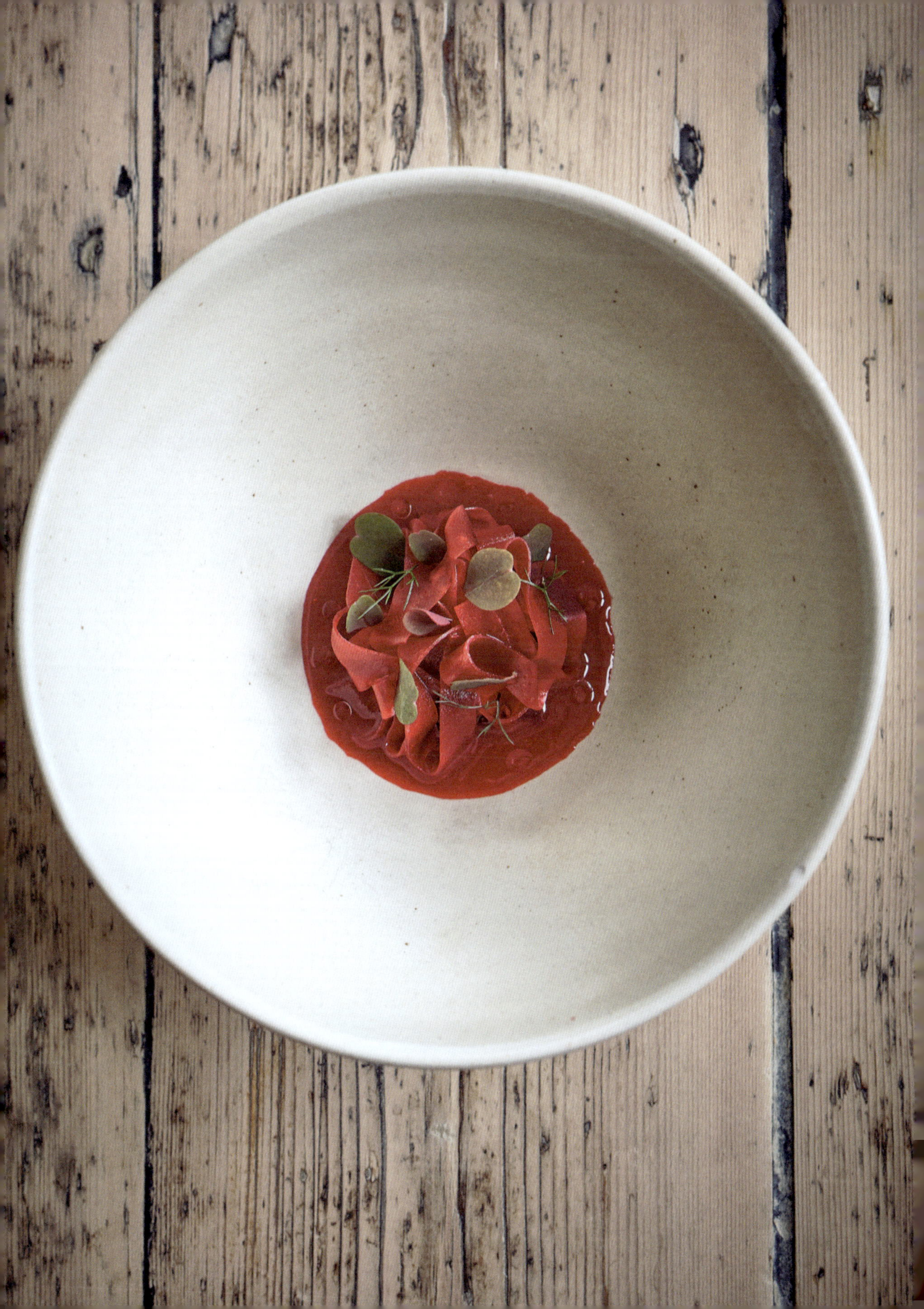

Forest Side, Lake District

Roasted Monkfish with Whey and Fermented Onion Sauce

Preparation time: 5 days | Cooking time: 12 hours | Serves 6

FOR THE KELP SEASONING
1kg fresh kelp

10 litres water

FOR THE ONION AND WHEY SAUCE
1kg white onion

20g fine Maldon sea salt

350g cultured butter

600ml fish stock

300ml whey

200ml double cream

FOR THE MONKFISH
2-3kg monkfish tail on the bone

1 litre water

80g fine sea salt

50g fish sauce

50g dried shiitake mushrooms

Lots of butter

FOR THE SHALLOT CONFIT
500g banana shallot

50g cultured butter

40g cabernet sauvignon vinegar

FOR THE ROASTED ONION PURÉE
1kg white onion

100g cultured butter

50g cabernet sauvignon vinegar

300ml vegetable nage

FOR THE KELP SEASONING
This is made in advance and kept as a larder item. Place the kelp and the water in a deep gastronorm tray, cover with cling film and tightly wrapped tin foil, then cook at 85°c for 12 hours. Pass off the kelp and reserve for another job… we turn ours into a seaweed jam for a snack. Reduce the kelp stock by half and then place into a dehydrator until all the liquid is gone and you have a white crystal or salt-like residue left. Blitz this until fine and keep in a Kilner jar.

FOR THE ONION AND WHEY SAUCE
We ferment our onions for 5 days so these need doing well in advance. Peel and slice the onion into 2cm pieces and mix with the fine sea salt. Vacuum down and keep at room temperature for 5 days.

FOR THE MONKFISH
Prepare the monkfish by trimming off any excess skin and blood lines but keeping it on the bone. Mix the water, salt, fish sauce and dried mushrooms in a pan over a low heat until the salt has dissolved and the mushrooms have rehydrated. Leave to cool to below 8°c. Place the monkfish in the brine for 25 minutes and then wash off with cold water. We need to leave this to air dry for at least 12 hours prior to using. Do this on a cooling wire in a fridge.

FOR THE ONION AND WHEY SAUCE
Pass off the onions from the liquid that will have been produced during the fermentation, reserving this. Place these in a pan with 250g of the cultured butter. We are going to sweat this off at a low temperature with a cartouche but it's really important not to get any colour on the onion. After around 1 hour of cooking, add the fish stock and whey. Increase the temperature and reduce by about a third. Pass this off and add the double cream, reduce again by a quarter, then season with the fermented onion juice and blitz in the remaining 100g cultured butter. Set aside for service.

FOR THE SHALLOT CONFIT
Peel and slice the shallots super fine lengthways. Place in a pan with some salt and the melted cultured butter. Sweat off for 20 minutes and then add the vinegar. Place a cartouche over the top and stir the shallot mixture every 10-15 minutes as the natural sugars will start caramelising. Keep scraping the bottom of the pan so that this flavour is mixed with the shallots and a jam-like consistency is created.

FOR THE ROASTED ONION PURÉE
We are going to make the onion purée using the exact same beginning stages we used for making our shallot confit. Once you have a jam-like consistency, add the vegetable nage and blitz in a Vita-Prep until smooth, then pass through a fine chinois.

To cook the monkfish, season it with the kelp seasoning, get a nice large pan super-hot with some grapeseed oil in and then carefully add the monkish tail. Seal until it has a nice even colour all the way around then reduce the heat and add a shedload of butter. Once the butter is foaming, use a ladle to baste the monkfish tail for around 2 minutes.

Take the monkfish tail out of the pan and pour the butter into a deep tray. Give it 5 minutes for the butter to cool and then place the monkfish in the butter at around 54°c for 8 minutes. This resting stage is really important for an even cooking of the monkfish.

Carve the monkfish off the bone; you should see a nice rainbow effect on the flesh which should be firm and not leaking any water.

Present the monkfish on a plate with the onion purée and shallot confit. I like to serve a grilled wild garlic leaf and some wild garlic flowers with this when in season. Serve the warmed onion and whey sauce at the table.

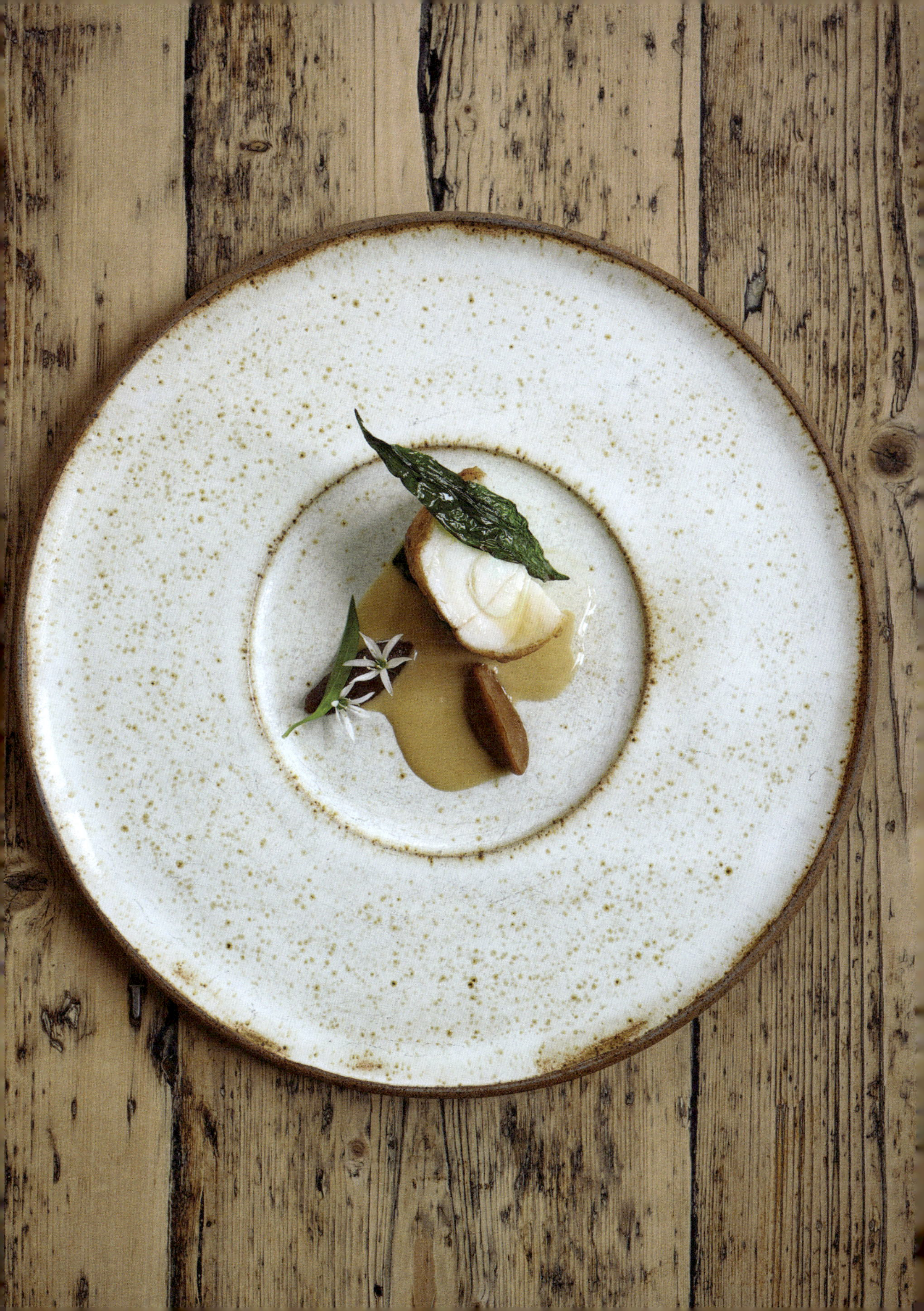

Forest Side, Lake District

Kitchen Confidential

HAFOD CHEDDAR GOUGÈRES

What's special about Hafod Cheddar?

We work closely with Andy Swinscoe at The Courtyard Dairy for our cheese trollies, so he gave us some of the Hafod to cook with and it was banging. Also, it's a super consistent cheese. A lot of cheeses change throughout the seasons, whereas with the Hafod we know we're going to get a very similar product every time. It's got a little bit of a punch to it as well, so the snacks that kick off our menu will build up to that, starting with gentler flavours before you get to the gougère which is just an amazing cheesy fondue mess. We needed a cheese with the right strength and texture – Hafod's not crumbly, there's almost a waxiness to it – and it's just got all the right characteristics.

Your fondue method for this recipe seems unusual…

Yeah, it's basically cooking out your egg yolks, milk and cream in a bain marie until they're like scrambled egg. Mix your cheese into that and somehow it makes a fondue with this gorgeous silky texture. You think it's not going to work because you've cooked all the moisture out of it, but it rehydrates and comes together so nicely. Then it gets 15 minutes in the Thermomix at 70°c and we pass it before filling all the gougères, which then go through the oven for 2 minutes.

Why are the gougères topped with 'cheap mild cheddar' as specified in your recipe?

We wanted to make a choux bun with a savoury craquelin on top to give the gougères a nice crust, so we tried it with all these different cheeses and some of them were too good in a way. The cheese wouldn't let the choux rise or cook to an even colour, etc. but eventually we just used a cheap catering cheddar that we get in for staff and it worked. You get a nice round gougère, the cheese melts and it forms a perfect coating. Honestly, it took us months to do it and anyone new to kitchen gives us a funny look when they see us getting the catering cheese out, but it all makes sense when you see how nicely the gougères rise and cook. Turns out cheap plastic cheese is the best way to do it! It's more for the texture than the actual flavour of the cheese of course, because you're not going to taste it over the fondue made with the Hafod.

BEETROOTS COOKED ALL DAY IN THEIR OWN JUICES

Where does this dish come into your menu?

The beetroot is course number four – it's a really nice, light, refreshing break after all the snacks and starters but before the slightly more indulgent mains. We're constantly changing the menu, but the beetroot has stayed on for months. Partly because people love it, and partly because we've got a room downstairs where we plant any roots we've got in sand and then we'll just keep them until they're gone. You get 18g of cooked beetroot on this dish, so it doesn't use up a lot of produce.

How does the dehydrating and rehydrating process improve the beetroot?

The dehydrating and rehydrating was something we saw maybe eight years ago at Blue Hill Farm at Stone Barns with chef Dan Barber, where they were working on these beetroots. The fructose in them had gone all jammy and we wanted something like that, so we juiced all the tiny ones which we couldn't cook and then cooked the rest of the beetroots in the juice. Dehydrating them takes out any excess water while leaving the sugars, then we know that compressing things is going to rehydrate them and create a different texture. They didn't end up jammy but instead we got a chewy wine gummy sort of texture which was phenomenal. We tried it with artichokes which was really good too – those were compressed in apple juice – so that whole process has given us this really cool technique, which also happens to preserve the ingredient for a couple of weeks.

What was the inspiration behind such a successful dish?

Instead of focusing on how to add more ingredients to make a better dish, we started to look at how to make a single ingredient better. So you're looking at it almost backwards, and that was a turning point for us – I'm not clever enough to bring loads of ingredients together, but what we can do is delve into each one. It just makes complete sense, especially with our own produce. It's what we believe in. Throughout this dish you've got loads of different textures and flavours – the nice chewiness, the freshness of the pickle, a light dressing which is made from the cooking liquor – which are almost entirely beetroot. I remember doing something similar at Andrew Fairlie's which was a beetroot and rhubarb dish, so it's always been something on my mind, but we've got it to a level where we're happy with it now.

ROASTED MONKFISH WITH WHEY AND FERMENTED ONION SAUCE

How integral is the monkfish to this dish, or do other fish work with the same flavours?

We've moved on to cod instead of monkfish for this dish and it will probably change again slightly as we get into summer with everything coming through from the garden: a nice little bean salad or something like that. With the cod, we steam it just to make it a bit cleaner. It worked great to give the monkfish that really hard sear, but for the cod we brine it and air dry it before steaming for 2-3 minutes at 65°c. We also make a stock with all the cooked bones and skin for the sauce, and all the oil that will sit on top of that stock is skimmed off, so the cod is brushed in its own oil to retain more moisture and flavour.

Do you always make stocks and sauces in house?

The fish stock and the vegetable nage (also used in this dish) are the main ones we make in house, just because of the size of our kitchen, and we already make 12 different sauces for the menu so it's full on for the guys. I'd always been a bit too proud to order stocks in but when we did make that change it made complete sense; we get some from the guys at True Foods who are class. The consistency is so important – if a stock gets left on an hour longer, it completely changes the flavour. Because the restaurant isn't open on Mondays and Tuesdays, we'll make all the stocks and pickles and brines then and store them ready for the week ahead.

Where did the idea for kelp seasoning come from?

Big Fred, a chef who used to work for us, spent three years in Japan so he had all these techniques like the dashi seasoning on the monkfish. I love that sort of thing and always ask how we can make it work for us. We've got to keep our identity but because I'm slowly understanding things like that more, we can evolve. Ultimately, it's about trialling those new techniques alongside what we do, which is about shedloads of butter, roasting, resting, cooking on the bone. I think it all makes up who you are and I'm certain that the way I'll be cooking in 10 years' time is different from what I'm doing now.

Forest Side, Lake District

Tell Us About Your...

Cooking style.

It's quite simplistic but natural. It's got a classical spine within it, so everything's done to enhance the flavour. The techniques we use are very relatable so if you were cooking 20-30 years ago, you'd be able to make one of our sauces. It would be the finishing touches, like the infusions, which are slightly different: classical undertones with some added natural and simplistic elements.

Kitchen garden.

What we grow in the beds, tunnels, greenhouse and wilder patches for foraged stuff dictates what we do 90% of the time. Some people think the process starts when the ingredient comes through the door, but actually you put a lot of work into it to make sure you're getting the right thing into the kitchen, whether that's building relationships with good suppliers or planting it yourself. That's why we grow so much in the kitchen garden because we know that it's all organic, there's no chemicals being used, and it's as fresh as you'll ever get.

Favourite ingredients.

Cheese, lots of cheese. I'm massively into cheese and I love trying super seasonal varieties. When vacherins come in, I'm all over them. Lobster and shellfish are special for me, probably from my time in Scotland. There was an oyster farm 2 minutes from where I used to live, and this Scottish salmon farm that let us go to the back door and pick up a few fish to stick in the car as there were huge trucks getting piled up with boxes to go all over the country. So I do have a big soft spot for seafood.

Essential equipment.

I'm a stickler for timers – the boys went through a period of everyone's phone alarms going off which just reminds me of waking up every morning. So I make sure everyone's got a timer now. A good quality knife is so important too; I just use a Mac knife and I've got a lovely slicer from Simon Maillet in Sheffield which we use on service every night, and a little paring knife too. We don't have a load of gadgets – just give me a timer and a knife and we'll be good.

Influences and inspirations.

We're blessed in a way because of where we are – even just going for a walk clears your head, but you're also looking at the bank and noticing something's about to come up – so all it takes is that one little flash and then suddenly you might have four ideas which all come together to make a dish. That's just how it seems to work sometimes. It's about sticking with the things that I love but also not being afraid not to follow a trend. The gougères are a perfect example – they were being served in the 70s but I'll still stick them on the menu because they're class. I've got to stay true to myself and make sure I'm not trying to reinvent the wheel, which is only going to make the guy on table seven go 'it was just alright' because I've been trying out some funky technique for the sake of it.

Dream places to eat.

I've never been to The Ritz but I'd love to go and just try everything. Then Gareth Ward's restaurant, Ynyshir in Wales – opposite ends of the spectrum in terms of what they do, but there's the same appreciation for the craft. I'd love to visit Kenny Atkinson's new gaff too. I love his food and being a northern lad, I've followed his career closely as he's always been a bit of a hero of mine.

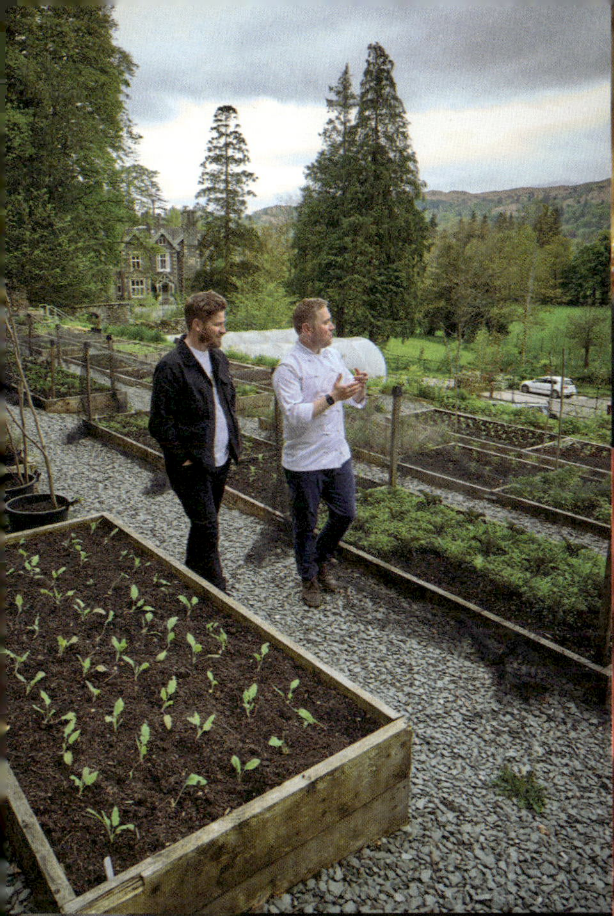
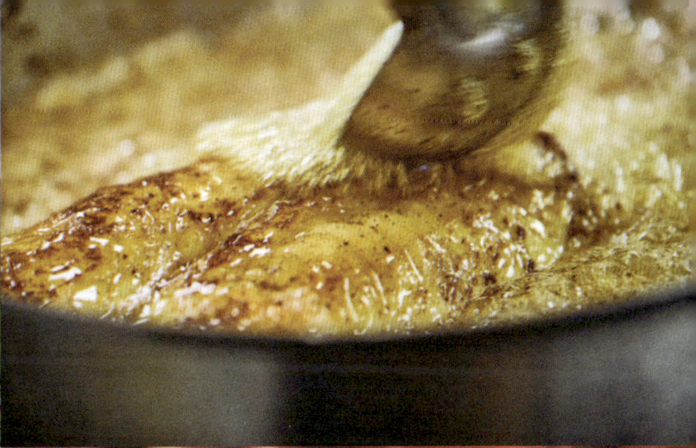
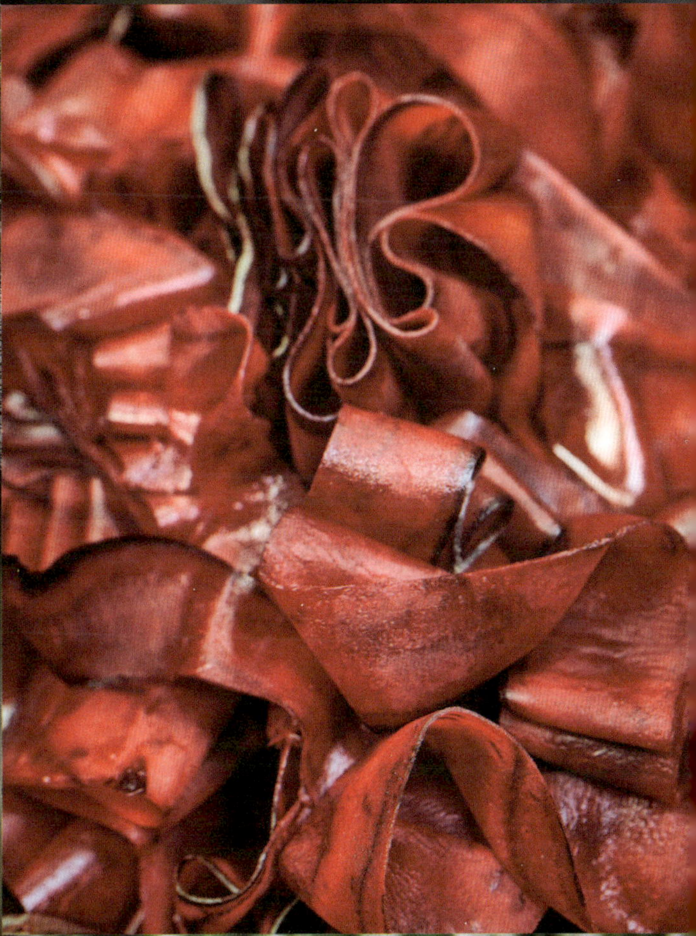
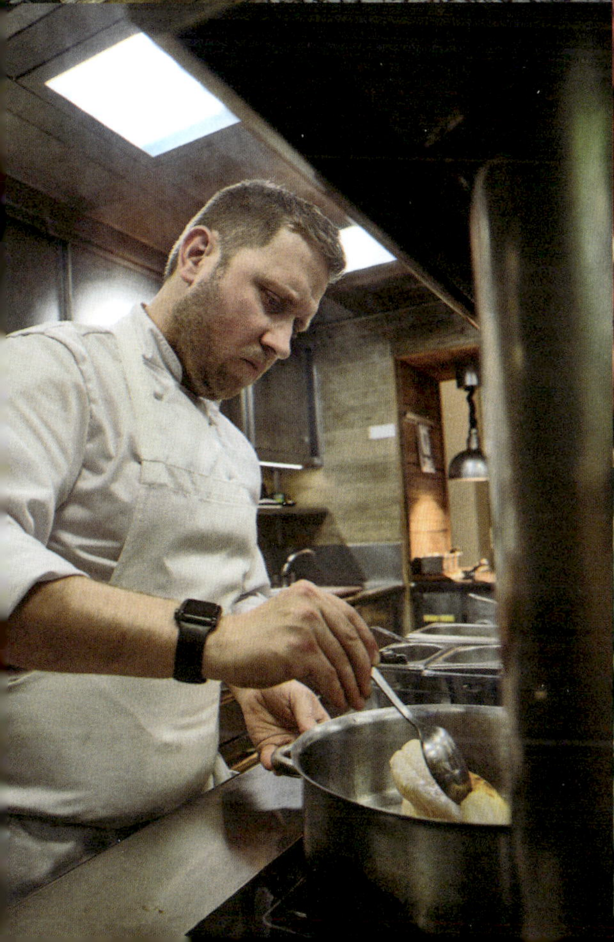
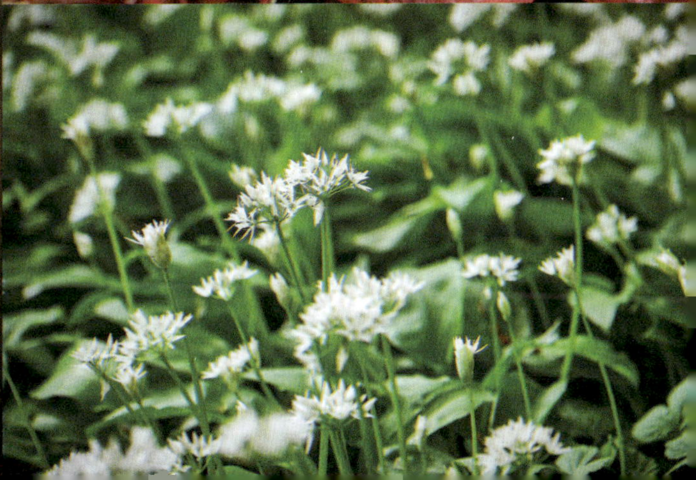

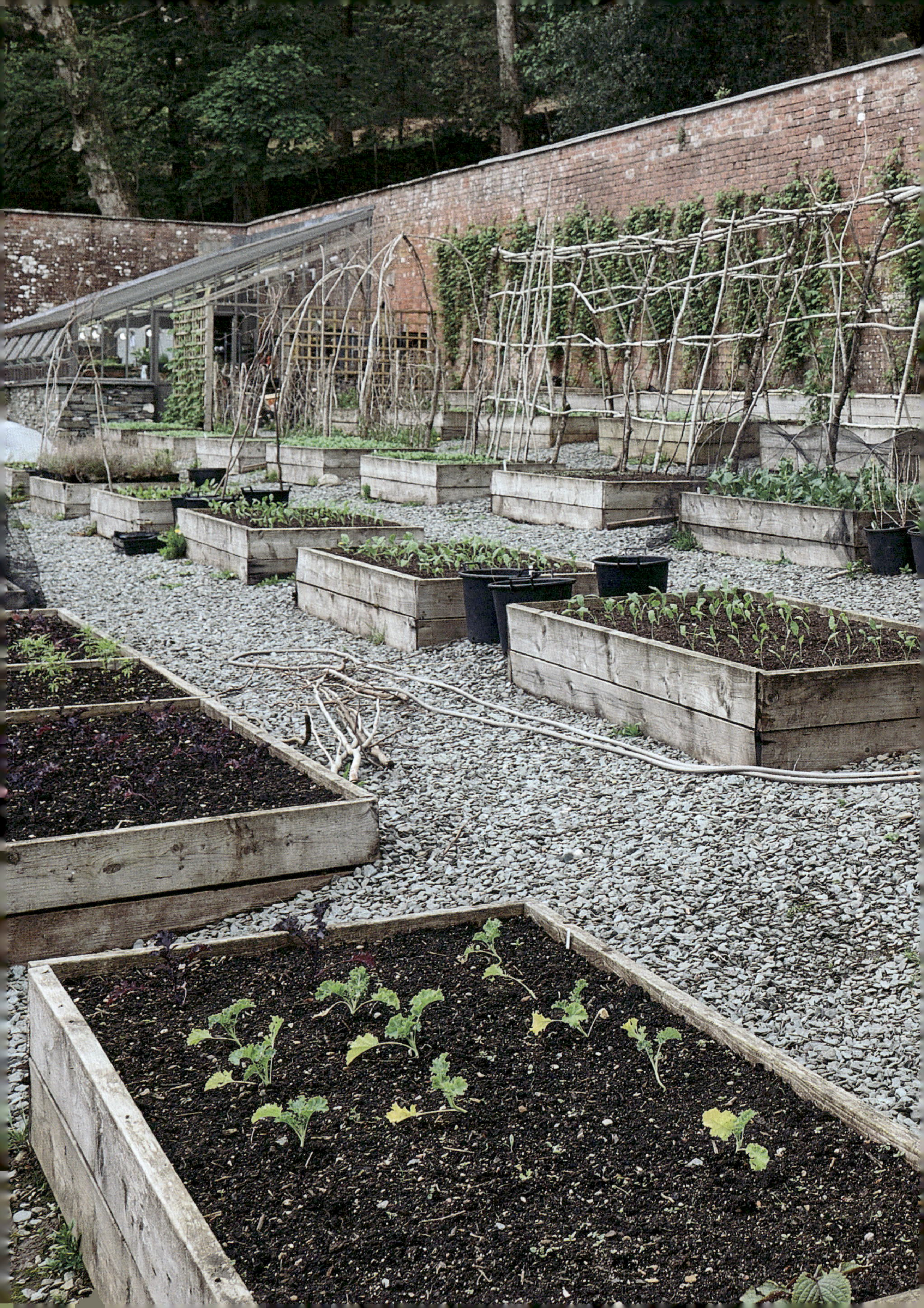

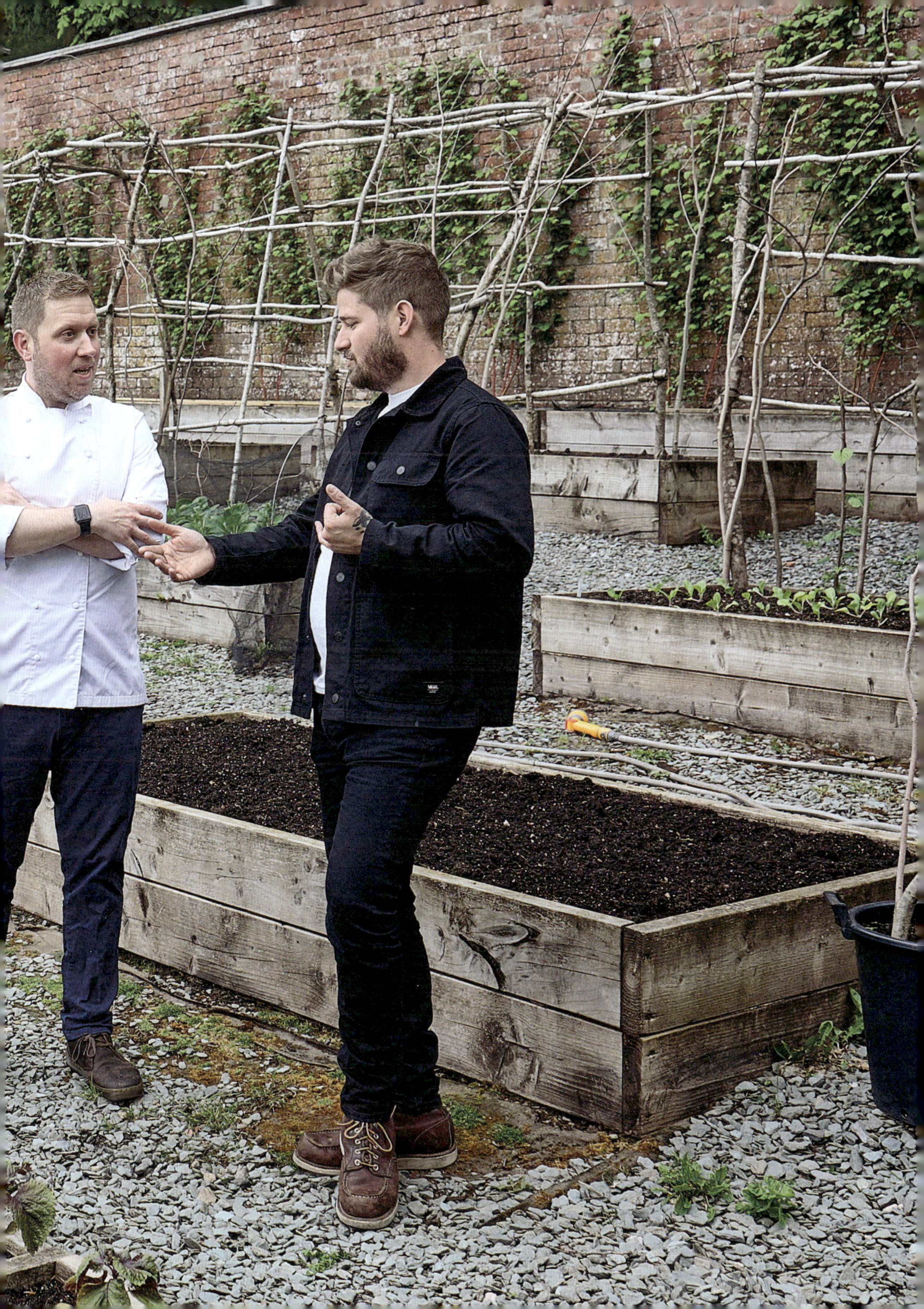

Da Terra, London

Rafael Cagali

Chef Rafael Cagali was born in São Paulo, Brazil, and moved to Europe at 21 where he began his career in restaurant kitchens. He spent years living in both Italy and Spain, working with the likes of Chef Stefano Baiocco at A Villa Feltrinelli, Chef Quique Dacosta and Martin Berasategui. After moving to the UK, Rafael went on to work at The Fat Duck and Yashin Ocean House before joining Simon Rogan at Fera at Claridges, and later took on the role of head chef at the eight-seater development kitchen, Aulis. He opened Da Terra in 2019, and the restaurant gained its first Michelin star that same year, quickly followed by a second in 2020.

Meaning 'from the ground' in Italian, Da Terra is set in the Edwardian Town Hall Hotel in Bethnal Green, East London. The restaurant has just 11 tables in an intimate yet lively setting looking onto the small open service kitchen. There are two tasting menu options – their full-length tasting menu as well as a lunch version – which guide diners through a flavourful journey that draws on the chef's origins and experiences.

How did you start out in the hospitality industry?

My mum had a restaurant so I grew up around the business but could never have imagined that this would be a career for me one day. When I came over here for the first time, I needed a job and found one as a potwash in the kitchen of a small place in west London. The hospitality industry is a beautiful one, open and vast, and I fell in love with it and worked my way up. This experience that you have is not just a career, it's a way of life. Hospitality gives you this and I don't know of any other career that would do that.

What influences and inspires your cooking?

My biggest influence is my Brazilian-Portuguese heritage and of course all the kitchens I have worked in. Da Terra is more about the produce for us – I don't say Da Terra is a Brazilian restaurant because it's far from it, but I am of course inspired by my country, our cuisine and ingredients, and we use these to guide what we do at Da Terra. Brazil is very much influenced by other cultures; it's a relatively young country with influences from all over the world. If you go south in Brazil there are Germans, Austrians, Portuguese, French, and North Brazil is mostly people of African descent, so you get the spices and ingredients like coconut milk. Growing up there amidst all those different cuisines and cultures has had a big influence on my cooking.

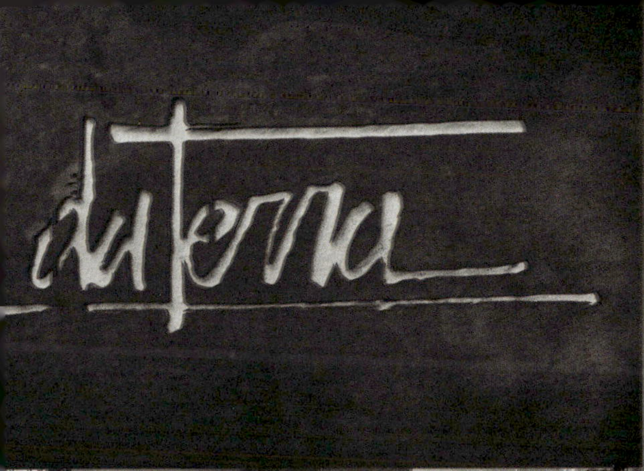
da terra

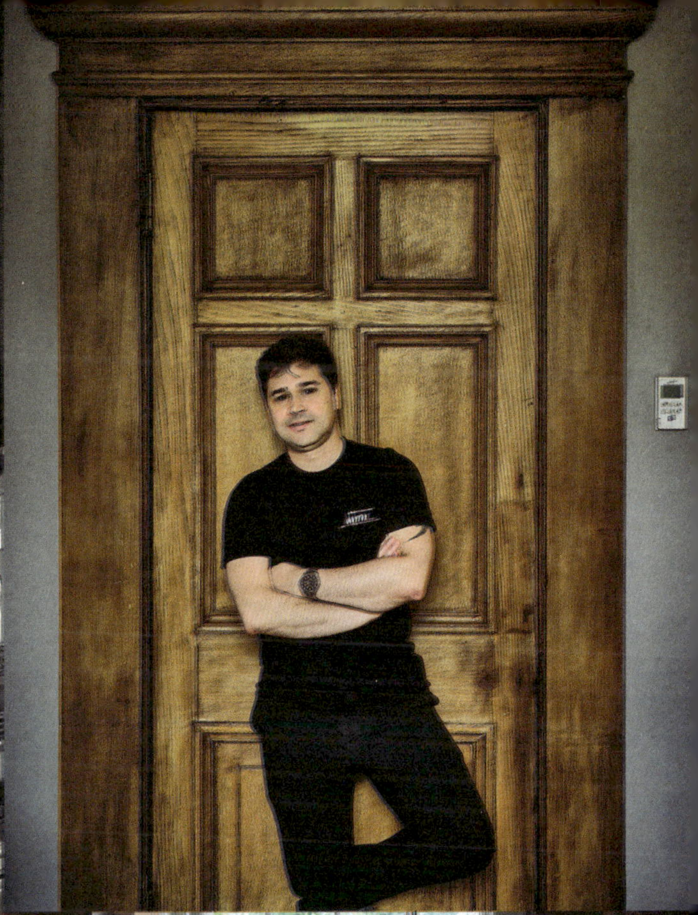

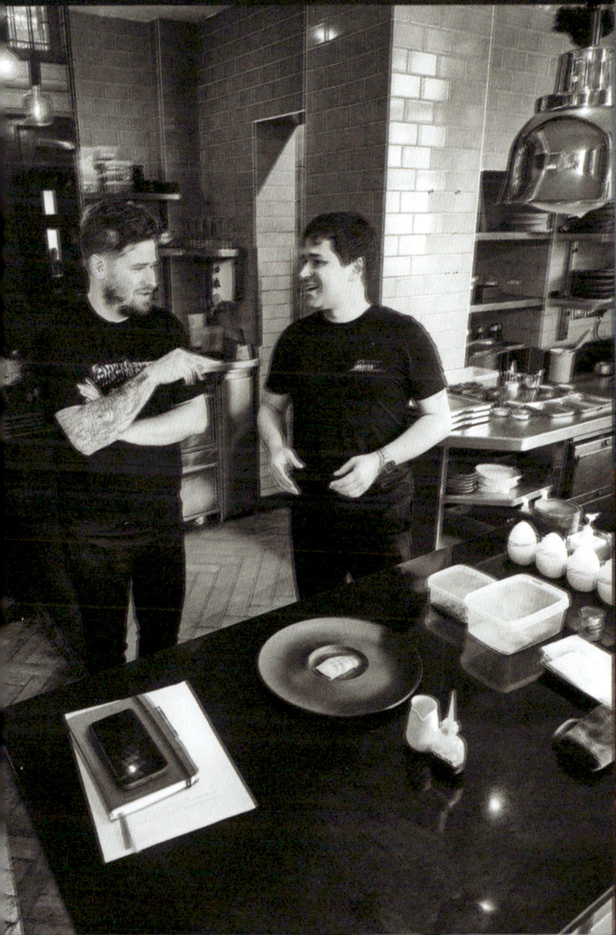

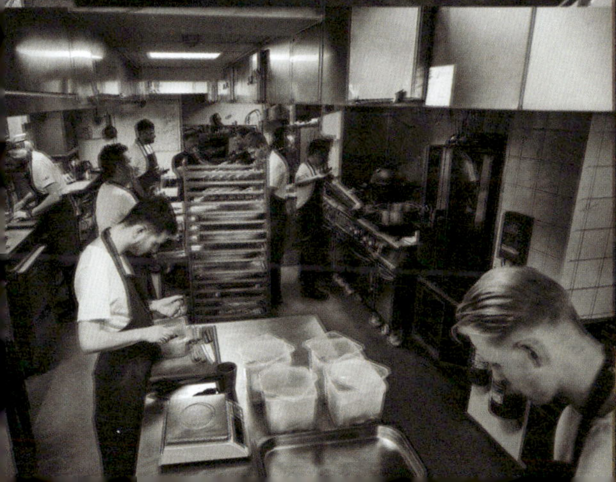

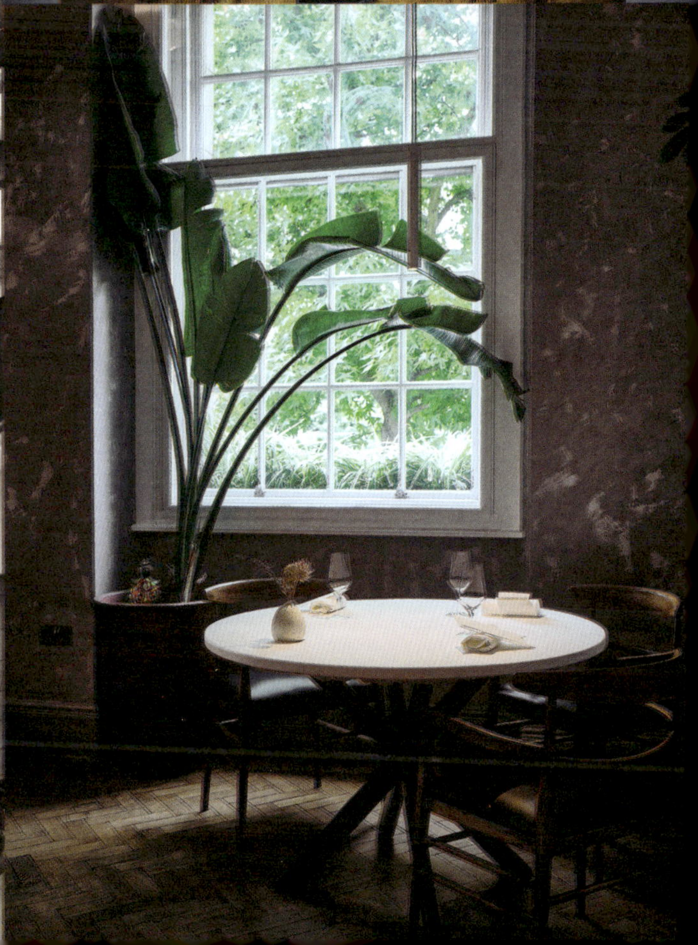

Da Terra, London

Where do your recipe ideas come from?

When I opened my own restaurant, it was liberating to be able to create a vision and implement it the way I wanted. What I'm thinking about most when creating a dish is always flavour, and how ingredients work together to add layers to a dish. With the pineapple dessert for example, we're adding Mexican tepache and using a fruit that doesn't grow in the UK, but I wanted to combine them because it's a great dish with good quality ingredients. Sometimes everybody ends up doing the same thing – in strawberry season there will be strawberry desserts everywhere. Most of our produce will come from Britain but I'm not going to hesitate to use certain ingredients from elsewhere if the result will be better. I'd go to any country for inspiration, as long as the ingredients are sustainably sourced.

Do you have any new projects in the pipeline?

I'm taking over the old Corner Room space in the Town Hall Hotel to open Elis, which will be a relaxed restaurant with à la carte dishes and a beautiful wine list curated by Noble Rot. It's exciting because I'll be able to buy a whole animal and use everything in an easier, more approachable way. As much as we do minimise waste at Da Terra by creating dishes with lots of different elements, people expect the prime cuts when it's a fine dining restaurant. Elis will mean that we can get more from the animal and we will be able to serve more rustic food.

How do you like to spend your time outside the restaurant?

Sunday is my day when I try to really switch off. Charlie and I like to take our dog Rollo for a walk, maybe grab lunch and relax because Saturdays at Da Terra are intense. When I can, I like to go to some of my favourite restaurants in East London: top of my list are Bistroteque, E.Pellici and Brawn. I also try to get back home to Brazil about every two years if I can to see my family and explore what's happening on the dining scene, everything from street food to fine dining.

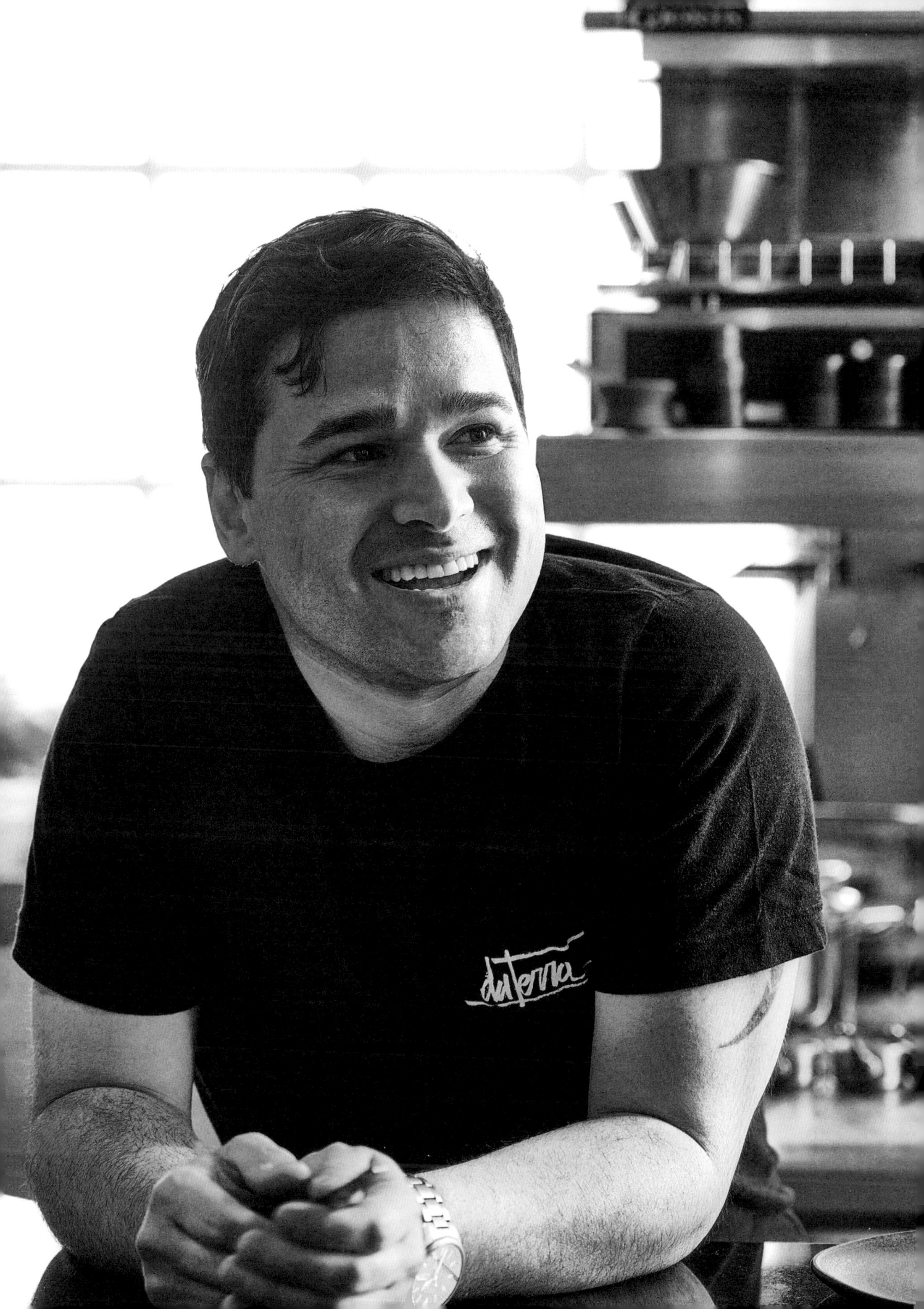

Da Terra, London

Herb Bouquet

Preparation time: 30 minutes | Serves 2

FOR THE BOUQUET

1 red endive leaf

2 chives

2 sprigs of coriander

2 marigolds

2 sprigs of chervil

2 nasturtium leaves

2 nasturtium flowers

2 fennel tops

2 mustard cress

2 rocket cress

2 oxalis leaves

2 sprigs of parsley

2 slices of duck ham

FOR THE FISH ROE MOUSSE

20g water

100g fish roe

150g sunflower oil

0.5g xanthan gum

Fresh lemon juice

Salt

FOR THE BOUQUET

Wash all the herbs in a bowl of iced water for a few minutes. Build them as a flower bouquet and wrap it up with a slice of duck ham. You can also use chives or cooked leeks to wrap up the bouquet.

FOR THE FISH ROE MOUSSE

Place the water and fish roe into a Vitamix. Blend to a paste, then emulsify in the sunflower oil and add the xanthan to hold the mousse. Season with lemon juice and salt to taste.

Place the mousse in an iSi canister and charge twice. Keep in the fridge.

TO ASSEMBLE THE DISH

Place the bouquet on your plate and then pipe the mousse from the canister to one side of it. Dust the mousse with a herb powder made from the dried ingredients of your bouquet – lovage for example – and serve.

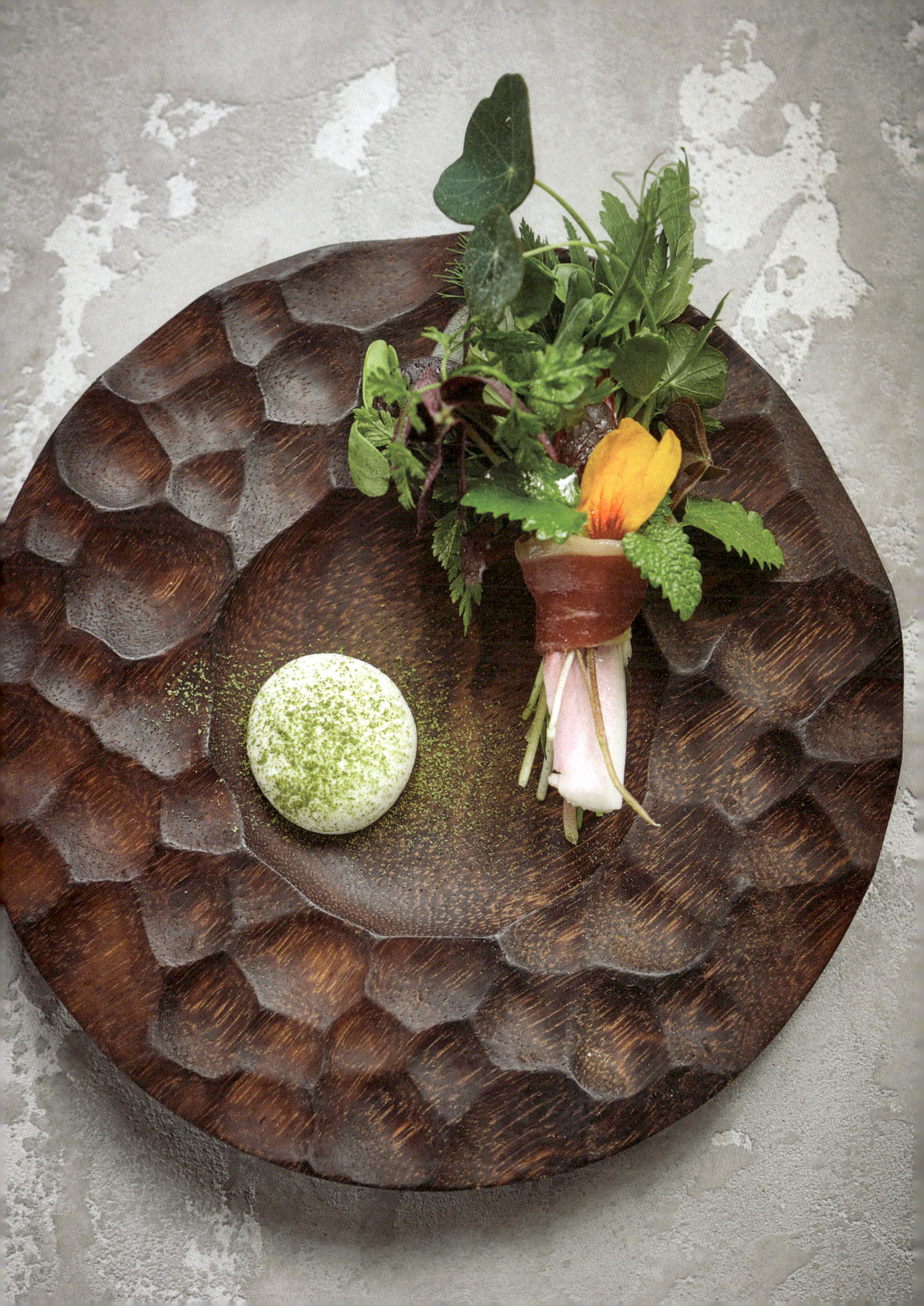

Da Terra, London

Pineapple, Coconut, Spice Biscuit

Preparation time: 4-5 days | Cooking time: 4 hours | Serves 6

1 pineapple

FOR THE COCONUT ICE CREAM

1kg whole milk

400g sugar

240g egg yolk

800g hung coconut yoghurt

FOR THE SPICE BISCUIT

160g butter

160g sugar

80g egg yolk

210g plain flour

5g ground cinnamon

2g baking powder

2g ground clove

1g ground nutmeg

TO SERVE

Coconut gel

Marigold sprigs

Mint oil

PREPARE THE PINEAPPLE

Peel the pineapple and place the skin into a large jar. Cover the skin with water and sugar at a ratio of 10:1 and leave at room temperature for 4-5 days. After this time, pass the fermented juice into a pan and reduce down until you have a syrupy glaze.

Prepare the pineapple according to your preference so it can be grilled or barbecued until just softened and starting to caramelise. We normally barbecue the whole pineapple before cutting it into rounds, then taking out the hard core and slicing the rounds really thinly. Brush the glaze made from the skins over the pineapple while barbecuing.

FOR THE COCONUT ICE CREAM

Bring the milk to a simmer. Mix the egg and sugar together in a heatproof bowl, then temper this with the hot milk and bring the temperature to 70°c. Keep the mixture at this temperature for 10 minutes, then place into the fridge and leave to chill for 4 hours before adding the hung yoghurt. Mix well to combine the yoghurt with the chilled egg mixture, then pass and freeze it. If you have an ice cream machine you can churn the mixture until frozen.

FOR THE SPICE BISCUIT

Mix the butter and sugar into a white paste. Gradually add the egg yolks until combined, then add all the dry ingredients and mix to a smooth dough. Rest the dough in the fridge or freezer for 30 minutes to firm up.

Shave the dough with a cheese grater onto a tray lined with parchment paper and bake at 180°c for until the biscuit crumb is your desired colour.

TO SERVE

Place the sliced pineapple in overlapping layers across the serving dish and then pipe dots of coconut gel on top of the pineapple. Garnish each dot of gel with a marigold sprig. Sprinkle the biscuit crumb either over the pineapple or onto a side plate, then place a quenelle of the coconut yoghurt ice cream on top. Pour some of the tapache (fermented liquid) into a small jug and split with some mint oil, then pour this over the dish (not over the ice cream) or serve on the side.

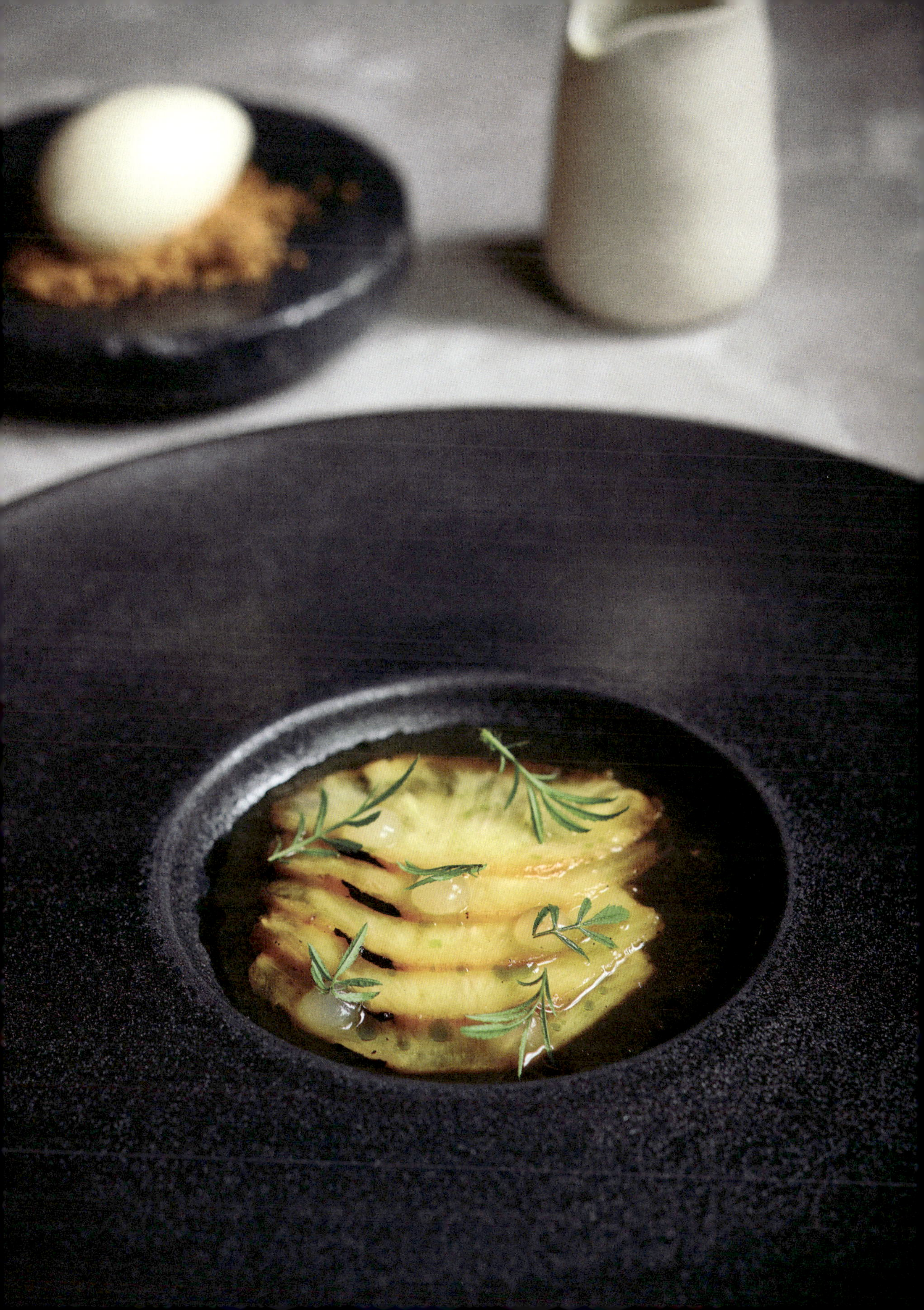

Da Terra, London

Moqueca – Brazilian Fish Stew

Preparation time: 30 minutes | Cooking time: 50 minutes | Serves 4

FOR THE SPICE PASTE
60g fresh ginger

20g dried shrimps

6g black peppercorns

6g ground turmeric

6g coriander seeds

4 fresh chillies

FOR THE SAUCE
20g garlic

500g onion

500g red pepper

300g green pepper

50g butter

500g tomatoes

80g dende oil (or a pinch of saffron for colour)

40g spice paste (see above)

100g okra, whole or sliced

3 litres fish stock

500g coconut milk

400g fresh cod

30g fresh coriander

20g chervil or parsley

1 lime, sliced

FOR THE SPICE PASTE
Blitz everything together with a bit of oil to form a paste.

FOR THE SAUCE
In a large pan with a lid, sweat off the garlic, onion and peppers in the butter without colouring them. Add the tomatoes and continue cooking. Stir in the dende oil and spice paste before adding the okra and fish stock. Simmer this mixture for 30 minutes with the lid on.

Add the coconut milk to the pan and simmer for another 10 minutes. Place the pieces of cod into the sauce and cook for another 5 minutes.

Chop the fresh herbs and stir them into the stew with the slices of lime, then leave the flavours to infuse for 5 minutes. I suggest serving this dish with plain rice and farofa (Brazilian toasted flour).

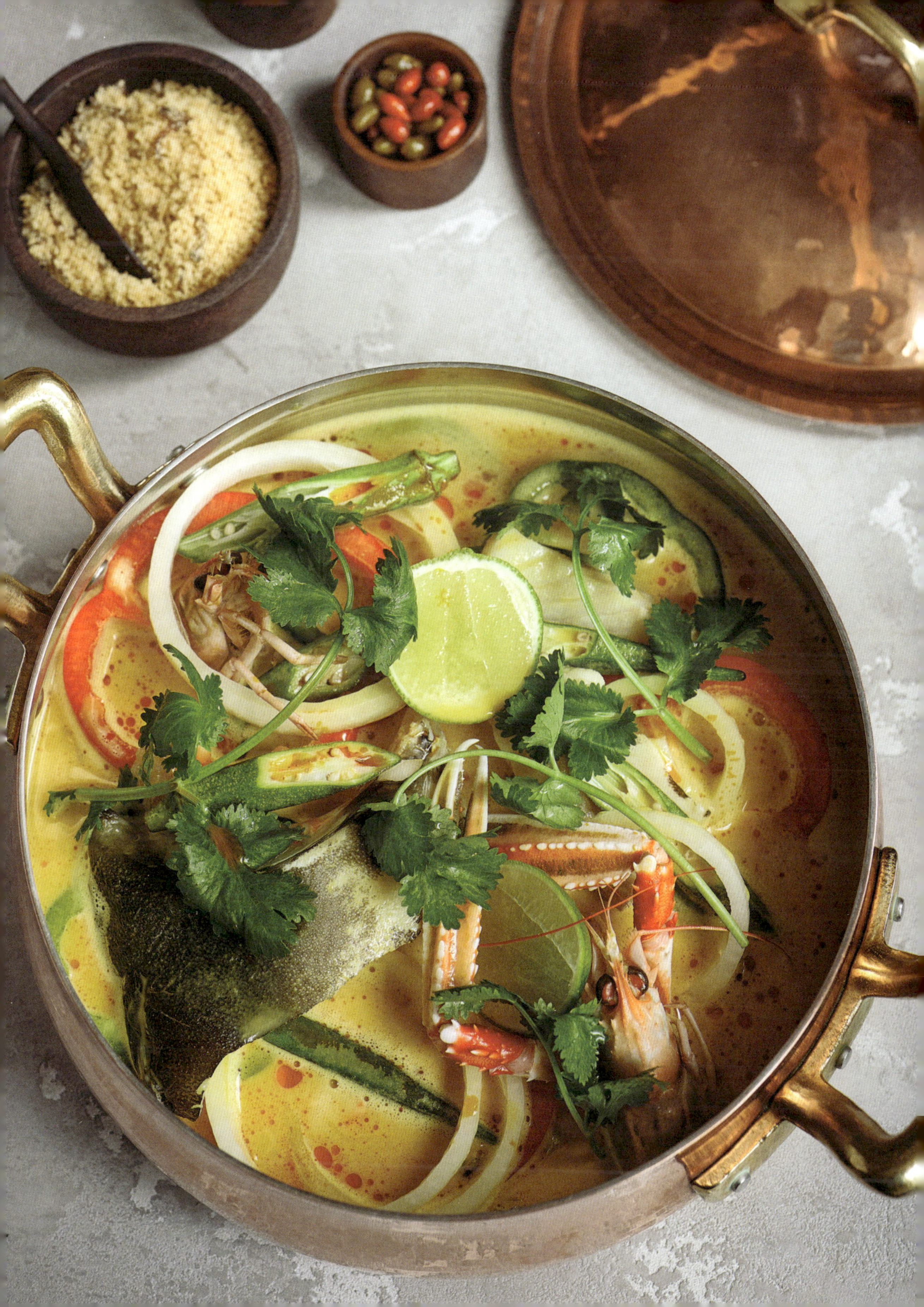

Da Terra, London

Kitchen Confidential

HERB BOUQUET

I've had this on the menu as a side dish before, but it could be a snack at the beginning of the meal or even towards the end as a palate cleanser. When you're coming into summer it's a great way to include so many shoots and cresses without serving a big bowl of salad, plus you can get in there with your hands and scoop up the fish mousse for loads of extra flavour. I've also done it with a brown butter dip before which adds a nice acidity and works like a dressing. We spray the bouquet with smoked vinegar and you can season it with salt and olive oil, too – treat it like a little salad.

I worked at a place in Italy years ago where all the herbs they used were growing in the kitchen garden, so we had a salad on the menu for the VIPs that included every single different cress, herb and edible flower, all in one big bowl. The flavours were just insane, like a burst of colour in your brain, and I took some inspiration from that to create this dish. We source the herbs from Infarm in London although we have marigolds in the back yard which can be used in season, as well as any herbs you can grow at home or forage like lovage, lemon balm, oxalis, pea shoots, nasturtiums, fennel tops…we just put it together depending on what's in season and what will create a really rounded flavour. You want to balance everything because there should be so many bursts of flavour in the mouth when you eat this.

We make the mousse here so when the fish comes in, we take out the roe which is cured and smoked to then make an emulsion. We usually use turbot roe as that's often in for other dishes. We also cure and dry the duck ham in house. That brings a saltiness to the dish. You can make a herb dust with whatever you're using in the bouquet to add extra flavour too. Generally there is a lot of work involved, for all the herbs to be collected and washed, then kept as fresh as possible, so when we did this for lunch and dinner we had to make it as close to service as possible. It looks very simple but I've seen chefs crying over this!

PINEAPPLE, COCONUT, SPICE BISCUIT

We currently have this dish on the menu. The pineapple skins are made into tepache which is a bit like kombucha, using a natural fermentation process with sugar for a few days to create a sweet, slightly alcoholic liquid. The tepache is served on the side with some mint oil which brings a nice freshness to the dish, as well as used to brush the pineapple while it's roasting on the barbecue.

For the biscuit, we use the technique of shaving it onto the baking tray from chilled or frozen to get a really fine crumb which then bakes quickly in a hot oven. You could roll it out like a normal biscuit dough, bake it between two trays, then cut out shapes if you wanted. The spices can include cinnamon, cardamom, nutmeg, clove or other warming flavours you want to try.

The gel is made from coconut water and garnished with marigold leaves. The coconut ice cream is set in a mould then sprayed with white chocolate in the restaurant, as from a service point of view that's easier and faster. All the elements on the recipe here are the same as those on the dish in the restaurant, I've just broken it down to make more of a home-cooked version. Although if you do have an ice cream machine it's beautiful. We sometimes include sagu on this too – it's like tapioca pearls but bigger and made from cassava flour. Sagu is a very classic old-school dessert in Brazil, usually served with a loose custard.

MOQUECA – BRAZILIAN FISH STEW

This is a typical dish from the north of Brazil called moqueca. There's lots of Afro influences in that cuisine like the coconut milk, spices and shellfish. I like to use okra as well which is quite popular in Brazil. We serve two types of chillies with this, biquinho and cumari. Biquinho chillies aren't spicy at all and are pickled so they give a nice pop of acidity and freshness, whereas cumari chillies have quite a kick. In this part of Brazil they love spicy food so I let people choose how much they want to add with chillies on the side.

If you've not come across it before, the dende oil used in this recipe is similar to palm oil but from the fruit of the palm oil tree. There are little berries on the trees which are pressed into oil and that's where the deep red colour comes from, which turns yellow when you heat the oil. That's what gives the stew its distinctive colour but you can replace it with a pinch of saffron if you can't find dende oil.

When we plate this in the restaurant, the fish and other elements will be portioned with the sauce on the side to finish off at the table. We normally cook the sauce classically and then pass it off. In the restaurant we use turbot that has been aged for a few days, or halibut, but cod is easier to source if you're making this at home. Traditionally it would include fish that you find in Brazil, cooked in the sauce. You can add a handful of langoustine heads or 200g fresh prawns to the stew at the spice paste stage if you like.

We call the side dish I've recommended 'farofa' which literally means toasted flour, so raw flour is tossed in a hot pan and becomes farofa. It's super traditional and very common in Brazil. We have many types of flour such as cassava and maize, but you can do it with any type. Here we toast the flour with hen of the woods mushrooms and Brazil nuts because I wanted to bring more nuttiness and earthiness to the dish. You can also make it by sweating off some garlic and onions in butter, then adding the flour to toast. It thickens the sauce a little bit and adds texture too. We would eat this stew with farofa as well as rice at home, as rice is a staple in Brazil.

The Little Chartroom | Eleanor, Edinburgh

Roberta Hall-McCarron

Roberta Hall-McCarron is the chef owner of The Little Chartroom in Edinburgh which she runs with her husband Shaun, who manages front of house. In 2021 they relocated the restaurant to a larger venue and used the original premises to open a wine bar with small plates, Eleanor. Roberta became chef de partie at The Kitchin after returning to her hometown of Edinburgh following stints in Glasgow, Northumbria and Dubai. She fell in love with the restaurant industry on work experience but always had an interest in food that stemmed from holidays on Scotland's coastline, enjoying sailing and seafood with her family. Having worked with Tom Kitchin for over three years, Roberta helped him to open a new restaurant called Castle Terrace, where she met Shaun. In 2018 they were ready to establish a restaurant of their own and renovated a former café to create The Little Chartroom, which met with immediate success and support from critics and locals alike.

"Our main ethos behind The Little Chartroom was to create a neighbourhood restaurant that you could come to once or twice a week. We want it to feel relaxed, warm and welcoming without any fussiness – almost like you were coming to our house for dinner – but still getting really tasty food that has lots of knowledge behind it. Shaun and I essentially created a space that we would like to eat in. The new site feels like a more grown up space where we had to stop 'playing restaurant' and be adults! It's been a very organic move although it was a big step – we went from having four chefs and two front of house staff to eight and five respectively. We've got a sommelier now and someone making the cocktails, but it hasn't made the restaurant any less informal. If you want to come in jeans and sandals, that's totally fine – we don't have a dress code because that reflects on your experience; if you feel relaxed in what you're wearing then you'll feel relaxed being out.

On the cooking side, it all comes down to 'is it tasty?' because we want people to get stuck into their meal and mop up every last morsel. If the answer is no, it's back to the drawing board. We work together as a team to create dishes, it's not just me or my head chef. When I was moving up through the ranks, I perhaps wasn't asked enough about what I would do on the dishes we were cooking, so it's great to give our team that opportunity even if they're relatively new to the role or the restaurant. Everyone's got different influences and experiences so it can only improve the dish, and it's better for the chefs because they're using their brains which is good for when they move on or become head chefs. When we opened the restaurant, that creative process was hard because Shaun and I had both come from a lot of structure working under someone else. Finding your own style takes a long time to figure out and you can't force it. There's definitely an identity to the food we do now, with lots of textures and different aspects of the same ingredient. It's so important to take stock as things grow and progress so you can continue to chart your own course."

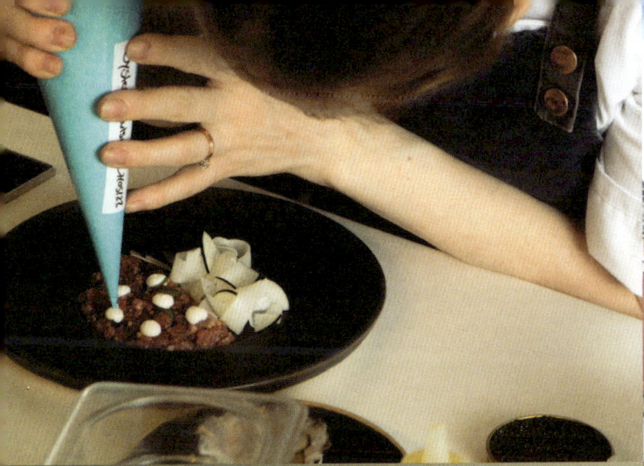

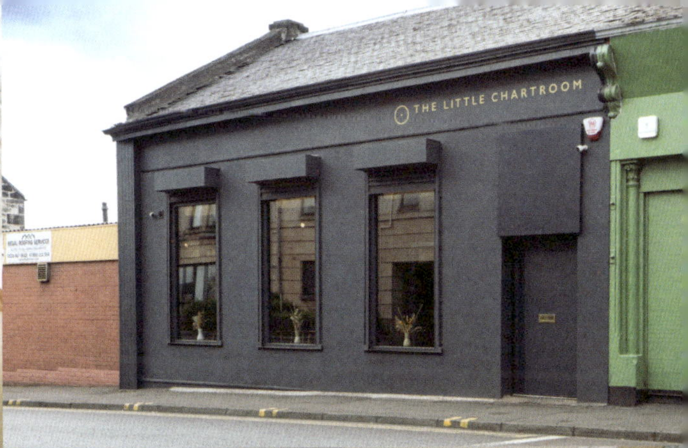
THE LITTLE CHARTROOM

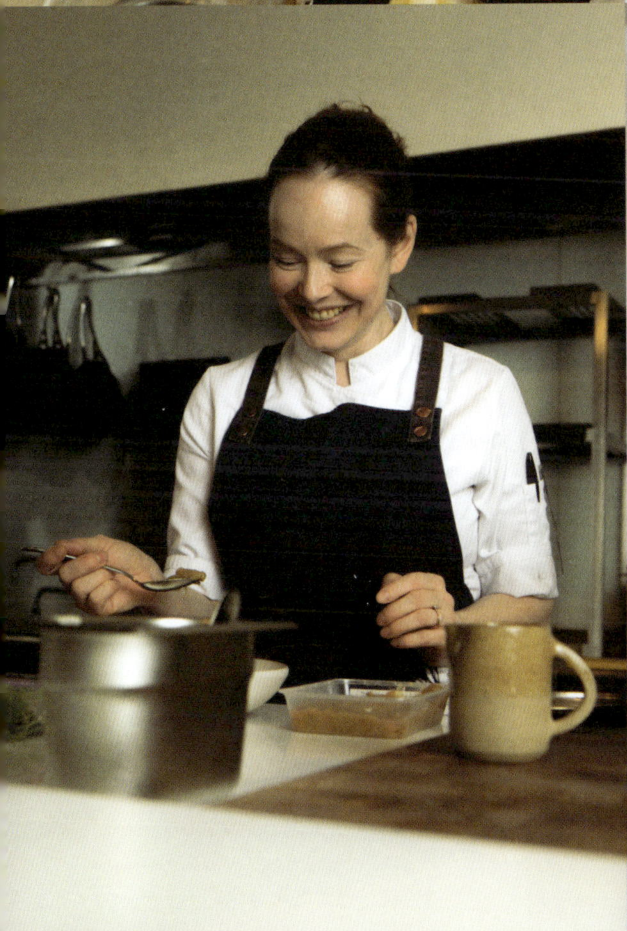

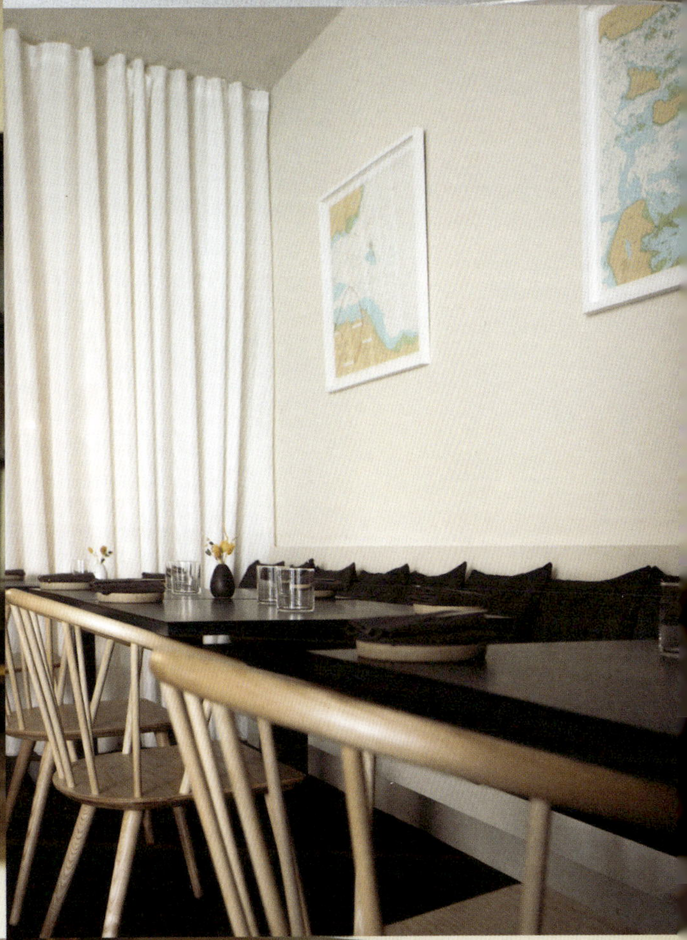

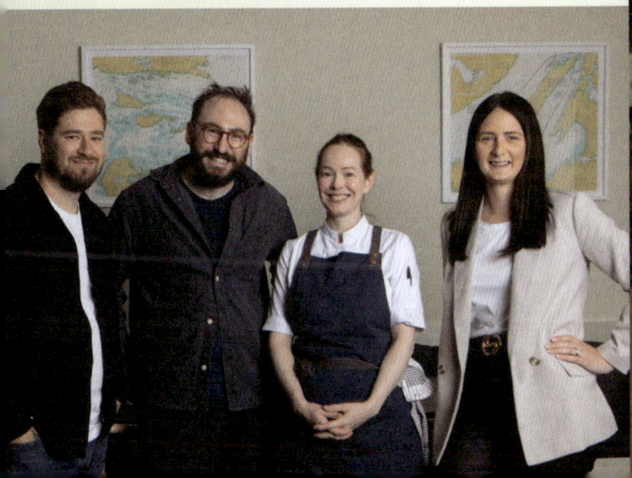

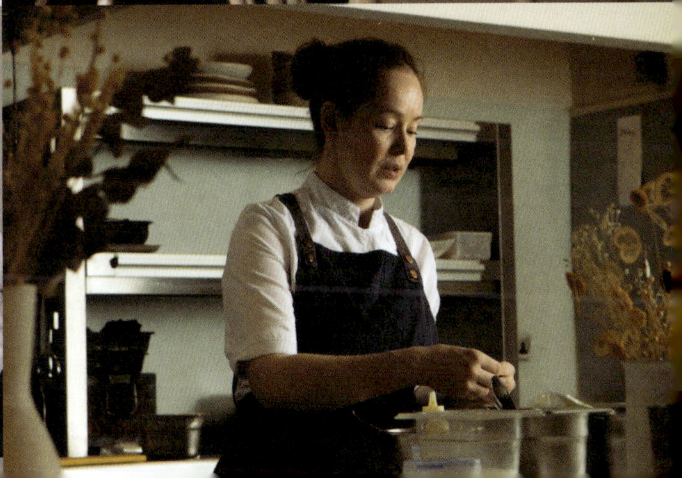

The Little Chartroom | Eleanor, Edinburgh

Mackerel, Gooseberry, Sunflower Seed Gazpacho

Preparation time: 3 hours | Cooking time: 10 minutes | Serves 4

FOR THE MACKEREL

4 fillets of mackerel, pin boned

50g caster sugar

50g fine salt

FOR THE GAZPACHO

65g sunflower seeds

15g bread

⅓ cucumber

½ clove of garlic

200g milk

15g sherry vinegar

5g olive oil

3g fine salt

Black pepper

FOR THE GOOSEBERRY JAM

660g gooseberries

50ml water

800g caster sugar

½ lemon, juiced

TO ASSEMBLE

100g samphire

FOR THE MACKEREL

Cure the fillets in the sugar and salt mix for 20 minutes. Gently wash the cure off and pat dry with paper towels. Place to one side.

FOR THE GAZPACHO

Toast all the sunflower seeds, putting 10g aside for garnish. Roughly chop the bread, cucumber and garlic. Combine the toasted sunflower seeds, bread, cucumber and garlic with the milk, sherry vinegar, olive oil, salt and black pepper to taste. Leave at room temperature, covered, for at least 3 hours. Alternatively, this can be mixed the day before and stored in the fridge. Blend the mixture until smooth, then taste and season accordingly.

FOR THE GOOSEBERRY JAM

Wash the gooseberries, then top and tail them. Set 35g aside and cut these into quarters for garnish. Place the rest of the gooseberries in a pot with the water and cook over a medium heat until they start to break down. Add the sugar and lemon juice, then boil until the jam reaches setting point (105°c). Remove the pan from the heat and allow to cool.

TO ASSEMBLE

Pick through the samphire, removing the 'woody' parts from the bottom, then blanch in boiling salted water for a few seconds. Refresh in iced water and drain.

Cut each mackerel fillet into 3 pieces and either lightly blow torch or lightly grill them on each side. Place the mackerel on the plate, then a couple of small dollops of gooseberry jam. Generously spoon the sunflower seed gazpacho around the mackerel and scatter with the fresh gooseberries. Chop the remaining sunflower seeds, sprinkle them over everything and finish with a few sprigs of samphire.

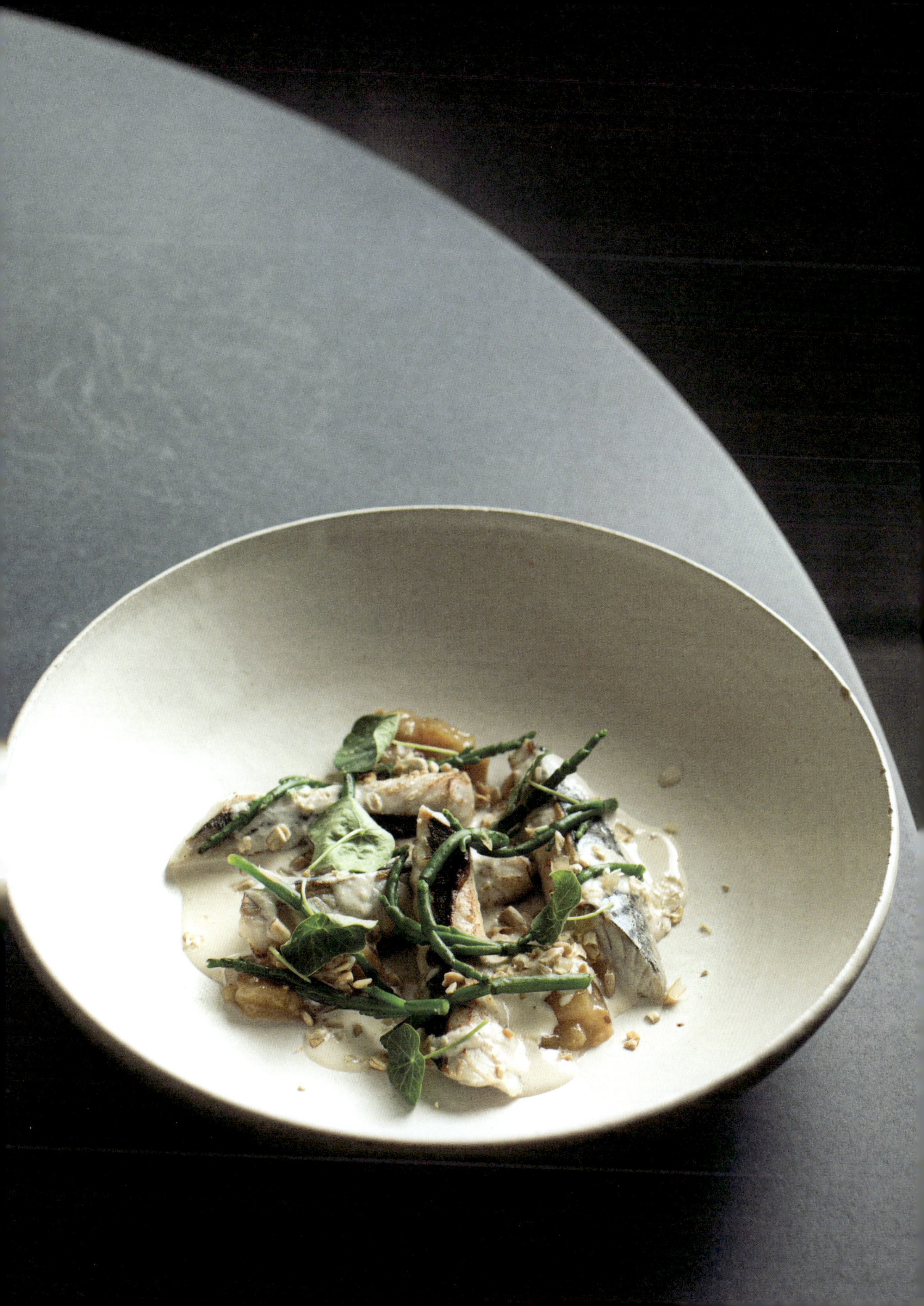

The Little Chartroom | Eleanor, Edinburgh

Beef Tartare and Oyster

Preparation time: 14 hours | Cooking time: 14 hours | Serves 4

40g fine salt (you may not need all this)

FOR THE VEAL JUS
4kg veal bones

6 carrots

1 onion

2 sticks of celery

200g tomato purée

FOR THE RED WINE SAUCE
4 shallots

1 slice of pancetta

10 black peppercorns

2 sprigs of thyme

1 bay leaf

1 bottle of red wine

FOR THE OYSTER CREAM
100g yoghurt

10 oysters

FOR THE PICKLED MUSTARD SEEDS
190ml water

30ml white wine vinegar

25g sugar

5g salt

2 sprigs of thyme

10 black peppercorns

50g mustard seeds

FOR THE PUFFED BUCKWHEAT
50g buckwheat

600ml oil

FOR THE BEEF TARTARE
200g beef rump cap (50g per person)

5ml cold-pressed rapeseed oil

6 oyster leaves, julienned

FOR THE RAW VEGETABLES
200g mooli

60g black radish

½ Granny Smith apple

TO ASSEMBLE
20g caviar

20 sprigs of wood sorrel

200g coarse salt

FOR THE VEAL JUS
Roast the bones at 180°c for 2 hours until golden brown, then place in a pot, cover with water, bring to the boil and reduce to a simmer. De-glaze the roasting tray with a little water and add this to the pot. Peel the carrots, onions and celery and cut into large pieces. In a warm pot, slowly caramelise the vegetables with the tomato purée. Add them to the stock and simmer for at least 12 hours, skimming off any fat. Pass through a chinois and reduce to sauce consistency.

FOR THE RED WINE SAUCE
Thinly slice the shallots and slowly sweat them down with the pancetta, cracked black peppercorns, thyme and bay leaf. Cover with red wine and reduce until almost dry. Repeat this twice more but only reduce the wine by half on the third reduction. Add the veal jus and reduce to sauce consistency. Pass through a fine sieve. (This recipe will make more than is required, but it can be frozen and goes well with beef and fish.)

FOR THE OYSTER CREAM
Hang the yoghurt in muslin for approximately 2 hours 30 minutes. Put 4 oysters aside and open the rest. Place these in a blender, removing any shell, and blitz until smooth. Pass through a sieve and gently mix the hung yoghurt and blended oyster together. Add a pinch of fine salt, taste and add more if necessary. Transfer into a piping bag.

FOR THE PICKLED MUSTARD SEEDS
Mix the water, vinegar, sugar, salt, thyme and peppercorns together. Bring to the boil, allow to cool and pass through a sieve, discarding the solids. Meanwhile, blanch and refresh the mustard seeds 6 times. Reheat some of the pickling liquid (reserving the rest) and cover the seeds.

FOR THE PUFFED BUCKWHEAT
Boil the buckwheat in salted water until completely cooked. Drain in a sieve and run under cold water for 10 minutes to wash off all the starch. Drain well and spread out on sheets of greaseproof paper. Place in a dehydrator for approximately 5 hours, checking regularly, or leave at room temperature for 2-3 days. There needs to be a small amount of moisture left.

Heat the oil in a small, deep pot to 210°c. Carefully place the buckwheat into the oil for a few seconds to puff up. Don't leave it in for too long as it will burn. Pass it through a sieve into another pot. Once drained, transfer it onto paper towels and season with fine salt.

FOR THE BEEF TARTARE
Trim any fat or sinew from the beef and dice into 0.5cm pieces. Mix the rapeseed oil with 30ml of the pickling liquid, then coat the beef in this mixture along with a good pinch of fine salt and pepper, 20g of pickled mustard seeds and the oyster leaf. Taste and adjust the seasoning accordingly.

FOR THE RAW VEGETABLES
Peel and thinly slice the mooli using a mandoline. Trim into 2cm wide ribbons. Thinly slice the black radish and cut into triangles. Thinly slice the apple and cut into batons. Season the radish and mooli with a pinch of fine salt.

TO ASSEMBLE
Place the 4 remaining oysters on a hot barbecue for 2 minutes. Warm the red wine sauce. Divide the beef tartare into 4 portions and spoon onto your plates in a demi-sphere shape. Place the mooli (approximately 30g each) and radish (approximately 10g each) on the other side. Place the apple batons on top and generously sprinkle with puffed buckwheat.

Put small dollops of caviar on top of the beef and generously pipe dots of the oyster cream on top of the beef. Finish with sprigs of wood sorrel. Mix the coarse salt with a little water and divide between small side plates. Pop open the cooked oysters, place on top of the salt, and cover with the warm red wine sauce.

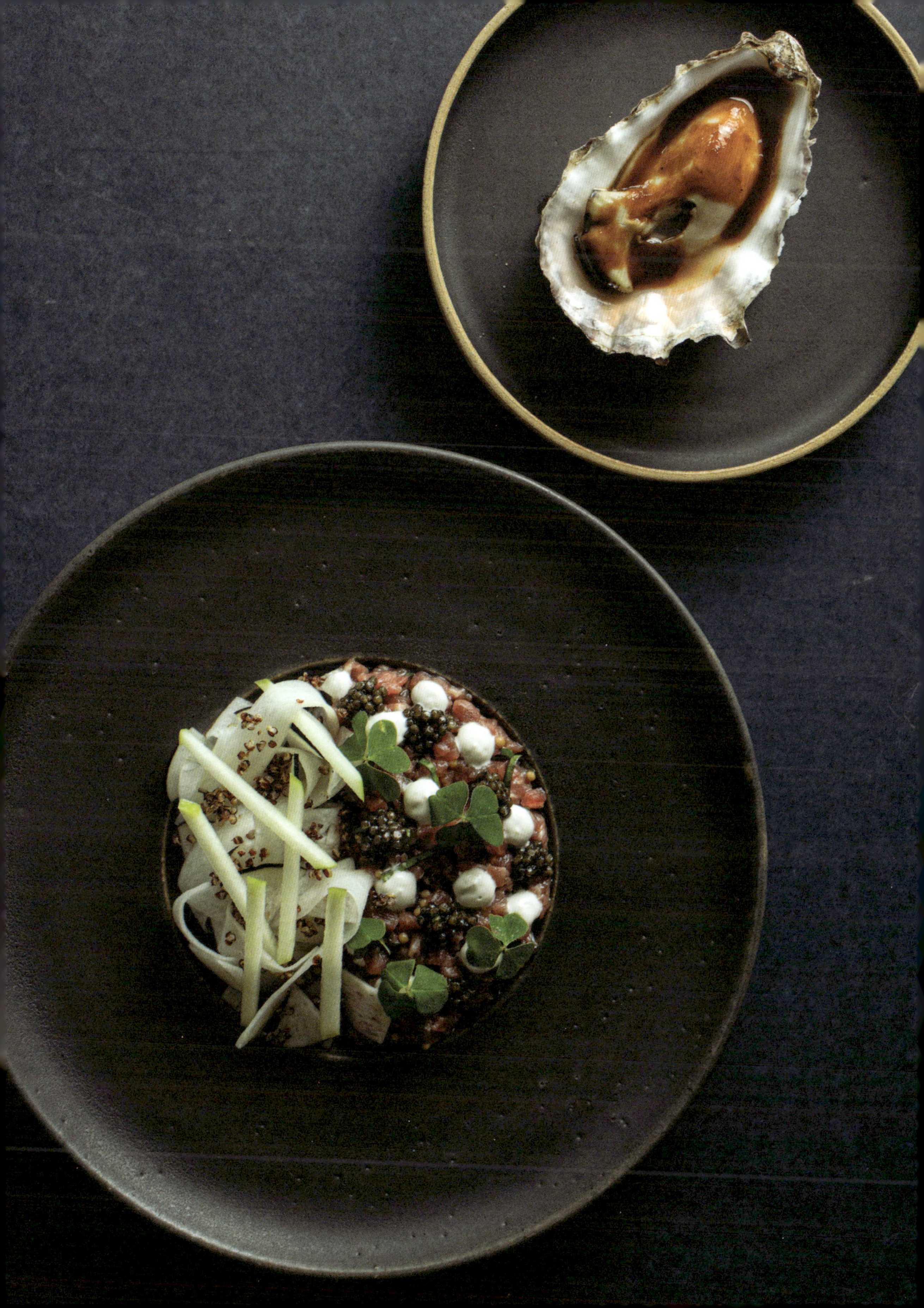

The Little Chartroom | Eleanor, Edinburgh

Duck, Radicchio, Rhubarb and Ginger

Preparation time: 1 week | Cooking time: 14 hours | Serves 4

2 duck crowns (approx. 1kg each)

120g treacle

FOR THE VEAL JUS

4kg veal bones

6 carrots

1 onion

2 sticks of celery

200g tomato purée

FOR THE DUCK LIVER SAUCE

4 litres chicken stock

400g veal jus

50g duck liver

20ml sherry vinegar

FOR THE RHUBARB AND GINGER PURÉE

1kg rhubarb, washed and trimmed

20g crystallised ginger

Pinch of fine salt

FOR THE BEETROOT MOLASSES

500ml beetroot juice

FOR THE PUFFED QUINOA

50g quinoa

600ml oil

TO ASSEMBLE

1 radicchio

10g chives, finely chopped

Buy your ducks a week in advance, take them out of the packaging and place on a wire cooling rack on a tray in the fridge. After 1 day of drying, brush the skin with treacle. Repeat every day. After 7 days, remove the duck breasts from the carcasses, trim and place back in the fridge.

FOR THE VEAL JUS

Roast the bones at 180°c for 2 hours until golden brown, then place in a pot, cover with water, bring to the boil and reduce to a simmer. De-glaze the roasting tray with a little water and add this to the pot. Peel the carrots, onions and celery and cut into large pieces. In a warm pot, slowly caramelise the vegetables with the tomato purée. Add them to the stock and simmer for at least 12 hours, skimming off any fat. Pass through a chinois and reduce to sauce consistency.

FOR THE DUCK LIVER SAUCE

Chop the duck carcasses into small pieces and roast at 180°c until golden brown. Strain off any fat, place into a pot and cover with the chicken stock. Bring to the boil and reduce to almost dry. Repeat twice more but only reduce by half on the last reduction. Pass the stock through a sieve, then add the veal jus and reduce to sauce consistency.

Finely chop the duck livers, then sweat them quickly in a very hot pan. De-glaze with the sherry vinegar, allow it to evaporate and then add the sauce.

FOR THE RHUBARB AND GINGER PURÉE

Juice 200g of the rhubarb and dice another 50g, setting this aside for later. Cut the rest into small pieces, place in a pot on a medium heat and sweat down. Add the rhubarb juice and crystallised ginger to cook gently until all the juice has evaporated and the rhubarb is soft. Blend until smooth, seasoning with fine salt to taste.

FOR THE BEETROOT MOLASSES

Place the beetroot juice in a pot over a high heat and reduce until it reaches a syrup consistency.

FOR THE PUFFED QUINOA

Boil the quinoa in salted water until completely cooked. Drain in a sieve and run under cold water for 10 minutes to wash off all the starch. Drain well and spread out on sheets of greaseproof paper. Place in a dehydrator for approximately 5 hours, checking regularly, or leave at room temperature for 2-3 days. There needs to be a small amount of moisture left.

Heat the oil in a small, deep pot to 210°c. Carefully place the quinoa into the oil for a few seconds to puff up. Don't leave it in for too long as it will burn. Pass it through a sieve into another pot. Once drained, transfer it onto paper towels and season with fine salt.

TO ASSEMBLE

Place the duck breasts skin side down into a cold pan on a low heat. Cook on this side until the fat has rendered down and is golden brown (approximately 6 minutes) and then turn up the heat to medium. Turn the breasts over to sear the other side and cook for a further 5 minutes. Remove from the pan and rest somewhere warm for 5 minutes.

Quarter and season the radicchio with salt, then barbecue or chargrill for a few minutes. Brush liberally with beetroot molasses and sprinkle generously with puffed quinoa.

Warm the rhubarb and ginger purée, then place a dollop on each plate with the radicchio next to it. Slice the duck breasts in half and place next to the radicchio. Warm the duck liver sauce, stir in the chives and reserved diced rhubarb, then serve.

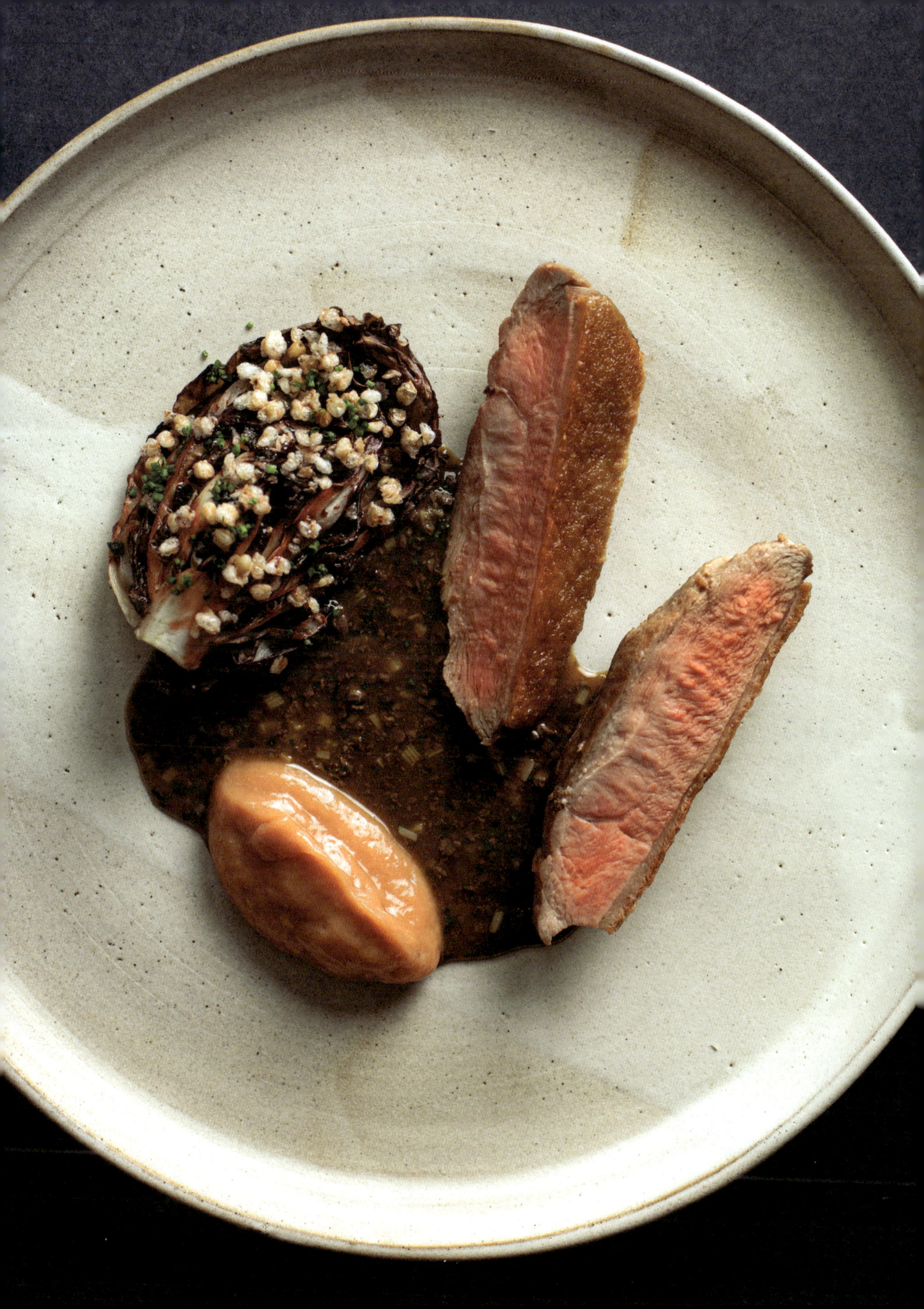

The Little Chartroom | Eleanor, Edinburgh

Kitchen Confidential

MACKEREL, GOOSEBERRY, SUNFLOWER SEED GAZPACHO

I love eating mackerel and ajo blanco, but I wanted to try something different that still had a similar texture, good flavour and was nut free. The sunflower seeds worked really well, and we have since found that using seeds in our cooking has opened up a lot of different choices for us in terms of being more experimental too.

Flavour-wise I find this dish really interesting; for me the smoky mackerel with the tart gooseberries and creamy gazpacho with a little bit of samphire creates a perfect balance. There's a richness to it as well as it being incredibly light and fresh. One thing I take into consideration every time I create a dish is the combination of textures: that's so important, as important as flavour. It's what balances the dish.

It's one of our more casual dishes that I think would be easy to replicate at home. All the ingredients are fairly accessible at the right time of year, although gooseberries do have a very short season – about a month – so if you really can't get them, forced or green rhubarb would work well with mackerel. I would use Salty Fingers instead of the samphire, but they're generally harder to get whereas you can find samphire in the supermarket these days.

Mackerel is one of my favourite fishes to work with. We source a lot from Peterhead in Aberdeenshire. It's such a versatile ingredient; you can make pâté or have it lightly cured, barbecued, grilled, raw as a tartare… it's absolutely delicious, and very good for you as well.

BEEF TARTARE AND OYSTER

Beef and oyster are obviously a classic pairing, but here you've got a cold beef tartare and cooked oysters with a warm red wine sauce. I like using traditional combinations with a modern twist and adding in hot and cold elements for contrast. In the restaurant, we serve the tartare and then follow with the cooked oyster a few minutes later.

We keep the tartare itself very simple and quite fresh because we want the oyster flavours and the pickled mustard seeds to come through. Daikon radish adds the bitterness and peppery flavour that's quite traditional with tartare, as it works so well to bring in that tiny bit of heat. The vegetables are raw and seasoned right at the last minute so it's a really nice, crunchy, fresh way to eat the beef. The tartare is finished with dollops of caviar and salty puffed quinoa. The oyster on the side is rich and indulgent with a generous spoon of red wine beef sauce.

Rump cap has great texture and quite lean meat that is versatile enough to serve raw or cooked. There's so much flavour, especially in the fat, although this doesn't get diced through the tartare. I think it's becoming a more popular cut that has been previously overlooked but we love using it in the restaurant. We've never really served the prime cuts – I find non-primes more interesting and versatile.

Shaun's wine pairing: For the tartare, we normally pair that with something fairly light and earthy that wouldn't overpower the oyster. A juicy red that lets the saltiness of the oyster come through works well. The temptation with the tartare is to go big but it's got to balance with everything.

DUCK, RADICCHIO, RHUBARB AND GINGER

The dry ageing process we use on the duck for this dish is great for allowing the skin to render down over time and then become incredibly crispy when cooked. It also strengthens the flavour of the meat, and the treacle adds a lovely sweetness. The balance of savoury, sweet, sour and salty flavours here references Chinese cooking in many ways. Thinking along those lines, if rhubarb wasn't available, plums obviously work so well with duck and ginger. I love the tartness that you get from green rhubarb; in many ways I prefer the summertime crop to earlier forced rhubarb as I think it's got better flavour with the extra bitterness.

I love the light and rich contrast of this dish, a simple clean garnish paired with the heavier, punchy liver sauce. We brush beetroot molasses over the barbecued radicchio which balances the bitterness in the leaf and sweetness from the beetroot perfectly. The rhubarb in the sauce also adds freshness and acidity, lifting the traditional finish of liver and chives. Our food should always sing with strong, punchy flavours: nothing's bland.

Making the most of our produce by working with whole animals, like we do with the duck in this dish, is really important to us. We like to use everything – there's an octopus dish on our menu that uses the tentacle for the carpaccio and the head to make a bolognese. It's nice to showcase all the different things you can do with animal produce. They've lived a life; they deserve to be respected and used in the best way. This approach also brings in more traditional aspects of cooking. The sauce on this dish, for example, is very traditional and something I learned maybe 15 years ago, but I've freshened it up with rhubarb dice to bring a bit more balance. It's one of my most favourite sauces that I've learned to do as a chef, and I think it brings a real meatiness to the dish along with great texture. I think every sauce should have something in it to add layers of interest, packing a punch not just with flavour but texture too.

The Little Chartroom | Eleanor, Edinburgh

Tell Us About Your…

Cooking style.

It's definitely evolved since opening The Little Chartroom. The food was very casual at the start, and I was still trying to figure out what my style was. Over time it has gotten more refined; it still has casual elements but more attention to detail. My biggest influences were working for Tom Kitchin and Dominic Jack. They were both classically trained with a heavy focus on French styles and techniques, using game, offal, and whole animals, so a lot of this resonates in the food I cook today. As time has gone on I've started branching out and experimenting.

Approach to produce.

Scotland has an abundance of produce, and you don't have to travel too far to reach it – fish, shellfish, game, mushrooms, berries, plants…we're spoiled! Game season is one of my favourite times of year, and I try to use all the different animals and birds that are available during that time. I have an amazing company that supplies our game; one of them is a gamekeeper and shoots a lot of the produce that we get in. To have that connection along with knowing exactly where the produce is coming from is what makes it all so much more special and fun.

Essential equipment.

I'd probably say a Thermomix – if that broke it would be like losing your arm! It depends though because when the menu changes, you'll suddenly find yourself using an aspect of the kitchen you've not used as much before. The barbecues, for example, are playing such a big part in our service now, more than in past years.

Favourite ingredients.

I love all the produce that has very short seasons because it feels extra special: greengages, damsons, blackcurrant leaf, fig leaf, cobnuts, tayberries, loganberries. We preserve some of the short season produce to add variety to the menu at different times of the year. I think you get to the point in any season where you're just waiting for the next one to start because you've almost exhausted everything that's available.

Life outside the restaurant.

Right now I'm taking a bit of time out with the wee one. Cooking at home can be tricky – I'm still waiting on my dream kitchen, so one pot wonders play a big part in what we eat, especially now with the baby. Anything that is really simple and quick does the job. All the creativity goes into the restaurant! When we're not working, Shaun and I like to eat out, so we do that a lot – it's nice to be on the other side sometimes when you work so hard. Storytelling is key when you're in a restaurant, and I love going out to eat and being surprised by what's put in front of me. Ynyshir's on our list but it's quite a mission to get to!

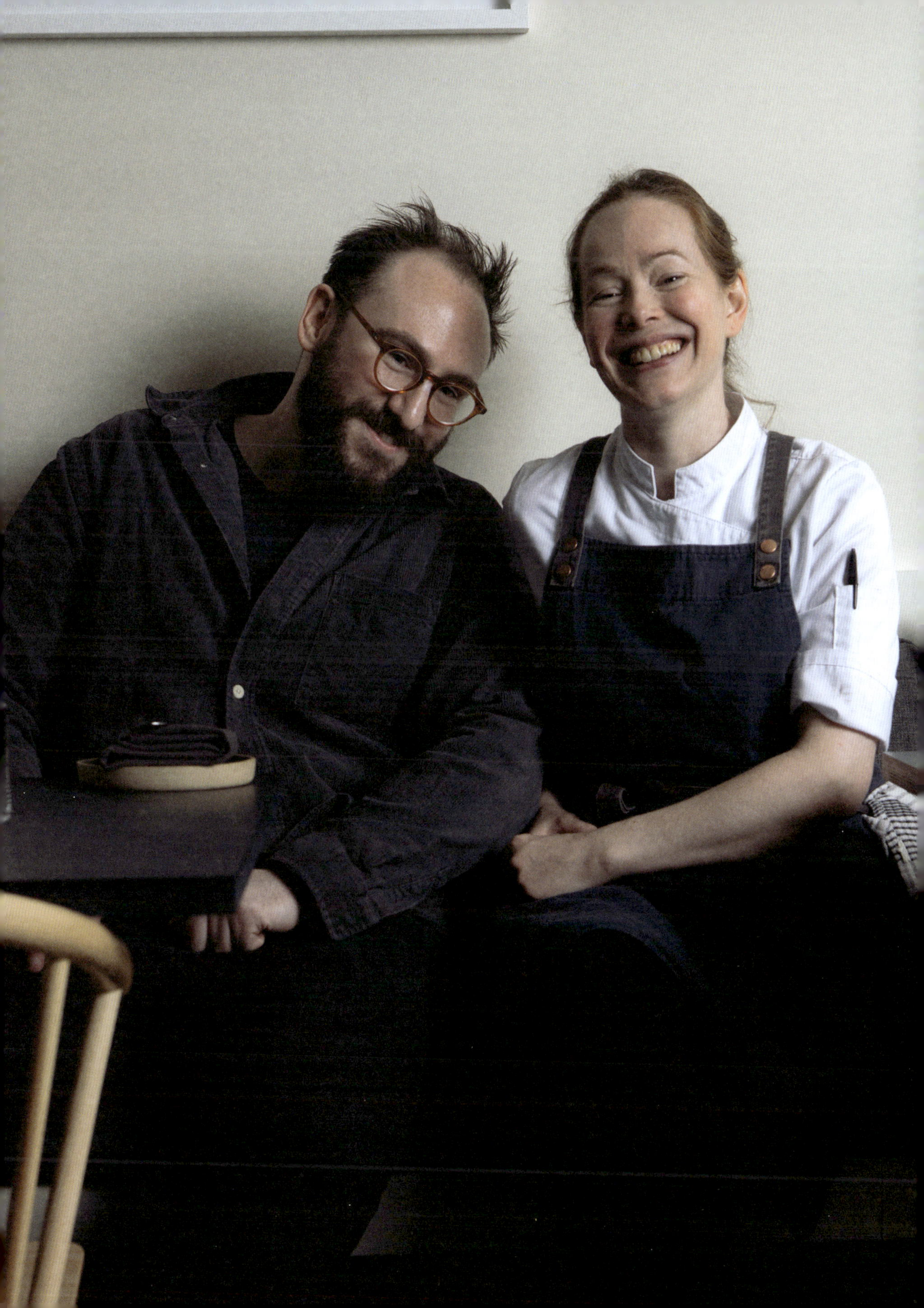

Restaurant Twenty Two, Cambridge

Sam Carter

Sam Carter began his career in hospitality by working in pubs, followed by training at Hambleton Hall under Aaron Patterson. He moved on to Maze, a Gordon Ramsay restaurant in London, by the age of 21 where he started as a commis chef and worked his way up to sous chef under head chef Tristan Farmer. After Maze, Sam spent 5 years at UBS BANK working his way up to head chef of their client dining. Sam met Alex Olivier – then a solicitor, now his wife and business partner – as teenagers whilst they were both working at their local pub in the Midlands. While Alex was completing her solicitor training in Peterborough, they decided to meet in the middle and move to Cambridge. Restaurant Twenty Two is their first restaurant and has been open since 2018, focusing on seasonal produce and a regularly changing tasting menu that guests enjoy in the intimate dining space of a Victorian town house.

Photo: Sam Carter

Restaurant Twenty Two, Cambridge

Tell Us Something We Might Not Know About…

Living and working in Cambridge.

It's such a small city, more like a town really. We've been here for seven or eight years now. It's a lovely city to live in with lots of green space, and you can still get into London in about 45 minutes for the weekend if you want to. Loads of people do the whole punting thing – it's a great place for a weekend away – so there are lots of tourists which means we get new customers alongside our regulars. We're only about an eight minute walk from the centre here on Chesterton Road.

Your favourite restaurants.

Me and my sous chef Caer went to Midsummer House for lunch a few months ago and I cannot believe it hasn't got a third star yet; it blew us away. The work that goes into it, the flavours, everything. A few more restaurants have opened around Cambridge recently which has been brilliant – it's so nice to have great places to eat on your doorstep. Adam Wood (formerly at Perilla) opened Garden House in 2021 and the food and setting are great. A group of us went the night before our wedding and he gave us the private dining room: it was amazing. Our friends Dan Fancett and Holly Minns have just opened a lovely French bistro across town called Fancetts which does an amazing value lunch menu – exactly what I want to eat. It's great to have so many independents and we really feel like part of the food community here. My favourite restaurant in London has to be Trinity. I love everything about the place.

What you've learnt from past experiences.

Our number one problem at the restaurant is space and over time we have learnt how important it is to maximise every inch! When we first started out, the kitchen was very different from how it is now, our equipment was very basic, and we barely had any storage. Over time, we have invested everything we can in getting better equipment and creating the most storage possible, and it has paid off so much. It has made the kitchen a much better place to work and, as a result, the food is ten times better. In the beginning, we barely took any time off and we were working constantly. In the hospitality business you are always going to do a lot of hours, but we have tried to make small changes here and there to improve things. We close one Saturday a month now so the whole team can have a whole weekend off and from Autumn we will be closing an extra lunch service to try and reduce the chefs' hours a bit. They might not be the best moves financially but, we found, the happier the team are the better the restaurant is!

Restaurant Twenty Two.

The stained glass window at the front has been there since the building was converted from a house to a restaurant in 1982 and it gives the place so much character. When we first got the keys, we thought about taking it out, but we are so glad we didn't! We love it now and it is a great reminder of the restaurant's history. We try and use local independent businesses as much as we can and have been lucky to find a couple of brilliant local artists who have created pieces for the restaurant which all include the stained glass window. We have gone for more colourful ones of local places and Cambridge scenes by Naomi Davis upstairs, and downstairs we have work by Georgina Burton who has created a few bespoke pieces for us, including a huge one of the front of the restaurant that we absolutely love.

Photo: Sam Carter

Restaurant Twenty Two, Cambridge

Turbot, Morels, Australian Winter Truffle, Sauce Bonne Femme

Preparation time: 45 minutes | Cooking time: 1 hour | Serves 10

10 x 70g portions of turbot

FOR THE PICKLED MORELS

100g morels, washed and sliced

250ml apple cider vinegar

150ml water

120g light brown sugar

50g dried mixed mushrooms

4 sprigs of tarragon

2 cloves of garlic, crushed

1 tsp black peppercorns

1 star anise

Salt to taste

FOR THE CONFIT GARLIC PURÉE

200g peeled garlic

75ml olive oil

50ml unsalted butter

150ml chicken stock

FOR THE SOURDOUGH CROUTONS

200g sourdough, 1cm diced

30ml good quality olive oil

3 sprigs of picked thyme

½ clove of garlic

FOR THE PICKLED MORELS

Add all the ingredients except the morels to a pan and bring to the boil. Simmer for 2-3 minutes to dissolve the sugar and allow the ingredients to infuse. Pour the warm pickling liquor over the morels and set aside.

FOR THE CONFIT GARLIC PURÉE

Bring the garlic to the boil 3 times, changing the water in between boils. After boiling for the third time, drain the water and cover the garlic in the olive oil. Slowly cook the garlic on a low heat until tender (this should take around 45 minutes). Once tender, drain off the oil and add the butter and chicken stock to the pan. Reduce until thick and emulsified. Blend in a blender until glossy and smooth. Season with salt and pepper. Pass through a fine chinois and put in a plastic squeezy bottle. Keep warm until plating.

FOR THE SOURDOUGH CROUTONS

Preheat the oven to 150°c. Coat the sourdough cubes evenly with the olive oil, picked thyme leaves and garlic. Bake in the oven for 8-10 minutes until golden and crispy.

Turbot, Morels, Australian Winter Truffle, Sauce Bonne Femme

Preparation time: 45 minutes | Cooking time: 1 hour | Serves 10

FOR THE TURBOT AND MUSHROOM STOCK
1 turbot carcass
350g chestnut mushrooms
3 white Italian onions
2 sticks of celery
20ml rapeseed oil
3 litres brown chicken stock
300g dried mushrooms (ideally morels)
30ml black truffle oil
2 star anise
1 garlic bulb
1 tsp black peppercorns

FOR THE SAUCE BONNE FEMME
250g truffle butter
200g chestnut mushrooms
200g banana shallots
4 cloves of garlic
2 sprigs of thyme
50ml Madeira
2 litres turbot and mushroom stock
150g double cream
150g crème fraiche
Truffle juice to taste
Lemon juice to taste
White soy to taste

FOR THE GARNISH
Sliced Australian winter truffle
Bronze fennel
Salty fingers
Picked sea fennel

FOR THE TURBOT AND MUSHROOM STOCK
Roast off the turbot bones on a baking tray in the oven at 180°c for 30 minutes. In a pan, sweat down the chestnut mushrooms, onion and celery in the oil. Add all the other ingredients to the pan and simmer for 90 minutes. Skim any impurities with a ladle as they rise. Pass through muslin cloth.

FOR THE SAUCE BONNE FEMME
Melt half of the truffle butter in a saucepan. Add the mushrooms, shallots, garlic and thyme and sweat down until translucent. Deglaze the pan with the Madeira and then add the turbot and mushroom stock. Reduce by half. When reduced, add the double cream. Reduce again until it reaches sauce consistency. Blend in a blender with the crème fraiche and emulsify in the remaining truffle butter. Pass the sauce through muslin cloth and season to taste with the truffle juice, lemon juice and white soy.

TO ASSEMBLE
In a non-stick frying pan, heat a generous dash of rapeseed oil. When medium-hot, add the turbot. Colour the fish until golden brown, then cool the pan slightly and add plenty of butter. Baste until the core temperature of the fish reaches 46°c. Finish with a ladle of chicken stock and a generous squeeze of lemon juice, then reduce this to a glaze that coats the fish. Put the fish in the centre of the plate and dress the top with croutons, pickled morels, garlic purée, sliced truffle, bronze fennel, salty fingers and picked sea herbs. Pour the sauce at the table.

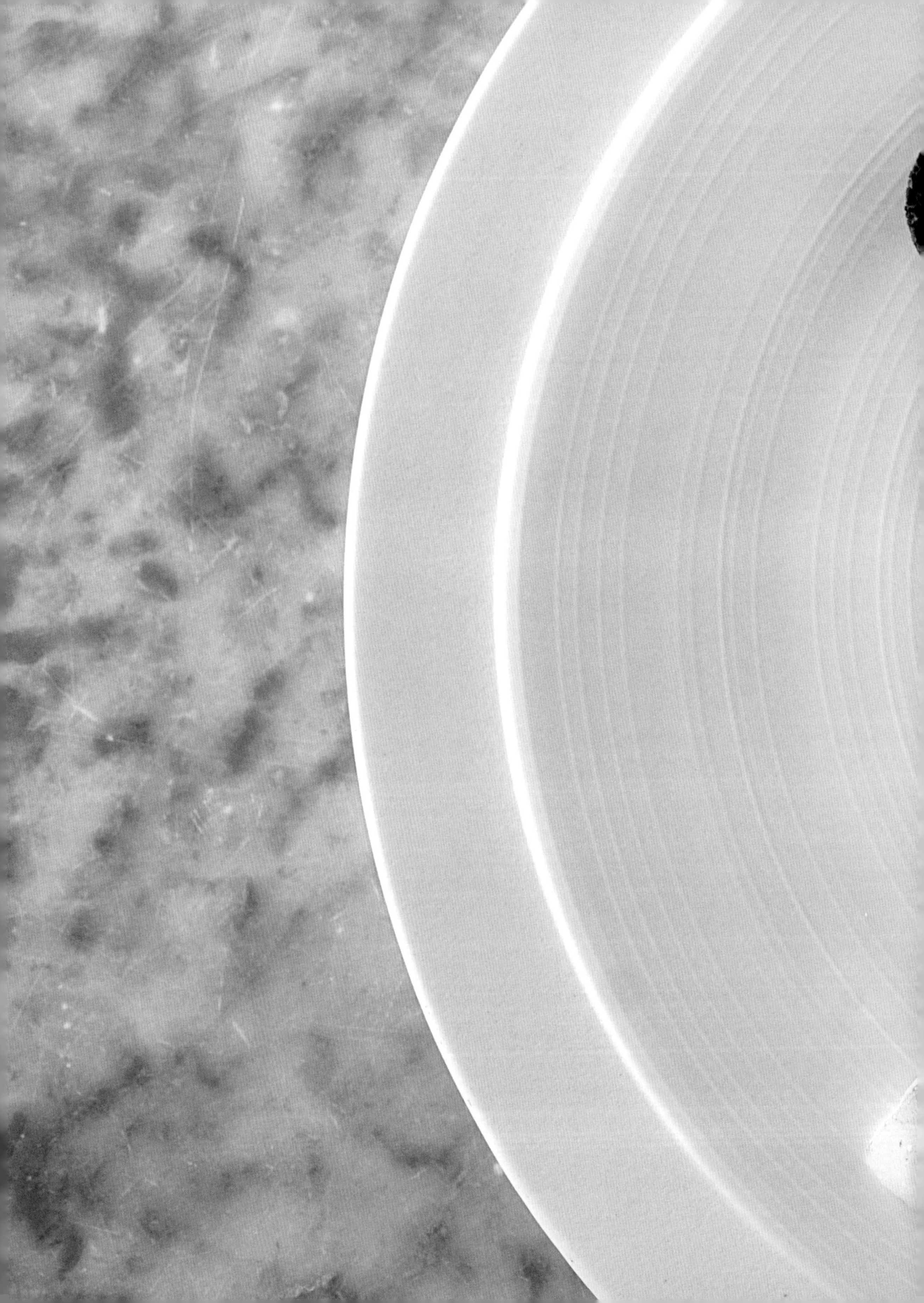

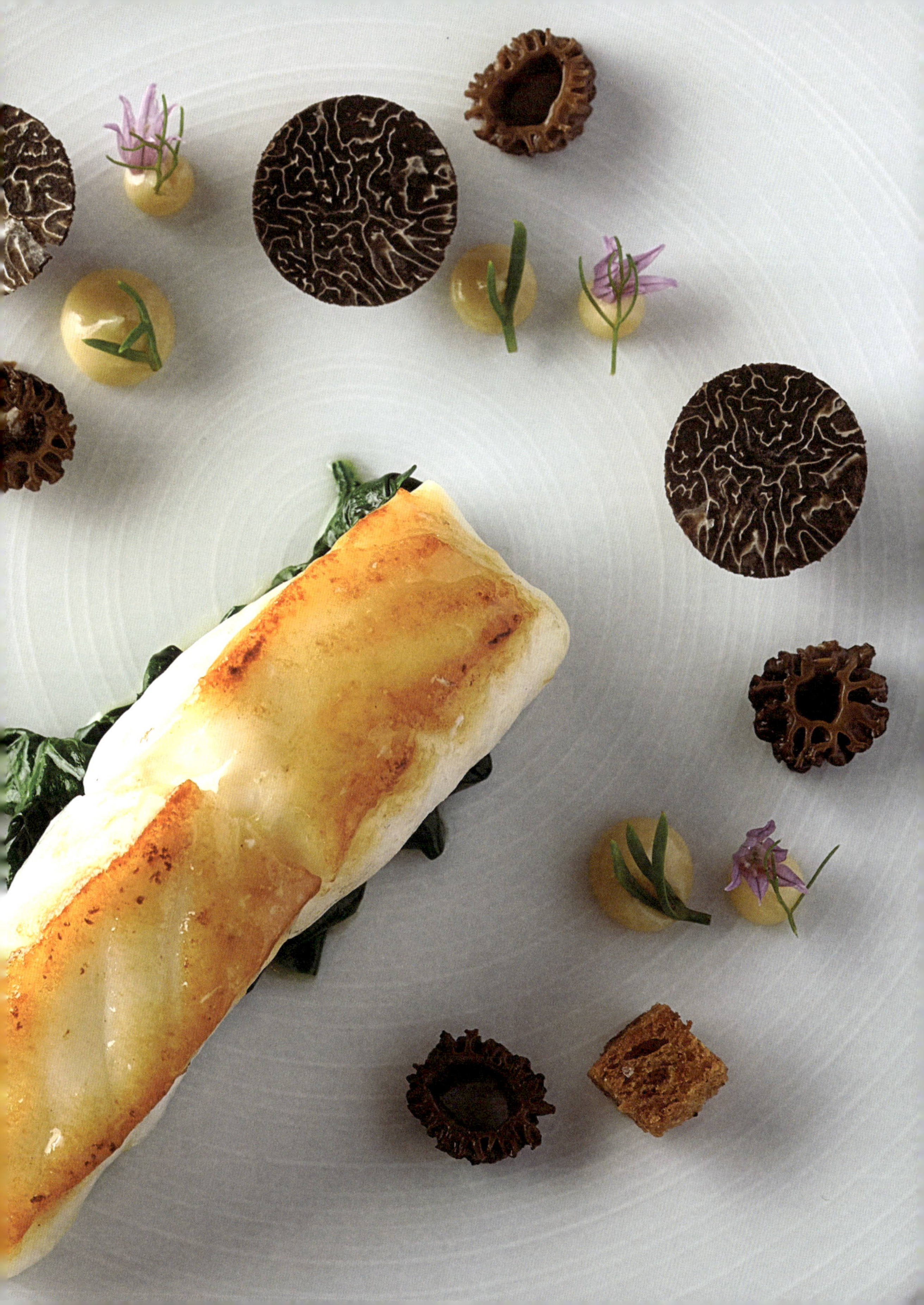

Restaurant Twenty Two, Cambridge

Lamb Moussaka

Preparation time: 30 minutes | Cooking time: 1 hour | Serves 10

FOR THE RAGU

30g lamb fat

1.4kg lean lamb mince

4 banana shallots

4 cloves of garlic

4 cinnamon sticks

4 tbsp ground cumin

4 tbsp smoked paprika

2 tbsp tomato paste

200g cherry vine tomatoes, halved

500ml lamb stock

6 tbsp chopped fresh basil

2 tbsp chopped flat leaf parsley

1 tbsp chopped fresh oregano

Salt and pepper, to taste

FOR THE LAYERS

2 large potatoes

2 aubergines

200g feta cheese, crumbled

100g gruyère, finely grated

FOR THE BECHAMEL

400ml full fat milk

20g lamb fat

10g butter

30g plain flour

150g Gruyère cheese

FOR THE LAMB FAT YOGHURT

30ml rendered lamb fat

3 cloves of garlic, crushed

2 sprigs of mint

1 sprig of thyme

1 sprig of rosemary

400ml Greek yoghurt

FOR THE RAGU

This can be made in advance, the day before is ideal so the flavours can develop. In a large pan, heat the lamb fat, add the lamb mince and brown. When the meat is nicely brown and caramelised, strain off the mince in a colander and set aside. Add the shallots, garlic and spices to the same pan and sweat down until translucent. Add the tomato paste and cherry tomatoes, give the tomato paste time to cook out (around 3 minutes will be enough) and then add the lamb mince back into the pan along with the lamb stock. Cook the ragu until the meat is tender and the ragu is thick and glossy. Add all the chopped herbs and adjust the seasoning with salt and pepper as necessary.

FOR THE LAYERS

Thinly slice the potatoes and season with salt and pepper. They will be assembled raw and will cook in the moussaka when it's in the oven. Slice the aubergine lengthways into 1cm slices. Season generously with salt and a pinch of ground cumin. Leave these for 10-15 minutes and then barbecue on both sides. Set aside the sliced potatoes and aubergines until you are ready to assemble.

FOR THE BECHAMEL

Bring the milk to a simmer in a saucepan and season with salt and pepper. In a separate pan, gently melt the lamb fat and butter, then add the flour and stir together to form a roux. Cook the roux gently for about 1 minute. Slowly add the hot milk while continuing to stir. The roux will thicken as the milk is absorbed. At this stage, add the gruyère and stir until melted. The roux needs to be quite thick for this recipe to help create layers.

FOR THE LAMB FAT YOGHURT

Heat the lamb fat in a saucepan until hot. Add the garlic and herbs and allow to cool. Add the yoghurt to a Thermomix and set to speed 3.5 and 45°c. When the yoghurt is at temperature, combine it with the lamb fat. Blend for 4 minutes at 45°c so all the fat is incorporated. Season the yoghurt to taste.

TO ASSEMBLE

Preheat the oven to 160°c. Place half of the lamb ragu into an ovenproof dish, add a layer of the sliced aubergine and cover with a layer of the bechamel sauce. Layer on all the sliced potato followed by another layer of the bechamel. Add the second half of the ragu, followed by a layer of the aubergine and finally the lamb fat yoghurt. Sprinkle over the crumbled feta and grated gruyère. Bake in the oven for 1 hour at 160°c. Serve with seasonal vegetables or a side salad.

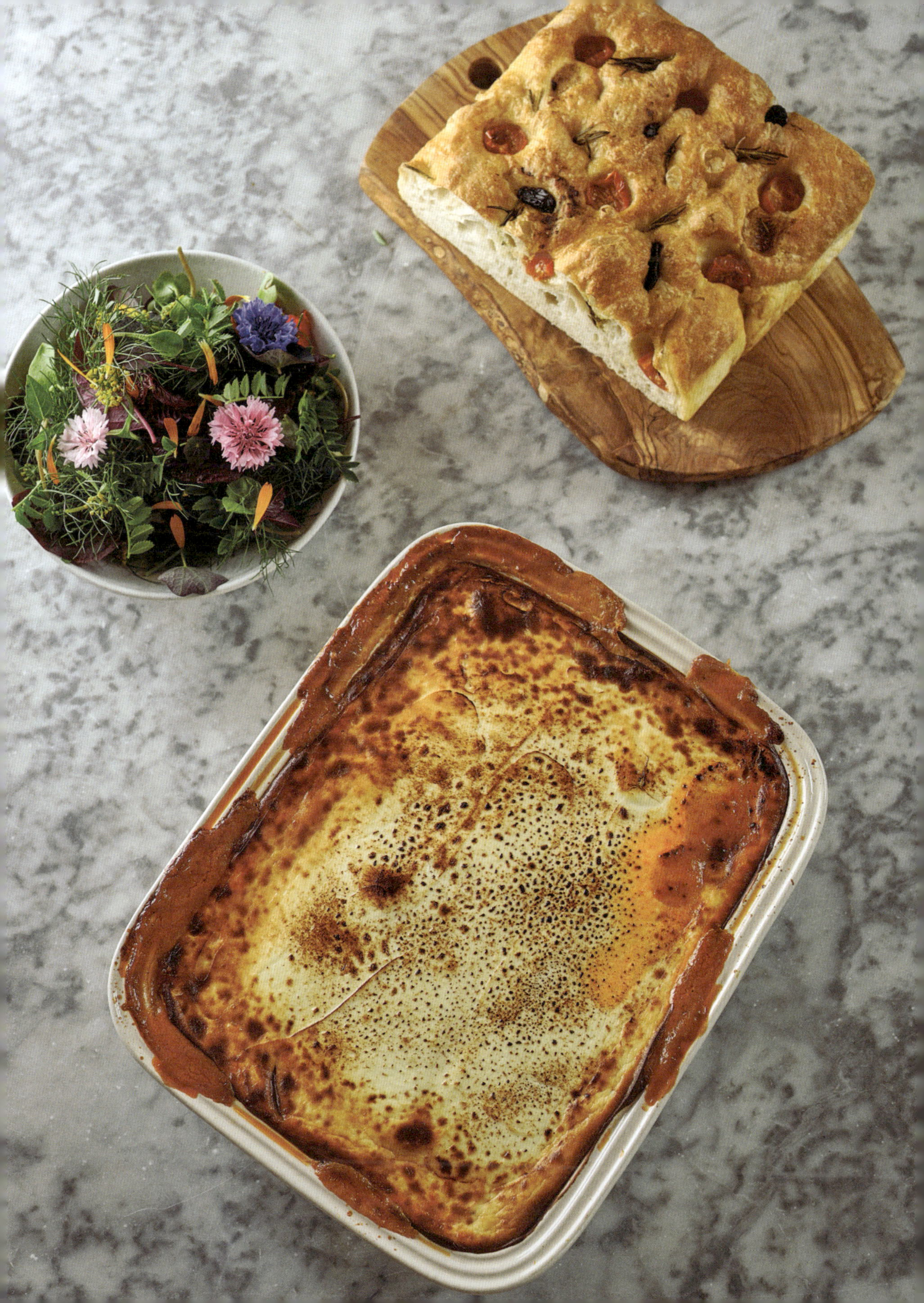

Restaurant Twenty Two, Cambridge

Tiramisu

Preparation time: 2 hours | Cooking time: 15 hours | Serves 10

FOR THE CAKE
80g egg yolks
170g sugar
60ml water
170g egg whites
140g plain flour
25g cocoa powder

FOR THE SET CREAM
1 leaf of silver gelatine
165ml double cream

FOR THE MASCARPONE MOUSSE
78g mascarpone
12g icing sugar
155g set cream (see above)

FOR THE COFFEE INFUSION
85ml milk
85ml double cream
18g freshly ground coffee

FOR THE MILK CHOCOLATE MOUSSE
14g caster sugar
30g egg yolks
150ml coffee infusion (see above)
2.5 leaves of silver gelatine
90g Valrhona Manjari 64% dark chocolate
270g Valrhona Jivara 40% milk chocolate
270g semi-whipped cream
Maldon salt, to taste

FOR THE CAKE
Preheat the oven to 200°c. In a KitchenAid mixer, start by whisking the yolks with half of the sugar. When the mixture starts to turn pale and reaches full volume, gradually add the water until fully incorporated and then set to one side. In a separate bowl, whisk the egg whites to stiff peaks and gradually add the remaining sugar until smooth and shiny. Combine the egg mixtures and fold in the sifted flour and cocoa powder. Spread the cake mixture on a Silpat mat to roughly 1cm thickness and bake at 200°c for 6-7 minutes.

FOR THE SET CREAM
Soak the gelatine in cold water and then melt into the cream. Pass and leave to set overnight.

FOR THE MASCARPONE MOUSSE
Leave the mascarpone out to soften. Once softened, beat by hand with a spatula until smooth. Whisk the sifted icing sugar and set cream together until soft peaks form. Combine this with the mascarpone and then transfer into piping bags.

FOR THE GATEAU
To assemble the gateau, stamp out the cake to the required size to fit in the moulds. Generously pipe the mascarpone mousse onto half the cakes, place the other half on top and set in the fridge.

FOR THE COFFEE INFUSION
Bring the milk and cream to a simmer, add the coffee and leave to cool. Pass through a fine chinois.

FOR THE MILK CHOCOLATE MOUSSE
To make the anglaise, combine the sugar, egg yolks and coffee infusion in a pan. Whisk together on a low heat while stirring constantly. Meanwhile, soak the gelatine in cold water. Once the anglaise has reached 82°c, add the gelatine and then pass the anglaise over the chocolate. Let it melt before emulsifying with a hand blender and leaving to cool, whisking regularly. When the anglaise has reached 37.5°c, whisk in half the cream and then fold in the remaining cream. Season with a pinch of salt and place in piping bags. Pipe the mixture into the moulds and then place each mascarpone gateau into the centre of each mould so it sits level. Freeze overnight before de-moulding onto a wire cooling rack, then place back into the freezer.

Tiramisu

Preparation time: 2 hours | Cooking time: 15 hours | Serves 10

FOR THE MASCARPONE ICE CREAM
524ml water

79g powdered milk

140g caster sugar

17g dextrose

8g glucose

6g super neutrose stabiliser

160g mascarpone

40g egg yolks

FOR THE MARSALA AND TAHITIAN VANILLA CARAMEL
450g caster sugar

300ml water

250ml marsala

30ml lemon juice

2 vanilla pods

9g agar agar

FOR THE WHITE CHOCOLATE SPRAY
300g Valrhona Opalys 33% white chocolate

200g cocoa butter

TO GARNISH
Tempered chocolate spirals

Gold leaf

FOR THE MASCARPONE ICE CREAM
Warm the water and add the milk powder, sugars and stabiliser until dissolved. Whisk the mascarpone and egg yolks together and then combine with the syrup. On a low heat, stir continuously and cook out to 85°c. Pass and chill over ice, then freeze into a Pacojet or churn.

FOR THE MARSALA AND TAHITIAN VANILLA CARAMEL
Add the sugar and the water to a heavy-based saucepan and reduce to a dark caramel. Add 200ml of the marsala with the lemon juice and vanilla pods. Whisk in the agar and bring back to the boil for 3 minutes. Leave to set overnight, then blend with the remaining 50ml of marsala until smooth. Pass through a fine chinois and transfer into a piping bag.

FOR THE WHITE CHOCOLATE SPRAY
Melt the white chocolate and cocoa butter together. While still warm, transfer the chocolate into a spray gun. Generously spray the mousses straight from the freezer, rotating them constantly to get an even coating. Place in the fridge to defrost.

TO PLATE
Remove the mousses from the fridge an hour before plating and dust with cocoa powder. Check your churned ice cream is at the right consistency before placing quenelles onto a frozen tray. In a zig zag motion, drizzle the caramel on top of the ice cream. Using a palette knife, carefully place the ice cream on top of the mousse and balance the tempered chocolate spirals over the ice cream. Finish by gently placing a few pieces of gold leaf on top.

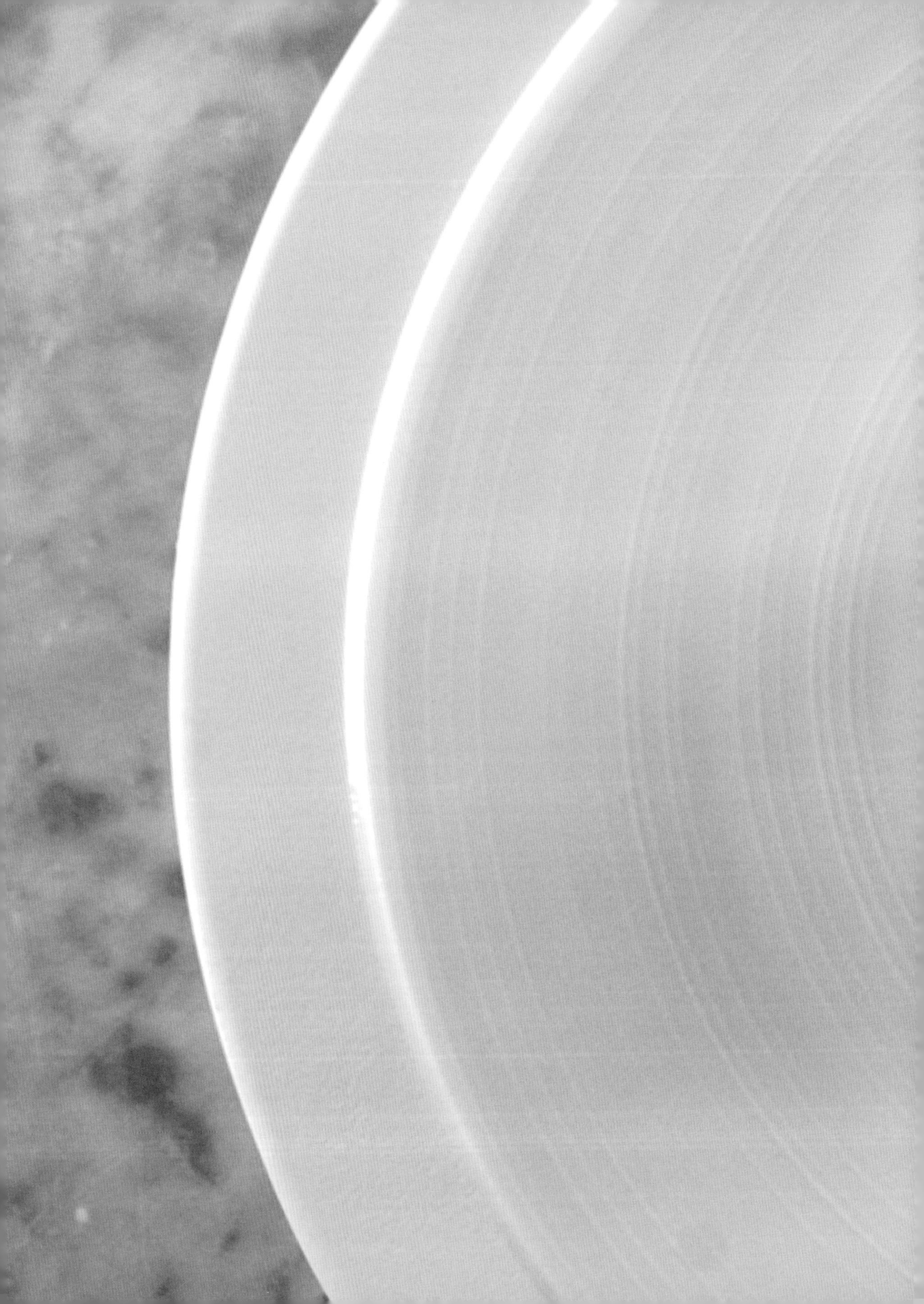

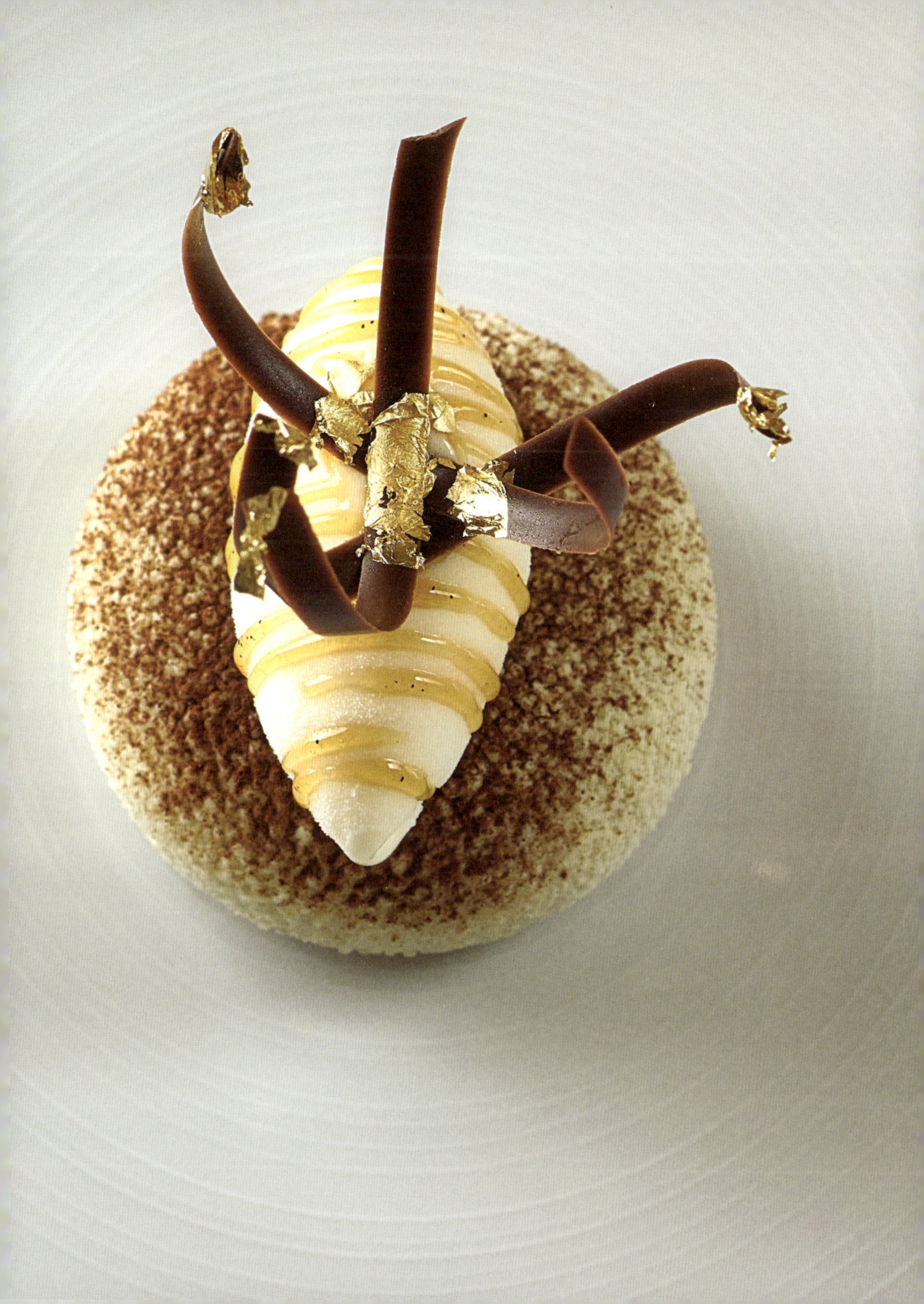

Restaurant Twenty Two, Cambridge

In The Kitchen

TURBOT, MORELS, AUSTRALIAN WINTER TRUFFLE, SAUCE BONNE FEMME

First on the plate is the confit garlic purée, then pickled morels, sourdough croutons and lots of truffle because everyone loves it. We've got truffle on another dish at the moment with Iberico ham and 5-year-old parmesan which is incredible. It's just the earthiness I think which goes so well with the mushrooms and garlic. We blend the truffle trim with cultured butter to make a truffle butter, which is added back into the sauce. It's very much the same ingredients as a traditional bonne femme but then we've added a few things like white soy and lemon juice. We made it and thought it needs a bit of this and a bit of that, and we're really happy with it now.

LAMB MOUSSAKA

I've made this a couple of times at home and for staff dinner. We had lamb on the menu so we were mincing the trim from the restaurant dishes to use up and avoid wasting what is otherwise a by-product. We use R&J Yorkshire's Finest for our lamb; it's the best I've seen and it's important to me to showcase British meat and support British farmers. We have got some really good local suppliers too, and one of our regulars, Rosemary Talbot, has an allotment down the road where she grows herbs, micro greens, leaves and flowers for us. It's great to have something picked in the morning and on the plate by lunchtime. Another one of our suppliers is a seed to feed micro farm, and he grows a lot of the salad and edible garnishes that we use. He's wicked, based eight miles from here, grows everything himself and picks it on the day he delivers. He gives me the seed catalogues and literally grows anything we want to order.

TIRAMISU

In this dish we've got a cocoa powder Joconde soaked in a coffee syrup, mascarpone mousse, Jivara mousse and mascarpone sorbet. You know when you get tiramisu you get cream with cocoa powder on top? We wanted to replicate that, so we sprayed all the layers with white chocolate and dusted the top with cocoa powder. Then we made the marsala caramel – that went through 6 or 7 recipes trying to get the caramel to stick. We ended up setting the caramel with agar and then reblending it so you get a nice thick consistency and it doesn't all drip off. It looks like it's going to be a heavy dessert but it's nice and light. When you're that far through a tasting menu, normally dessert would be the one that gets pushed to the side a little, but not many people leave this. If I see tiramisu on a menu somewhere, I'd definitely order it, so I wanted to take something I loved and put my own stamp on it.

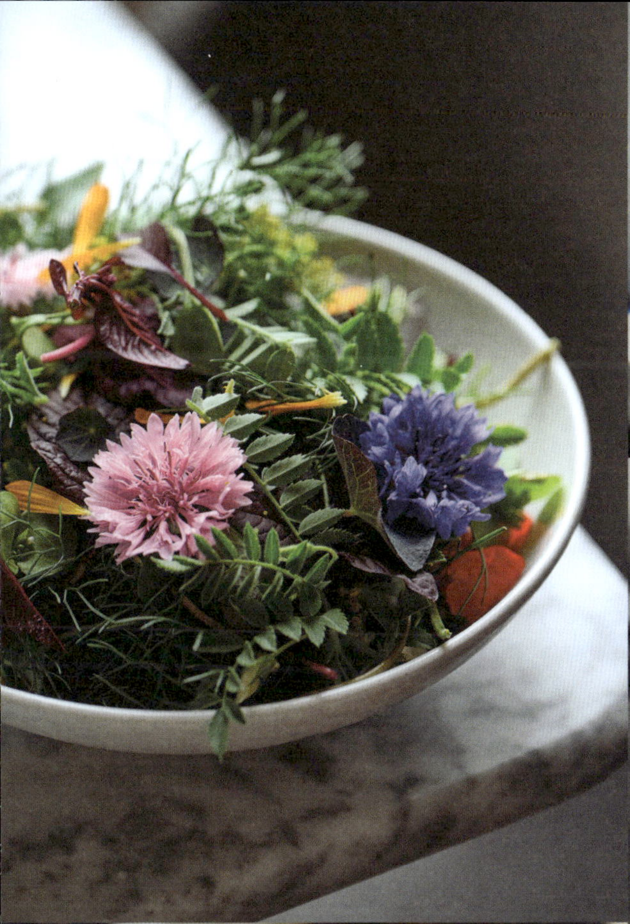
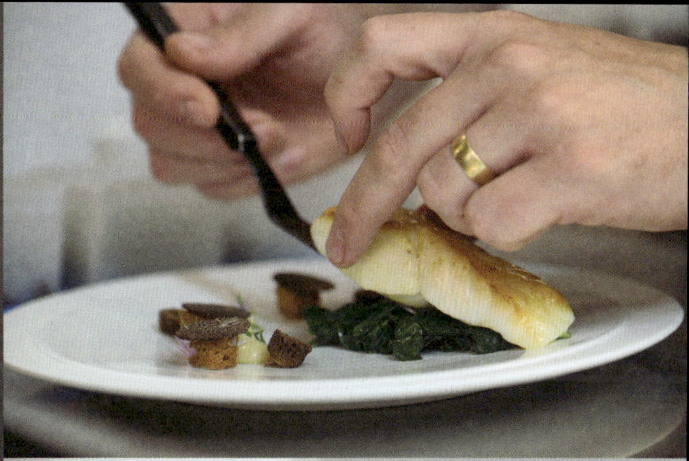
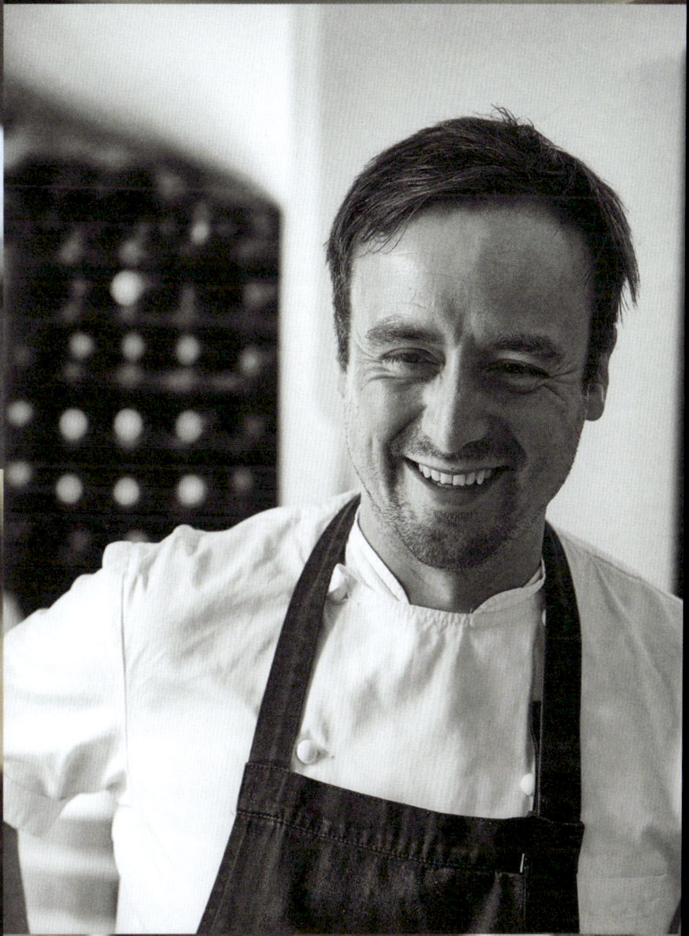
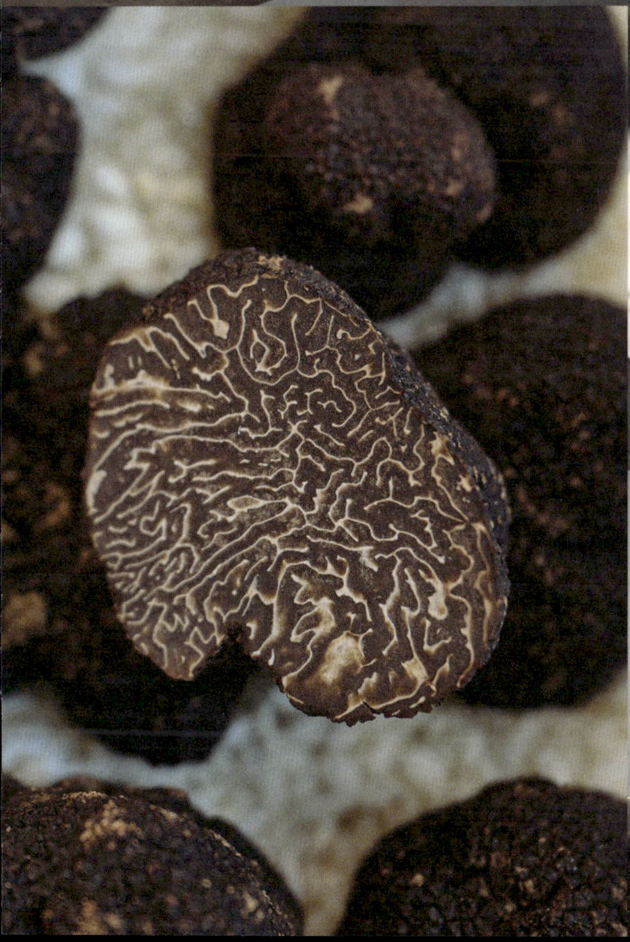
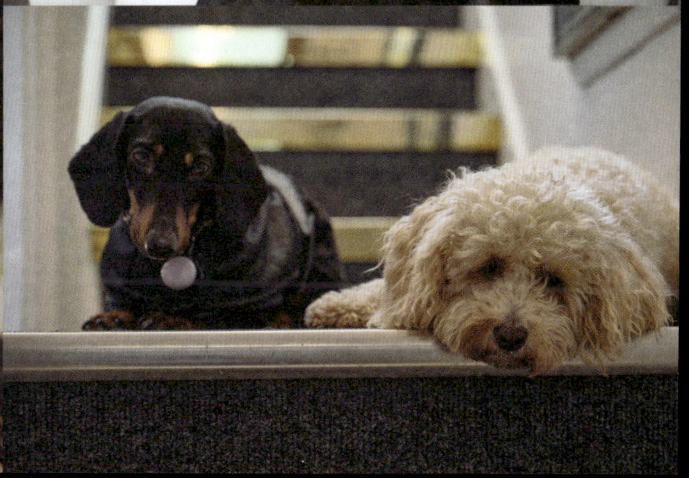

Restaurant Twenty Two, Cambridge

In The Restaurant

Alex and I got the keys to Restaurant Twenty Two in 2018. It's been a restaurant since 1982 in various forms – Italian, classic French – although it's always been called Restaurant Twenty Two. When we came in it was quite dated. Everything was green and pink, tablecloths everywhere, really stuffy – like your grandma's living room. We spent about four months gutting it, including getting rid of about six layers of carpet, so the rooms felt a little bit bigger after that!

We've got a private dining room upstairs for four tables of two or a table of ten, with exactly the same offering as the main restaurant on the floor below. Although being a beautiful old Victorian townhouse gives the restaurant lots of character, it means the kitchen, restaurant and private dining room are split over three floors which has its challenges!

Alex and I actually ate in the restaurant about 3 months ago for the first time; we had a cancellation at quarter to nine and as we'd already done the majority of service, we went out and came back in the front door to sit down and have the full menu. I've never seen the restaurant from that side before and it was a really proud moment to see what the team can do.

Caer is my senior sous chef who came on board when he was 20 and has been with us ever since, having started as a commis chef and been recently promoted to senior sous chef. Our front of house team are absolutely brilliant; they are so passionate about the food and giving the guests the best experience we can. Similar to Caer, we have Mel who has been with us from the very start and is amazing with the guests. She has built up brilliant relationships with our regulars, remembering their special occasions, likes and dislikes. The small details are so important, making them feel special every time they visit: that's what it's all about. We have a very special guest who comes in every couple of weeks for lunch and she gets treated like royalty every time. We love to hear her feedback on new dishes, she doesn't hold back! Having guests who choose to come back time and time again and spend their hard-earned money with you is the ultimate compliment.

Our menu is super seasonal. For example, we'll have wild garlic and lamb on and then we'll swap it over to use aubergine instead when that comes in, so the dishes change based on what is tasting best. It's what all chefs say but it's true and it makes total sense to get everything when it's in peak condition. We like to source locally where possible but it's more about the ingredient and the flavour. We're not doing anything ground-breaking and our flavours are quite classical, modern British cookery.

We made a bit of a buzz opening in Cambridge because there were surprisingly few good restaurants here when we first opened. Everyone came and the locals seemed to like us, so we have been able to keep doing what we love and grow a little. There are 14 full-time members of staff here now, compared to three chefs and three front of house when we opened. It's not an easy ride and the crazy food prices are one of many things making life more difficult for our industry – I feel a bit like we're being filmed at the minute, like someone's going to turn round and say it was all a joke… but we still do it. I could easily just close and sell up or whatever, but I love it and can't imagine doing anything else. Everyone talks about unsociable hours but when everything's going to plan and the team are singing, there's nowhere else I'd rather be on a Saturday night. When I'm tired at the end of the week, I like the feeling of what we've accomplished. Obviously there's a lot more pride in having our own place than working for someone else. It's a different ballgame when it's your name above the door.

Photo: Sam Carter

KOL, London

Santiago Lastra

Santiago Lastra has worked in professional kitchens since the age of 15 and travelled the globe as a chef, accepting invitations at high profile establishments including London's Tate Modern and Hija de Sanchez in Copenhagen. He returned to his homeland to launch NOMA Mexico in 2017 and was instrumental in the concept as Rene Redzepi's right-hand man. Following this experience, which involved travelling and getting to know the traditions and personalities behind Mexican gastronomy, he realised that there were only a few examples of authentic Mexican cuisine in the world. The concept of KOL was born on a beach in Tulum, shaped from a desire to be one of the few who did represent Mexico in a genuine way. Since launching the restaurant in London, Santiago has been awarded the title of GQ Best Chef 2021 while KOL was named La Liste's New Arrival of the Year 2021 and recognised as one of the top 35 restaurants in the UK in the National Restaurant Awards.

"I had the idea for KOL when I was living and working in Mexico for Noma. Having worked for a full year before the Noma Mexico pop up – organising the research trips; visiting communities, restaurants and markets; working with indigenous farmers; commissioning people to make crockery – I wanted to do something similar that would promote the quality of Mexican culture and cuisine to the rest of the world. So, I wrote a list of what the next country or city that I moved to would have. I wanted it to be multicultural and English speaking, with open-minded people who liked spicy food and Mexican culture (or at least knew what it was).

I had created pop ups in over 30 countries and lived in Taiwan, Russia, Ukraine, Turkey, Germany, and Italy among others, but London was the place I thought would work best for my concept. I moved to the UK without knowing anyone and started from scratch, travelling around the country for research, meeting other chefs and looking for investment and business partners. KOL opened in the middle of the pandemic, and it's my first restaurant, so it was pretty complicated. But now we are in a great position where we can enjoy the journey.

The word col means 'cabbage' in Spanish when it's spelled with a c, and the idea was to represent things that are undervalued but can be special when you put them in the right context. For us, that context is Mexican culture and cuisine with British ingredients. A lot of people think that Mexican food is not very good, or at least not well represented, and outside Britain people often think that British food isn't very good either. We want to show that they can be incredible."

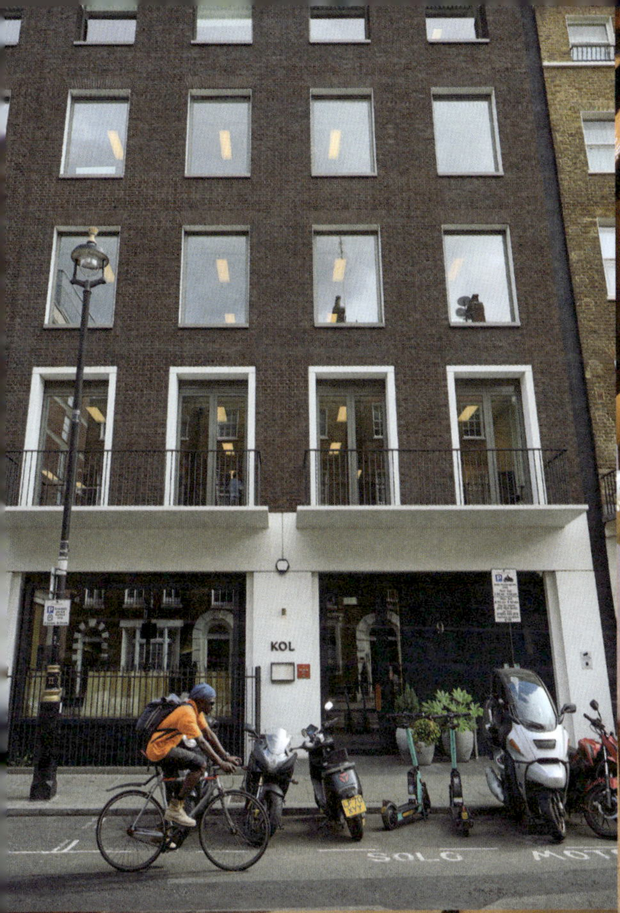
KOL
SOLO

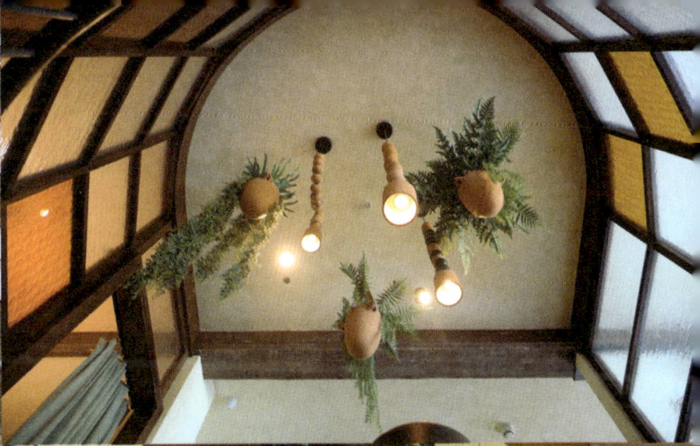

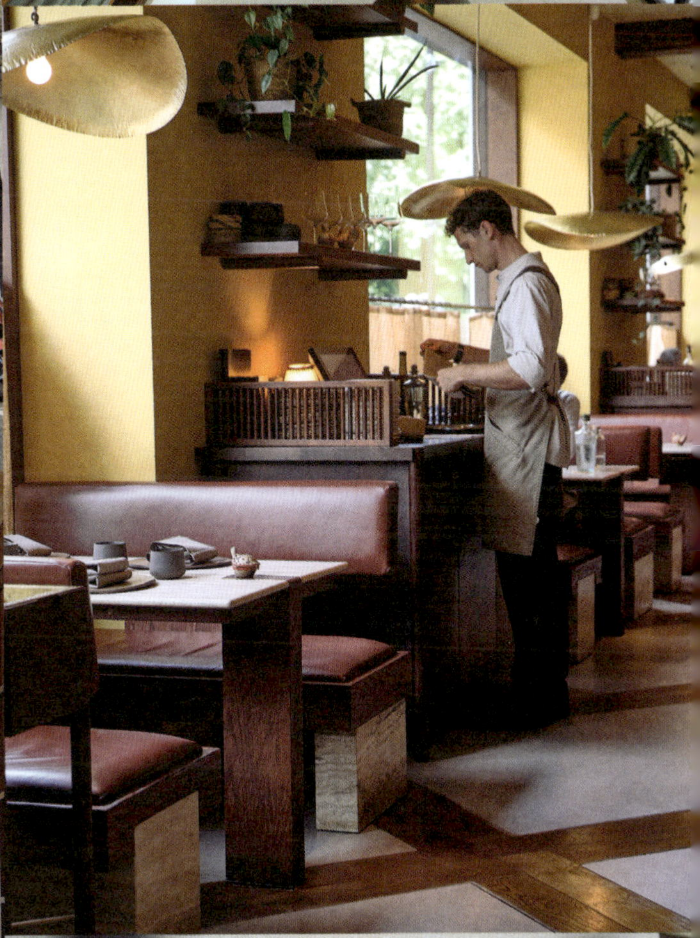

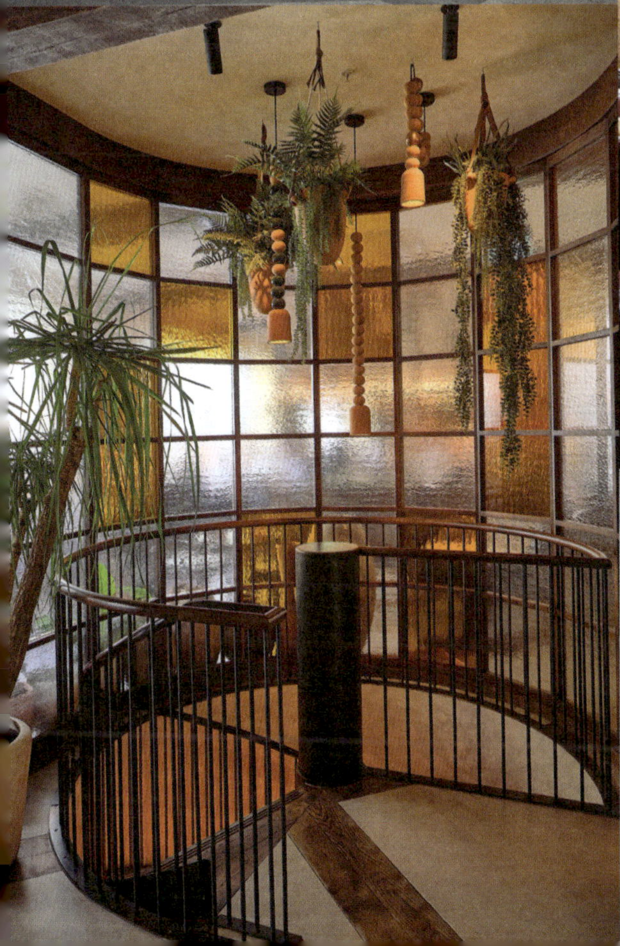

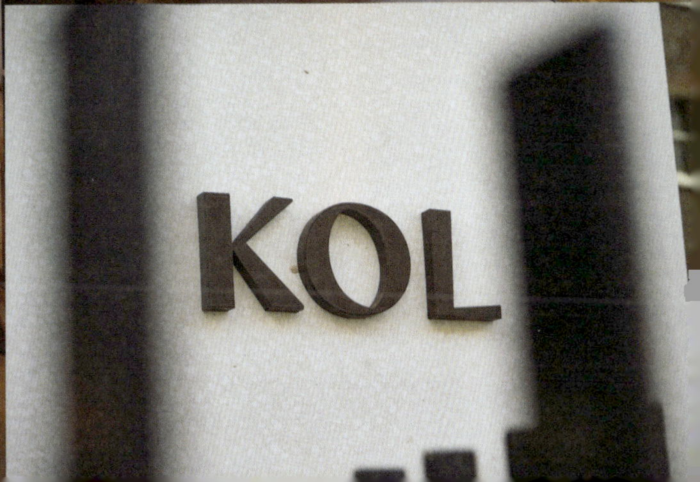
KOL

KOL, London

Buñuelos with Brie Ice Cream and Sea Buckthorn

Preparation time: 12 hours | Cooking time: 3 hours | Serves 10

100ml walnut oil

FOR THE BUÑUELOS
500kg plain flour

60g caster sugar

5g baking powder

5g fine salt

300g water

1 egg

45g butter, melted

80g brown sugar

40g ancho chilli powder

FOR THE ICE CREAM
56g British brie

100g milk

114g cream

80g sugar

1.5g stabiliser

22g egg yolk

FOR THE SEA BUCKTHORN PASTE
50ml sea buckthorn juice

10g sugar

2g agar

1g pectin

FOR THE BUÑUELOS
Mix all the dry ingredients together in a KitchenAid with the leaf attachment. Add the water, then once it has been absorbed add the egg. Once the mixture has homogenised, add the melted butter. Keep mixing until the dough is smooth and shiny. Let it rest, covered, for at least 30 minutes in the fridge and then portion into 40g pieces. Press these pieces into circular shapes with a rolling pin to approximately 20mm thickness. Let the dough rest at room temperature and then deep fry in vegetable oil at 200°c. Drain off the excess oil and then toss the buñuelos with the sugar and chilli powder. Reserve at room temperature.

FOR THE ICE CREAM
Break the cheese up and add it to the milk and cream in a saucepan. Bring to the boil, then add half the sugar with the stabiliser when it reaches 40°c. In a separate bowl, whisk the remaining sugar with the egg yolk. Once the milk mixture comes back to the boil, slowly pour a small amount into the egg mixture and whisk to combine, then pour this into the pan and cook the combined mixture to 82°c. Chill overnight. The next day, hand blend and pass. Place in a Pacojet beaker and freeze.

FOR THE SEA BUCKTHORN PASTE
Bring the juice to the boil with half the sugar. Mix the remaining sugar with the pectin and agar, then add this to the boiling juice while whisking. Keep whisking until the mixture thickens and homogenises. Take the pan off the heat, let it cool down and then blitz to a paste.

TO FINISH
Place the sea buckthorn paste on the bottom of the bowl with a spoon. Make a quenelle with the ice cream, place this on top and then finish with walnut oil. Serve the buñuelos on a separate plate.

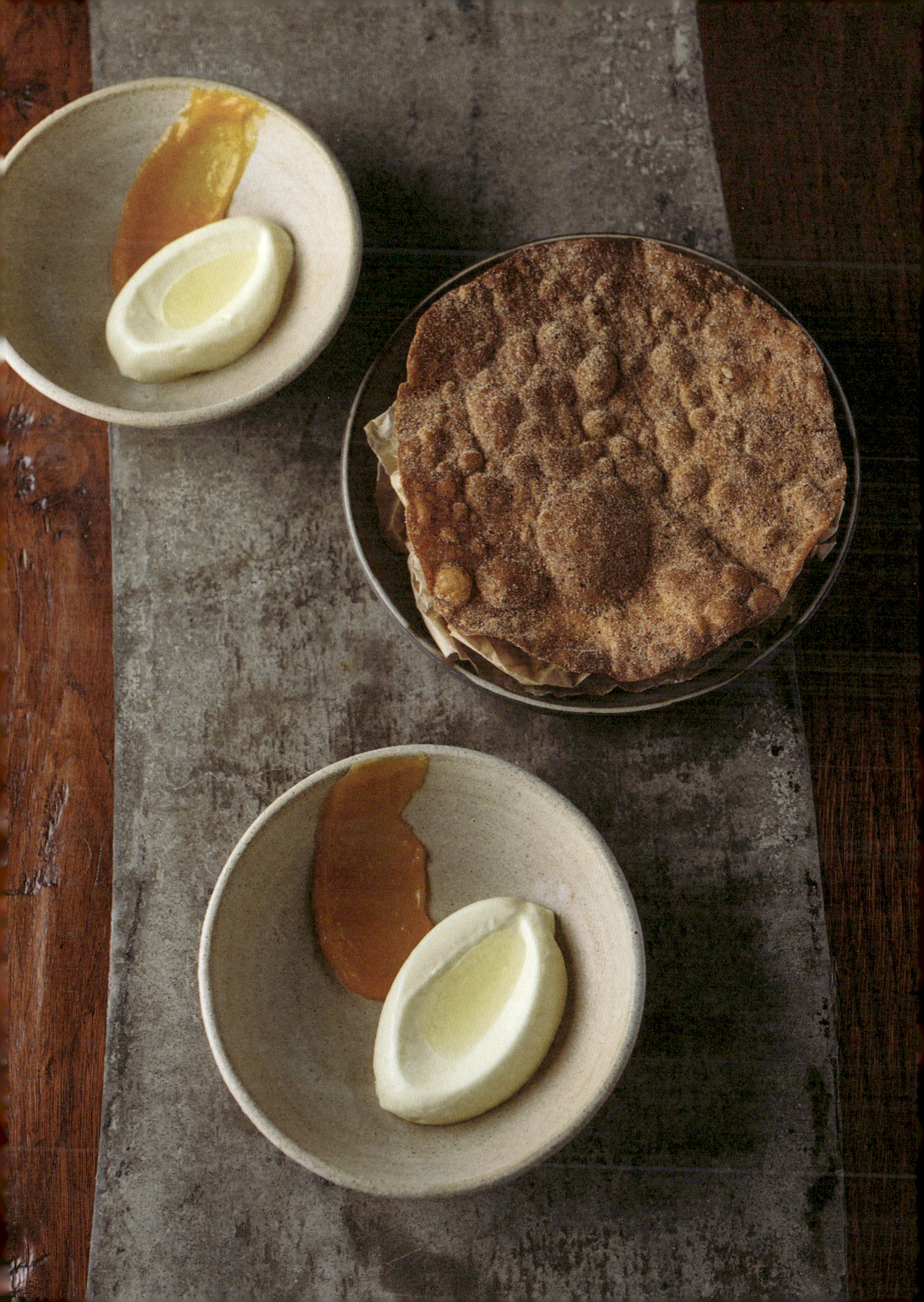

KOL, London

Crab Empanada

Preparation time: 2 hours | Cooking time: 1 hour 30 minutes | Serves 12

250g white crab meat

250ml crème fraiche

FOR THE ADOBO

200g tomatoes

80g onions

10g dried guajillo chilli

10g dried pasilla chilli

10g dried mulato chilli

6g chipotles in adobo (from a can)

2g garlic (1 clove)

1g salt

FOR THE SALSA

12.5g guajillo chilli

8g dried habanero

1 arbol chilli

50g achiote

1 litre rapeseed oil

170ml guajillo oil (see method or shop-bought)

2 egg yolks, pasteurised

5ml fermented gooseberry juice (or lime juice)

5ml kombucha

FOR THE MASA TORTILLAS

350g corn masa harina

350g water

3g fine salt

FOR THE ADOBO

In a hot pan, char the tomatoes and onions (cook until dark, not burnt). Once the tomatoes and onions are cooked, blend the dried chillies to create a powder. Add the rest of the ingredients to the pan and blend until smooth, then pass through a fine strainer and reserve.

FOR THE SALSA

First, make the guajillo oil (or it can be bought ready-made) by blending the chillies, achiote and rapeseed oil in the Thermomix at 70°c for 4 minutes. Strain through a cheese cloth and reserve.

Next, make an emulsion by whisking 170ml of the guajillo oil with the egg yolks until light and foamy. Add the gooseberry juice and season to taste with salt. Add the kombucha and mix to incorporate.

FOR THE MASA TORTILLAS

Mix the ingredients together in a bowl and work with your hands until homogeneous, then reserve the dough at room temperature with a wet towel on top. Make the tortillas à la minute. Take 35g balls of the corn masa dough and press with a tortilla press (between 2 plastic sheets or parchment paper) to create circles that are 13cm in diameter.

FOR THE EMPANADA

Mix the crab meat with half the adobo and season to taste. Place the mix inside the masa circles and gently fold the masa to create a semicircle, pressing the borders with your fingers to create an empanada (make sure the masa doesn't break in the middle). Deep fry the empanadas in vegetable oil at 190°c until it stops bubbling. Dry the empanadas with kitchen paper and leave to cool down at room temperature.

TO FINISH

Serve the empanada in the middle with the crème fraiche and salsa in separate containers.

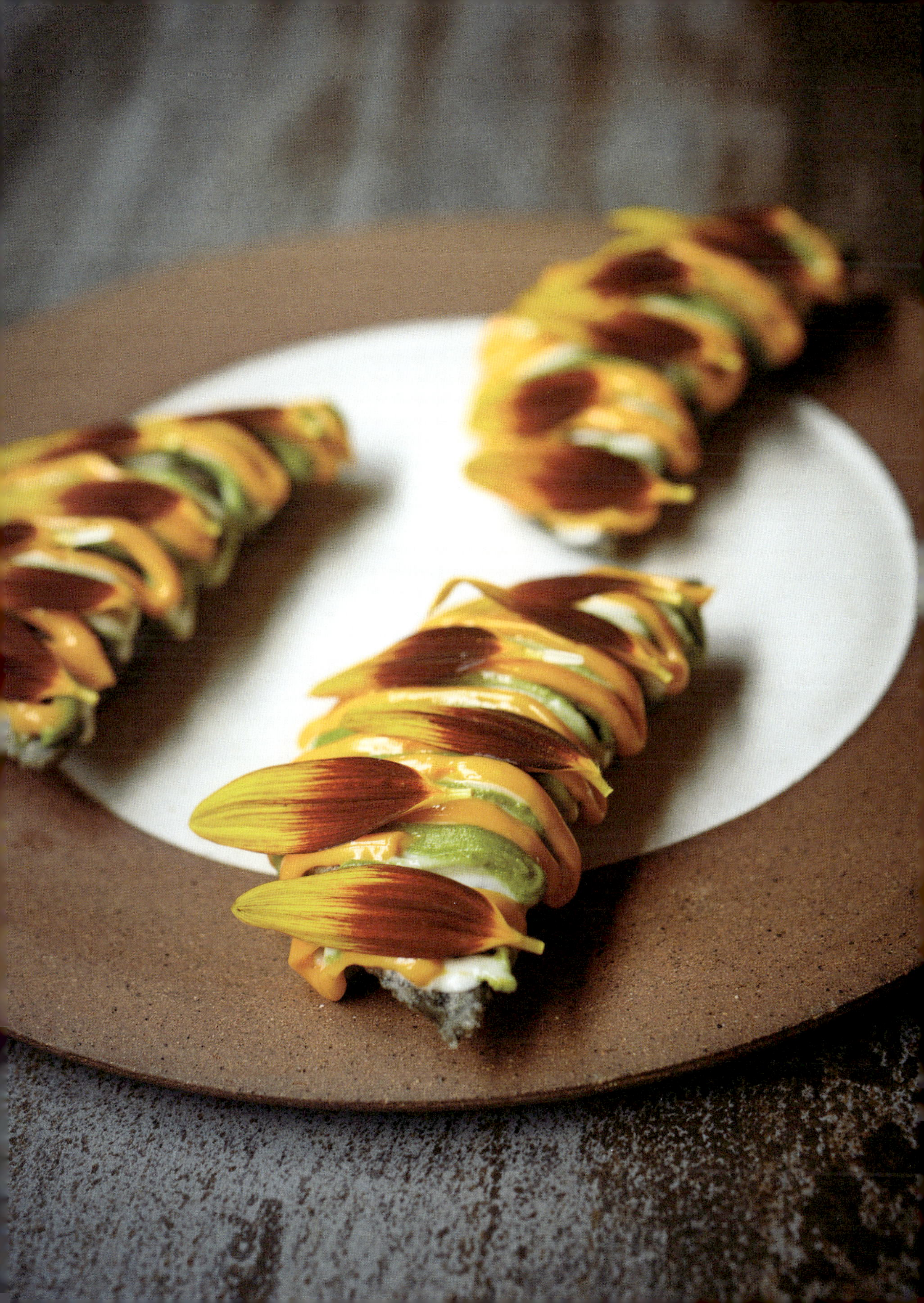

KOL, London

Pork Cheek Carnitas Tacos

Preparation time: 8 hours, plus marinating | Cooking time: 4 hours | Serves 4

1kg pork cheeks

Pork skin chicharron

FOR THE MARINADE

310ml vegetable oil

40g peeled whole garlic cloves

40g picked parsley

10g salt

FOR THE BEANS

10 bay leaves

10g black peppercorns

10 pasilla chillies, cleaned

20 ancho chillies, cleaned

20 dried arbol chillies

1.2kg whole tomatoes

600g black beans, soaked

400g onions, quartered

6 cloves of garlic

2.5 litres water (approx.)

30g dried Atlantic wakame seaweed

30g dried woodruff

200g lamb fat

FOR THE XNIPEC

200g red onion, sliced

80g pickling liquid (see method)

60g fermented gooseberry liquid

60g sour kombucha

10g scotch bonnet, deseeded and sliced

1g dried oregano

FOR THE SALSA

250g roasted gooseberries

250g blanched and roasted pear

40g white onion, charred

20g garlic, toasted and peeled

40g honey

4g Thai chilli, sliced

4g fine salt

TO SERVE

4 corn tortillas or pointed cabbage leaves

Wild herbs, to garnish

FOR THE MARINADE

Blend all the ingredients in a Thermomix at 70°c for 4 minutes. Cover the pork cheeks in the marinade and leave overnight.

FOR THE PORK

Cook the marinated pork cheeks at 70°c for 2 hours until tender. They can be mixed with pork fat, or lardo for a better result, then chopped finely and served with chicharron made with the skin.

FOR THE BEANS

Put the bay leaves, peppercorns and chillies in a piece of muslin cloth and tie up to make a bag. Combine the remaining ingredients except the woodruff and lamb fat in a pot and simmer, then add the bag of spices and leave until the beans are cooked.

Once cooked, remove the seaweed from the mix and let it rest. Remove the bag of spices and then blend the bean mixture until smooth. Pass it through a fine strainer. To finish, refry the beans with fat (lamb fat is recommended) and infuse with the woodruff.

FOR THE XNIPEC

Make up the pickling liquid by combining water and white vinegar at a ratio of 10:1, then adding cider vinegar to this mixture at a ratio of 10:1.5. Briefly flash fry the red onions in a pan with a dash of water to soften but retain their colour. Remove them from the pan and then add the liquids, scotch bonnet and oregano.

FOR THE SALSA

Blend all the ingredients together until smooth, then pass through a fine strainer and season to taste.

TO SERVE

If you are using cabbage to make the tortillas, separate the leaves and cut into discs of 15cm. Otherwise, follow the recipe for masa tortillas on page 218 but portion into 35g balls, press out and then cook in a hot dry pan for about a minute on the first side, then flip and cook for about 30 seconds, then flip again so it puffs up which will happen very quickly. Alternatively, you can use fresh shop-bought tortillas.

Serve the pork cheek carnitas in a warm bowl, with the beans, salsa and xnipec in separate bowls. Make tacos with all the ingredients in the cabbage leaf discs or corn tortillas, topped with wild herbs.

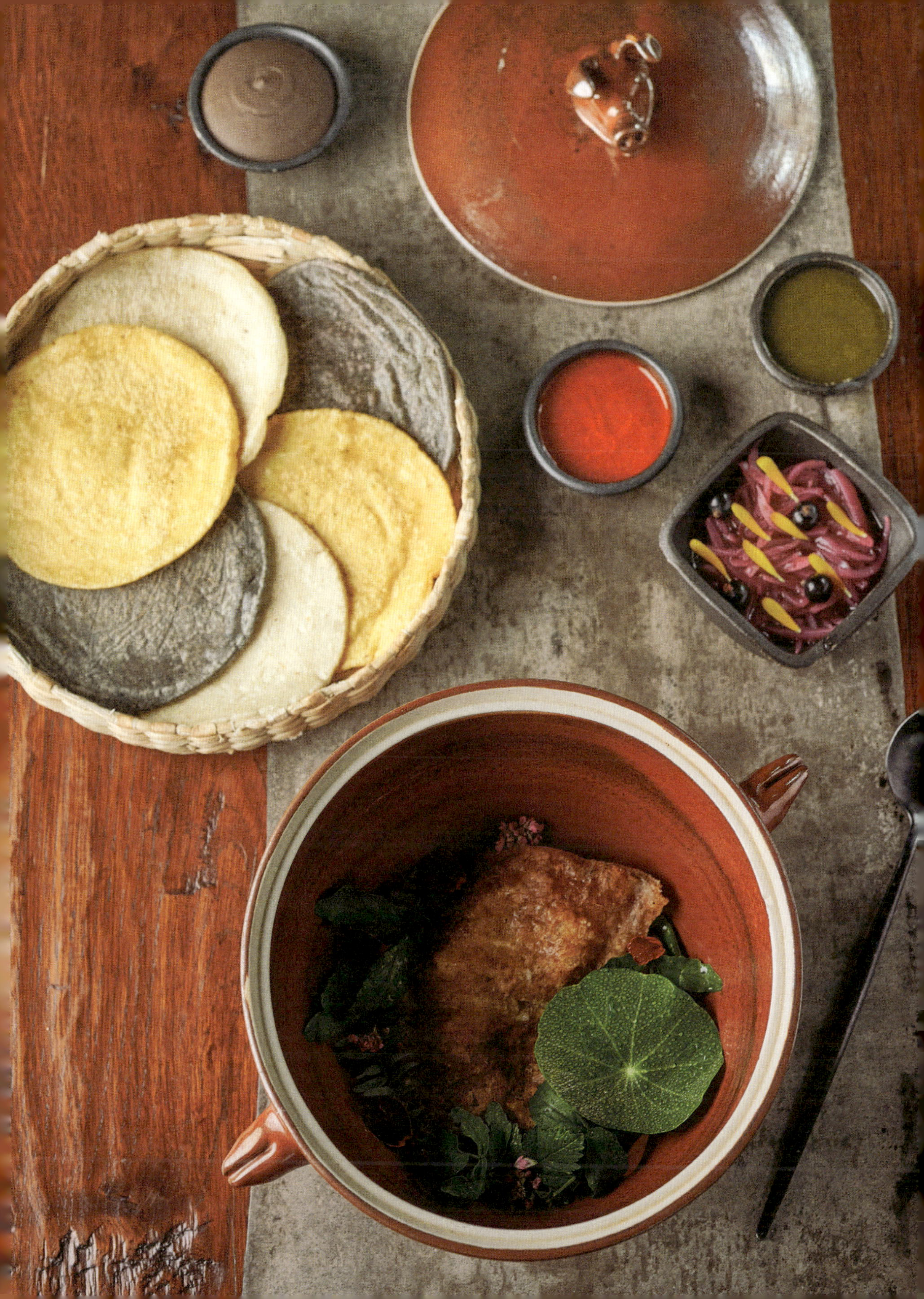

KOL, London

Recipe Notes

BUÑUELOS WITH BRIE ICE CREAM AND SEA BUCKTHORN

Traditionally, buñuelos are a sweet food, dusted with sugar and served with a fruit sugarcane syrup, normally made with guava. For this dish, our inspiration was also a cheeseboard from the UK, so the buñuelos is the cracker, the ice cream is the cheese, and the sea buckthorn jam is like a compote. The walnut oil is the nuts you would have with the cheese, so the idea comes together from British inspiration presented in a Mexican way.

The ancho chilli in this dish has a sort of peppery flavour and is not too spicy. It has some earthy notes too and a flavour of raisins. Ancho chilli is the green poblano chilli when it's fresh – because in Mexico chillies have a different name when they are fresh from when they are dried. It's one of the most easily available dried chillies, and you can find them here in the UK.

CRAB EMPANADAS

In Mexico, we call these empanadas when they don't include cheese – a quesadilla has cheese but empanadas don't. You can also call these pescadillas because they include fish. A crab filling would be traditional in Mexico, but the crab inside will be prepared slightly different from the way we do it at KOL. Normally it would be a little bit less punchy, with a tomato sauce, so the crab will be whiter with a watery dressing. I think this version of the filling isn't thick enough, so we use a mixed chilli adobo instead of tomato sauce which gives the crab a little more texture.

I use several different types of chillies in the adobo for this dish because the perfect dried chilli doesn't really exist, so they ideally need to be mixed for the best flavour. The guajillo is important for colour but it's not spicy enough, and the pasilla is too sweet, while the mulato is more spicy and earthy. In Europe, chillies are just chillies, but in Mexico every single sauce or preparation will include the name of the chilli because they're so important to the dish. We would never just call something a 'chilli sauce' – it would sound really odd to a Mexican!

Part of the KOL concept is that we don't use ingredients that don't naturally grow in the UK, so we use gooseberry juice to give the salsa in this dish a citrussy flavour and acidity instead of lemon or lime. The alternatives we use depend on the season – we tried plum and quince juices – and we are still learning what works best. Fermented gooseberry juice has a really interesting tart flavour, and we ferment the fruit itself with 2% salt for two weeks, then blend it so we end up with a paste as well, which is used in many other recipes. The kombucha adds a little bit of sweetness because the gooseberries can be briny, savoury and sour so it balances the salsa.

PORK CHEEK CARNITAS TACOS

In the south of Mexico, refried beans are flavoured with avocado leaves which have a really interesting fragrance, like a bay leaf but sweeter, and woodruff reminds me of that, so in recipes that call for avocado leaves I use woodruff. I wanted to find something British that is really specific in terms of the flavour it brings to the beans. It makes the beans taste sweet without adding any sugar, and woodruff is similar to tonka bean as well, so it adds a vanilla-like flavour. We also use seaweed to give the beans a really nice umami flavour.

Chicarron is the Mexican equivalent of the pork scratchings you get here in the UK. We make the chicarron for this dish ourselves, and there are so many recipes out there, but you can just buy it. You can steam the pork skin for about 3 hours at 90°c and then dry and fry it, or you can bake it – ours is done this way, whereas the ones you can buy are deep fried.

KOL, London

Q&A with Santiago Lastra

What was it that first interested you about food and cooking?

I don't have a beautiful story about my mum cooking or my grandparents making dinner with me, it was nothing like that! When I was 15, I saw this recipe for a crab dip on the back of a Ritz Crackers box in the supermarket, and I decided to cook it at home. Everyone in my family liked it, so I decided to go back to the supermarket and buy a booklet of recipes. They were Italian and I began to really enjoy making them all, so I tried some work experience at a local Italian restaurant. From the first moment, I fell in love with everything about it – the kitchen, the uniforms, the smells, the cleaning, everything! I knew that it was something that I wanted to do for the rest of my life. I worked 12 hour shifts there every day after school for the next three years. I had never loved or enjoyed anything more in my life, and I couldn't believe they paid me for it! That was a huge turning point for me.

Having travelled extensively, do you find you're inspired by flavours from all over the world?

For me, being able to unlock flavours through new ingredients is really exciting. At KOL, the more that I learn about British produce, the more I can use it. In the beginning, my concept was more about Mexican ingredients and flavours but the more I discover this country, the more it flips. Our main goal is still for our food to taste Mexican – that's pretty much the only rule we have – and the inspiration and techniques can come from anywhere, but the ingredients are from the UK. I work directly with farms so that we can ask what produce they have a lot of, then we create a menu based on that. We make sure that every dish has a story about Mexico behind it too.

What are you most passionate about as a chef?

That's a really good question because the thing is, when you have a restaurant it's different. You don't cook as much, and I do enjoy cooking a lot – when you feel that you're part of your craft. Like when you're cooking a whole animal in the bonfire, and you can feel when it's cooked – it's intuitive. That's one of the things I love the most, but what motivates me now is being able to create something. When we're changing the menu and we try something that's never been made before, it gives me joy. I also really like to help other people, and if you can do both then you have a reason to be alive. You're doing something that you love, creating something that hasn't been made before in this world, and you can also work with other people that inspire you, while helping your community. That's the dream.

What's your favourite ingredient to cook with?

It's going to sound quite obvious, but I would say chillies – all the chillies! Mexico is the birthplace of chillies and they are the only ingredient that I can't work without. The moment that we don't use chillies here at KOL, the food just becomes British. Which is great, but not our concept. Using chilli is not about making things spicy, it's about layers of flavour, complexity, warmth, freshness, passion. The level of spice is so important to the experience. Chilli is what we cannot live without in this restaurant; we share a palate for spice now. Last year I went to a great restaurant in Paris with my head chef Ben, and he said to me 'you know, this dish is great, but with chilli…?' and I thought, yes!

Do you consider your cooking more technical or more classical?

We try not to mess with ingredients — that's really important — because it's a shame and I think you have to respect nature. At the same time, our main goal is to be able to craft flavours. It's not about doing something that tastes like something else — we don't want to trick the guests, we want to give pleasure with flavour, and represent culture. Whatever it takes to do that may or may not use technology, but we want to do it in the most natural way possible. We don't use any chemicals in the food, we don't do foams with siphons and things like that. We use nature to craft flavours and give pleasure, as best we can with the experience and the technology we have right now.

What direction are KOL and your own cooking journey heading in?

I think there's something very important about tradition and innovation. I believe that tradition was innovation at some point, like when a pizza or fish and chips or a sandwich was new. When these traditional recipes were innovative, they were made in a way that made sense at that time and in that context. You do your thing to feed other people and make them happy with what you have. I think sometimes as chefs we disconnect with this humble meaning of feeding others by becoming very ego-driven and creating dishes just to look good or showcase many techniques. Cooking is about how we can use what we have in a new way — in your own way. It's a process of adding new traditions to the world. I'm very interested in how something you create can become normal for people — that's the next level, even more than being innovative.

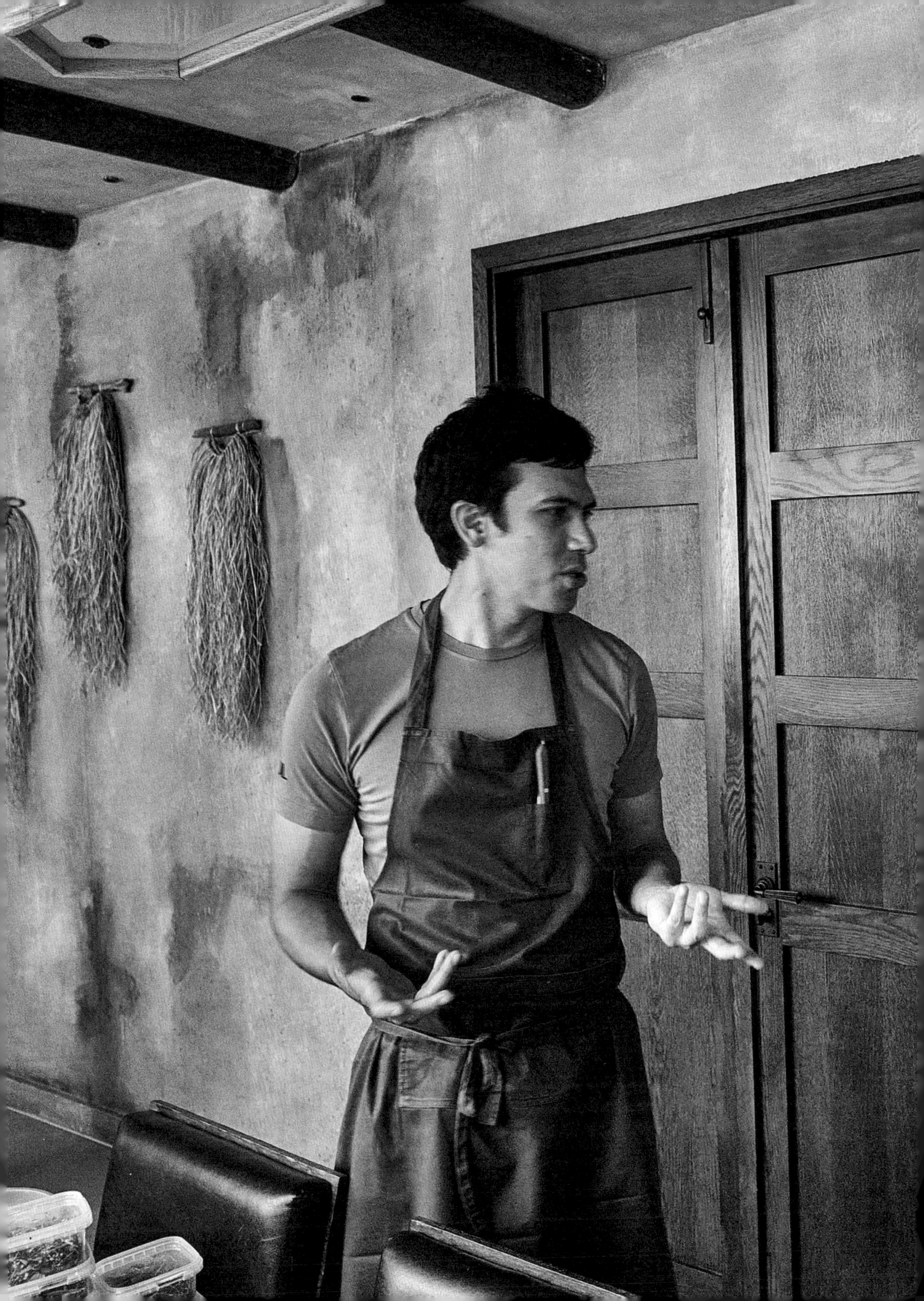

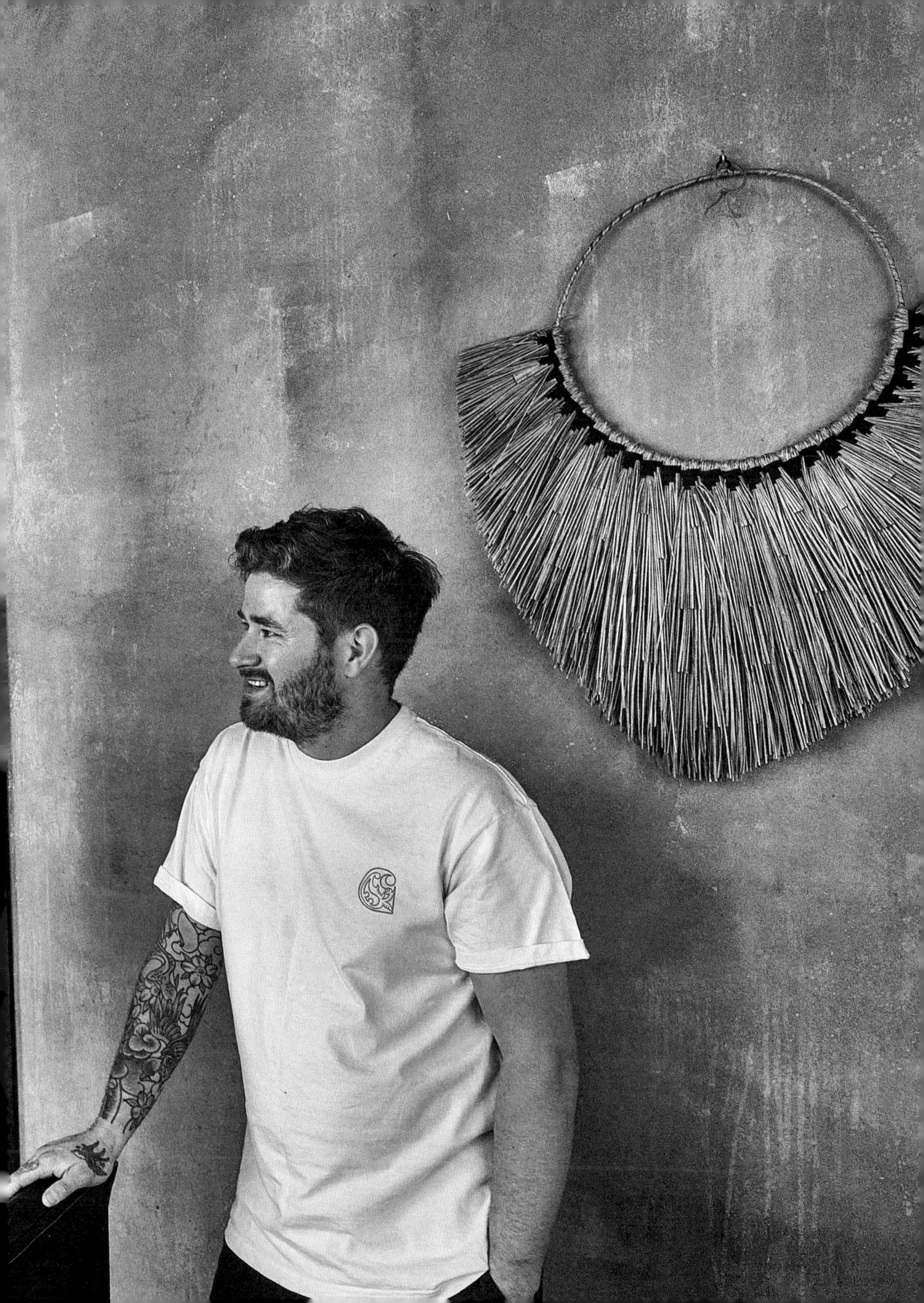

The Grill by Tom Booton, London

Tom Booton

Tom's career began at the age of 15 in a local restaurant, where he rose through the ranks. Tom moved to London in 2013 where he worked as a commis chef and sous chef before taking up the position of head chef for Alyn Williams at The Westbury. He was approached by The Grill at The Dorchester to become their youngest ever head chef after the hotel's director dined at The Westbury. Tom has also worked in restaurants in New York, Copenhagen and Iceland.

Having started so young, did you always want to be a chef?

I fell into cooking really, never left after work experience in a kitchen at 15. The first chef I worked for wanted to know what my parents did, so I told him: my dad was in the Army and my mum was a nurse. All he said was "you'll be a good chef" which I didn't get at the time, but I do the same thing now. When I employ people, I always ask what their parents do because it's quite an interesting question and I've found that most good chefs have very hard-working parents, though of course this isn't always true. We are always on the lookout for new talent, and we all need to continue promoting what a great career choice hospitality can be. That includes going into schools or colleges and inspiring the next generation.

Can you describe your current cooking style?

I know that a lot of chefs say it, but we always try and get the best ingredients – whether that's ribeye or mushrooms – and just cook them with love and passion. The whole idea of revitalising The Grill at The Dorchester was to create modern British cuisine. My food is informed by the setting to some extent, but I didn't want the menu to reflect a misguided assumption that it's all about formality at The Dorchester. Just as we do across the entire hotel, I want to surprise and excite people with a new and enjoyable experience.

Which other restaurants do you most want visit?

JÖRO has been on my list for a while (sorry Stacey and Luke!). The good thing about the industry today though is that we're all well connected because of social media. There's an openness now that I believe you wouldn't have got 20 years ago, which is for the better. We are all on a journey together; the food in this country is amazing now. When I travel it always makes me remember how great it is here in Great Britain, especially for produce.

What's your go-to meal or cuisine when you're not working?

My girlfriend Rachel and I both love Indian food and we've got a couple of really great local Indian restaurants. Sunday night curry, beer and watching TV to finish off the week is my chill time.

You've already travelled quite a bit – do you see yourself living and working anywhere else?

I'm from Colchester, so I've not gone far from home. There are a few nice villages in Essex so maybe one day it would be quite interesting to do something similar to Tom Kerridge, Paul Ainsworth and many others who have launched businesses in an area. I do like London though, and we've got something really great here. The hotel took a massive gamble in appointing and trusting me as head chef at 27 and they've been very good to me. We want to change things up a little bit and we've got a lot more planned.

THE GRILL

The Grill by Tom Booton, London

Beef Ribeye, Stuffed Potato, Mushrooms, Chive Mayonnaise

Preparation time: 2 hours, plus resting | Cooking time: 6 hours | Serves 4

500g beef shin

1 litre water

100g salt

50g brown sugar

1 glass of red wine

500ml veal or beef stock

50g red wine vinegar

Salt and pepper

8 Charlotte potatoes

50g chives, finely chopped

2 x 300-400g dry-aged ribeye steaks

100g butter

A few cloves of garlic

A few sprigs of thyme

500g different mushrooms

FOR THE CHIVE MAYONNAISE

400g chives

400g oil

60g egg yolk

10g chardonnay vinegar

8g English mustard

3g salt

15g sugar

15g lemon juice

150ml vegetable oil

FOR THE BEEF SHIN

This should be done the day before your dinner party. Once the meat is braised it will keep for up to 5 days in the fridge (or 3 months in the freezer). Firstly, make the brine by boiling the water, salt and brown sugar then leaving to cool. Place the beef shin into the brine and leave for a minimum of 4 hours or overnight.

Preheat the oven to 150°c. Wash the shin well in a bowl of water then dry on a tea towel. Preheat a large frying pan on a high heat, add some oil and then carefully place the shin in the pan and begin to caramelise all around the joint. Remove the shin and deglaze the pan with the red wine, then add the stock and place the shin back into the pan. Cover with baking paper then tin foil and place into the oven for 4-5 hours until the meat is tender.

Once cooked, leave the beef shin to rest for 1 hour. Meanwhile, transfer all the cooking juices to a pan and start to reduce them slowly. Pick the rested beef into nice small pieces, fold through the reduced cooking liquid and season with salt, pepper and red wine vinegar. Add garlic and herbs if you wish. Cool and place into the fridge ready to use.

FOR THE CHIVE MAYONNAISE

Firstly, make the chive oil by roughly chopping the chives and blending them with the oil in a food processor for 5-10 minutes. A Thermomix would be perfect for this as we want the oil to reach 75°c so the chlorophyll splits and we get a vibrant green colour. Pass the green oil through muslin cloth or kitchen paper and let it hang to drip through naturally. You can make this in advance as the oil will keep in the fridge for a couple of weeks.

Place the egg yolk, vinegar, mustard, salt, sugar and lemon juice into a jug and begin to blitz using a handheld blender. Slowly start to drizzle in 150ml of the chive oil and the vegetable oil while blitzing. If it is getting too thick, add a splash of cold water.

FOR THE STUFFED POTATOES

Preheat the oven to 180°c and place the potatoes on a tray. Bake for 35-45 minutes until cooked through, then leave to cool. Carefully remove the top of the potatoes lengthways and begin to carefully scoop out the insides, being careful not to damage the skin. Save the insides for another dish and place the skins back in the oven for 5 minutes to harden slightly. When you are ready to plate, reheat the braised beef shin, spoon this into the potato skins and top with fresh chives.

FOR THE BEEF RIBEYE AND MUSHROOMS

Heat a large frying pan over a high heat until smoking. Season the steaks heavily with salt and pepper, then place them into the hot pan to sear on each side for 2-3 minutes. Add the butter, garlic and thyme and baste the steaks for 1-2 minutes. Remove from the pan and leave to rest for 8-10 minutes in a warm place. Add the mushrooms to the same pan and baste them in the lovely beefy butter until done to your liking. Season with salt, pepper and a touch of red wine vinegar at the end.

TO SERVE

Place a big dot of the chive mayonnaise onto the plate, followed by the hot stuffed potato skin. Halve the ribeye and place on each plate, top with the mushrooms and finish with a lovely beef sauce.

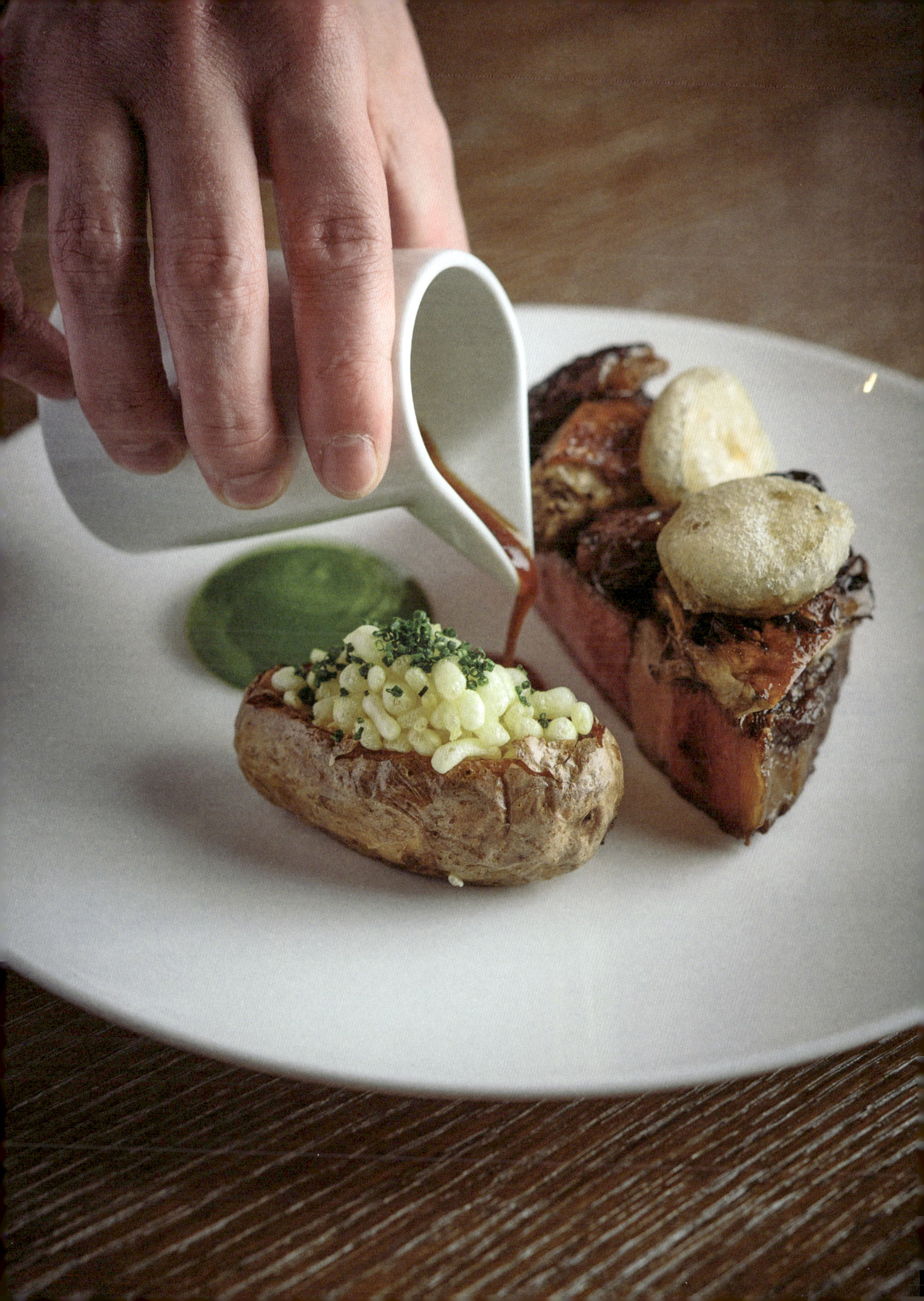

The Grill by Tom Booton, London

Ham, Egg and Chips with Roasted Pineapple

Preparation time: 12 hours | Cooking time: 2 hours | Serves 4

2kg large potatoes (choose ones that are great for frying)

25g table salt

20g cornflour

200g clarified butter

1 pineapple

4 Cacklebean eggs

8 thick slices of the best ham from your butcher

FOR THE CHIPS

Firstly, make sure you have 2 identical deep dishes or trays for cooking and pressing the chip terrine in the fridge overnight. Line one of these well with baking paper. Preheat the oven to 190°c while you peel and finely slice the potatoes (2mm) using a mandoline. Season with salt and mix well.

Start to layer up the potatoes in the lined dish in neat rows. Every couple of layers, sprinkle with a light dusting of cornflour to help them stick together. Keep going until you have used all the potatoes (you should have around 3-4 layers with a light dusting of cornflour on top).

Place the other dish on top and squeeze hard to extract as much liquid as you can out of the terrine, pouring it off. Once done, pierce several holes in the potatoes and pour over the clarified butter. Cover with baking paper and then tin foil. Bake in the preheated oven for 2-3 hours.

Once cooked, remove from the oven and place the other dish on top, squeezing to extract more liquid. Place in the fridge overnight with some weight on top. The next day, carefully remove the terrine from the trays and cut to any chip size you want (I do 8x2x2cm chips). Deep fry your chips for 5 minutes at 180°c to get them golden and crisp.

FOR THE PINEAPPLE

Preheat the oven to 180°c and trim off the leafy part at the top of the pineapple so it fits into your oven when standing upright in a tray. Roast it like this for 45 minutes, then remove and leave to cool fully. Once cool, skin the pineapple and cut into chunky discs like you get out of a tin. Remove the core of the pineapple if you wish.

FOR THE EGGS

Put a non-stick frying pan on a medium heat, add a little oil and carefully crack in the eggs. Once the eggs have been in for 2 minutes, add a small splash of water and cover the pan with a lid. Turn the heat off and leave to finish steaming for 2 minutes until the yolks are still runny but the white is cooked.

TO SERVE

Remove the ham from the fridge 15 minutes before serving to bring it to room temperature. Place the lovely golden brown, crispy chips on the plate followed by slices of the thick-cut ham, then the eggs and the disc of pineapple. My idea of a perfect meal to be honest!

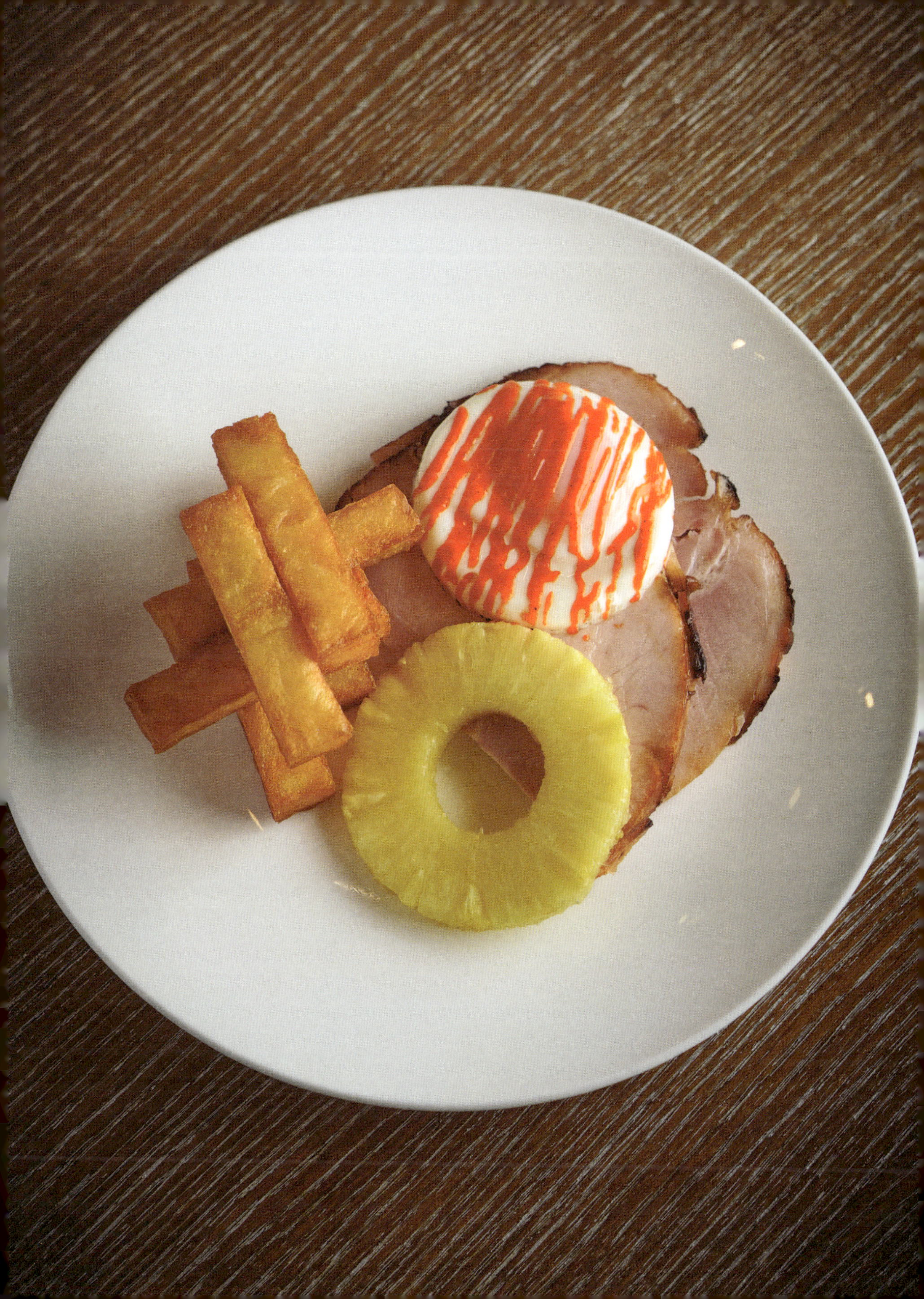

The Grill by Tom Booton, London

Lobster, Carrot Bisque, N25 Caviar

Preparation time: 12 hours | Cooking time: 3 hours | Serves 4

4 whole native lobsters (500-600g)
2.5 litres shop-bought carrot juice
12g agar agar
2 sheets of gelatine, soaked in ice water
1 fennel bulb, cut into mirepoix size
1 carrot, cut into mirepoix size
1 banana shallot, cut into mirepoix size
1 stick of celery, cut into mirepoix size
1 star anise
1 glass of white wine
25g Pernod
1 tsp tomato paste
500g fish stock
30g butter
50ml cream
50g sea purslane
1 bunch of dill
N25 caviar

FOR THE LOBSTERS

Ask your fishmonger to prepare your lobsters: we need 4 tails with the sacks removed, 4 heads cut into quarters and 8 claws. Firstly, we are going to freeze the lobster tails overnight, flat and wrapped in cling film, then defrost them in the fridge the next day. This process helps the shell release from the protein as well as tenderising the meat. Once defrosted, carefully begin to crack and remove the shell from the tails. Spike them with metal kebab sticks to keep them straight when roasting.

Bring a large pot of water to a strong boil, add the lobster claws, turn the heat off and poach for 6 minutes. Remove and cool in ice water, then crack the shells to remove the meat. Save all the shells for the bisque and the claw meat for the side salad or another dish.

FOR THE CARROT GEL

Place 2 litres of the carrot juice into a large pot and reduce to 800g (take care that it doesn't boil over and make a mess). Pass the carrot juice through muslin into a clean pan over a high heat and whisk in the agar agar for 2 minutes. Remove from the heat and stir in the bloomed gelatine sheets until dissolved. Season with salt and then set over a bowl of ice or in the fridge until rock hard.

Remove the set carrot gel from the fridge and blend (it may need a touch of water to get it going, but it is very important you don't make it too wet) to a smooth texture. Taste and season with salt and a touch of vinegar if needed. Transfer the gel into a piping bag and store in the fridge.

FOR THE LOBSTER BISQUE

Place a large pot on a medium heat, add oil followed by the lobster heads and begin to lightly colour (you are not looking for a heavy roast here as we don't want the bisque to be bitter). Remove the heads from the pan, then add all the mirepoix veg and star anise. After 5 minutes, deglaze the pan with the white wine and reduce, followed by the Pernod. Add the tomato paste and cook out for 3 minutes, then add the lobster heads and claw shells.

Pour the fish stock and remaining 500g of carrot juice into the pan and bring to a boil. Reduce the liquid by half, then pass the bisque through muslin or a tea towel into a smaller pan and reduce by half again. Now add the butter and cream to thicken the sauce and make it delicious! Taste to check whether it needs lemon or carrot juice to freshen the sauce before serving.

TO SERVE

Preheat a large frying pan with oil and season your prepared lobster tails with table salt. Carefully place them skin side down in the pan and begin to roast on a high heat. Treat the skin side of the lobster in 3 stages so you can get maximum roasting on all angles. Once you are happy with this, turn the tails over and lightly colour the other side on a lower heat for 2 minutes. Remove from the pan, pour over all that lovely lobster oil and leave to rest for 5-10 minutes.

Reheat the bisque sauce. Place a large dot of the carrot gel on a warm dish and garnish with the herbs, followed by a big spoonful of the caviar, then add the rested lobster tail and finish with the warm lobster bisque.

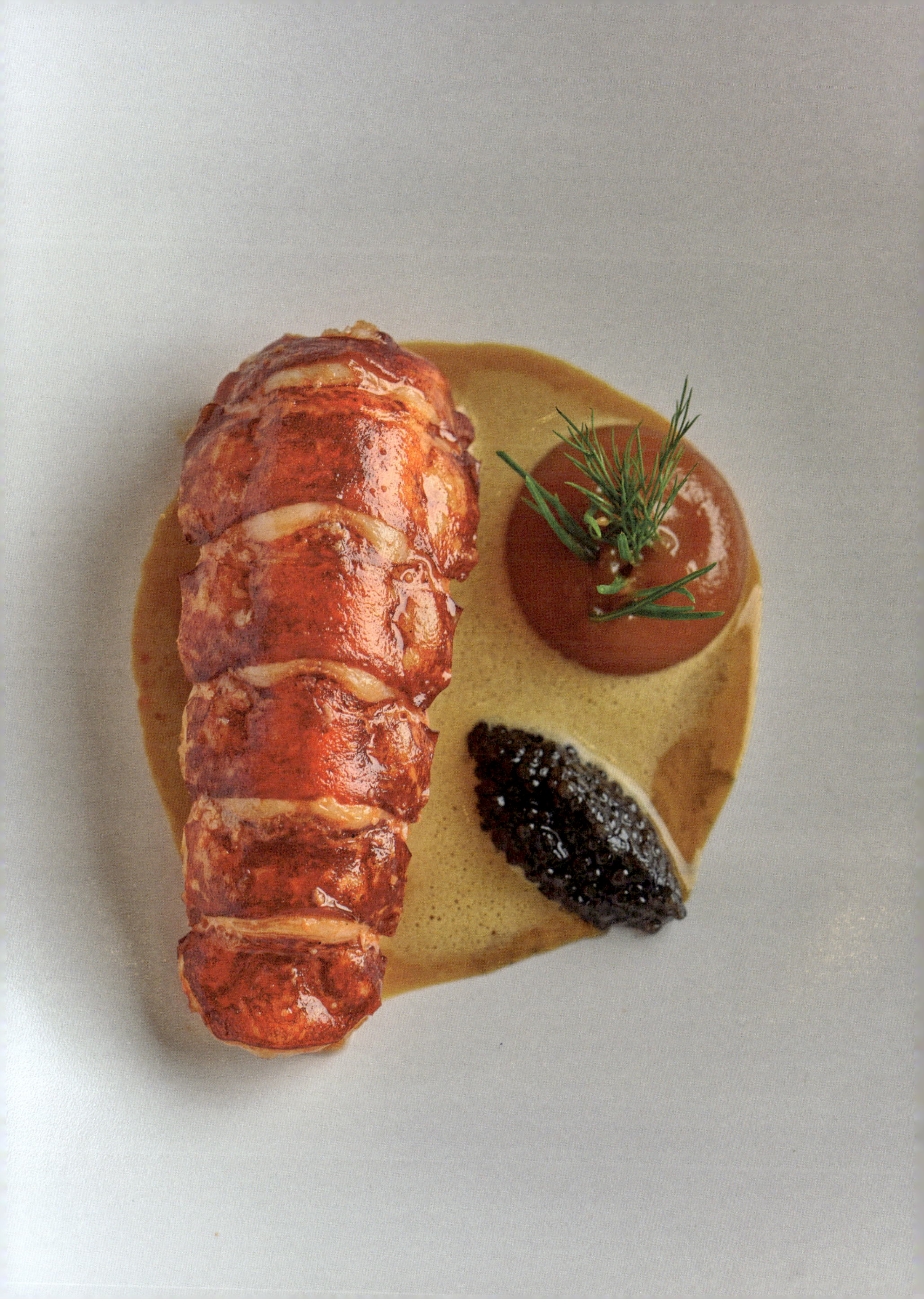

The Grill by Tom Booton, London

In The Kitchen

BEEF RIBEYE, STUFFED POTATO, MUSHROOMS, CHIVE MAYONNAISE

The key to this dish is fantastic quality beef from our local butcher, always cooked in loads of butter. The stuffed potato element is nostalgic for me as it reminds me of my mum cooking me loaded skins when I was a kid. For the beef sauce, we like to finish it off with lots of lovely beef fat from the pan and the resting juices to give it real beefy oomph.

HAM, EGG AND CHIPS WITH ROASTED PINEAPPLE

Everybody loves these chips, we can't take them off the menu now. We have to make around 80-100kg a week when we are busy. I do feel sorry for the garnish team sometimes, but they are worth it! We serve nine in a portion; I did this on purpose because we wanted customers to fight over the last chip since there's an odd number. This is a take on a dish we presented on our lunch menu before but would be perfect for a Saturday night home treat. It's a nice take on an old British classic. Roasting the pineapple whole just elevates it from the tinned pineapple rings you might normally use, and we made some sriracha sauce from scratch in the restaurant, which is amazing with this dish.

LOBSTER, CARROT BISQUE, N25 CAVIAR

This was one of the first dishes I ever made, back when I was at The Westbury under Alyn Williams. One of the chefs who now works with me came to eat at The Dorchester when he was still at The Hand & Flowers, and he had this dish, which he said was the reason he wanted to come and work with me. It's a simple dish, but the sauce is the key. When you've got caviar and lobster you don't need to mess around with anything else really. Shellfish is probably one of my favourite things to cook with and the freezing process really tenderises the lobster – we do it with scallops as well – and it also minimises waste.

My Food

There's nothing I wouldn't cook with, even if I don't particularly enjoy eating it. For some reason, I often don't really enjoy the things that everyone thinks are luxurious, or expensive ingredients; sometimes I feel like they are overused. I come from a humble background where we didn't eat beef fillet and truffle; the older I get, the more I enjoy eating simpler food. Don't get me wrong, when the luxury ingredients are cooked well, I do enjoy them. I can respect everything and as a chef you can be creative with how you cook and present that ingredient. I think we all forget sometimes that food is very subjective and everyone has their own opinion. I generally think food should be simple and clean… it's just cooking at the end of the day. It's just food. I know we all get worked up in this 'cheffing world' but I think the way that food is becoming cleaner and simpler at the moment is really good. I've been in London since 2012 and when I first moved here you had foams, jellies, gels and powders on every dish. I remember a restaurant I visited a few years ago and there was one of those three ingredients on almost every single dish on the tasting menu, and one day I tried the foams and it just tasted awful. There was too much focus on the visual rather than the taste. All our dishes at The Dorchester only ever have around four to five elements on them. For me, it's a lot harder to create simple well-cooked delicious food than it is to do complicated dishes, you give yourself nowhere to hide on the plate and have to really focus on cooking those few elements perfectly.

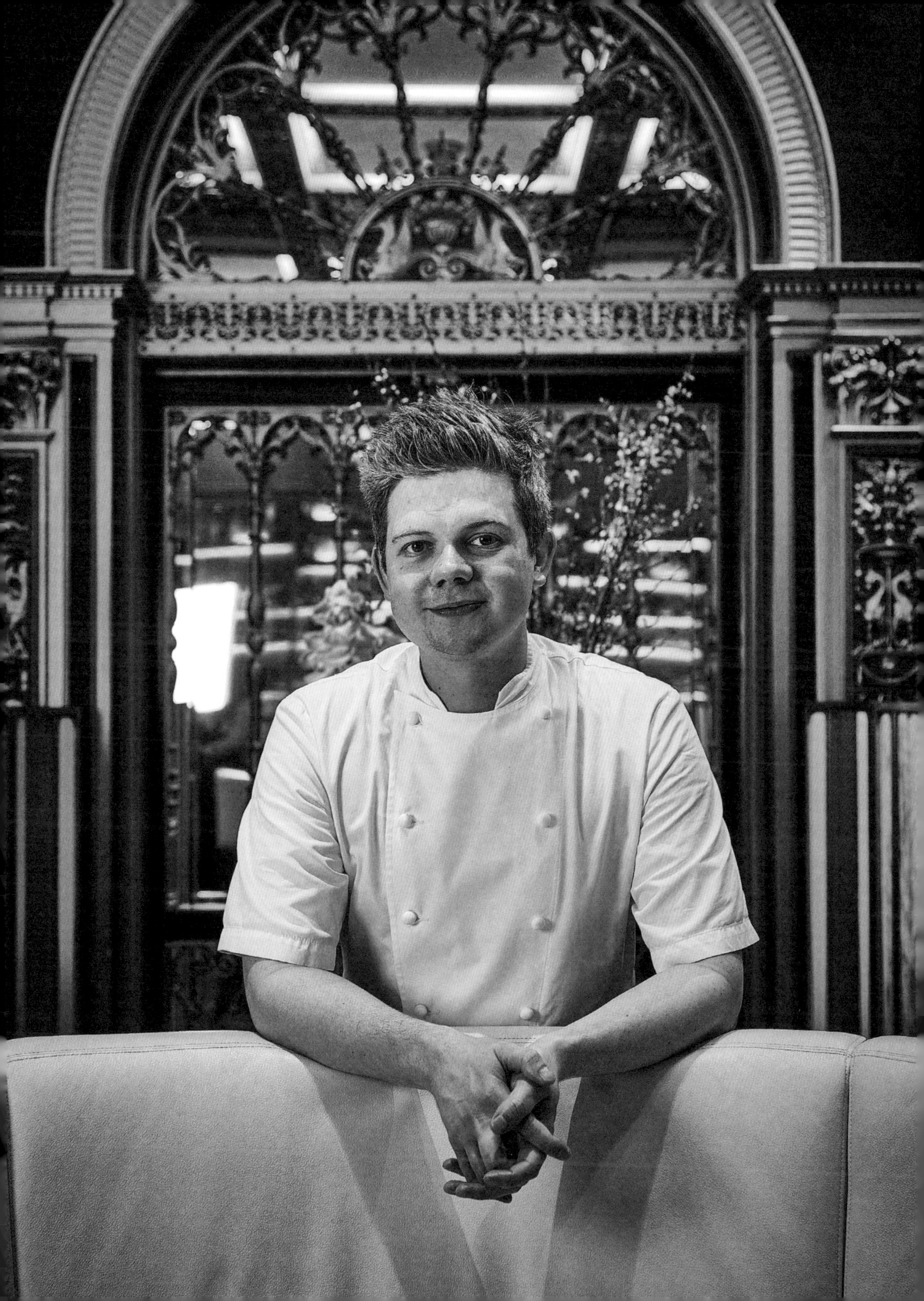

In The Restaurant

The Grill at The Dorchester

In some big grand hotels with restaurants, it can feel like there's a barrier between the guests and the staff, but we try and make the service feel really relaxed and approachable here. I want the team to show their own character and bring some personality to work. A typical Saturday night is 90 covers and there's normally three chefs out in the dining room during service on the chef's counter. We all work very closely as a team so if the front of house are really busy we'll just take the plates ourselves, and if we're busy they help us out too. I do really enjoy breaking down that barrier between guest and chef; I want my chefs to meet our guests and see the massive smiles on their faces. This makes the chefs feel pride in what they do and so they should!

As we are in a five-star hotel setting, you have to be ready for anything – last minute bookings happen every day so you need to be prepared. We also have a really flexible menu that changes daily. A lot of restaurants nowadays have rules and regulations, but we just try and look after the guests as much as we can. We make sure every single front of house team member is trained really well, learning every single element on the dishes so we can accommodate our guests. I hate when the front of house team have to say 'let me just go and check with the chef to ask if we can do that'.

There are 14 of us on the rota including me and we have about eight to nine chefs in here for a full service. Everyone's been here a long time, relatively speaking, so most of my team have done nearly every section by now and they know the drill. We move the chefs around the kitchen quite a lot though to keep everyone on their toes. They all get three days off a week, and I am very big on that as they deserve it for working super hard the other four days. Work life balance is such a super important subject, and I am a big supporter of that. I am in the middle of trying to teach myself to let go more and take my days off. I am really big on getting all the chefs involved in everything we do, I believe in being transparent, I can let the chefs be creative with food and express themselves but also teach them the business side of things. 14 heads are much better than just mine!

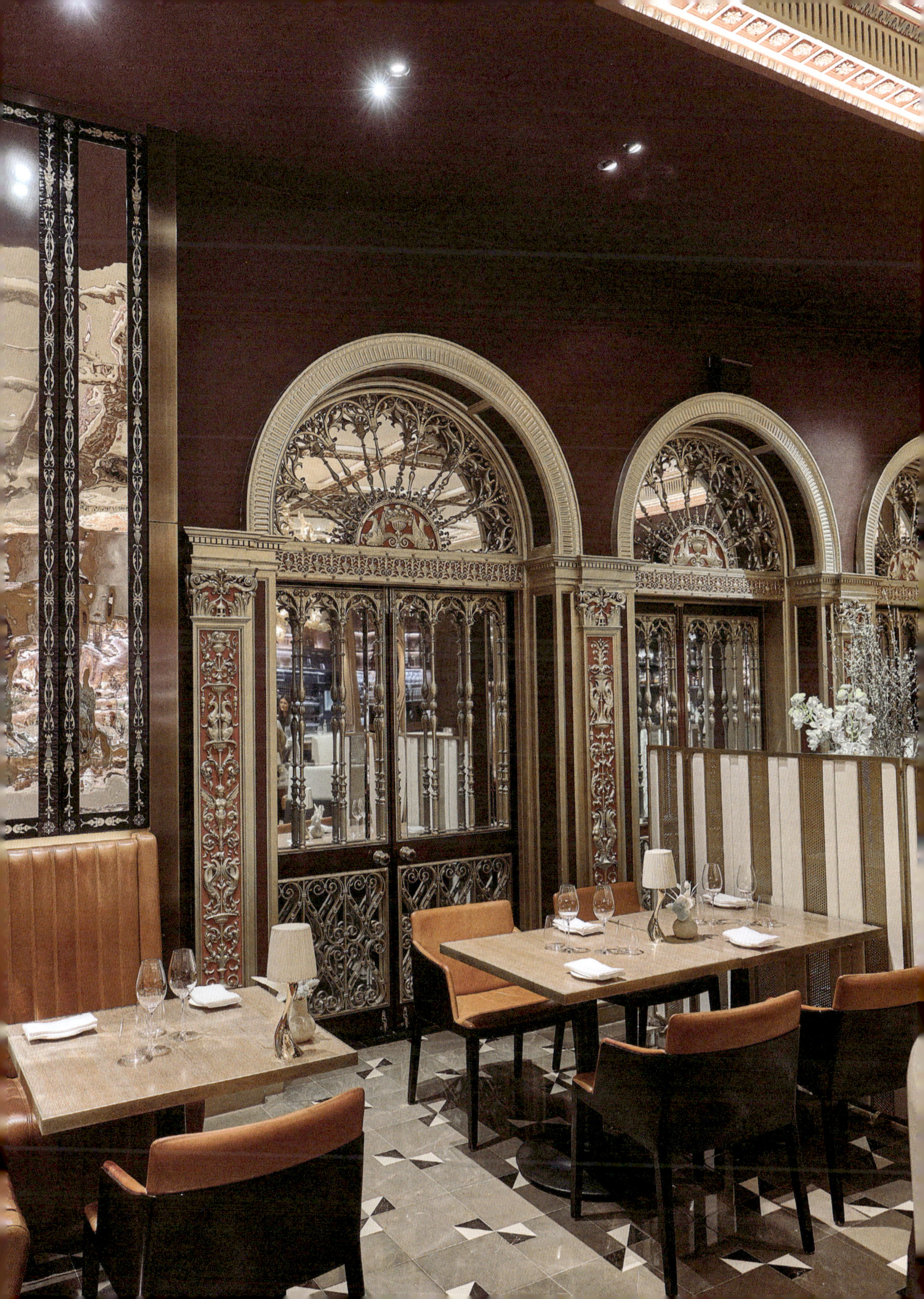

Cornerstone, London

Tom Brown

Chef Tom Brown earned a Michelin star in 2021 for Cornerstone, his first restaurant, which is based in Hackney Wick and serves a seafood-focused menu in a relaxed atmosphere. His approach to casual dining stems from the sense of "immediate gratification" that drew Tom to cooking in the first place, paired with unfussy but flavour-packed dishes that start with great produce. Having begun his career in Cornwall, Tom worked under chefs including Bryn Williams, Paul Ripley at Rick Stein's restaurant and Nathan Outlaw. The latter gave Tom his first head chef position at The Capital where he stayed for two years, during which time which he reached the finals of Great British Menu 2017. In 2018, Tom decided to set out on his own and opened Cornerstone to wide acclaim.

"Because I grew up in Cornwall, and worked for Nathan for a long time, it made sense that when I moved on to my own place I stuck to what I was good at. Fish and seafood are quite close to my heart as well; I used to go fishing with my dad a lot when I was younger, and fish was the first thing I ever cooked. I think when you're surrounded by great produce – whether that's seafood, meat or vegetables – you feel an affinity with it, but I also think we can source better fish than most other places in the UK. I still source a lot of my produce from Cornwall and have been buying fish off the same people for ten years now. I'd happily go for a pint with any of them – that's my rule.

"At Cornerstone, dishes are developed according to what produce is available. I remember years ago I went to a restaurant and commented on the menu being produce-led, to which the chef said 'how can you have a menu without produce?' so I felt like an idiot. He was right of course, because if you haven't got it to start with the dish won't be good, especially with seafood. If you want to see a group of chefs get excited, put some nice fresh fish in front of them; nothing gets people's imagination and passion flared up like fish. It's a whole creature and there's a real connection to something that's truly wild. We know next to nothing about the sea, so you're bringing this almost alien thing into the kitchen and somehow turning it into an amazing thing to eat.

"For me, if you can't get excited about the ingredient, there's no point getting started. The cliché of 'less is more' with fish and seafood is so true; if you don't have something that's blowing your mind to start with, then you've run out of track already. I like to think of fish not as fish, if you know what I mean. Fish restaurants are quite formulaic: fish pie, dover sole, fish with brown butter… it's all quite traditional and samey: 'this fish must be done this way with this'. I like to think we don't need to cook that way, like the squid cacio e pepe which I created based on my favourite pasta dish, or monkfish with peppercorn sauce, as if it was a steak. There is room for the classics, obviously, but I like to think we're the fish restaurant for people who don't like fish. As an ingredient, it's so varied and two species of fish are different things in the same way that chicken and pork or asparagus and cabbage are totally different. To just say 'fish' is such a broad sweep, and then the scope of where to go with that one ingredient is huge. Monkfish, for example, can be raw, poached, cured, fried, roasted in butter and all those things are so different. That's what floats my boat.

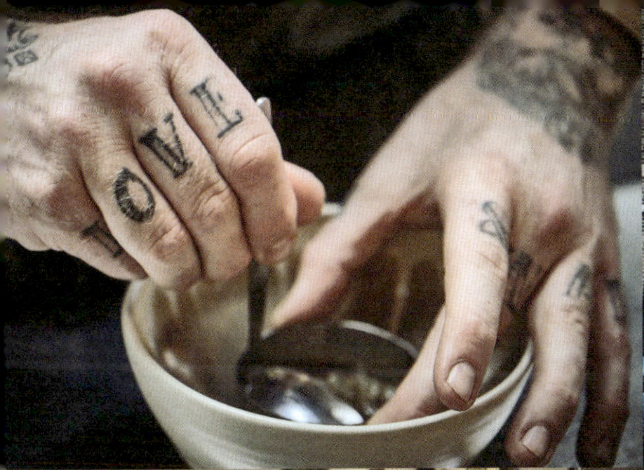

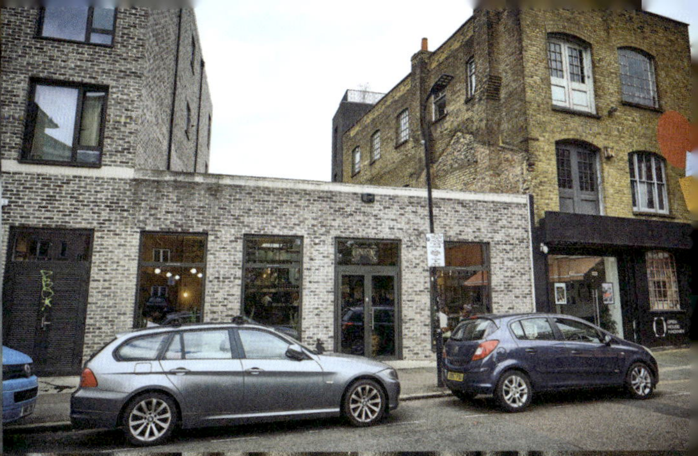

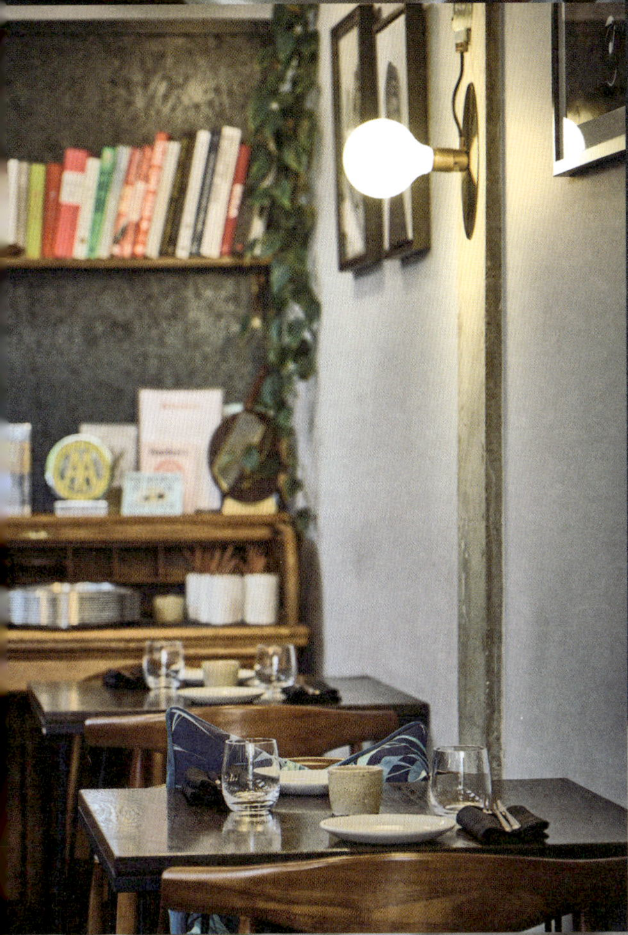

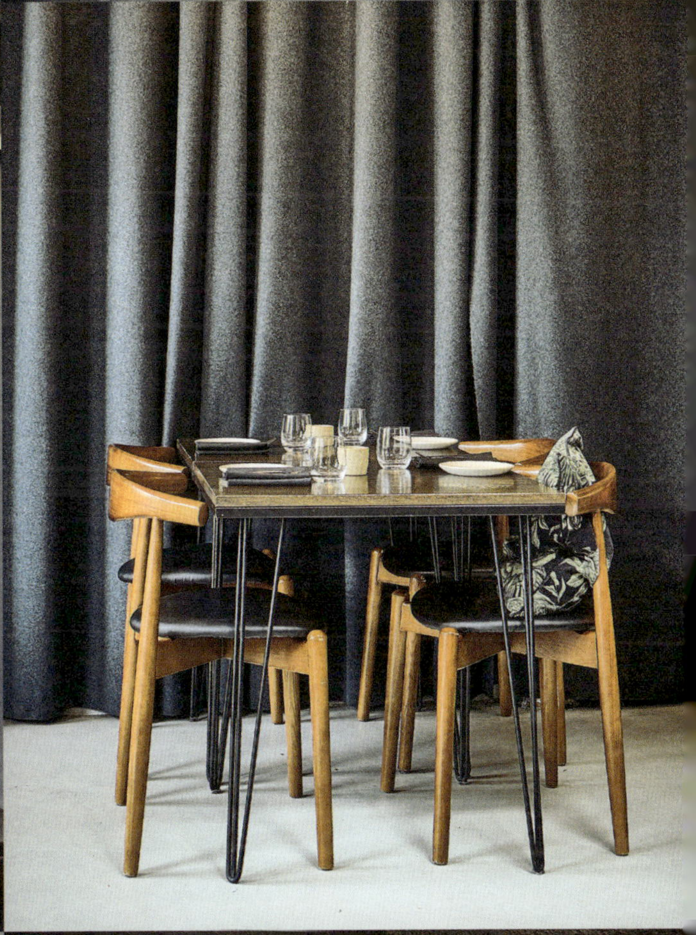

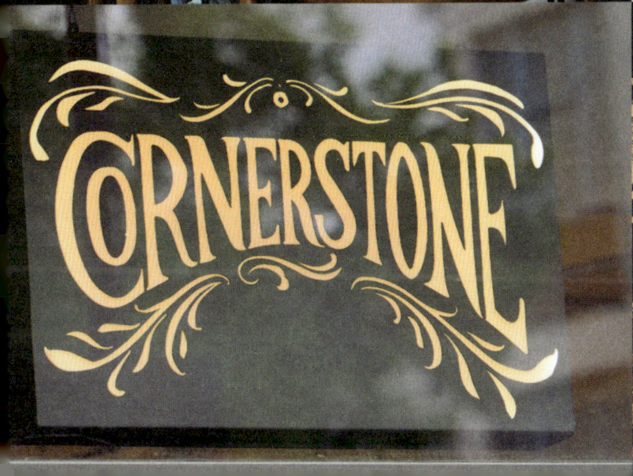
CORNERSTONE

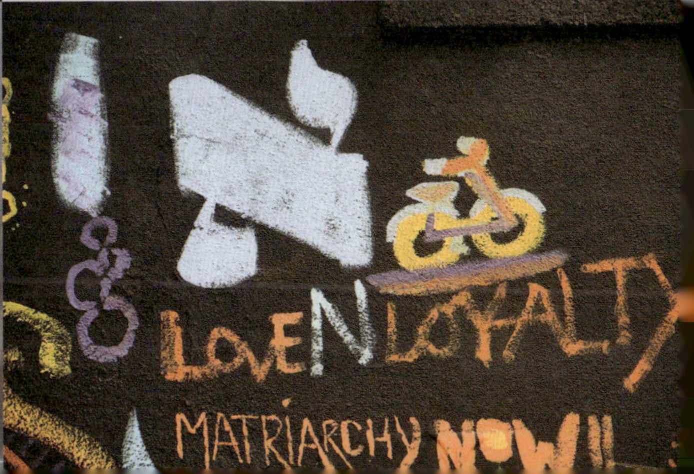
LOVE N LOYALTY
MATRIARCHY

Cornerstone, London

"I just want everyone to come into the restaurant and have a good time. I always think of what we do as chefs, and on the wider spectrum now as restaurateurs, as being facilitators for happiness. Why do people go out to a restaurant? Maybe it's their birthday, or they haven't seen their mum for ages, or they're going on a date – whatever the occasion, we're the middlemen, just there to make them happy. It's not about getting people in to massage your own ego. That's why I set up like this – with the open kitchen in the centre of the restaurant – because I want to bask in that short term gratification. I can make something and see people smiling about it within ten minutes. That's honestly what it's all about for me; the feeling when you cook something perfectly or make something beautifully is what drew me to this job.

"I moved to London to feel like I'm back in Cornwall. Hackney Wick feels like a little village; I live a five-minute cycle from the restaurant, bump into people I know every day, say hello to the people in the shop when I come down from my flat. It's such a soulful community and I love it so much. People worry about gentrification and that must have its drawbacks – we're part of that to some extent I guess – but for me I just think it's a beautiful part of the world. We've been here since 2018 although it doesn't really feel like that because of the pandemic, but in another way it feels like we've always been here. Opening Cornerstone in Hackney Wick didn't come from a savvy business decision, but I thought if I could do something here it might open doors for other things. Gastronomy was so centralised in London – Mayfair, Chelsea and the Soho and Shoreditch scenes – but people actually live in East London so it makes perfect sense to be within that area. You do get people who come from all over the country because they've watched Great British Menu or they're Michelin followers, which is great, but you've also got locals. I've got no plans to go elsewhere, unless it's somewhere really hot and I can open an oyster bar on a beach in Mexico.

"The top of my list of restaurants to visit is actually JÖRO. Seriously, me and my head chef James say it all the time. In this industry there are chefs that fall into two brackets: defensive and territorial ones who don't like people asking for recipes and want to talk negatively about something before talking positively, then the others, the good guys. We look at other people's food constantly and talk about how amazing it is – there are so many places I want to eat. A few that I really like around here are Black Axe Mangal in Highbury and Islington; it's literally the perfect restaurant. I love places where the restaurant, in a non-egotistical way, is an extension of that chef's personality. I think that's the only way you get artistic perfection. Gareth's place in Wales [Ynyshir] is the best food I've ever eaten. It's unreal, he's untouchable. Da Terra is the best food I've eaten this year, easily, and the thing I loved there is that it's so warm for something that looks like it could be so 'stiff two star'. The one that I'd like to go in the rest of the world is Saint Peter, Josh Niland's fish place in Australia. He's a constant source of inspiration and inadequacy anxiety. I just try and look at everyone else's food in a positive light. I love this industry so much and so many of the people in it. It is like a family. We don't see much of each other because everyone's so busy, but it's true what people say about real friends, that when you see them again it's like no time's gone by. Those are the people I properly care about."

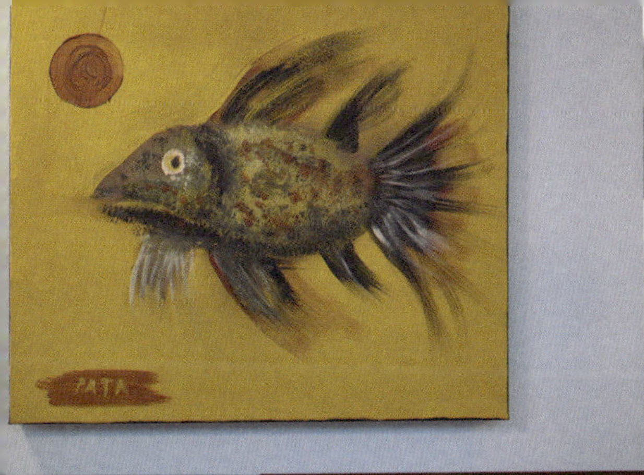
PATA

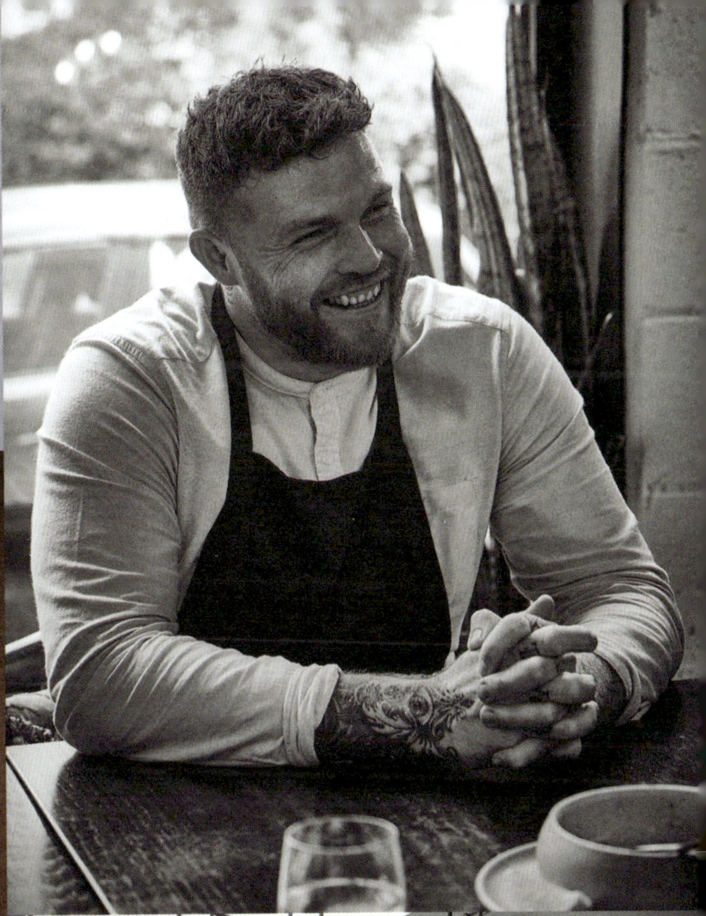

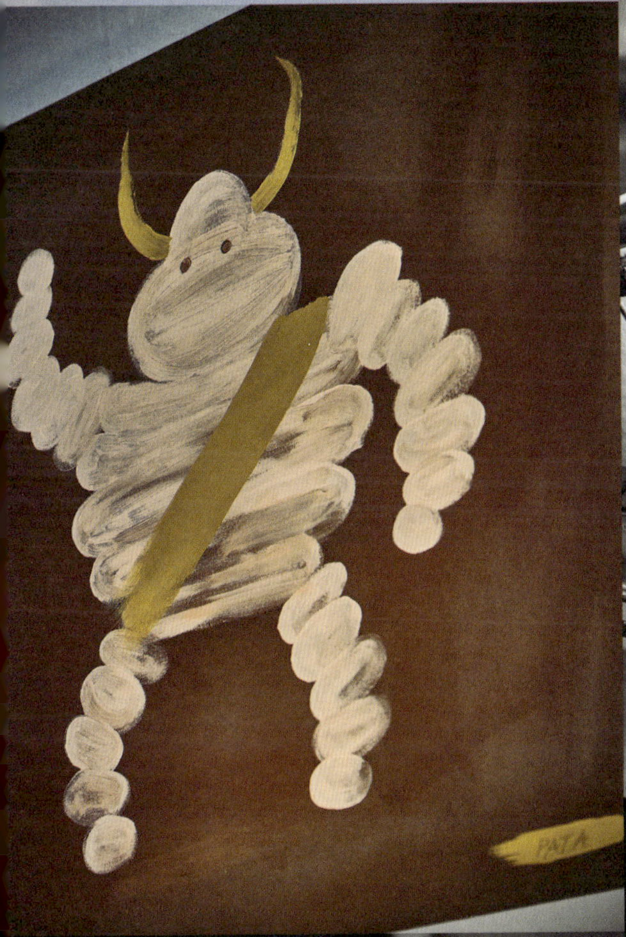
PATA

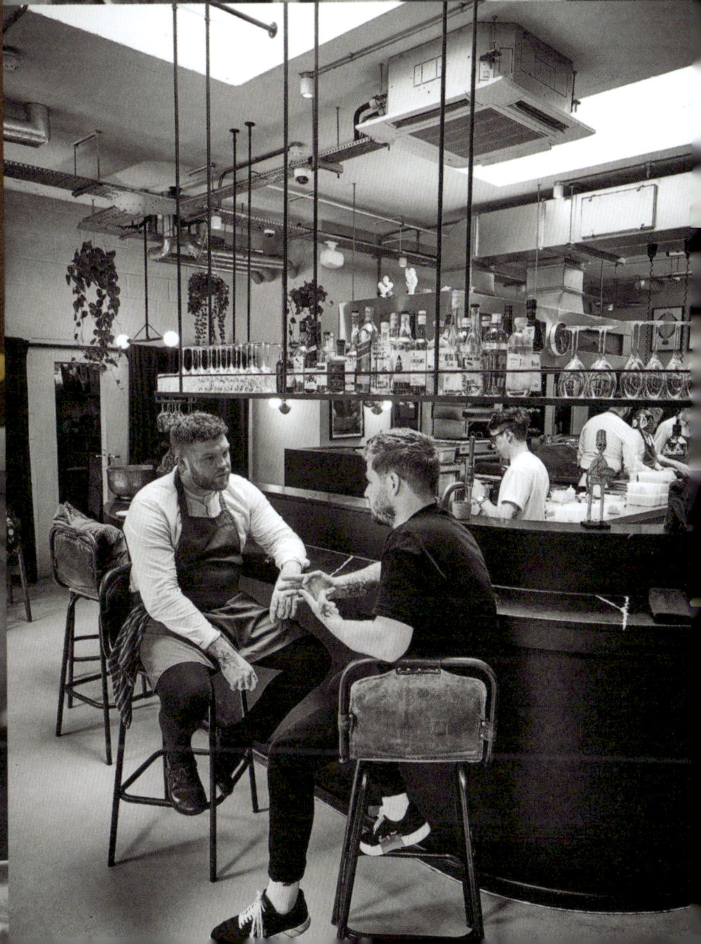

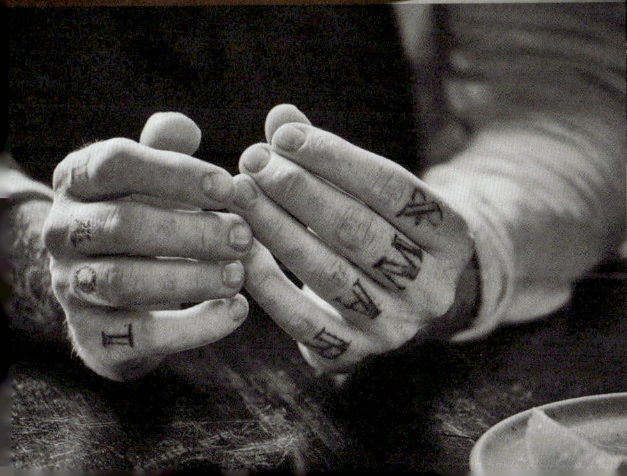

Cornerstone, London

Sea Bream Tartare, Egg Yolk, Soy, Seaweed

Preparation time: 30 minutes, plus 4-6 hours curing | Serves 4

FOR THE BREAM TARTARE

50ml clear honey

200ml dark soy sauce

1kg bream fillet, skinned and pin boned

1 pinch of dried seaweed powder

FOR THE PONZU DRESSING

2 fresh jalapeño chillies

100ml light rapeseed oil

100ml ponzu sauce (ideally yuzu)

FOR THE GARNISH

4 Clarence Court eggs

1 small packet of furikake (we use the Daihoku brand which is a blend of nori and bonito but whatever you want to use is fine)

TO CURE THE BREAM

Mix the honey and soy sauce together, then generously cover the bream with this mixture. Leave the bream in the fridge to cure for around 4-6 hours, depending on the thickness of the fish. Turn the fish over every hour or so to ensure it cures evenly. Once done, the bream should feel slightly firm, as if it has been 'cooked'. Wash the cured fish under cold running water, pat dry and set aside.

FOR THE PONZU DRESSING

First, slice the jalapeños roughly and put them into a small pan along with the rapeseed oil. Bring the oil up to 80°c and then remove from the heat. Leave it to cool completely and infuse further, then strain the oil and mix it with the ponzu sauce.

Now dice the cured bream as finely as possible. Mix it with a touch of the chilli ponzu dressing to help bind it along with a pinch of the seaweed powder and some additional salt to season if necessary.

Firmly press the tartare into a ring in the serving bowl to make a burger shape, then press a small dent into the top. Repeat this to make 4 portions, then separate the eggs and gently nestle a yolk into the dent on top of each bream tartare. Spoon 2-3 tablespoons of the ponzu dressing over the egg yolks. Sprinkle on the furikake and serve immediately.

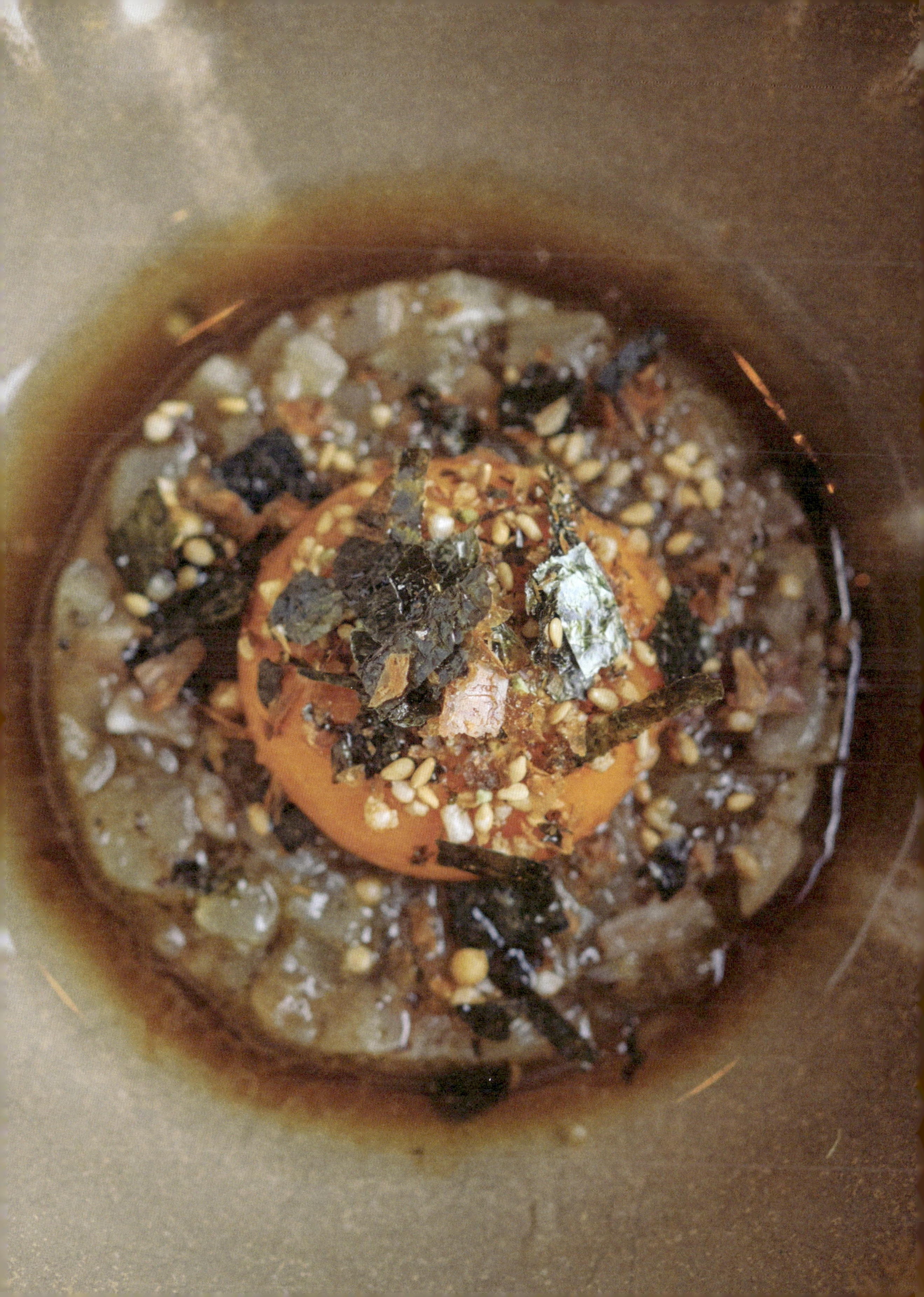

Cornerstone, London

Smoked Mackerel Pâté with Treacle Soda Bread

Preparation time: 10 minutes | Cooking time: 35-40 minutes | Serves 4

FOR THE TREACLE BREAD

Knob of butter

475ml milk

225g plain flour, plus extra for dusting

225g self-raising flour (or another 225g plain flour + 1 tbsp baking powder)

50g porridge oats, plus 1 tbsp for sprinkling (optional, for texture)

2 tbsp black treacle (or maple syrup, honey, pomegranate molasses or golden syrup)

1 tsp bicarbonate of soda

1 tsp sea salt

FOR THE PÂTÉ

500g smoked mackerel, skinned and boned, flesh flaked (alternatively use any cooked or smoked fish such as salmon, sardines or tinned crab meat)

350g cream cheese (or crème fraiche or cottage cheese)

50g plain yoghurt

1 tbsp horseradish sauce (or Dijon mustard or wasabi paste)

1 lemon, juice only

Sea salt and freshly ground black pepper

FOR THE TREACLE BREAD

Preheat the oven to 200°c/180°c fan/Gas Mark 6 and grease a loaf tin with the butter. Mix all the ingredients together in a large bowl until a soft, sticky dough is formed. Place in the loaf tin and sprinkle the remaining oats on top (if using).

Bake the soda bread for around 35–40 minutes, or until the loaf is golden-brown on top and sounds hollow when tapped on the bottom. Place on a wire rack to cool.

FOR THE PÂTÉ

Place all the ingredients in a large bowl and mix well. Do not blend, as this recipe makes a rough textured pâté. Season with salt and pepper to taste and serve with the soda bread.

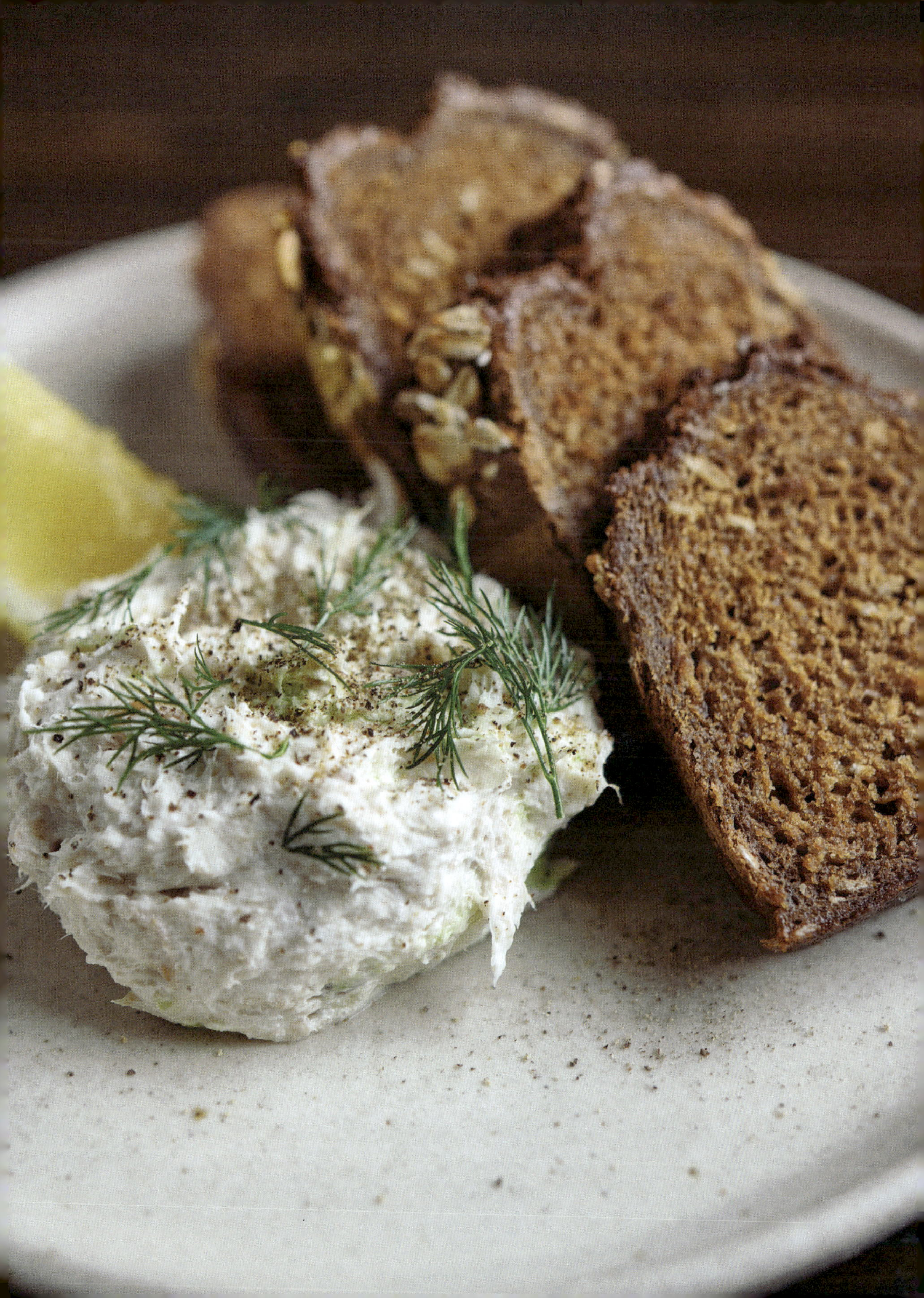

Cornerstone, London

Squid Cacio e Pepe with 36 Month Aged Parmesan

Preparation time: 24 hours | Cooking time: 45 minutes | Serves 4

500g squid hoods, cleaned and trimmed

650g dried white beans, soaked overnight

½ a carrot, peeled and roughly chopped

½ a leek, trimmed and roughly chopped

½ an onion, peeled and roughly chopped

1 stick of celery, roughly chopped

3 sprigs of thyme

1 clove of garlic

1 tsp salt

265g parmesan, plus 50g to serve

Extra virgin olive oil

Black pepper

PREPARE THE SQUID

Split the squid hoods lengthways and flatten them out. Lay the hoods on top of each other in a stack, vacuum pack and freeze overnight.

FOR THE SAUCE

Drain the soaked beans and put in a large pan. Add the chopped vegetables and cover with 2 litres of water. Bring to the boil and simmer for 40 minutes, until the beans are tender.

Add the thyme, garlic and half a teaspoon of salt to the beans, then pour the mixture into a tray to stop the cooking process, reserving all the liquid. Leave to cool.

Once cool, strain the stock into a clean measuring jug, discarding the vegetables. Put the beans into a clean bowl and pour over enough of the stock to cover them.

Pour 900ml of the remaining stock into a pan and bring to the boil. Add the parmesan and remaining salt. Remove from the heat and blend with a hand blender. Allow to cool, then put in the fridge overnight. The following day, strain the liquid into a clean pan and reheat.

TO SERVE

Slice the squid very finely on a meat slicer to create the 'pasta' and then pan fry in a hot pan with a little olive oil for just a few seconds.

Divide the squid 'pasta' between 4 bowls and grate over the remaining parmesan, then pour in the reheated cheese sauce. Drizzle the dish with the olive oil and season generously with freshly ground black pepper.

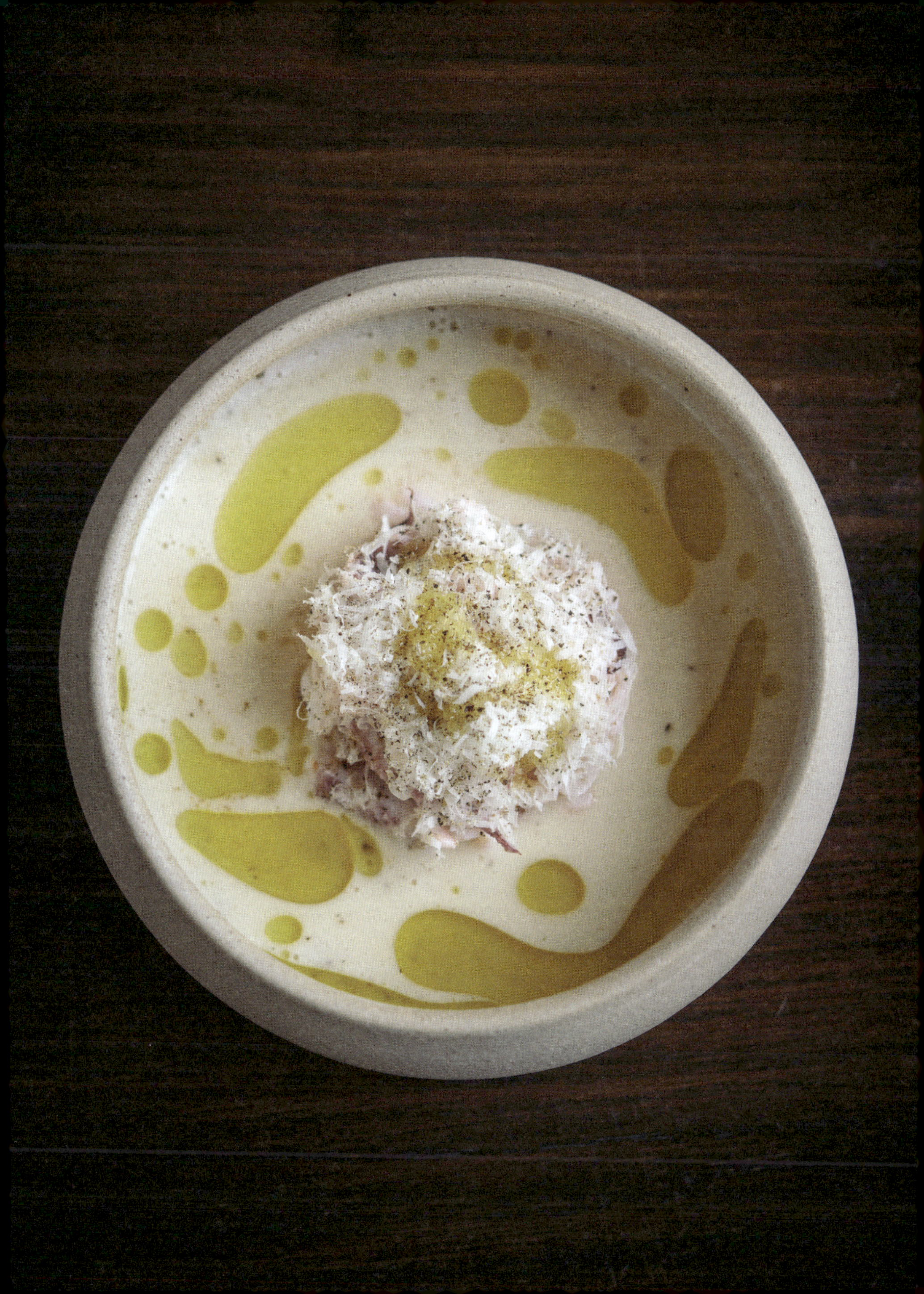

Cornerstone, London

Recipe Q&A

SEA BREAM TARTARE, EGG YOLK, SOY, SEAWEED

Chef's Tip: This dish is meant to be mixed together before you eat it, so we do that at the table for guests in the restaurant.

Where do you recommend sourcing good bream or would other fish work if that's not available?

We used to do this dish with grey mullet but bream is the most consistent in terms of quality.

Were the Japanese flavours in this dish inspired by travels or other influences?

I went to the place where the soy sauce we use is made, just outside Tokyo. I don't feel that I know that much about Japanese cuisine so I would never say that it's a Japanese dish, just that it tastes nice with those flavours. I tasted all the ingredients and worked backwards.

What's special about Clarence Court eggs?

They're great quality but any egg with a really rich yolk is good here. Everyone always thinks that we've cured it because the yolk is so dark in colour but it's just raw.

SMOKED MACKEREL PÂTÉ WITH TREACLE SODA BREAD

Chef's Tip: We would use Secret Smokehouse for the mackerel if we made this in the restaurant; it's just round the corner and only a small operation but building up a good reputation.

When would you make this at home?

I rarely cook at home to be honest, but this is a nice easy one – if we're going to my mum's at Christmas, she always asks me to make this pâté.

There are lots of ways to adapt this recipe, have you got any favourite variations?

This one really, as written. I did that when it was lockdown to allow for what people could and couldn't get so it was designed to be adaptable. It's accessible too as you don't need to find fresh fish – you can do it with tinned fish, even tuna or tonnato. We did a mussel one in the restaurant that's literally a chicken liver parfait in terms of the technique – reduction, shallots, all that, then mussels poached and blended down with lots of butter. We keep the nicest mussels back and pickle them, along with pickled brown shrimp, cockles and gherkins – you need sharpness alongside the rich pâté. It's really old school, tastes like something you'd get at the Savoy, and it looks beautiful.

SQUID CACIO E PEPE WITH 36 MONTH AGED PARMESAN

Chef's Tip: This one's very quick to put together during service – all the work goes into the prep. The sauce should have a little bit of thickness, so we soak the white beans, drain and blanch them, strain them off, then put the cheese into that cooking liquid so you've got all the starch to 'hold' it. Then we blend a few of the beans back in to give it a little bit of body. It's more viscous rather than watery that way. Then it's just pan frying the squid and bringing it together with more cheese.

How do you prepare the squid for this dish?

Split the hoods down, open them, layer them in little blocks, shave them on the slicer, marinade them in a bit of oil and shave it when it's frozen. I like the legs in there as well for some texture.

Would any white beans work in this recipe or do you have a preference/recommendation?

It doesn't really matter but we tend to use coco or haricot blanc. Butter beans are a bit too sweet.

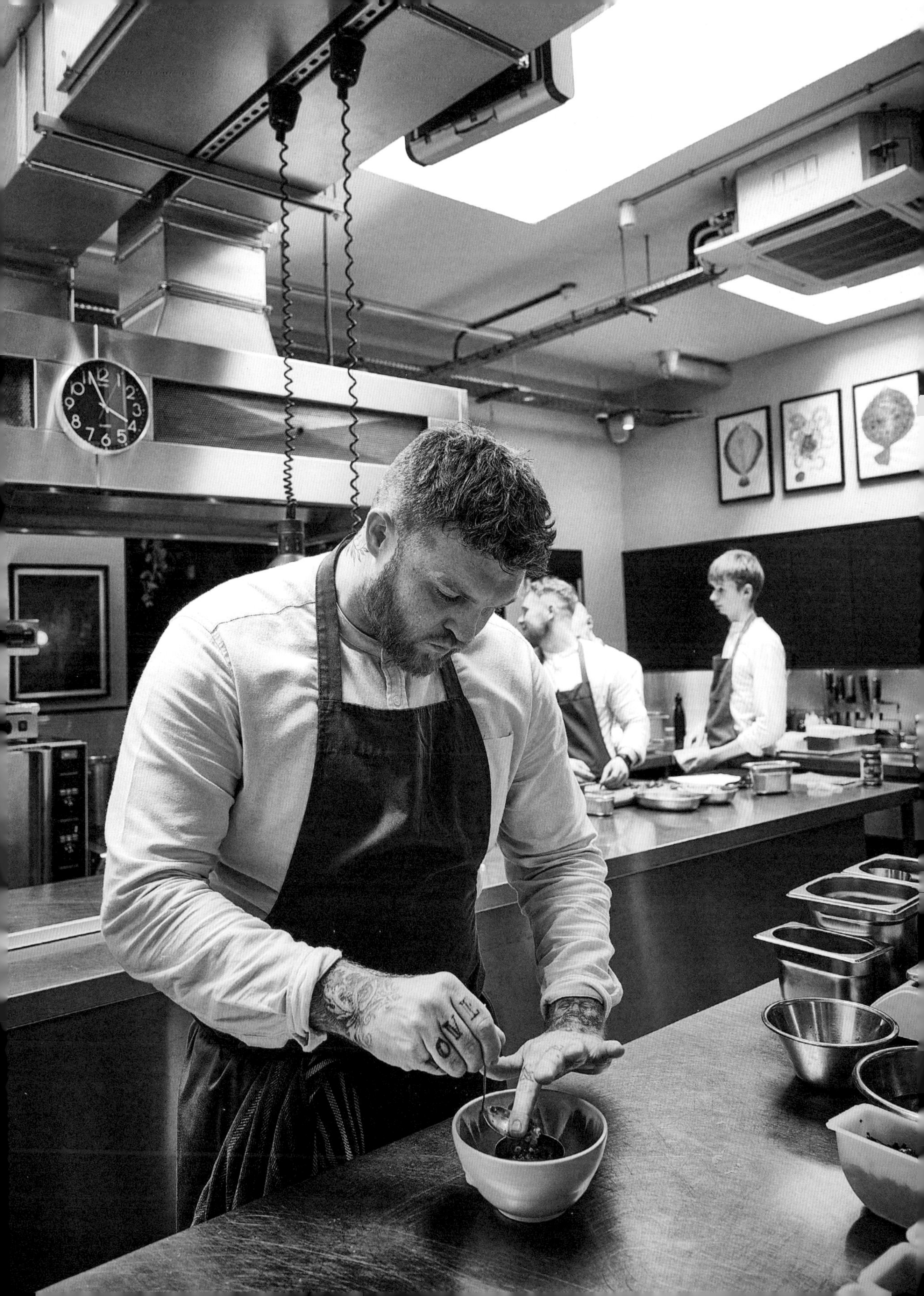

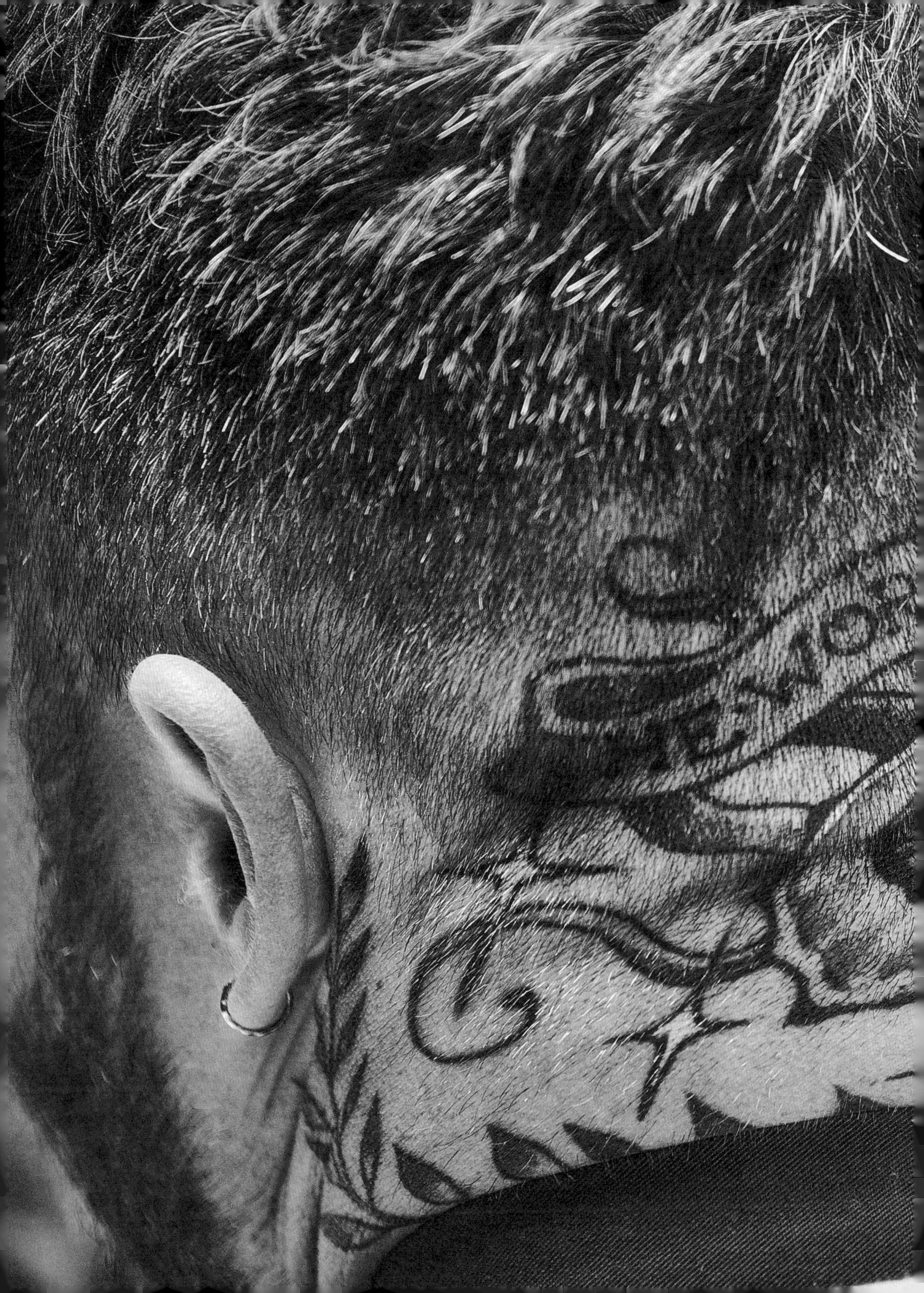

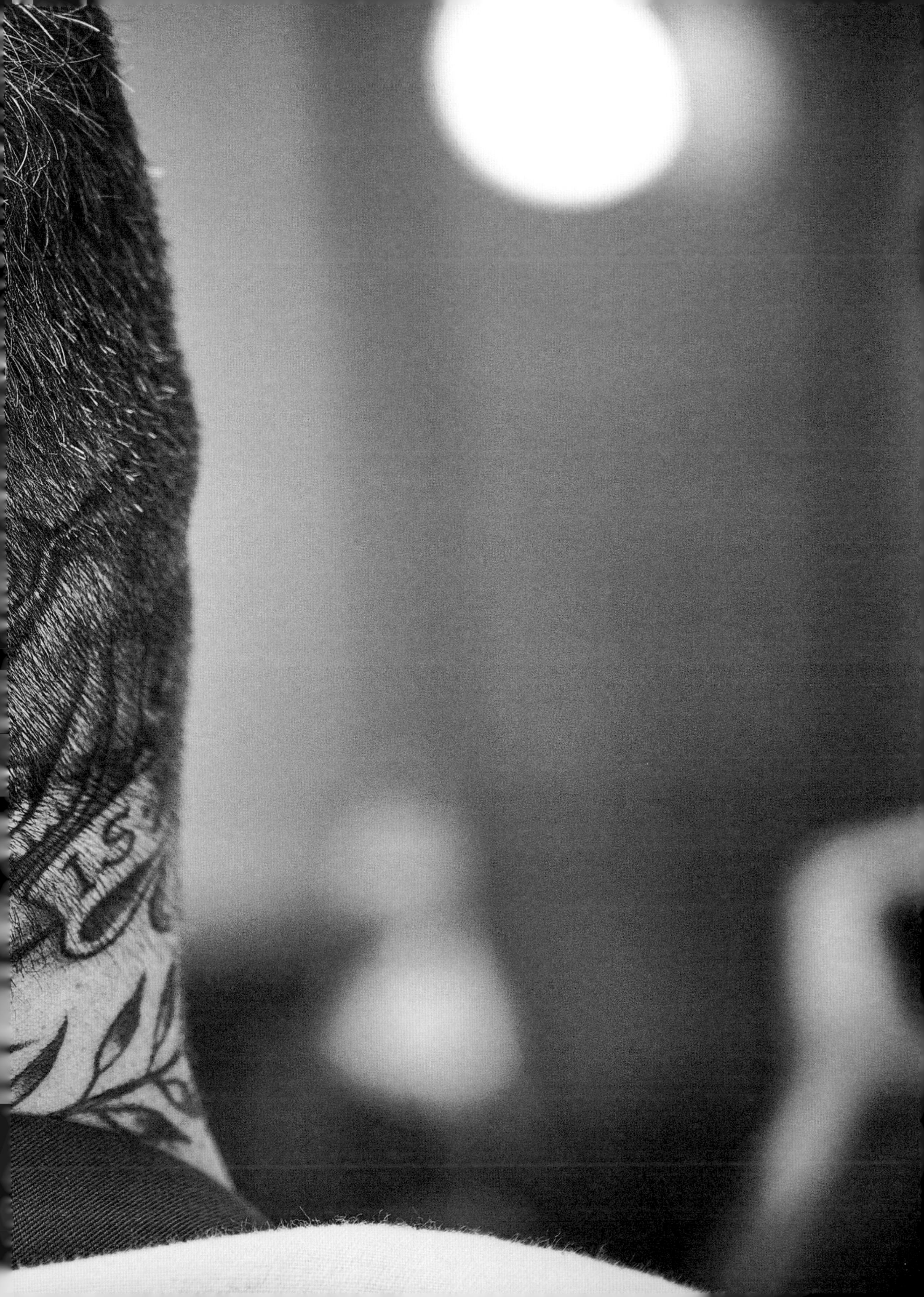

The Black Swan at Oldstead | Roots | Made In Oldstead, Yorkshire

Tommy Banks

Tommy Banks became Britain's youngest Michelin starred chef in 2013 and won Great British Menu in 2016 and 2017. The Black Swan at Oldstead is run by the Banks family who have lived and farmed in the area for generations, with Tommy heading up the kitchen and his brother James front of house. In 2018 they opened a new restaurant, Roots York, with business partner and family friend Matthew Lockwood, then in March 2020 Tommy and the team launched Made in Oldstead amidst the first lockdowns which offers another take on the fine dining experience through food boxes to enjoy at home. All three ventures use produce grown, foraged and preserved on the farm in Oldstead to creative dynamic menus based on a highly creative 'field to fork' ethos.

Where does your inspiration come from as a chef?

For me, the farm feels like a really important part of the business: the whole thing's centred around it. Only a few years ago, we didn't do anything on the farm because it didn't pay. Our family's original livelihood was just going to wrack and ruin and we'd become chefs instead, which saddened me, whereas now I wish I could spend more time on it. The farm is the most exciting bit for me, especially now we've been able to bring some animals back.

Who do you admire within the industry?

I think about it from a business point of view much more these days and the chefs who inspire me are the ones reducing working hours, creating better paid jobs and changing the industry for the better. It's also about getting the message out there that food shouldn't be cheap, because that means unsustainable and unethical farming practices within systems that pay badly and offer a poor quality product. As independent restaurateurs, that's where we can change the narrative. My dream is that at 45 I'll be working with the same guys as I am now, because we've created great jobs so they won't want to retrain and leave the industry. It's so important to retain those skills and knowledge. That's become a big part of my philosophy, especially since the pandemic.

What are you most proud of in your career so far?

Establishing Made In Oldstead during the first lockdown felt really positive, because we were able to buy stock from producers and suppliers who were otherwise closed, turn it into a dish and meet what quickly became a huge demand for our 'finish at home' food boxes. Everyone was able to continue working and getting paid, we were able to employ more people who had been made redundant or maybe would have left the industry – because it's normal working hours at the food production facility we now run for MIA – and keep those skillsets within the industry. To me, that felt massive and having started from our own kitchen it's become a key part of what we do here.

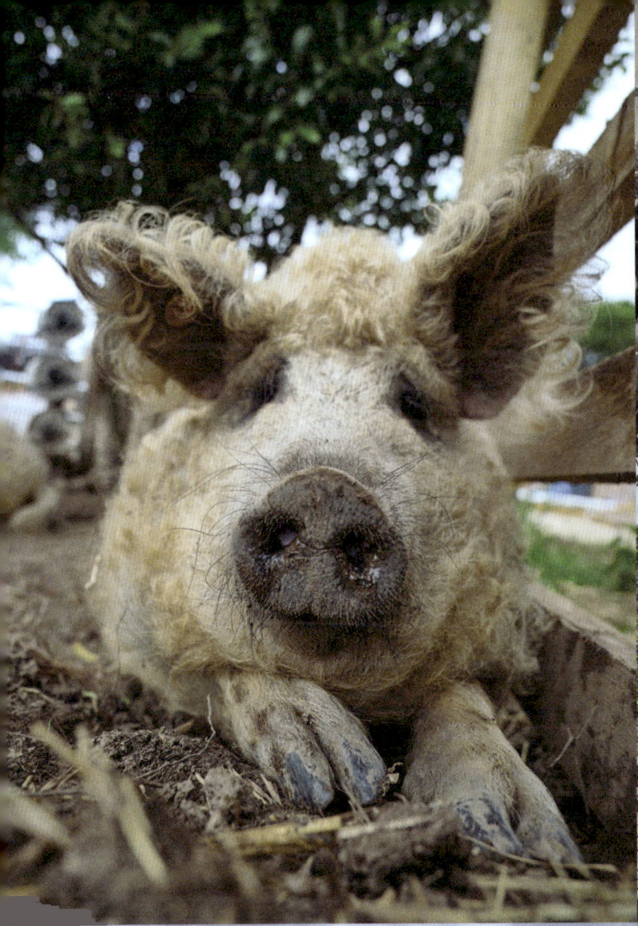
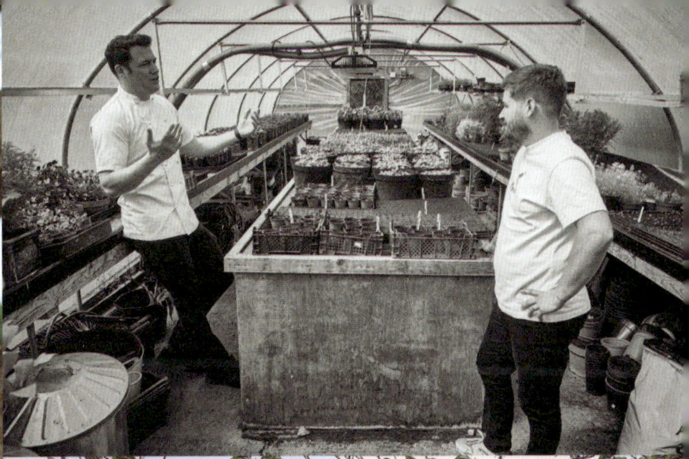
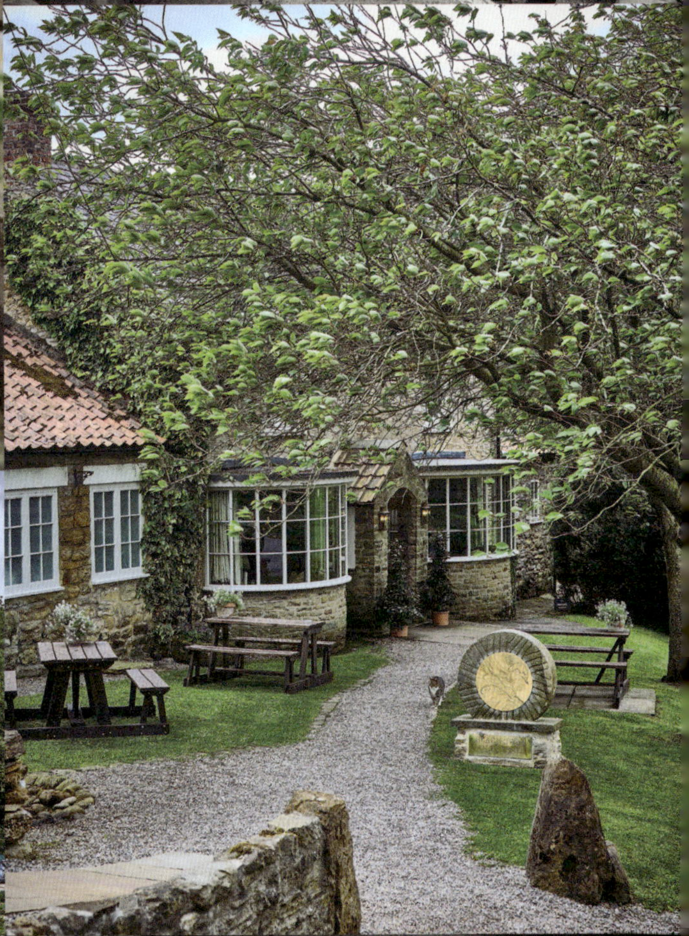
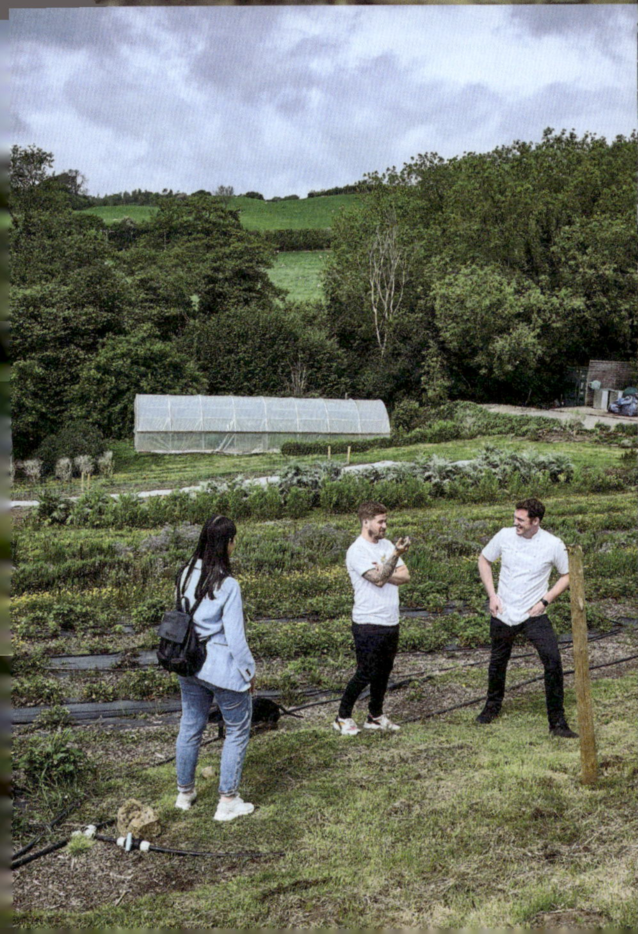
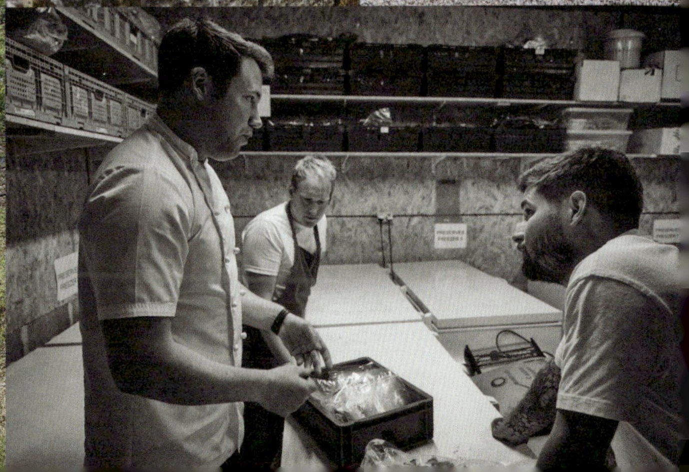

The Black Swan at Oldstead | Roots | Made In Oldstead, Yorkshire

Beef Short Rib with Glazed Beetroot and Hazelnut Gremolata

Preparation time: 1 hour | Cooking time: 4 hours | Serves 4

1kg beef short rib

50g salt

1 litre beef stock

100g hazelnuts

70g panko breadcrumbs

1 tsp dried thyme

1 lemon, zested

1kg raw beetroot, washed and stalks removed

200g beetroot juice

50g honey

5 radicchio heads, ends removed and leaves picked

FOR THE SUMMER OIL (OPTIONAL)

1 litre grapeseed oil

Summer herbs of your choice (we used lovage, lemon balm, lemon verbena and parsley)

TO MAKE THE DISH

For the summer oil, combine all the ingredients and infuse for 1 week. If you want it quicker, carefully heat the grapeseed oil to 60°c, then add your herbs and infuse overnight.

In a lidded container large enough to fit the short rib, combine the salt with 1 litre of water and whisk until dissolved. Add the short rib and refrigerate overnight or for up to 48 hours. When ready to cook, remove the short rib from the brine, rinse and pat dry.

Preheat the oven to 160°c or 140°c fan. In a large casserole dish or pan, cover the short rib with beef stock. Cover with foil and cook in the oven for 4 hours. For the final 20 minutes, remove the foil to allow the short rib to glaze. On a separate baking tray, roast the hazelnuts for the remaining time.

Remove the short rib from the oven and leave in a warm place to rest. Reserve all the reduced stock for the sauce. In a food processor, blend your roasted hazelnuts with the panko breadcrumbs, thyme and lemon zest into a coarse crumb. Set aside.

Next, make your glazed beetroot. Put the whole beets into a roasting tin and cook for 40-45 minutes, until soft to al dente, but not shrunken. Remove from the oven and leave to cool. Carefully rub the skin away with a paper towel or rubber gloves, then cut the beetroot into large pieces and place them back in the roasting tin. Mix the beetroot juice and honey together, season well and pour over the beetroot. Return to the oven until the beetroot is sticky and glazed, about 25 minutes.

If needed, increase the oven temperature to 200°c or 180°c fan and return the short rib to the oven on a greaseproof paper-lined baking tray for 15 minutes to warm up. After 5 minutes add the glazed beetroot (if this has been prepared in advance and then cooled). Meanwhile, put a little oil into a saucepan over a medium heat and add the radicchio leaves. Season well and coat the radicchio with the oil. Cook, stirring frequently, until the radicchio is tender and starting to brown, about 5-8 minutes.

Top your short rib with the hazelnut gremolata and serve with your glazed beets and radicchio. Drizzle the plate with your summer oil if using.

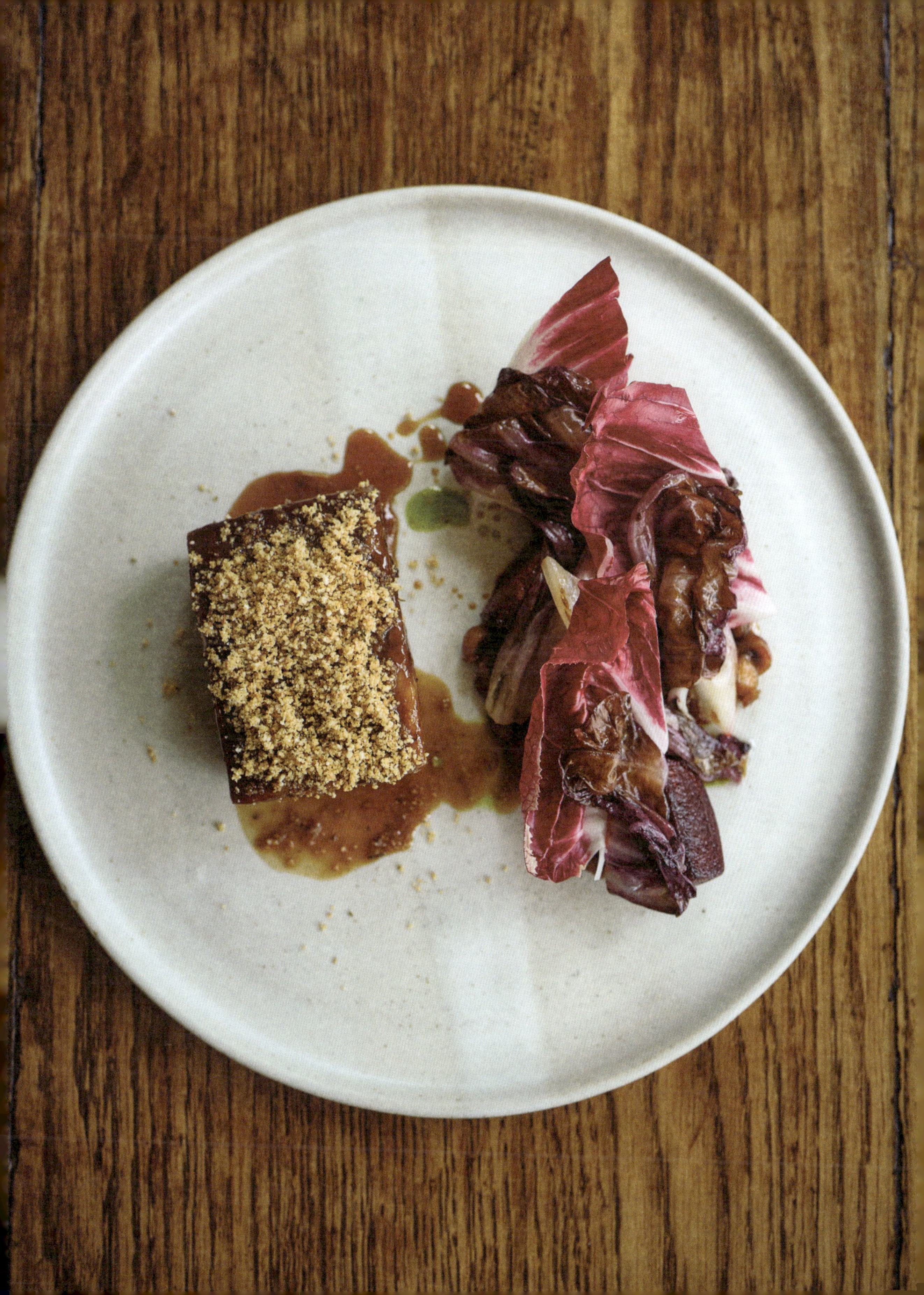

The Black Swan at Oldstead | Roots | Made In Oldstead, Yorkshire

Sea Buckthorn, Chocolate & Chestnut

Preparation time: 1 hour 30 minutes, plus overnight | Cooking time: 20 minutes, plus overnight | Serves 20

FOR THE CHICORY ROOT CRUMBLE
- 135g butter, softened
- 70g dark brown sugar
- 125g plain flour
- 2 tsp chicory root syrup (or shop-bought Camp coffee)
- 1½ tsp baking powder
- 1 tsp salt

FOR THE CHESTNUT ICE CREAM
- 250g roasted chestnuts
- 750ml whole milk
- 17 large egg yolks (300g)
- 150ml double cream
- 135g sugar
- 50g honey

FOR THE CHOCOLATE AND CHICORY ROOT GANACHE
- 250ml whole milk
- 250ml double cream
- 5 large egg yolks (about 100g)
- 1 tsp chicory syrup (or shop-bought Camp coffee)
- 250g 75% dark chocolate

FOR THE SEA BUCKTHORN GEL AND TUILE
- 1 litre sea buckthorn purée (if you can't make this, you can use shop-bought boiron)
- 50g sugar
- 20g agar agar

FOR THE SEA BUCKTHORN MERINGUE
- 300g sugar
- 35g glucose
- 4 egg whites
- 120ml sea buckthorn purée, reduced by half (or boiron, as above)

FOR THE CHICORY ROOT CRUMBLE
In a large mixing bowl, cream the butter and sugar together until light and fluffy, about 4 minutes. Add the remaining ingredients and mix until a paste is formed. Wrap in cling film and freeze. Preheat the oven to 180°c or 160°c fan and line a baking tray with greaseproof paper. Grate the frozen crumble mixture onto the lined tray and bake in the centre of the oven for 15 minutes. Halfway through the cooking time, break up the crumble a little and turn the tray. Remove and leave to cool.

FOR THE CHESTNUT ICE CREAM
Break the roasted chestnuts into small pieces with a rolling pin, then put them into a large saucepan over a low heat with the milk. Do not allow it to boil and once hot, remove from the heat and leave to infuse for 3 hours. Pass through a sieve and reserve the chestnut infused milk.

Pour the infused milk back into the saucepan along with the remaining ingredients. Cook for 8 minutes, whisking continuously, until thickened. Skim any aerated mixture off the top and discard. Pour into your ice cream machine and churn according to the manufacturer's instructions.

FOR THE CHOCOLATE AND CHICORY ROOT GANACHE
In a heavy-based pan over a medium heat, combine all the ingredients except the chocolate and heat to 85°c, whisking continuously. Allow mixture to cool to about 70°c and continue to cook for 10 minutes. Add the chocolate a bit at a time until fully melted and combined. Pour the ganache into a container and leave to set in a refrigerator overnight.

FOR THE SEA BUCKTHORN GEL AND TUILE
In a large saucepan, combine all the ingredients and bring to the boil. Pour onto a shallow tray and leave to set. Once set, blend in a food processor until completely smooth. Pour half the gel into a piping bag and store in the refrigerator until ready to use.

Pour the remaining gel onto a greaseproof-lined tray and spread out. Dehydrate at 65°c until crispy. If you don't have a dehydrator, leave in the oven at 60°c overnight. Break into jagged pieces, approximately 4cm, and store in a sealed tub until ready to use. Make sure the tub's base is covered in salt with greaseproof paper on top to absorb any moisture.

FOR THE SEA BUCKTHORN MERINGUE
In a large pan over a medium heat, heat the sugar and glucose with 65ml of water to 118°c. Meanwhile, whisk the egg whites using a stand mixer with a whisk attachment, or electric handheld whisk in a large bowl, until stiff peaks are formed. Now slowly pour the hot syrup into the egg whites while whisking, avoiding the beaters. If using electric beaters, keep turning the bowl to ensure all the egg white is combined with the syrup. Once all the syrup has been incorporated, continue to whisk the mixture for 2-3 minutes until thick and shiny. Leave to cool.

Once completely cool, add the reduced sea buckthorn purée to the meringue and mix to combine.

Preheat the oven to about 70°c fan and line a baking tray with greaseproof paper. Spread the meringue mixture onto the tray and cook in the oven for 3 hours. Leave to cool completely before breaking into shards.

TO SERVE
Place 1 tablespoon of chicory root crumble in the middle of a bowl and make a small indent. Place one rocher of ganache and one rocher of chestnut ice cream next to each other on top. Pipe dots of sea buckthorn gel around the dish. Finally, take equal amounts of meringue and tuile and alternate them across the top of the ganache and ice cream.

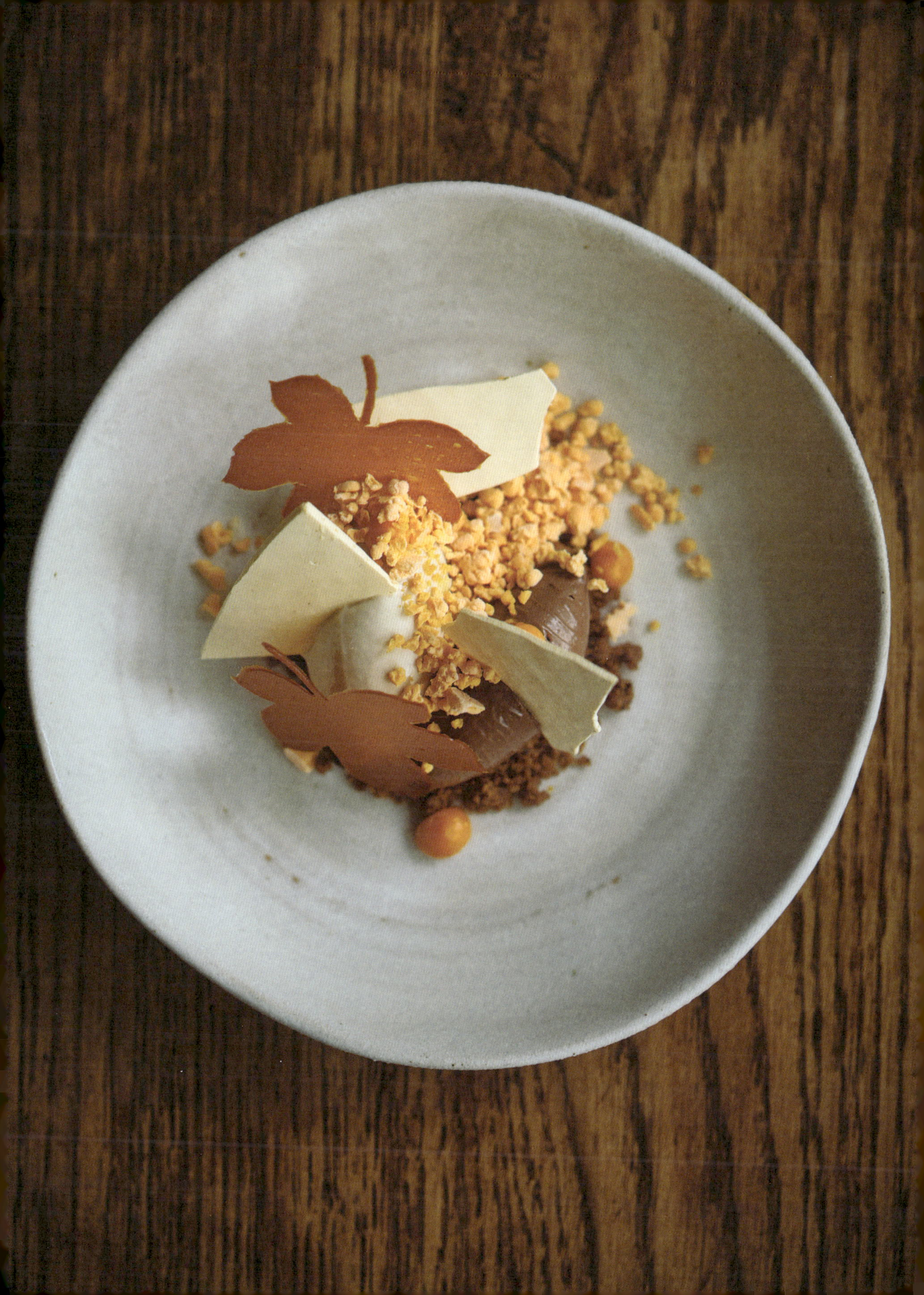

The Black Swan at Oldstead | Roots | Made In Oldstead, Yorkshire

Devilled Crab Toast with Brown Crab Custard and Caviar

Preparation time: 1 hour 10 minutes, plus proving | Cooking time: 1 hour 5 minutes | Serves 14

FOR THE BRIOCHE
- 1kg strong white flour
- 130g caster sugar
- 50g yeast
- 2 tbsp salt
- 200ml milk
- 10 large eggs (approx. 550g)
- 500g butter

FOR THE BROWN CRAB DASHI
- 1 tsp oil
- 200g shallot, sliced
- 3 cloves of garlic, crushed
- 500g brown crab meat
- 12g dashi granules

FOR THE BROWN CRAB CUSTARD
- 200ml brown crab dashi
- 250ml double cream
- 65ml whole milk
- 4 medium egg yolks (about 80g)
- 1 large egg
- 20g dashi granules

FOR THE PARSLEY OIL, SAUCE AND PICKLED PARSLEY STEMS
- 250g parsley, leaves picked and stems reserved
- 750ml sunflower oil
- 350ml mussel stock
- 250ml chardonnay vinegar

FOR THE PARSLEY EMULSION
- 3 large egg yolks (about 60g)
- 2 tbsp Dijon mustard
- 1½ tbsp elderflower vinegar
- 1 tsp flaky sea salt
- 320ml parsley oil

TO SERVE
- 280g white crab meat
- Tabasco
- Pickled dill
- Caviar

FOR THE BRIOCHE
Put all the dry ingredients into a mixing bowl with a paddle attachment and combine. Add the milk and eggs, mix for 12 minutes, then add the butter bit by bit until a dough is formed. Turn out the dough onto a floured surface, stretch and fold it, then place into a floured container to prove for 1 hour. Repeat the stretching process, then prove for a further 3 hours.

Halve the dough, shape into loaf tins and cover with cling film. Leave to prove overnight in the refrigerator. The next day, preheat the oven to 200°c or 180°c fan. Remove the cling film and bake the loaves for 45 minutes. Slice once cooled and leave ready to serve with the crab custard.

FOR THE BROWN CRAB DASHI
In a large frying pan over a medium heat, heat the oil and then add the shallot and garlic. Fry until soft, about 5-6 minutes. Add the brown crab and cook for a further 2 minutes. Add 800ml of water with the dashi granules and simmer for 20 minutes, ensuring nothing sticks to the bottom of the pan. Remove from the heat, strain and cool. This will make more than is needed but can be frozen and used in other recipes requiring dashi.

FOR THE BROWN CRAB CUSTARD
Add all the ingredients to a large bowl and mix with a hand blender until a custard is formed. Season to taste. Add 50g of custard to 14 ramekins. Cling film tightly and place in a steamer over a rolling boil for 15-20 minutes. Remove the cling film and serve warm.

FOR THE PARSLEY OIL, SAUCE AND PICKLED PARSLEY STEMS
Blanch the parsley leaves for 10 seconds and then refresh in iced water. Squeeze all the water from the leaves then finely chop and leave to dry on kitchen towel. Meanwhile, heat the oil to 70°c and transfer the parsley to a food processor. Add the hot oil and blitz for 6 minutes on a medium speed, then 9 minutes full speed (no heat if using a Thermomix).

Cool the oil over ice overnight, then hang in muslin cloth and collect the strained oil in a bowl below. Reserve all the remaining pulp and transfer this to a clean food processor with the mussel stock and salt to taste. Blend on full speed for 4 minutes, then pass the sauce through a sieve and chill over ice.

Place the parsley stems into a jar with the chardonnay vinegar and leave to cold infuse for 12 hours.

FOR THE PARSLEY EMULSION
Add all the ingredients except your parsley oil to a blender. Slowly add in the oil while the blender is running until emulsified, then taste to adjust the seasoning.

TO SERVE
Fry your brioche portions in butter until golden on all sides. Dress the white crab meat with Tabasco and place one large tablespoon on top of your brioche. Pipe 4 pea-sized dots of parsley emulsion on top of the crab and dress each dot with a dill frond.

Meanwhile, heat a small amount of parsley sauce (around 2 tablespoons per pot) and split with 1 teaspoon of parsley oil. Place half a teaspoon of the pickled parsley stems in the centre of the crab custard and spoon the split sauce around the stems. If using, add a generous amount of caviar on top and serve alongside your brioche toasts.

TIP: To make your own mussel stock, combine 3kg mussels with 4 cloves of garlic, 3 shallots, 750ml white wine and a small bunch of parsley. Cover and bring to a boil. Turn the heat down and cook for 15 minutes, then remove from the heat and allow to steam for a further 15 minutes. Pass through a colander then a muslin cloth and reserve your fresh mussel stock.

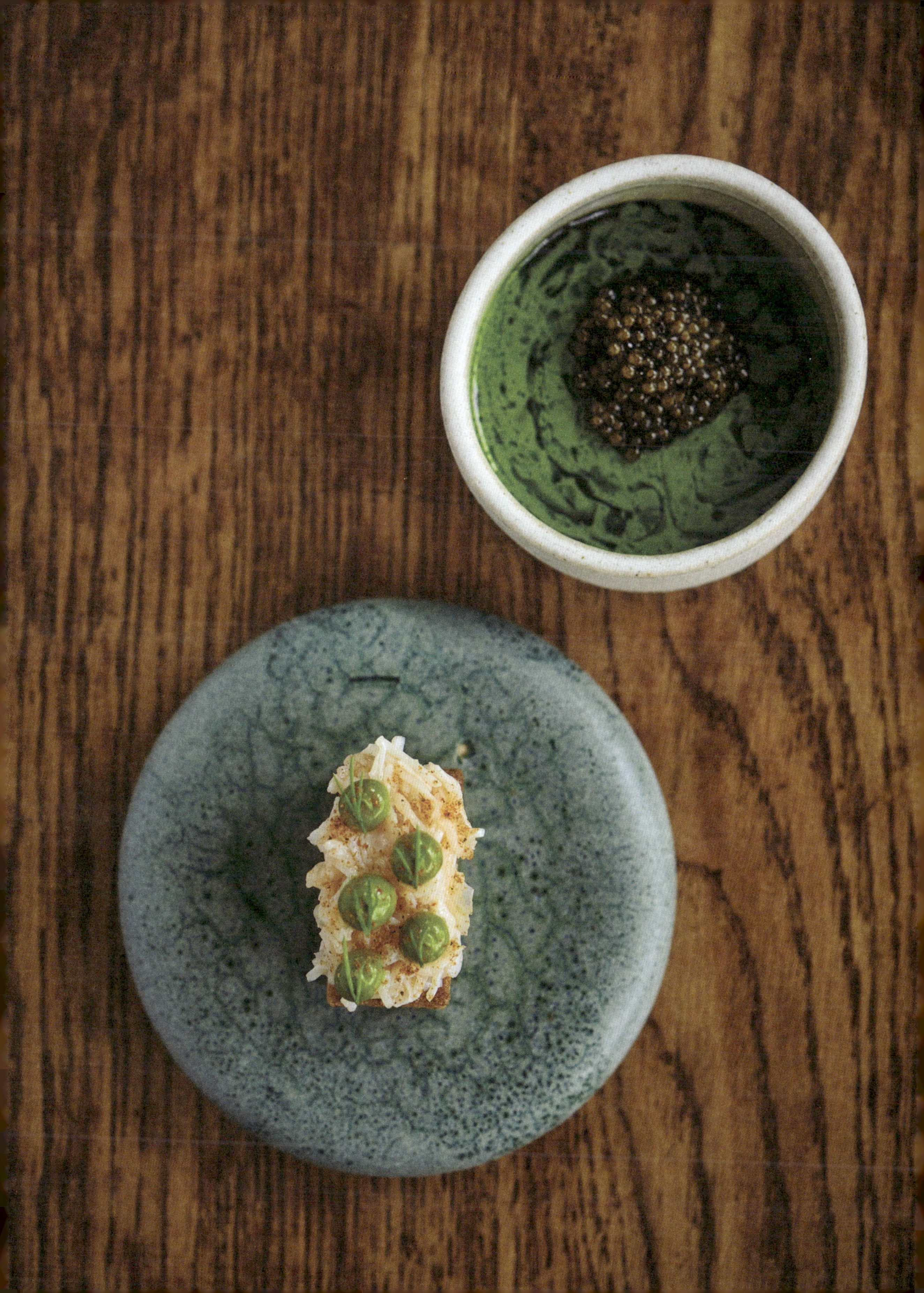

The Black Swan at Oldstead | Roots | Made In Oldstead, Yorkshire

My Recipes

BEEF SHORT RIB WITH GLAZED BEETROOT AND HAZELNUT GREMOLATA

This dish is currently a main course from Made in Oldstead, so each element will be prepared, cooked, packed up and boxed for you to finish at home. The mise en place is all done by us so it only takes 10 minutes – the presentation might not always look exactly like ours but it tastes the same! As a chef, you have a whole range of crockery to work with and you know that certain things work really well in particular dishes. We work with a few local potters now, mainly 'Jane the Potter' who designs all the pottery around dishes we develop. We do try to keep MIO dishes really simple because if people can't recreate them, it sort of ruins the experience. We put more development into the dishes for Made in Oldstead than anything else because there are more variables to consider. Everyone has a different oven at home, for example, so we take that into account and make sure it's adapted for a normal kitchen set up.

SEA BUCKTHORN, CHOCOLATE & CHESTNUT

Sea buckthorn is native to coastal areas of the UK, but we've got about 20 or 30 bushes here in the garden just outside the restaurant, and then down at the farm we have one bank which is really sandy so it's planted across there too. It's an invasive species so it grows fast and can be foraged by snapping the branches off, although it's horrible to gather because it's got huge spikes! One of the best things to do is to freeze it and then just knock it and all the berries fall off. I love sea buckthorn's flavour and it's quite oily when juiced or puréed which creates a nice mouthfeel.

For this dish, the sea buckthorn purée and juice goes into a tuile, meringue and granita. Normally you wouldn't use so much in a dish because the flavour can be overpowering, but this needs loads of acidity to cut through the rich chocolate and chicory ganache. We don't use chocolate a lot – it's quite heavy on a dessert after a full tasting menu – but we wanted to use some of York Cocoa House's produce because it's so good and the people who run it really know their stuff, even visiting the producing countries a couple of times a year to work with farmers first hand.

I don't think anyone else uses chicory root in the way we do; you can buy chicory essence and it's the flavouring in things like Camp coffee substitute, but we grow and process it from scratch. Chicory root is the same species as the chicory plant but a slightly different thing, like celeriac and celery, and it looks like a parsnip's ugly cousin – longer and gnarlier – which we peel and slice very thinly on a mandoline. That's dried out in a really low oven to make blonde-coloured chips, then you whack those in the oven to roast until they get really dark, and the whole place smells of coffee, and finally make the roasted chicory into a powder which almost looks like cocoa but tastes like coffee. I love coffee but it can be quite dominant, whereas chicory takes flavours better.

DEVILLED CRAB TOAST WITH BROWN CRAB CUSTARD AND CAVIAR

This dish is from the menu at Roots and uses the pickled parsley stems, parsley emulsion, oil and sauce that's all made on site at Oldstead. We grow all the parsley in the kitchen garden to make the oil, which also creates a pulp that we use for the sauce, and freeze them both until we need them.

Will Lockwood, the head chef of Roots, says this about the dish:

I suppose the dish is based on some pretty classical concepts but I believe it has improved massively with use of some amazing produce, some help from our farm and stock of preserves but also the use of more up to date cooking and technique.

Firstly, for the toast there are two concepts: sweet shellfish on buttery brioche and the other, Devilled Crab. We did very little to change these and with good reason, they are classics after all. We use fermented chilli and elderflower oil which are grown and preserved on the farm in Oldstead, to make it more unique to us. To make it more decadent we fry the fingers of brioche in clarified butter to make them beautiful and crisp to contrast with the softness and richness of the caviar and the custard. After a long search, we found the best possible crabs from Penzance, towards the southern tip of Cornwall and gently steam them until pearlescent and meaty.

Lastly, the custard and parsley sauce. The custard is based on your classical Royale but very gently steamed at lower temperature to achieve a soft, rich and delicate texture which is more akin to your now very popular Japanese chawanmushi. The brown crab meat gives you a punchy, savoury seafood flavour, wonderful alongside the sweet claw meat on the toast. The parsley sauce is unrecognisable from the green-speckled white sauce you may have encountered before. It is packed with fresh green herb flavour. Made using pulp from parsley oil production on the farm, it gives vibrant flavour, colour and a velvety texture to the sauce. The custard is finished with a big dollop of Petrossian Daurenki caviar to really add to the luxurious texture and flavour of this two-part dish.

The Black Swan at Oldstead | Roots | Made In Oldstead, Yorkshire

Our Approach to Food

We plan all our produce a year in advance, so we're kind of working backwards towards the menu. We'll work out what Roots needs for a year, what The Black Swan needs, what we need for any events we've got coming up – radishes and turnips in the first week of June, for example – and that all goes into the schedule for our farm and kitchen garden. It's taken years to get to this level of organisation though. We used to just grow stuff and then try to use it up, which doesn't work very well. You need to plan ahead. Of course, from a creative perspective you don't want to be thinking 'so next August I'm going to put this dish on the menu' because you're going to have other ideas in the meantime. It's more about growing the ingredients that we know we want. For instance, we love new potatoes so we'll always grow plenty and then decide what to do with them nearer the harvest.

In the kitchen garden, which is just outside the restaurant at The Black Swan, we grow a lot of fruit and herbs as well as things like chillies, peppers and tomatoes in our heated tunnel. The benches in there are also used for propagation which use the waste heat from the energy we generate to cook with to start the life of our produce. Lemon verbena's my favourite herb so we have a whole tunnel of that, which we make beer with and use in a lot of cocktails too; we work closely with Cooper King Distillery to make drink bases with all sorts of ingredients that we can harvest here at their best.

There are certain things that we don't grow anymore because it's not cost effective. Hispi cabbages, which are quite difficult to grow well and pest-free, are very cheap and very good quality so we buy those in. But if you take peas for instance, ours are phenomenal because we pick them so small and you can't buy that quality. Then a lot of other produce is grown purely to be preserved in large batches, like chicory root.

We also forage ingredients to be processed, whether it's blossoms or flowers or wild herbs, so they can be stored and ready to use for a whole year. It's almost the opposite of seasonal cooking because it's not reactive, it's proactive. Our dry store is full of ingredients we've produced ourselves, so rather than just being able to replace those whenever we need to from a supplier, that store needs to last for maybe 15 months.

We have a lot of meat on our farm – like our Mangalica pigs which we make streaky bacon and charcuterie from – but we also work with R&J, an awesome local butchers and farmers who really know their stuff and have a longstanding relationship with us. Fish is probably the only thing we go a little bit further afield for, because I think different things are better from different places. We do have a local supplier for certain fish like cod and monkfish, that do better in cold water, and some really nice turbot from the Channel. I think shellfish is better the further north you go though, so our lobsters, langoustines and scallops all come from Scotland. We also use Flying Fish in Cornwall and our head chef has been able to go out fishing with them and see it all first hand on the exchange programme we set up with them.

I was very into the self-sufficiency approach when I was a bit younger, to the detriment of certain things. I wouldn't have bought a fish from Cornwall back then because it felt too far away but compared to say, the banana I'd eat for breakfast, that distance is nothing. Ultimately, everyone wants to win more accolades and make the best restaurant you possibly can, and it's all down to the best produce. I'd rather source from slightly further afield than compromise on the quality but most of our ingredients do come straight from our own farm and garden – that growing and preserving cycle is the basis of it all.

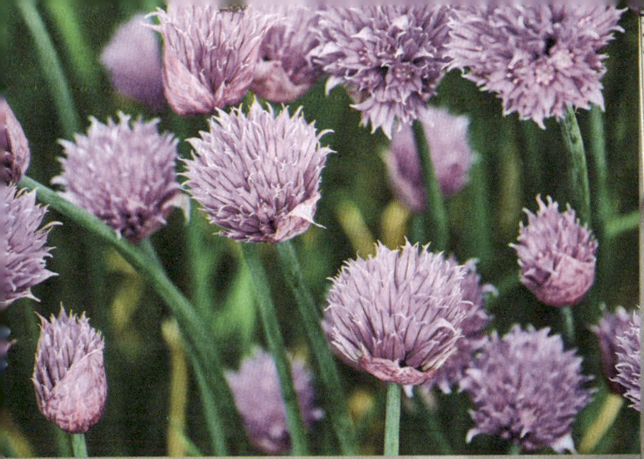

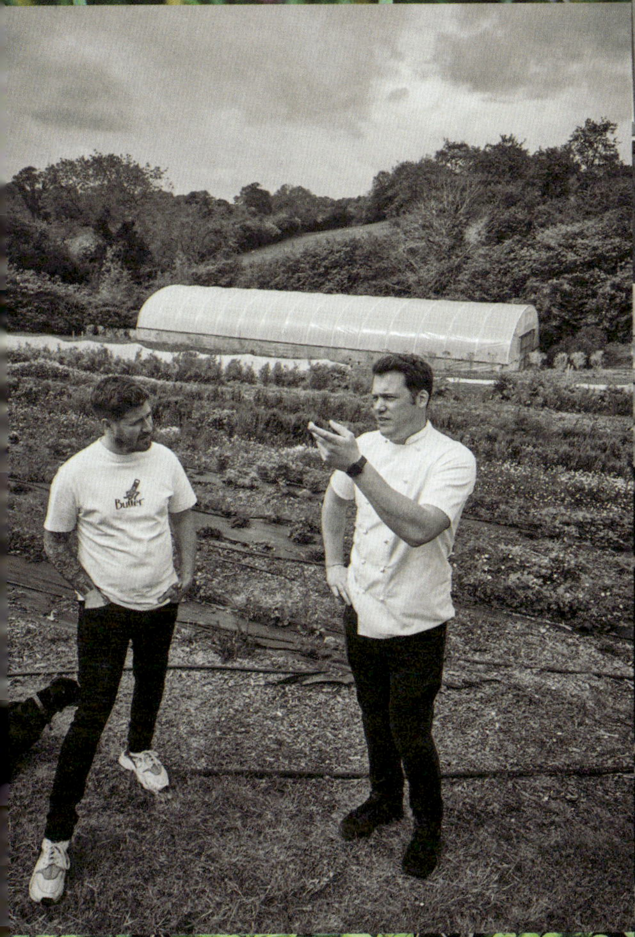

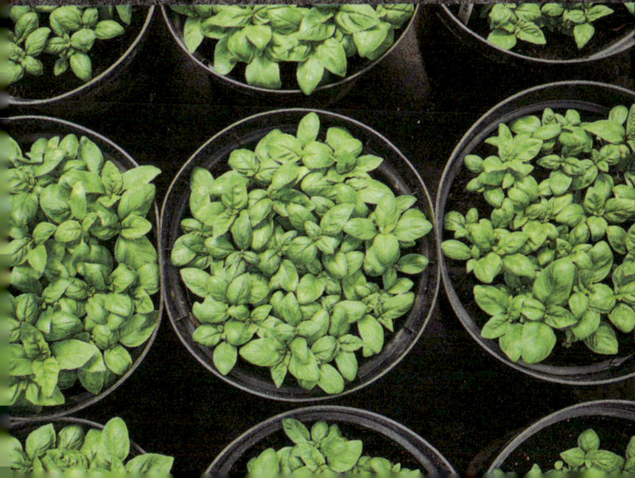

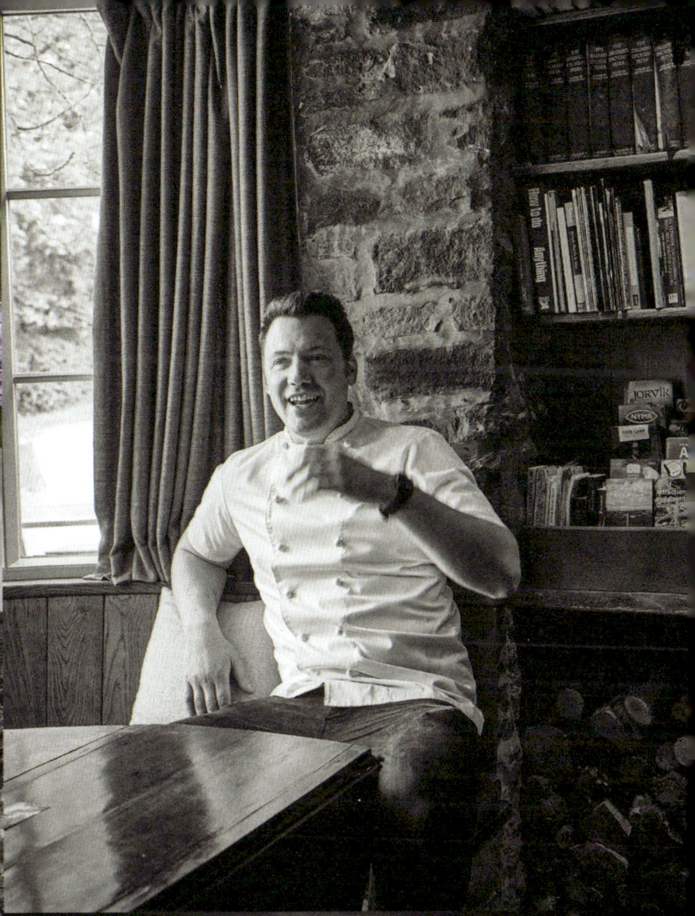

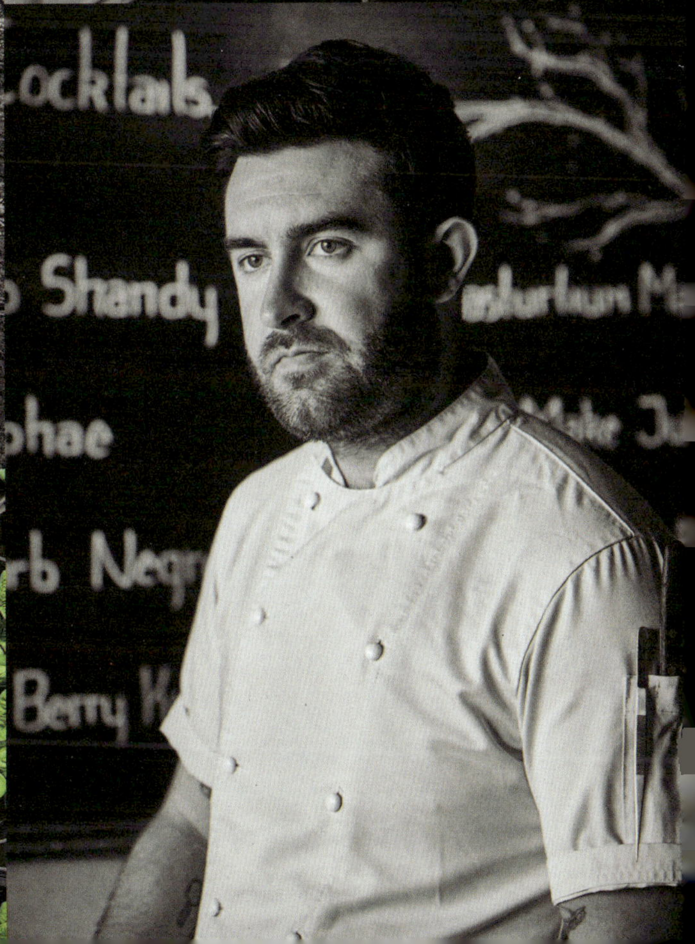
Cocktails
Shandy

PLEASE LET ME KNOW IF YOU TAKE ANY STOCK FROM THIS STORAGE FACILITY!
Thank You,
Chef Dickie Lad. X

PALACE OF PRESERVES

'PRESERVES 2'

PRESE
FREEZ

Fallow, London

Will Murray & Jack Croft

"Jack was the chef de partie on my section at Dinner by Heston Blumenthal when I first moved to London for work as a commis chef. We worked together for about four and a half years there and the beginnings of Fallow's concept was basically us trying different ideas with the waste you get in a fine dining restaurant. We'd take things like turbot cheeks and come up with new dishes to use them – that's where the whole thing stemmed from, so we've always been inspired by surplus produce.

The story of how that concept turned into a restaurant is all very organic to be honest; there was no 'eureka' moment. Following a few pop ups and residencies, including Carousel and Crispin, we had a great opportunity with a restaurant residency on Heddon Street. It was just the two of us and one waiter at first, then we grew very slowly, one member of staff at a time. We got to define the food we wanted to do bit by bit, and we had numerous lockdowns throughout our whole tenure there, which obviously wasn't great in general but benefitted us because every few months we'd be able to stop and reflect when the restaurant had to close again. So that gave us time to analyse and take stock on what we were doing to make it better. We were only meant to be there for three months, but it ended up being a year and a half because of lockdowns, so out of a disaster we got to build a nice team and a pretty solid concept.

The second site, where we are now, again came out of lockdown; the restaurant that used to be here closed and the landlord – who also owned our previous venue and was brilliant with us – had seen the positive reaction to our food. We found ourselves in a restaurant setting that we'd never usually have had the opportunity to get, being fairly inexperienced when we came here. It was a risky move because we only had a month's cashflow to open, so the renovation and fit out was completed within five weeks. We brought the whole team with us from our previous residency and have been continuously growing since then, both as chefs and as a concept.

At Fallow, we marry using surplus produce with doing large amounts of covers, so we can buy whole animals in and use every single part of them. That's what generates a lot of the new ideas – we might have to use up lots of pig skin, or lamb tongues – and we also ask our suppliers what's left over. Often this approach takes a lot more work at our end, prep wise, in order to use those ingredients. For example, we've been trying to work with spent hens for about three months now, and we'll keep going until we find something that works. The principle is that it doesn't go on the menu, despite our ethos, unless it tastes absolutely banging. We're not using these ingredients simply because they're sustainable; the food still needs to be of a standard that we both agree is amazing. As two head chefs, we often don't agree, but that dynamic is part of what improves our food. Either of us can have an idea and be working on something, then we'll come together to discuss it, but it has to be worthy of the menu and we have to be proud of it."

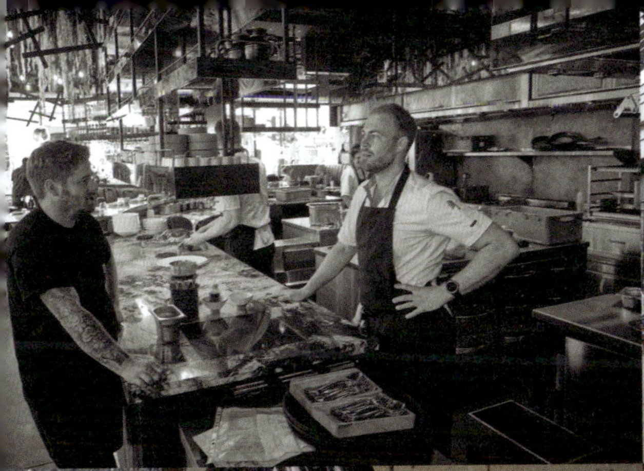

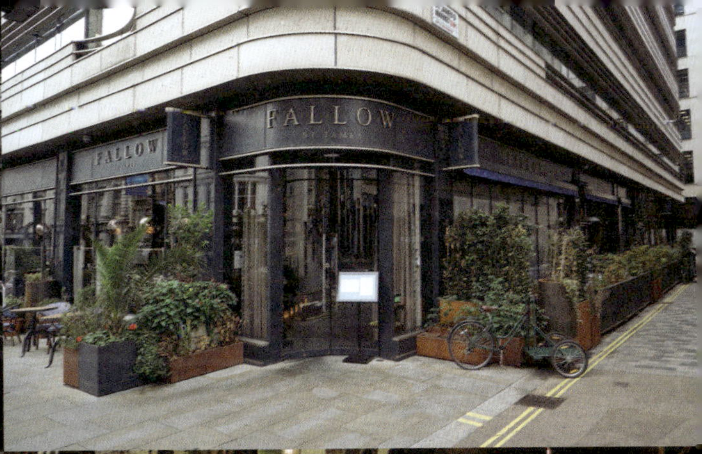
FALLOW
FALLOW

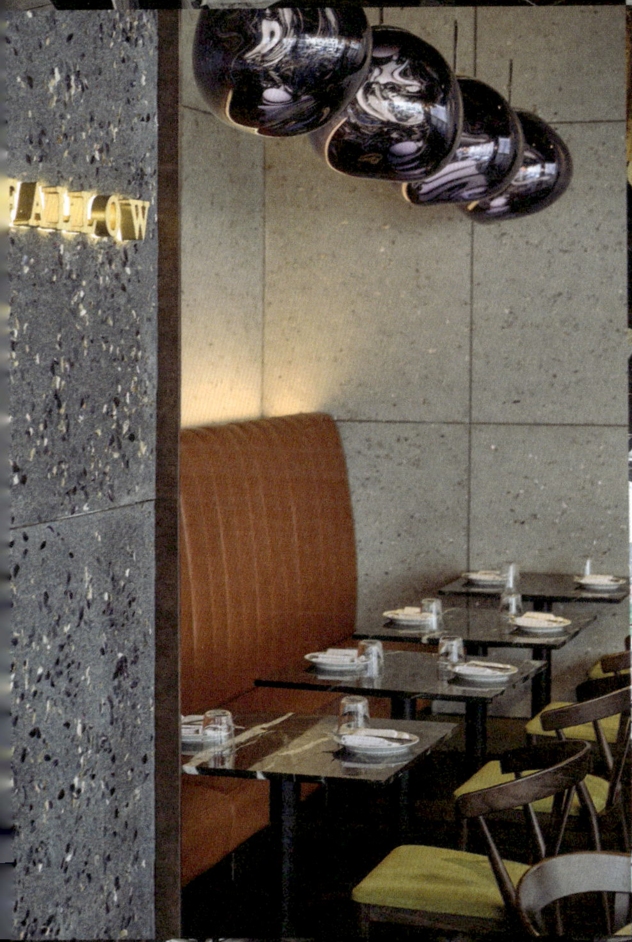
FALLOW

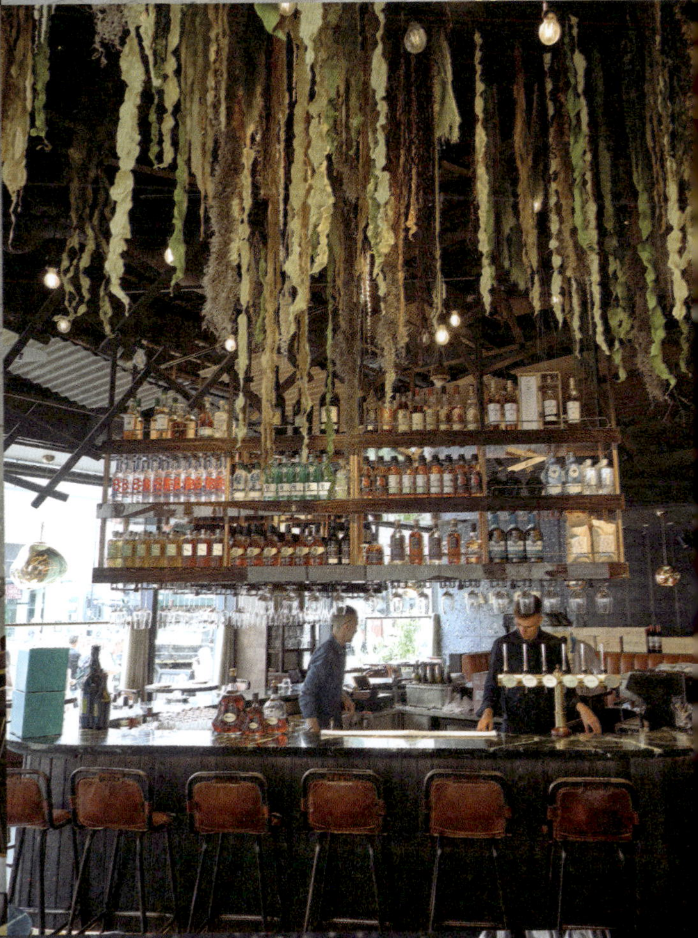

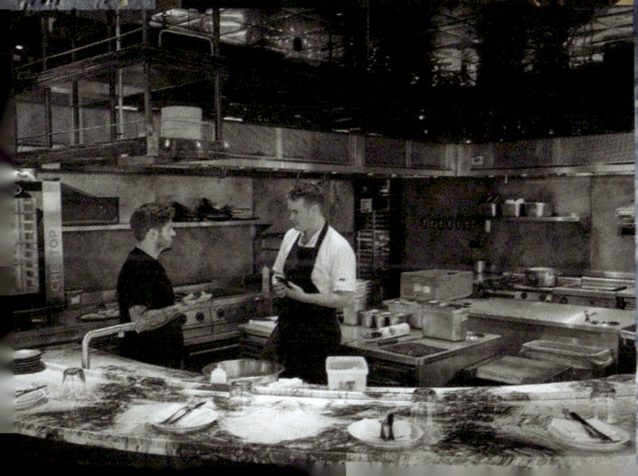

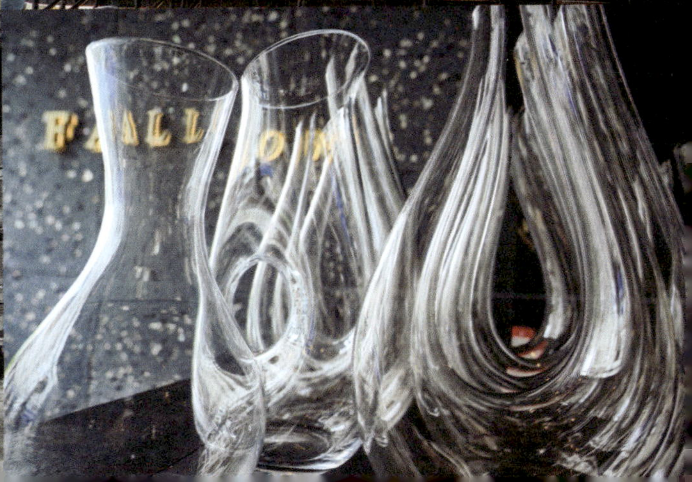

Fallow, London

Leek, Hen Of The Woods

Preparation time: 45 minutes | Cooking time: 2 hours | Serves 4

FOR THE CONFIT LEEKS
10 whole leeks
350ml rapeseed oil

FOR THE GREEN OIL
Leek tops
Cavolo nero
Grelotte tops
Spring onion tops
Parsley
Rapeseed oil

FOR THE LEEK CRUMB
10 leek roots
35g rice flour
12g onion powder
180ml cooking oil
100g panko breadcrumbs
100g dehydrated parmesan

FOR THE CONFIT GARLIC
250g garlic
150g rapeseed or vegetable oil

FOR THE HEN OF THE WOODS
1 head of hen of the woods mushroom
20ml rapeseed oil
20ml lemon juice
5g fresh parsley
5g confit garlic pulp

FOR THE LEEK TOP MAYONNAISE
30g pasteurised egg yolk
25ml Chardonnay vinegar
5g Dijon mustard
8g salt
300g smoked leek oil

FOR THE CONFIT LEEKS
Cut off and reserve the leek tops and roots. Place the leek centres into a deep baking dish and cover with the oil. Place a cartouche over the leeks and cover the tray with foil. Cook the leeks at 140°c for 2 hours until a knife goes through them with no resistance. The oil can be reused many times for confit leeks or used as leek-infused oil in cooking or dressings like the mayonnaise below.

FOR THE GREEN OIL
The key to this part of the recipe is firstly collecting all the green elements you will be using to make the oil, and always use at least 50% cavolo nero. Use the leek tops you reserved earlier here.

Prep all your elements, removing any yellow parts and blanching separately in boiling water to ensure maximum colour and cook each ingredient to its potential. You want them to be just cooked and tender; for leek tops this will be approximately 2 minutes, whereas parsley will be 5 seconds. Drain and then squeeze as dry as possible.

Mix together and roughly chop all your ingredients, then weigh the total amount you have. Now weigh out twice the amount of rapeseed oil. For example, 500g blanched greens = 1kg rapeseed oil.

Place the oil and all the blanched chopped greens into the Thermomix. Set the temperature to 70°c and the timer to 7 minutes, then blend on speed 8. Once the time is up, pour the mixture into a coarse chinois set over a fine chinois with a blue J-cloth in the middle.

Place the draining set-up into the blast chiller to drain until cold, then very gently squeeze to get a little extra oil out. This can then be checked for colour and poured into a small plastic bottle or container. Place in the freezer for later use.

FOR THE LEEK CRUMB
Use the leek roots you reserved earlier here. Simmer them in boiling water for 10 minutes to soften slightly, then remove and dry with paper towels. Coat the roots in the rice flour and a pinch of salt, then deep fry in oil at 170°c until golden and crispy. Coat in the onion powder and then use scissors to cut the roots into small pieces.

Place the cooking oil into a wide pan and bring to 180°c. Add the panko breadcrumbs and whisk until golden brown. Carefully pass the hot oil through a sieve and dry the golden panko crumb on paper towels. The oil will be good to use again.

Combine the panko crumb, parmesan and crispy leek root in an equal ratio.

FOR THE CONFIT GARLIC
Peel the garlic and lightly pulse in the Thermomix. Combine this with the oil in a large pan, mixing to fully incorporate. Confit on a very low heat until soft and sweet, approximately 2 hours. Blend with a hand blender until smooth. Keep the leftovers as great pantry item.

FOR THE HEN OF THE WOODS
Sauté the mushroom with the rapeseed oil until golden and tender. Deglaze the pan with the lemon juice, fresh parsley and confit garlic.

FOR THE LEEK TOP MAYONNAISE
Place the egg, vinegar, mustard, and salt into the Thermomix with the butterfly attachment. Set to speed 4 and gradually add the smoked leek oil until fully emulsified.

FOR THE FINISHING TOUCHES
Dress the confit leeks with hen of the wood mushroom, leek crumb and green oil. Top it off with your homemade leek top mayonnaise!

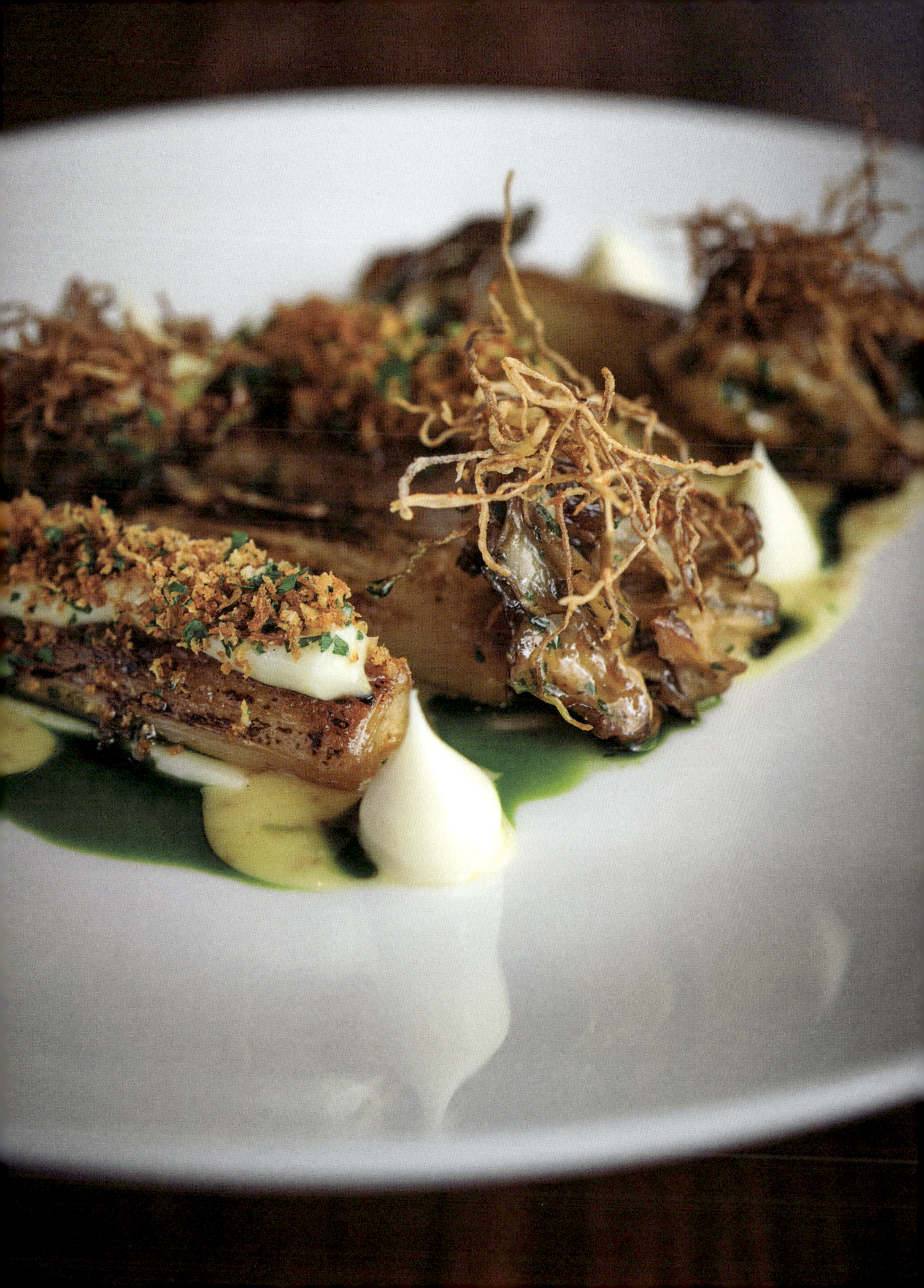

Fallow, London

Cod's Head, Sriracha Butter Sauce

Preparation time: 6-8 weeks | Cooking time: 1 hour 20 minutes | Serves 2

FOR THE SRIRACHA

20kg red chillies

2kg peeled garlic

2% salt brine

100g gluten-free soy sauce

80g light brown sugar

40g white wine vinegar

40ml water

1g xanthan gum

FOR THE COD'S HEAD

1 large cod's head

Salt

Cooking oil

FOR THE BUTTER EMULSION

1kg unsalted butter

500g water

FOR THE GREEN OIL

Leek tops

Cavolo nero

Grelotte tops

Spring onion tops

Parsley

Rapeseed oil

FOR THE FINISHING TOUCHES

Fresh lemon juice

FOR THE SRIRACHA

Remove the green stalks from the chillies, cut the chillies into small pieces and place into 2 large white buckets. Place 1kg of garlic in each bucket. Cover the chillies and garlic with 2% brine, then lay a sheet of parchment over the top and put a plate over that to keep it all submerged. Leave in the container to ferment for 4-6 weeks.

Combine 1kg of the fermented chillies and garlic (no liquid) with the remaining ingredients in a Thermomix jug and blend on speed 10 for 4 minutes. Pass the sauce through a fine chinois into a large pan. Continue blending until all the chillies have been blended.

Place the pan onto the stove and bring the sauce to a boil to stop the fermentation. Chill down the sauce overnight. The next day, taste and adjust the sauce. It's now ready!

FOR THE COD'S HEAD

Remove the gills and thoroughly dry the head. Liberally season with salt and cooking oil, then cook over very hot charcoal until the flesh reaches 62°c.

FOR THE BUTTER EMULSION

Cut the butter into 1cm cubes. Place the water into a small pan and gently heat on a low heat. Gradually add the butter, whisking to emulsify. Once all the butter is fully melted and emulsified, blitz with a handheld blender to fully incorporate.

FOR THE GREEN OIL

The key to this part of the recipe is firstly collecting all the green elements you will be using to make the oil, and always use at least 50% cavolo nero. If you have no green trimmings, just cavolo nero can be used to make the oil.

Prep all your elements, removing any yellow parts and blanching separately in boiling water to ensure maximum colour and cook each ingredient to its potential. You want them to be just cooked and tender; for leek tops this will be approximately 2 minutes, whereas parsley will be 5 seconds. Drain and then squeeze as dry as possible.

Mix together and roughly chop all your ingredients, then weigh the total amount you have. Now weigh out twice the amount of rapeseed oil. For example, 500g blanched greens = 1kg rapeseed oil.

Place the oil and all the blanched chopped greens into the Thermomix. Set the temperature to 70°c and the timer to 7 minutes, then blend on speed 8. Once the time is up, pour the mixture into a coarse chinois set over a fine chinois with a blue J-cloth in the middle.

Place the draining set-up into the blast chiller to drain until cold, then very gently squeeze to get a little extra oil out. This can then be checked for colour and poured into a small plastic bottle or container. Place in the freezer for later use.

FOR THE FINISHING TOUCHES

Pour 1 part sriracha and 3 parts butter emulsion over the cod's head. Drizzle the green oil over the dish, then finish with lemon juice and salt to taste.

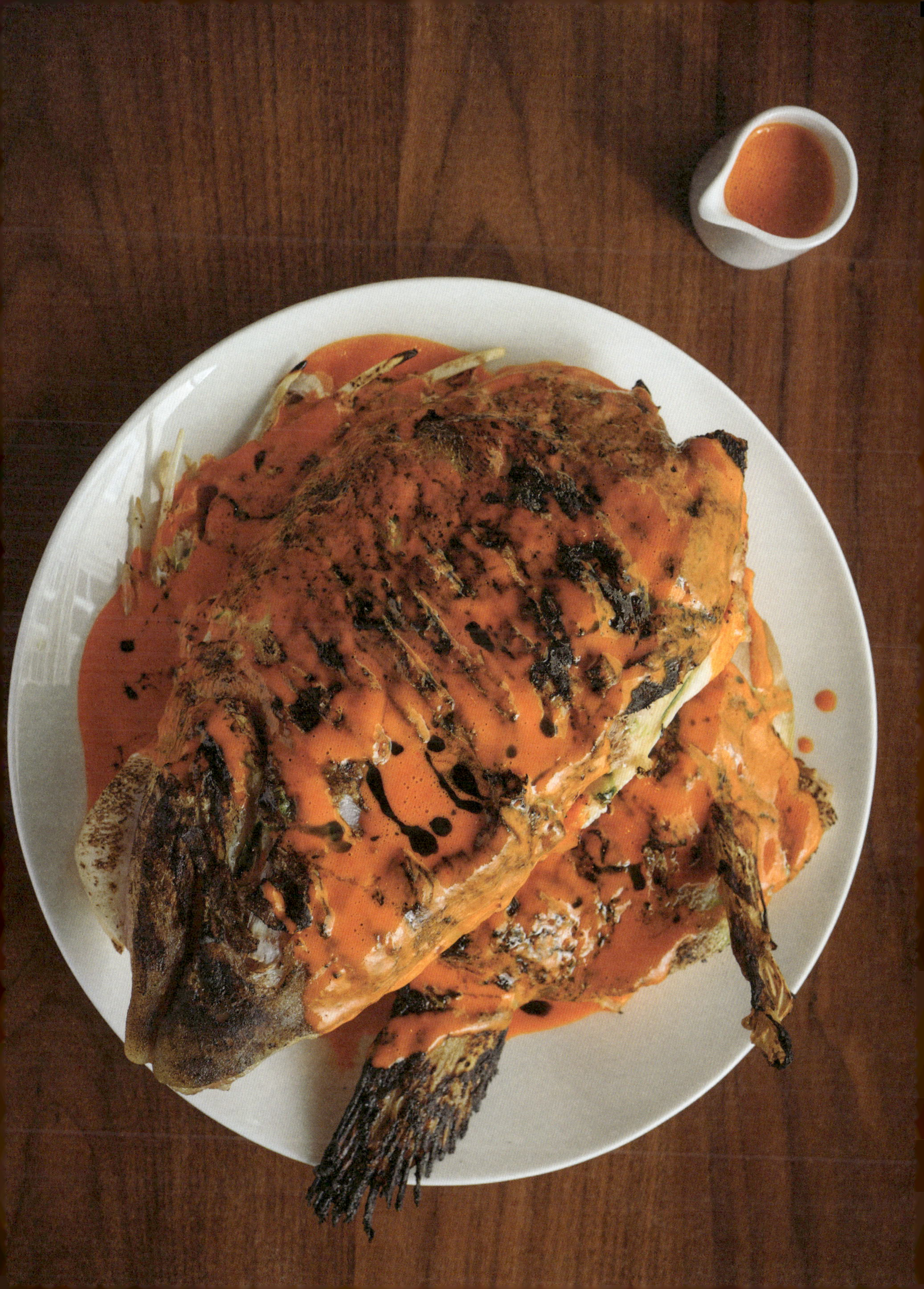

Fallow, London

Corn Ribs, Lime

Preparation time: 15 minutes | Cooking time: 10 minutes | Serves 4

FOR THE CORN RIBS
4 corn on the cob
240ml neutral oil
Lime wedges

FOR THE KOMBU SEASONING
100g coriander seeds
60g black peppercorns
15g cumin seeds
800g dehydrated kombu dashi kelp
340g smoked sweet paprika
200g kosher salt
180g fermented chilli powder
150g garlic powder

FOR THE CORN RIBS
Cut the corn cobs in half, then stand them upright and cut from the top into quarters. You should get 8 corn ribs per cob. Deep fry the corn ribs in oil at 170°c for 4 minutes. Deep fry a second time in oil at 190°c for 3 minutes.

FOR THE KOMBU SEASONING
Toast all the whole spices and then set aside to cool. Blitz the kelp to a fine powder and then place in a large bowl. Add the paprika, salt, chilli powder, and garlic powder. Blitz the toasted spices to a fine powder and finally mix them with the rest of the seasoning.

FOR THE FINISHING TOUCHES
Generously season the deep-fried corn ribs with your kombu seasoning. Serve with wedges of lime to be squeezed over the top.

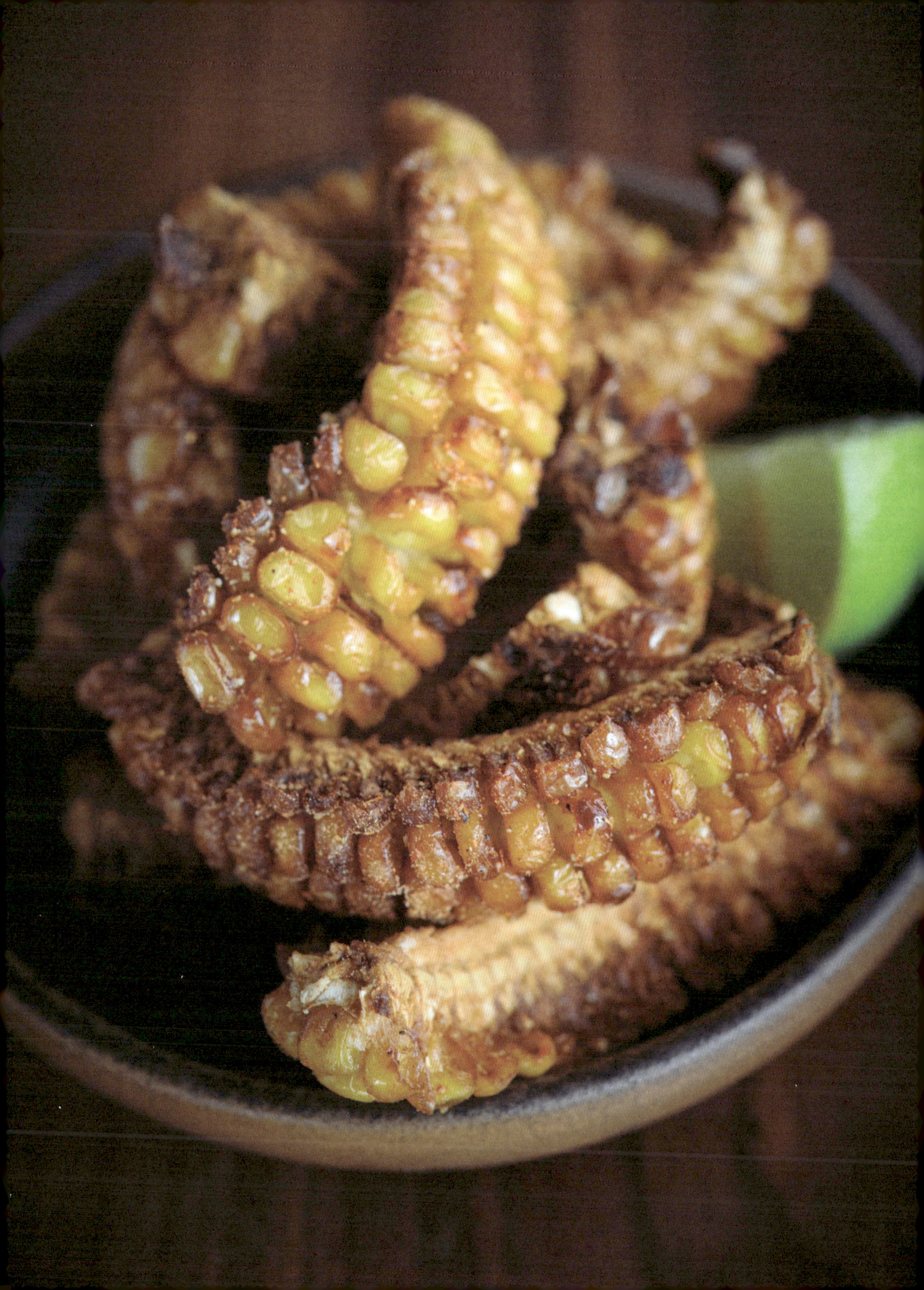

Fallow, London

Kitchen Confidential

LEEK, HEN OF THE WOODS

Did the concept of this dish develop through a no-waste goal for the leeks or come about naturally?

We do have a kind of 'root to stem' approach to using leeks. We use the surplus tops to make the leek oil for a smoked mayonnaise, then we confit the stems in that same oil so they have a really nice smoky flavour, and we clean, blanch and deep fry the roots for an extra oniony crisp to the dish. So many people are used to just cutting the tops and roots off to chuck them away, whereas you can use both of those things and they all complement each other nicely. It's just about getting people to think a little bit about how they can reduce waste when cooking at home. This dish is basically a take on a classic leek vinaigrette, done our way.

Was the green oil developed to use up elements from other dishes or specifically for this one?

It's a recipe that works very well with a lot of dishes because it uses up a lot of surplus products from around the kitchen. Predominantly we make it with green leek tops, but you can also put parsley and cavolo nero stalks in there – it's a versatile thing to make regularly. We always try to find a use for the whole ingredient before we use it on the menu, so whenever we put a new dish on, it directly affects other dishes that are on the menu at the same time and needs to be well-rounded.

Why were hen of the woods mushrooms chosen to accompany the leeks in this dish?

The texture and roasted flavour almost resemble meat in a way, so it's a way of making vegetarian dishes more interesting by adding umami richness, which can be often missing with those dishes. There are lots of different ways you can cook hen of the woods: confit, slow cooked, barbecued, roast. In our opinion, just getting it super crispy with a nice crust on it, and adding the simple flavours of garlic, lemon and parsley just works really well with it so there's neutral flavour, it's not too complicated.

COD'S HEAD, SRIRACHA

What inspired you to make your own sriracha?

When chefs cook the food that they want to eat, they're going to be cooking at their highest level, and we like hot sauce. This sriracha stemmed from a lockdown when we had loads of chillies in the fridge and we decided to ferment them. We were popping into the restaurant every now and then, and we made a batch of sriracha with the fermented chillies because we thought why the hell not? When you're designing dishes, quite often you use what's in the kitchen around you, so the sriracha now goes into quite a few things like dressings. We've done a dish where we used the brine from the sriracha, and the pulp goes into numerous dishes on the menu. Ultimately, we really enjoyed that first batch so we ended up using it more and more.

How does cooking the cod's head over charcoal to 62°c create the best flavour?

They're very robust – there's so much gelatine, connective tissue, skin – so it's a very well protected piece of meat that can take quite a lot of heat. The most important thing is that when you hit 62°c all the meat starts to fall off the bones really nicely, and then it just needs to rest for a good amount of time. The story with the cod's head is that one morning we called up our fish supplier to ask what was in the bin that day. He sent us loads of monkfish heads but when we cooked them the flesh recoiled and ended up looking like Alien vs Predator so we couldn't put those on the menu – it was too terrifying. There were a couple of neglected cod's heads at the bottom so we sawed them in half and had a go with those, putting them on the menu with a sriracha butter sauce. Then Fay Maschler walks in on our first pop up and of course, the first thing she ordered was the cod's head. Her review said it was her favourite dish and after that we had people coming in just to try it. We've never taken it off the menu since and the hardest thing has been getting the supply network right, because it's not an easy thing to have as your signature dish. We started by taking the lion's share of all the cod's head coming into Billingsgate and now we've got seven ships that fish off the Outer Hebrides – instead of cutting off the heads and using them for crab bait, they bring them back to shore for us. It's tricky but great that we're seeing a slightly positive change in the food system because we sell so many. They now come pristinely packaged like a premium piece of cod and are more expensive because we've pushed the price up by creating so much demand. The idea that we've been throwing them away before now is crazy.

CORN RIBS, LIME

How do the different frying temperatures affect the corn ribs?

It's exactly like the process of making twice-cooked chips, so the first stage is softening and the second is to crisp them up. It helps to get them super crisp at the end when you blanch them before, although if you're cooking them at home, you'll get almost the same result with just one fry at 165°c for 7 minutes.

What is the kombu seasoning based on, or is this your own invention?

Initially we'd designed a seasoning to go on chicken feet that included lots of different spices from cayenne pepper to dried seaweed. Once we started making our own sriracha, we had all this pulp left over – because we want the sriracha to be quite smooth, we pass it through a chinois and end up with a lot of pulp – so we blended that and thought about what else we could use it for. It went well with the kombu seasoning and once we ramped up the production of the sriracha we got so much pulp that we altered the recipe. It's predominantly a fermented chilli kombu seasoning now, with a few other spices in there. It evolved over time and was one of those happy accidents that started on one of our residencies when we found this dry store with loads of Japanese seasonings in. It took us ages to work out what they were, but some of those are still in the current version of the seasoning, like the seaweed and dashi. People sometimes ask what they can use instead of this at home, and we usually recommend Old Bay Seasoning which you can get from supermarkets or online.

Fallow, London

Q&A with Will Murray & Jack Croft

How would you describe the food at Fallow?

We focus on bold flavours, driven by conscious creativity and surplus ingredients. Nothing about our food is too outlandish; a lot of it's just subbing in different ingredients that people may not have used before. For example, we use salmon belly instead of salmon fillet, spent hen instead of chicken… we aim to think outside the box but work from classical ideas and techniques. It's just a slightly different thought process, driven by what we love and are passionate about.

Where do your recipe ideas come from?

Will – We work completely differently and if you put both of us in the same body, we'd be a really good chef. I'm not as classically trained as Jack, and I tend to get obsessed with a certain thing – like maybe a duck head – for months and months, then move onto the next thing once that's finished. Jack's more inspired by what comes in seasonally, speaking to the suppliers, and what he's seen when he's eating out. Usually, it all comes together into something we're really happy with.

Jack – Often I'll taste a dish when I'm eating out, or read about a technique, and want to apply that approach to an ingredient that we've been working on. We always have a bank of ingredients that we want to use, so eating out might give me an idea about how to present it or what would work well with it. That's the beauty of the restaurant industry and the whole reason I got into cooking is because I love eating out, even more than cooking!

Are there other chefs or restaurants that particularly inspire you?

Will – Absolutely, what we're doing is not by any means new; kitchens have been finding interesting ways to use their waste products for ever, and like most 'new' things it's an old trend that comes back around. Silo has been a massive inspiration to the whole industry in terms of sustainability, especially in terms of practices within the actual restaurant and how chefs work. I think there's a lot of chefs out there who are championing low intervention wines, local menus, limited waste, sustainable products… generally speaking, a lot more chefs are taking a hell of a lot more interest and an active role in more sustainable food.

Jack – There's a lot of inspiration out there on Instagram too. Since the growth of that platform, I can scroll for a few minutes and see ten restaurants doing ten amazing dishes. That makes me think 'I need to up my game' so I find that inspiring. It's never ending, so it makes you realise that you know nothing and the possibilities are just endless. The food scene in the UK in general has taken such a step up in the last five years and I love seeing other chefs do what they do.

What would you say to younger chefs coming into the industry?

Will – I think you have to get rooted down somewhere that's doing a lot of stuff in-house and stay there for a good long time. Ideas and creativity are everywhere but the hardest things to learn as a chef are the work ethic and managing other people. The most important thing though is that you're cooking the food that you want to cook.

Jack – Youth in a kitchen is fundamental: they add enthusiasm, atmosphere and energy, which is essential when putting in the hours. The important thing to remember is that it's a craft that takes patience, time and devotion to master. I'm not saying you have to slave away for years and years, just dedicate a certain amount of time to one place to really understand what they do.

Which ingredients are you most excited about cooking with at the moment?

Will – We're pretty set on mushrooms as an all-encompassing, mystifying, insane ingredient… they appear on our menu in desserts, fresh, smoked, pickled, sautéed… I just think it's such a cool and varied, relatively undiscovered ingredient.

Jack – I'd say venison because one of the best things about Fallow is the versatility of being able to buy in whole animals and really have some fun, get creative. Butchering is one of my favourite parts of the prep because you get all these ideas – different braises, charcuterie, staff meals – and I love that process. Incidentally, the name Fallow was originally to do with a fallow year – doing things slowly with respect for the land – and then it was a happy accident that we fell in love with fallow deer as well. And that they're an invasive species so really good value!

When you're not in the restaurant, what do you like to do in your time off?

Will – I've got a little girl, so I spend my days off with her. Or I'll be messaging Jack, talking about work!

Jack – It sounds really boring, but Fallow isn't just a job for me – if I'm not working, I'll be going out for dinner. On a Sunday morning I might go for a coffee with my missus, and we'll talk about where to go for lunch! I'm sure that's not going to be the answer forever, but at this point in our journey, we're so ingrained in what we're doing here and planning what we want to do next. It might be things that evolve out of the restaurant – like being part of this book – but it's all food and drink related for sure.

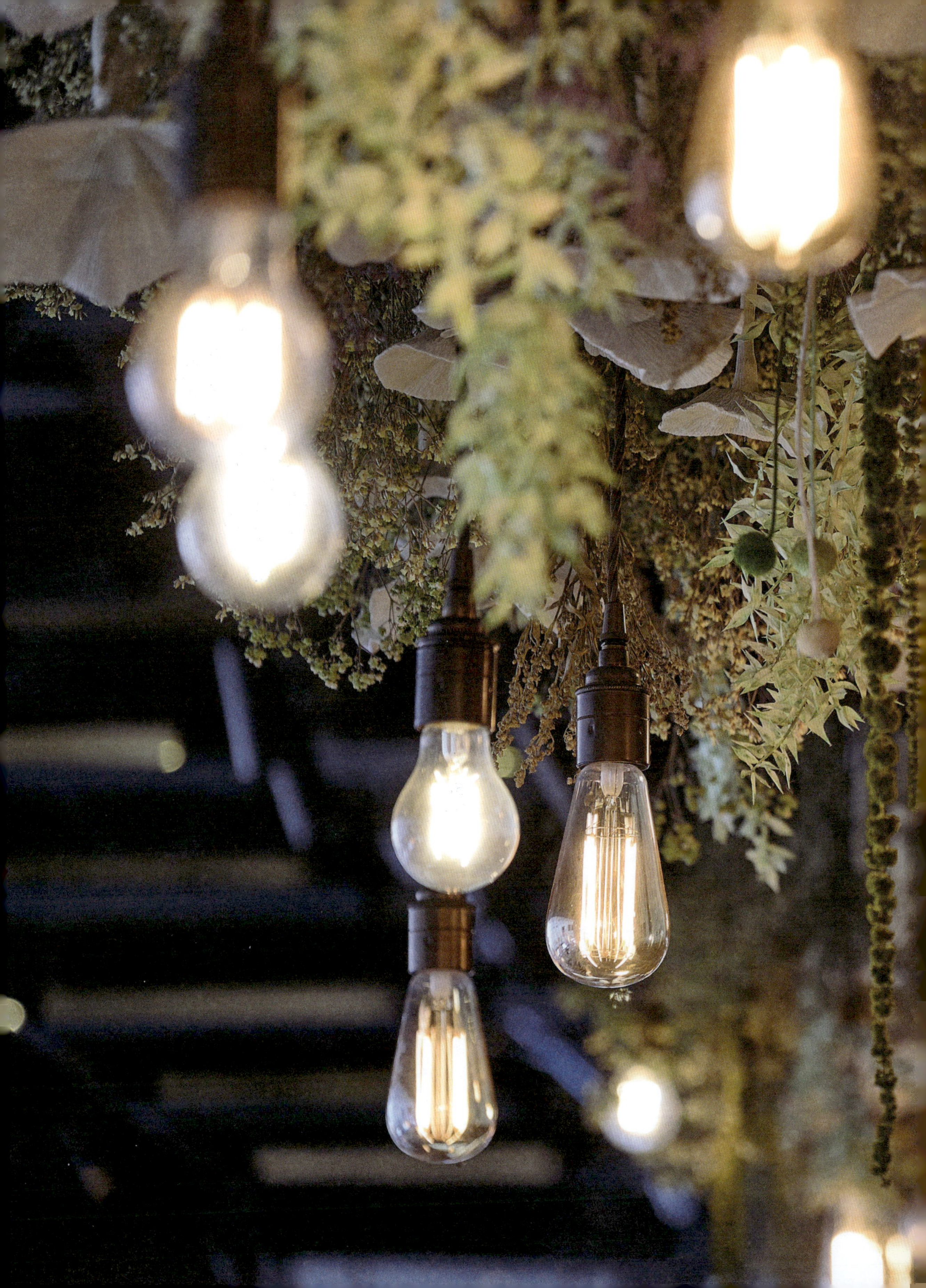

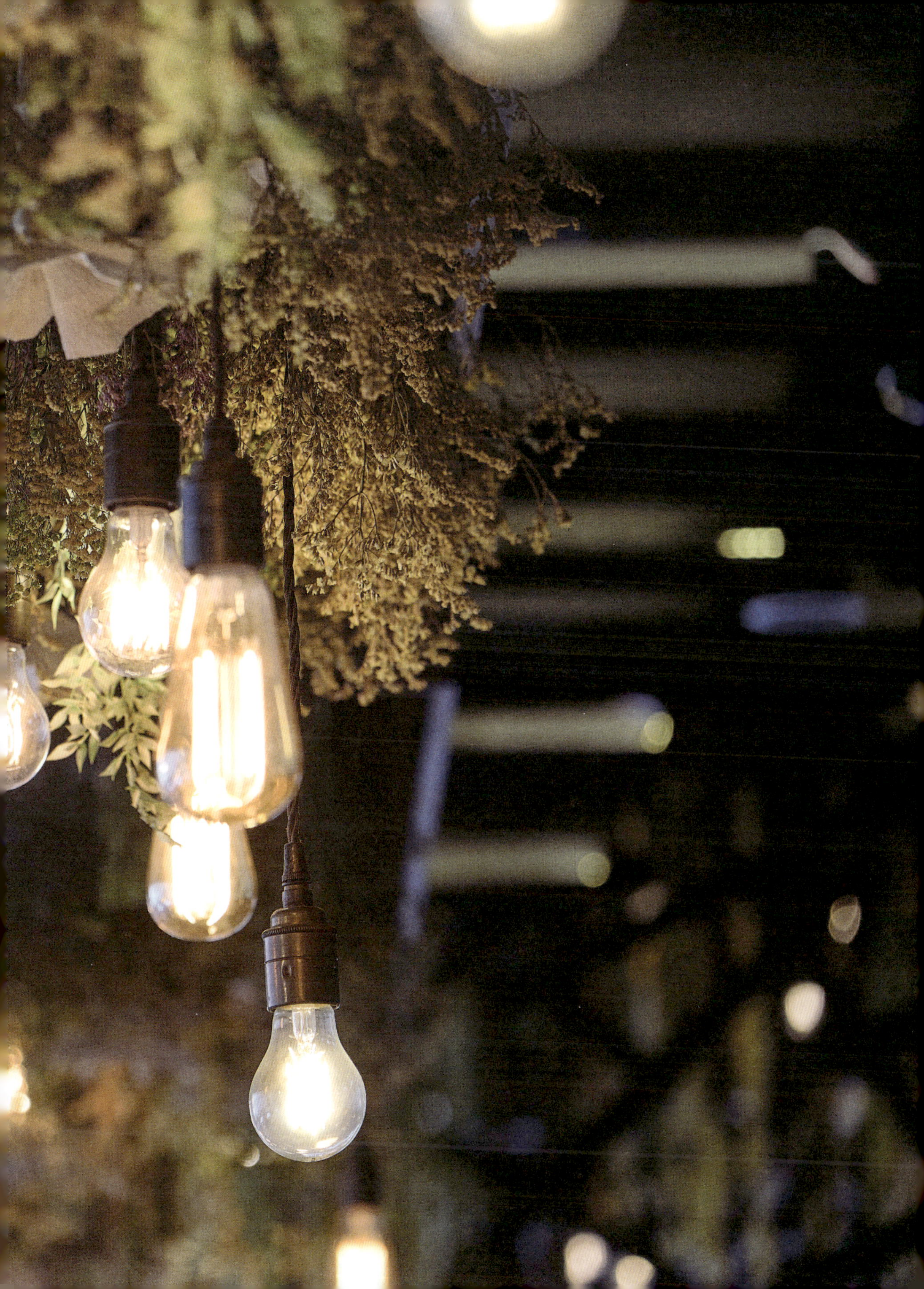

Behind The Pass

Directory

THE BLACK SWAN, ROOTS, MADE IN OLDSTEAD
Chef/Proprietors Tommy Banks & the Banks family
Website tommybanks.co.uk
Instagram @blackswan_oldstead @rootsyork @madeinoldstead @tommybanks

CORNERSTONE
Chef/Proprietors Tom Brown
Website cornerstonehackney.com
Instagram @cornerstonehackney @cheftombrown

DA TERRA
Chef/Proprietors Rafael Cagali
Website daterra.co.uk
Instagram @daterrarestaurant @rafacagali

FALLOW
Chef/Proprietors Will Murray, Jack Croft & James Robson
Website fallowrestaurant.com
Instagram @fallowrestaurant @willmurraychef @jcroftchef

THE FOREST SIDE
Chef/Proprietors Paul Leonard, Andrew Wildsmith
Website theforestside.com
Instagram @the_forest_side

THE GRILL BY TOM BOOTON
Chef/Proprietors Tom Booton & Dorchester Collection
Website dorchestercollection.com/en/london/the-dorchester/restaurants-bars/the-grill-at-the-dorchester
Instagram @bootontom

HJEM
Chef/Proprietors Alex & Ali Nietosvuori
Website restauranthjem.co.uk
Instagram @restauranthjem @a.nietosvuori

HOUSE OF TIDES
Chef/Proprietors Kenny & Abi Atkinson
Website houseoftides.co.uk
Instagram @houseoftides @solstice_ncl

JÖRO, KONJÖ, HOUSE OF JÖRO, AXL
Chef/Proprietors Luke & Stacey Sherwood-French
Website jororestaurant.co.uk
Instagram @restaurant_joro @cheflukefrench

KOL RESTAURANT
Chef/Proprietors Santiago Lastra & MJMK Restaurants
Website kolrestaurant.com
Instagram @kol.restaurant @kol.mezcaleria @santiagolas

LE COCHON AVEUGLE

Chef/Proprietors Josh & Victoria Overington
Website lecochonaveugle.uk
Instagram @lecochonaveugle @joshoverington

LEE WESTCOTT
(NEW VENTURE COMING SOON)

Chef/Proprietors Lee Westcott
Website leewestcott.com
Instagram @leewestcott

THE LITTLE CHARTROOM

Chef/Proprietors Roberta Hall & Shaun Mccarron
Website thelittlechartroom.com
Instagram @thelittlechartroom @chef_roberta_hall

NORTHCOTE HOTEL & RESTAURANT

Chef/Proprietors Lisa Goodwin-Allen
& Stafford Collection
Website northcote.com
Instagram @northcoteuk @chef_lisa_allen

THE PACKHORSE

Chef/Proprietors Luke Payne and Emma Daniels
Website thepackhorsehayfield.uk
Instagram @thepackhorsehayfield @lukepayne92

PAUL AINSWORTH AT NO6

Chef/Proprietors Chris McClurg, Paul & Emma Ainsworth
Website paul-ainsworth.co.uk
Instagram @no6padstow @chrismcclurg

PLATES

Chef/Proprietors Kirk Haworth & Keeley Haworth
Website plates-london.com
Instagram @kirk_haworth @plates_london

RESTAURANT 22

Chef/Proprietors Sam Carter & Alex Olivier
Website restaurant22.co.uk
Instagram @restaurant22_cambridge
@samcarter_22

YNYSHIR

Chef/Proprietors Gareth Ward & Amelia Eriksson
Website ynyshir.co.uk
Instagram @ynyshirrestaurant @garethwardchef

For the latest news and updates visit:

EPICURIA
EPICURIA
BUNCH THEORY
Achillée
TARA
CONDRIEU
2019
CIÙ CIÙ
Piceno
APHROS
VINHÃO
2018
Davenport

HOUSE OF JORO
NATURAL GIN
GORDON RAMSAY ★★★ CHEF
Cook It Raw
Simon Rogan
THE COOKBOOK
WYLIE DUFRESNE
WITH PETER MEEHAN
wd~50
THE COOKBOOK
Lisboeta
Nuno Mendes
HOG
RICHARD H. TURNER
fish TOM AIKENS
CALLWEY
TIM RAUE MY WAY
John Chantarasak
KIN THAI
ALBERT ADRIÀ
TAPAS
TICKETS CUISINE
The Gaijin Cookbook
Ivan Orkin and Chris Ying
OFF DUTY
DAN TOOMBS
THE CURRY GUY THAI
PIERRE GAGNAIRE REINVENTING FRENCH CUISINE
HESTON BLUMENTHAL
TOTAL PERFECTION
Preservin
Bronson
F*ck It, I'll Start Tomorrow
TODAY'S SPECIAL
20 LEADING CHEFS CHOOSE 100 EMERGING CHEFS
mattos
estela
SALUMI
THE CRAFT OF ITALIAN DRY CURING
TOM KERRIDGE
DANIEL PATTERSON
COI
STORIES AND RECIPES
benu
corey lee
Atelier Crenn
NOPI
Contra Wildair
A VERY SERIOUS COOKBOOK
The Nordic Baking Book
BO BECH IN MY BLOOD
ROOT
1 MUSCAT
blanc d'argile
ORGANIC

Acknowledgements & Contributions

Authors

Luke French, Stacey Sherwood-French

Editor

Katie Fisher, Meze Publishing

Chefs

Alex Nietosvuori, Ally Thompson & Team Hjem / Chris McClurg & Team Paul Ainsworth at No6 / Gareth Ward, Amelia Eiríksson & Team Ynyshir / Josh & Victoria Overington & Team Le Cochon Aveugle / Kenny Atkinson & Team House of Tides / Kirk Haworth & Team Plates / Lee Westcott / Lisa Goodwin-Allen & Team Northcote / Luke Payne & Team The Packhorse / Paul Leonard & Team The Forest Side / Rafael Cagali & Team Da Terra / Roberta Hall-McCarron, Shaun McCarron & Team The Little Chartroom / Sam Carter, Alex Olivier & Team Restaurant 22 / Santiago Lastra, Ben Morgan & Team KOL Restaurant / Tommy Banks & Team The Black Swan at Oldstead / Tom Booton & Team The Grill at The Dorchester / Tom Brown & Team Cornerstone / Will Murray, Jack Croft & Team FALLOW

Design

Paul Cocker & Phil Turner, Meze Publishing

Cover: Nik Daughtry & Jon Daughtry, DED Studio

Photography

Tim Green / Clair Irwin / Simon Burt

With special thanks to

Our (Stacey & Luke's) personal teams – at JÖRO, House of JÖRO and KONJÖ, for consistently delivering and keeping up the standards and then some, especially at times where we are working away – thank you all so much.

All the incredible producers, farmers, growers, hunters, foragers, fishers, designers, painters, crafts people and makers. Without you all, none of us would be able to produce what we do in our restaurants every day.

There are many unbelievably talented people that wanted to contribute to this project, but not all could commit this time round. We all share so much with each other, whether it be recipes, tips, suppliers of ingredients, equipment, knowledge, personal support, positive mental health and encouragement to help us all continue to move forwards and be better at what we do, personally and professionally. Stacey and I want to say a huge thank you to you all; you know who you are. We love you all.

Photo: Zachary Turner

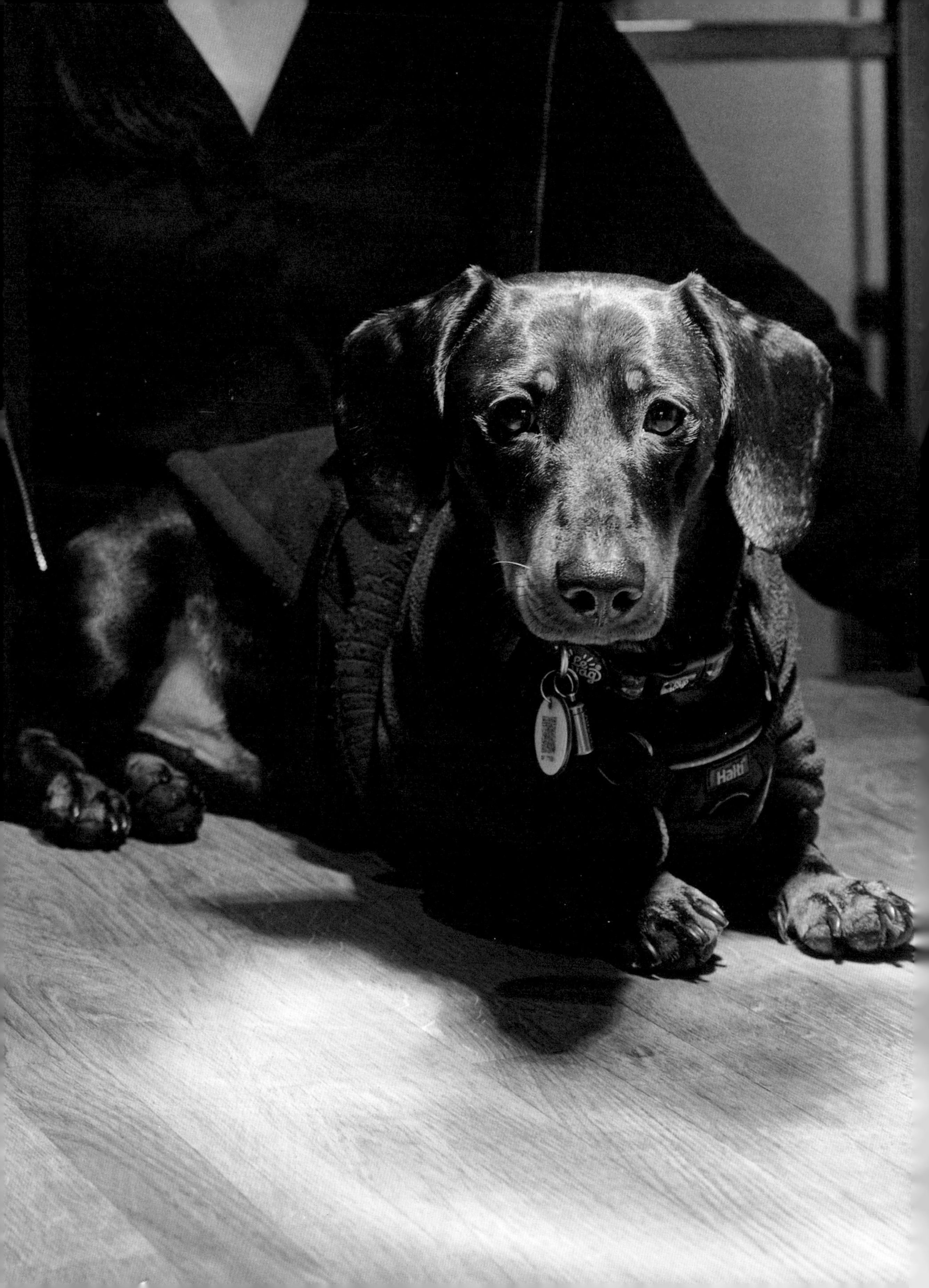
Halti